St Bernard's Football Club

or when the well ran dry!

By George H Park

Produced and Published
by
George H Park
15 Royal Crescent
Edinburgh
EH3 6QA

Email: georgepark@btinternet.com
Website: www.stbernardsfc.co.uk

Printed
by
Thomson Litho Ltd, East Kilbride

Contents

Foreword by Bob Crampsey

Acknowledgements

Introduction

Chapter 1
The Early Years (1878 to 1882) *Page 1*

Chapter 2
The Days at Old Powderhall (1882 to 1889) *Page 7*

Chapter 3
The Logie Green Days (1889 to 1899) *Page 16*

Chapter 4
A brief stay at New Powderhall (1899 to 1901) *Page 41*

Chapter 5
Back at the Royal Gymnasium (1901 to 1917) Page *44*

Chapter 6
New Logie Green used for the Revival (1919 to 1924) *Page 64*

Chapter 7
Home again for the last time (1924 to 1942) *Page 70*

Chapter 8
The Arsenal Stadium Mystery *Page 97*

Chapter 9
Some Odds and Ends *Page 99*

Appendix 1
The Players

Appendix 2
Results and Team Line Ups

Appendix 3
Some Prominent Officials

Foreword

Goodbye St Bernard's

There is an intriguing mystery about the third Edinburgh football club, St Bernard's and its closing.

There was at first sight nothing odd about the club although their ground, the Gymnasium, was slap bang in the middle of town. There were a handful of turnstiles, a rickety grandstand, a scene of pleasant struggle.

On pre-war Saturdays a comparative handful of elderly men could be seen making their way to the exotic water pavilion.

The life of St Bernard's had been hard, rarely enough to do more than scrape a living. Every year supporters would solemnly assure each other that this year would be different.

Fat chance, the years clanked slowly by until 1937/38 that is, when Saints drew Motherwell in the Scottish Cup in the quarter finals.

Still that success did not necessarily bring immediate wealth. However a semi final with a crowd of 30,000, to be followed right away by another 30,000 in the replay, and another yet again in the second replay against East Fife, must have swelled the coffers. At the outbreak of the Second World War St Bernard's were on a better financial footing.

In August 1939 the Saints were playing in the Scottish League, Division 2 when war broke out. This led to a period of near anarchy until there could be a more permanent arrangement. Saints played out the remainder of the first season of the hostilities in a regionalised Eastern League. After a season of inactivity the Saints found themselves in a North Eastern League comprising of clubs deemed surplus to the top league in Scotland, the Southern League. The two big clubs, Hearts and Hibs would obviously have been delighted to lever St Bernards from the top drawer. This was accomplished when their reserve teams replaced Saints and Leith Athletic for the following season.

In June 1945 further negotiations were needed to enable St Bernard's to rejoin the League. The call went out to wealthy fans to save the Saints.

Alas! There were no wealthy patrons, or at any rate in sufficient numbers. With every year the links weakened, and somehow the money leaked away and in increasingly quick quantities.

So, no knight on the white charger which led to the beginning of the end for the famous club.

St Bernard's have held a special interest for me and I was exceedingly pleased to be given the opportunity to write a foreword to George's book.

Bob Crampsey

Acknowledgements

Bearing in mind that it is over 60 years since the Saints played their last match, former players have passed on, and even the young supporters in the last days of the club are now old men, personal reminiscences are difficult to obtain. It has been necessary therefore to rely on newspaper coverage for the most part. Fortunately Edinburgh is well served with good libraries. Many are the visits I have made to the National Library but more so the Central Library both on George IV Bridge. The staff of the latter has been particularly helpful and I am most grateful to those in the Edinburgh Room for their help and guidance.

In 1995 a number of events were held in the city to commemorate the centenary of St Bernard's winning the Scottish Cup including an exhibition of photographs and other memorabilia held in the Edinburgh Room of the Central Library. It was organised by Andy Mitchell, who is currently Head of Communications at the SFA, and the late John McLennan. In terms of popularity and as a focal point for people with an interest in the Saints it proved to be a great success and much information was gleaned from old players and supporters on that occasion.

It would be inappropriate not to mention the late Jimmy Allardyce whose personal scrapbook has proved to be invaluable to those researching the history of the club. I never met Jimmy but I am sure our paths crossed in London Street in the early 1960s on the way to our respective works. After all you did not see many people wearing St Bernard's scarves at that time!

Jimmy Allardyce (right) at the Gymnasium

Others I have spoken to over the years include Stewart Tulloch, Jim Stewart, Jimmy Hogg of the Edinburgh Room, Sid Sinclair, Lawrie Reilly of Hibs and Scotland fame, Andrew McErlane, Denis Allan, David Speed, Alan Cunningham, Ian Brash, Ronnie Hall, Tommy Hall, Ronnie Hall Jnr, Anne Hepburn, Fraser Simm of the Heriots Trust, Bunty Gibson, and John Bremner. All have been helpful with anecdotes about the club and the area in general.

My research really started in 1984 and given the long time span it is not surprising that some friends and neighbours who have assisted with information have passed on. These include Pym Simpson, John Tulloch, George and Freda Clark, members of the family of the late McDonald Lyon, Gavin Mouat, Davie Walker, Willie Ramsay and George Campbell.

While I have tried to maintain some sort of record of those who have helped, undoubtedly I will have omitted somebody and I trust that anyone who falls into this category will not be too upset.

My own family however deserves a mention. My late father fostered my keen interest in football and my late uncle Joe was the nearest to a Saints supporter of all my relations albeit a part time one, as he really supported the Hearts. Perhaps the most surprising item of information that came to light was when I spoke to my cousin Robert Cowan and he revealed that he was a grandson of James Sneddon the goalkeeper of the Scottish Cup winning side. Robert recalls that as a very wee boy he was coached by Jimmy in the technique of goalkeeping.

I have consulted many publications over the years too numerous to list here but the following deserve a mention as being particularly helpful:

'The Scotsman' newspaper
'The Edinburgh Evening News' newspaper
'The Evening Dispatch' newspaper
'Historic Saints of Edinburgh' by George Campbell
'St Bernard's Football Club' article in the SFA Annual of 1896
'Who's Who of Scottish Internationalists' by Douglas Lamming
'Heart of Midlothian FC – a pictorial history 1874/1984'
'The Hearts – The Story of Heart of Midlothian FC' by Albert Mackie
'Hibernian – The Complete History' by John R Mackay

Malky McCormick of the Daily Record for his permission to include the caricature of Bob Crampsey. Roy Preston, the brother of Tommy Preston, for his proof reading of the book - not a straightforward task!

CCLASP is a children's cancer and leukaemia charity based in Leith, run by parents whose children have been affected by various types of cancer. Since being set up in 1994 by Valerie and Bill Simpson after their own son Robert was diagnosed with leukaemia, it has provided invaluable support to families during the most devastating time of their lives. Its patrons include former footballers Paul Kane and John Hughes, the Falkirk manager and I am pleased to lend my support by donating all the proceeds of this book to such a worthwhile cause.

Finally very special thanks to Billy Hunter of Motherwell FC and Scotland fame and his wife Rona whose help and encouragement have proved to be invaluable. Billy, an author of four books, has provided the necessary drive in converting my dream of writing a book into reality.

George H Park

Unfortunately the death of Bob Crampsey was announced just prior to the book going to print. In addition to writing the foreword his help and inspiration assisted enormously. Bob was very interested in being the first read of the book and my personal memory of him was his suggestion that a friend does not read the book (they would say it was good anyway! – a sure sign of his pawky humour.) He will be sorely missed.

St Bernard's Football Club

Introduction

From a very early age I have had an interest in the old St Bernard's Football Club. This has largely stemmed from living in Royal Crescent, Edinburgh in a flat overlooking the site of the club's old ground, the Royal Gymnasium. The club played their last match the year before I was born but the grandstand remained intact on the site until 1948 before being dismantled and moved to Old Meadowbank the home of Leith Athletic FC and the Edinburgh Monarchs speedway team. I would be about four years old at the time and I just remember the outline of the old stand protruding above the street level of Royal Crescent. The Gymnasium ground was situated at a level of 40 feet below the street.

My interest then lay dormant for many years until the late 1970s when I was appointed Accountant of the Royal Bank of Scotland branch in Queen Street. Whilst sorting out some old records there I happened upon a copy of an old Branch Inspection Report compiled in 1946 that contained a reference to the St Bernard's Football Club Grand Stand Company Limited and an overdraft in the books of the branch that was causing some concern! Unfortunately other items from the same period had been destroyed, as it would have been useful to see the bank account itself in the ledgers and indeed confirm what other accounts relating to the football club were held at the branch to get a fuller financial picture.

However this discovery was to trigger off many years of research that has culminated in this book, as I just had to find out more about my 'local club'.

Early on it became obvious that no official club records existed as minute books, in particular, would have been an invaluable source of information. Files of the limited companies were available in the Scottish Record Office and plans of the various grandstands were available for perusal in the Edinburgh City Archives. The records of the Scottish Football Association have been consulted and I am most grateful to all of these organisations for their help.

At the outset I resolved to obtain as many team line-ups as possible and in this aspect I have largely achieved what I set out to do but it has not been easy. Early on I found that libraries, for whatever reason, did not always retain the same edition of a particular newspaper. For instance the final Saturday Sports edition of the *Edinburgh Evening News,* a very useful source, might be kept for a three-month spell only to be followed by a similar period when the lunchtime edition prevailed. This necessitated looking elsewhere for the match reports very often in libraries outwith the city. This of course added greatly to the time required.

Just when it looked as if a visit to the British Library, Colindale Library in London which stores many Scottish newspapers not available in the libraries here would be needed to finalise the research a great initiative came to the rescue in the shape of the Newsplan 2000 Project. This undertaking involving the Heritage Lottery Fund and the UK Regional Newspaper Industry ensured that microfilm copies of the 'missing' newspapers came home, so to speak, and were available in the libraries in Scotland. This was a great boost to my endeavours and I am most grateful to this enterprise and indeed the staff of all the libraries I had to visit or correspond with throughout the country.

Although time consuming, carrying out the research required for the book has been a very enjoyable experience in many ways, like trying to piece a large jig saw puzzle together.

Given its proud history it is disappointing that a club like St Bernard's had to fold. The loss of their ground in my view was a major factor but if it had not happened when it did, a move to a less central location would have become almost inevitable as the traffic volumes increased in the 1950s. Finding a suitable site and the finance to build a new ground would have been very difficult.

George H Park
Edinburgh 2008

Chapter 1
The Early Years

The late 1870s and early 1880s saw a rapid growth in the number of football clubs in Edinburgh of both the association and rugby codes. The round ball game in particular was in its infancy in the city. Most written records that were made around that time have long since gone, and such is the case with the St Bernard's Football Club. It is therefore difficult to establish the exact origins of the club without minutes, for instance, to consult. In the circumstances the researcher has to rely mainly on the very limited press coverage of the time. However all is not lost, as a way of recognising St Bernard's Scottish Cup win of 1895, the *Scottish Football Annual,* in a short article on the history of the club, states the date of foundation to be 1878 and in fact narrows it down to 'a Sabbath in September'. The meeting was held in Buchanan's Temperance Hotel, 114 High Street, Edinburgh, a popular meeting place for football teams. Additionally, an official club publication – the Prospectus issued much later in 1924 offering shares in The Saint Bernard's Grand Stand Company Limited confirms the year of inception. There is however reason to believe that the origins go back a few years before then.

It has to be borne in mind that rugby football was the first of the two codes to be established in town and was particularly strong in the Stockbridge area, where the Edinburgh Academical Football Club, the oldest in Scotland, had been formed almost 20 years earlier. In fact the first ever rugby union international between Scotland and England had already been hosted at it's Raeburn Place ground in 1871. It is not surprising therefore to find only rugby being played in that part of the city around that time. Players were establishing association football elsewhere in the city, principally at the East Meadows, where both Hearts and Hibs had been playing for two or three years.

The clubs playing rugby in the public park in Stockbridge were United and St Bernard's. If coverage of matches in the press was anything to go by these clubs did not play many times. *The Scotsman* reports on a match played on 6 November 1875 at Kirkcaldy where the local side of the same name was beaten 1-0 by the United. This was the first time a report on one of their games appeared in the press. St Bernard's followed them into the sports' columns with a 'draw' against United on 15 January 1876. Other matches covered were against local clubs Comely Bank, St Vincent and St George, and Cronstadt from Leith. A 2-0 win by United against St Vincent on 1 December 1877 was quoted as being the last match played by United using rugby rules, and we find the association rules being employed the following March by United against the Hearts second XI in a 2-0 defeat. *The Scotsman* of 8 April 1878 in a 'Review of the Season' article states: 'The United is a convert from the rugby code. Notwithstanding that many of their former members are now in 3rd Edinburgh Rifle Volunteers and Brunswick they have played some very good matches'.

Very often, the match against the Hearts second XI is stated to be the first ever played by St Bernard's Football Club, but strictly speaking this is not the case as it was really against United. The change of code was attributed to a lack of rugby fixtures, and United and St Bernard's decided to merge soon after into a football club using the name of the latter.

The newly-merged clubs did not join the Edinburgh Football Association for season 1878/79, probably due to the fact that their formation date was too late for anything to be done about it. It must be assumed that matches were being played against other clubs of a similar standing that season, but no details appear in the press. Football of the association variety was taking place in Stockbridge however, by Brunswick FC, formed in 1877 from members of their cricket club, playing on a private ground called Brunswick Park at Raeburn Place. Their clubhouse Veitch's Tavern was located nearby.

Edinburgh's first association football team, the 3rd Edinburgh Rifle Volunteers, founded in 1874, was also reported to have moved to Stockbridge Park in what was to be their last season. Some sources link the demise of the Volunteers and the creation of St Bernard's, by suggesting that there was a direct link between the two events. However such evidence as there is, would suggest that they were not one and the same club. This statement is based on the fact that the last line-up appearing in the press of the Volunteers in October 1878, is completely different from the first available for St Bernard's exactly a year later. Certainly three members of the Volunteers, namely, Tom Fraser, Frank G Watt, and John Creyk all became associated with the Saints in an official capacity, but this seems to be the only link. Fraser was a very prominent athletic official eventually becoming President of the SAAA in 1898/99, as the St Bernard's FC representative. Watt on the other hand made his name in football as manager of Dundee FC before joining Newcastle United.

The Saints became members of the Edinburgh Association for season 1879/80, it being reported in the *Scottish Football Annual* that the club had a membership of 30, with captain George Heathcote on the Edinburgh Committee. This rise in status brought the club to the attention of the local newspapers, with results and sometimes brief reports appearing on a regular basis in *The Scotsman, Edinburgh Evening News and the Edinburgh Courant*.

George Heathcote

One match, which did not appear in the press but has been mentioned in various histories since, concerns the day when Hibs were due to play Hearts in an Edinburgh Cup tie at Mayfield. For some reason the Hearts did not turn up. Hibs obviously had their suspicions beforehand and had the young St Bernard's team 'waiting in the wings' to take their place. This went some way to placating the large crowd that had turned up and the Saints were paid the sum of £5 for their trouble. It is said this windfall was divided up amongst the team members!

Results also appear in the press for a second XI suggesting that the previous season had been far from inactive as the lack of press coverage might lead us to believe.

Matches against the more prominent clubs also contained team line-ups, and on 18 October 1879, losing an away match against the University 1-0, we find the first Saints team so listed. The team was A Anderson, G Heathcote, W Waugh, J Wilson, A Masterton, G McBeth, W Lamb, J Dunn, H McLennan, W Laurieston and H Paton. It was an early rule of the club that players had to reside north of Heriot Row in the districts of Stockbridge and Canonmills in the valley of the Water of Leith. An examination of the 1881 Census shows George Heathcote then aged 21 and his brother William living at 12 Dean Street. Other team members lived in Haugh Street, Saunders Street, Jamaica Street, Cumberland Street, India Place and elsewhere in the specified area. St Bernard's was also the parish and town council ward name for this area so it would be logical to name the team after it. The ward name disappeared in 1975 following local government reorganisation with the parish name lasting longer but only until 1992.

The original colours of the club were white jerseys with a red waistband, white knickers secured below the knee and red stockings. On the breast a badge depicting the Doric rotunda of St Bernard's Well was woven in red. The well itself is a well-known landmark situated on the banks of the Water of Leith between Saunders Street and the Dean Village. It is named after St Bernard of Clairvaux who by legend is reputed to have sought refuge nearby in the twelfth century whilst attempting to raise soldiers for the Second Crusade. The well has been closed for over half a century now but was famous for its mineral waters said to taste like 'the washings of a foul gun barrel'!

The first ground of the Saints was Stockbridge Park a public park situated where the tenements of Comely Bank now stand. This had originally been 'John Hope's Park'. John Hope the philanthropist, who was closely associated with the 3rd Edinburgh Rifle Volunteers, had rented a field of ten acres extent behind Raeburn Place from Mr Rochied of Inverleith in 1854 to provide a playground for the youth of the area. It only lasted for one year due to the landlord being unwilling to renew the lease for reasons unknown. The Town Council subsequently opened it again. The Saints used a pitch in the northwest corner of the park in the vicinity of the present day Dean Bowling Club.

This early period is referred to as the 'Horn Lane Hall days'. Horn Lane, now long since gone, was located between India Place and Saunders Street. It ran parallel to them and was entered off what is now Gloucester Street. There was a large Mission Hall with seating for 250 that was used by the Independent Order of Good Templars as a meeting place. To what total extent the Saints used the hall is unclear but most certainly at this time the general meetings of the club were held there. Horn Lane was later known as Church Place.

In that first season in the Edinburgh Association the Saints lost narrowly to both Hearts and Hibs, the latter game being in the Second Round of the Edinburgh Cup, but beat the longer established Brunswick and Hanover and most of the other clubs that played. It could be said they had begun to establish themselves quickly. It is understood that St Bernard's were never defeated in the two years spent in Stockbridge Public Park.

Season 1880/81 saw the ambitious club move from the public park to the Royal Gymnasium Grounds situated between Royal Crescent and Eyre Place. This facility was shared initially with the declining Hanover FC, the smaller park being used by St Bernard's. The Royal Patent Gymnasium to give the ground its full name had been an amusement and recreational park created in 1861 by a John Cox. By the time the Saints moved in however the emphasis was on athletics and football and the change saw St Bernard's make further progress. That season saw results for a third XI called the Stockbridge XI appear in the press. As the table of the statistics for the three that season shows all were doing well.

	P	W	D	L	F	A
1st Eleven	28	19	0	9	143	43
2nd Eleven	22	13	4	5	105	37
3rd Eleven	11	8	1	2	47	23

Not widely known is the fact that St Bernard's had a brief stay at some time as tenants of the first Tynecastle Park, across the road from the present ground, before the Hearts moved in. One of the matches there was the 2-1 home win over the Hearts on 19 February! A publican who had moved to Gorgie from Stockbridge suggested the move no doubt with business motives in mind. Things did not work out as it was too far from Stockbridge for the Saints' followers to walk; the tramcars did not go there at that time.

This season saw an important addition to the playing ranks in the shape of goalkeeper James Baillie. He proved to be a great clubman playing for the Saints for 14 seasons during which he was captain at one stage. On occasions he played at centre forward before turning to refereeing when his playing days were over. Saints were now finding the measure of the other local clubs as evidenced by wins over both Hearts and Hibs. All fixtures at that time were friendlies and the standing of any particular club could be judged by the quality of its fixture list. The only exceptions were the cup competitions organised by the various associations. The Saints had the distinction of reaching the final of the Edinburgh Cup that season where their opponents were the Hibs. This match was played on Hibs' first ground at Easter Road,

James Baillie

where the present Hibs' Supporters Club is situated in Sunnyside. St Bernard's must have thought they had at least one hand on the cup when they stormed into a four goal lead by half time. Normally such a lead would have been enough to ensure success but they reckoned without a great fight back by the men in green that levelled the game at 4-4 in the final minute. Such an opportunity did not arise the next time with Hibs winning 1-0 in the replay. Sandwiched between these two games the same two clubs contested the Edinburgh 2nd XI Cup Final. No consolation was forthcoming to the Stockbridge club however in losing 7-1 this time. Still St Bernard's had done well to reach both finals so soon into their existence, and it was no disgrace to lose to a Hibs' club that was in the middle of a run of winning both trophies three years in a row.

Season 1881/82 saw St Bernard's join the Scottish Football Association. This of course meant they were now eligible to take part in the Scottish Cup, now in its ninth year. At the time the early rounds were drawn on a geographical basis and the first round brought the Saints a home draw against the Hearts. A McBeth goal with the Hearts goalkeeper putting his jersey on the wrong way round, and cursing his luck, was all that was needed to set up a second round tie with the Hibs. This match saw the opening of a new stand at the Hibs' ground and a reported attendance of 6000 for an eagerly anticipated match. Again only one goal of a difference separated the sides at the end of a keenly contested game, but it was the men from Stockbridge whose interest in the competition was ended. For the second season running St Bernard's met Hibs in the final of the Edinburgh Cup, this time at Tynecastle. In front of a crowd of 8000 the game followed a totally different pattern to that of the previous year. This time it was the team from Easter Road that built up a 4-0 lead at half time. Saints were unable to retrieve the situation, only scoring twice after the break. The final of the 2nd XI Cup was reached yet again with Hearts winning by a score of 2-0 at the third attempt. In reaching these finals, albeit without success, St Bernard's had firmly established themselves as one of the leading clubs in the city alongside Hearts and Hibs. For instance it was reported that the Saints had entertained their opponents from Lenzie to dinner in the Café Royal, no less, after their match. Of 121 members it was reported that 79 were playing members of the club so turning out three teams presented no problems. Towards the end of the season, and reflecting their continuing rise in status, the Saints were able to acquire the use of the Powderhall Grounds for their home games. This was done through the good offices of Mr W M Lapsley whose main interest was pedestrianism, and who was the tenant of both the Royal Gymnasium and Powderhall both principally venues for athletics. This was the original Powderhall, opened in 1870, which was situated next to the banks of the Water of Leith, and is currently occupied by the city's Cleansing Department.

WM Lapsley

Chapter 2
The Days at Old Powderhall

Saints had been developing a habit of reaching the finals of the two local cups but missed out the following season. It was perhaps appropriate, therefore, that a new competition was introduced in the shape of the Rosebery Charity Cup to remedy the situation. Gifted by Lord Rosebery the aim was to raise money for charity in the east of Scotland, much in the same manner as the Glasgow Charity Cup instituted in 1877 had been doing in the west. The introduction of competitions for this purpose reflected the increasing drawing power of the game and the attendant financial benefits. St Bernard's took advantage of the extra competition and reached the first final losing 2-0 to Hearts. In the Scottish Cup first round Hearts gained revenge for their defeat the previous season by winning 4-3 after a 1-1 draw. In the Edinburgh Cup Edinburgh University beat the Saints 2-1 in the fourth round. University teams by the very nature of that type of organisation varied in strength from year to year. However Edinburgh University was a particularly good side at that time containing John Macdonald, Dr John Smith and R M Christie all full internationalists for Scotland.

Saints had been acquiring good players themselves including George McKenzie and Jamie Lowe from the Brunswick. The demise of that club prompted the *Scottish Athletic Journal* to opinion that the Brunswick players had joined St Bernard's en bloc. Other players to join the Saints, following a rescinding of the 'Heriot Row Rule', were Sandy Robertson from Hanover, Robert Bryce from Edina and George Drummond from St James's. Another change saw the third XI renamed the Glenogle XI presumably after the Glenogle Road 'colonies' which would prove to be a useful recruiting ground for the club. It was all go and St Bernard's joined the Scottish AAA that season. August saw their first annual sports event held at Powderhall. Many clubs held annual athletic sports during the summer but over the years the Saints turned out to be particularly successful in this sphere. This was not surprising, given that W M Lapsley a noted sport's promoter in his own right and Tom Fraser a future President and Honorary Treasurer of the Scottish AAA, were in their ranks. In all, 31 meetings were held between 1882 and 1924 at Powderhall, then the Gymnasium, and lastly at the Marine Gardens in the final years leading up to the First World War. These meetings revolved around a format of athletics and the almost mandatory five-a-side football. However in an innovative move the sports committee introduced seven-a-side rugby from 1901 to 1903. The line up of clubs for this competition was not dissimilar to the famous Melrose event itself. The seven from Hawick RFC go on the record of having won the St Bernard's Sports twice.

Just when things appeared to be running smoothly in season 1883/84, a major blow lay in store for the club with the defection of some of their best players to Lancashire clubs, who were understood to be paying their players. Officially they did not, as professionalism was not legalised in England until 1885, but it was common knowledge that their Scottish recruits were being financially recompensed. Saints, as indeed many other Scottish clubs so affected, were up against it as they were still strictly amateur, and within a short space of time we find Sandy Robertson, Jamie Ross and George Drummond (all Preston North End), Robert Bryce and Robert McBeth (both Accrington) heading over the border. The subsequent success of these players, in particular with the famous Preston North End 'Invincibles' of the late 1880s, would lead us to believe that St Bernard's would have become very strong had they held on to them. Of course the same could have been said of all other Scottish clubs in the same position. There is no doubt that at least Drummond and Ross would have been good enough to play for Scotland but they were never capped. The Scottish Football Association frowned on professional players and suspended those involved. The Scottish clubs themselves were virtually powerless to do anything about the situation. It would have been understandable to find considerable friction between the clubs on either side of the border as a result but this appears not to have been the case. Ironically we find Saints embarking on their first tour of Lancashire to play these clubs! In the space of four days over the New Year period they played Accrington, Blackburn Olympic and Great Lever, a team from Bolton. Defeats in the first and last of these games were more than compensated by a meritorious draw with the Olympic who had won the FA Cup the previous March. In this they had a little help from a friend of the club George Drummond who came across from Preston to help his old mates.

It became fashionable for the Edinburgh clubs to bring their old boys back from Lancashire to help them in the Rosebery Charity Cup and the Saints were no exception. Saints played the Hibs in the final, with a side augmented by Drummond and Robertson of Preston North End and Bryce and McBeth of Accrington. The first game finished 1-1 but Saints lost the replay 0-1 despite the inclusion of the same guests. Earlier on in the season the Saints had lost 0-7 to Hibs in the Edinburgh Cup final with no help. To round off the season the Saints entertained the famous Preston North End at Powderhall losing 2-3. Emigration also posed a problem, W Collie and J Robertson left for Australia but not before receiving gold pendants from the club in appreciation of their services. Over the years St Bernard's were to similarly honour a number of players in this manner.

Sandy Robertson | Jamie Ross | George Drummond

The older generation of football followers in Edinburgh will recognise in the portraits three of the North End "Invincibles," A. Robertson on the reader's left, Ross, jun., in the centre, and G. Drummond on the right. All three were connected with the St Bernards, and Robertson and Drummond finished their football careers with the North End, Ross, on the other hand, being identified with other clubs after the break-up of the famous combination. The photographs from which the portraits were taken, were kindly lent by Mr David M'Queen, Hanover Street.

By now the reader will be aware that St Bernard's' record in cup finals had been a fruitless one. In season 1884/85 there was to be no such setbacks for their supporters, as they did not reach any finals! In fact the season was to be a disappointing one results wise with an early exit from the Scottish Cup as well at the hands of the team from West Benhar a mining village situated near Harthill. In beating the Saints 5-1, the locals gained revenge for a 7-0 Scottish Cup defeat in Edinburgh the previous season. The community of West Benhar no longer exists. Despite a lack of playing success St Bernard's continued to thrive with a reported membership of 200. An early season *Scottish Athletic Journal* stated that they would have difficulty in selecting the first XI with so many good players available. Subsequent events, as is sometimes the case, proved otherwise. On the social side the annual sports were abandoned that year and a large-scale picnic was held instead of the annual supper.

On the wider football front what was to be a unique match took place at the grounds of Merchiston Castle School on 28 March 1885. The event was the semi-final replay of the FA Cup between Queens Park and Nottingham Forest. The first game at Derby Cricket Ground had been drawn 1-1 and the compromise to replay in neutral Edinburgh saw the Queens win 3-0. For the second season in succession Blackburn Rovers met Queens Park in the Final and added to their previous season's success. In a bold initiative, the Saints invited the winners to play at Powderhall 19 days after the Final. On 23 April 1885 before a crowd of 6000 the Saints beat their famous visitors 2-0. This was accomplished with a little help from their friends and we find James Lundy, James McLaren, James McGhee and Willie Cox all prominent Hibs players augmenting the ranks. This season saw James Hutton join the club from the Northern, one of the Stockbridge minor clubs, and a useful nursery for the Saints. James a forceful halfback, was highly regarded by his contemporaries and was to represent the Saints for seven seasons.

The start of season 1885/86 saw an alteration to the Powderhall enclosure with the grandstand being taken further back leading to a widening of the pitch. The ground had been the first option for the aforementioned FA Cup semi-final replay the previous season, but perhaps the narrowness of the playing surface had been the reason it did not meet the criteria for the FA Cup tie. Another change saw James Baillie take over from George Heathcote as captain of the club.

An exciting prospect was the pairing of Hearts and the Saints in the first round of the Scottish Cup at the ground of the former. The defeat of the Stockbridge team by 2-5 was responded to by a protest to the SFA on the grounds of an infringement of a registration rule by their opponents. This was upheld by the ruling body. A replay was ordered two weeks later at the Saints ground, but still the Hearts won by the only goal. Protests were commonplace at this time in the history of the Cup competition. Despite the disappointment of the national trophy, in the local competitions Saints were back in the habit of reaching all the finals and you may have guessed it losing them! The Edinburgh Cup went to the Hibs who won 5-1, the second XI version to the Hibs reserves winning 2-0 and the Rosebery Cup to the Hearts who won 4-1 albeit after a 0-0 draw. Andrew Jackson (Cambuslang), William McKinnon (Dumbarton) and Charles Heggie (Rangers), all internationalists, were the players 'imported' for the Charity Cup but to no avail. The lack of cup success prompted new captain Baillie to say that he thought the Saints would never win a cup, but if they did, they would probably lose it on the way home! Old boy George Drummond, whilst never to gain international honours for Scotland, was 'capped' by his adopted country, when he lined up for the Players (professionals) against the Gentlemen (amateurs) at the Oval in March, and scored their goal in a 1-2 defeat.

Not covered in the story so far is the subject of representative honours gained by St Bernard's players. As will become clear it is particularly significant to raise it in the section covering the 1886/87 season. Inter association matches were commonplace at this time and regular matches were played by the Edinburgh FA (later to be the East of Scotland FA) against Ayrshire, Lanarkshire, Dunbartonshire, Renfrewshire, and of course the Glasgow FA, for obvious reasons the most important game of the season. Not only was Scottish opposition encountered, across border matches also took place against the associations of Sheffield, Cleveland, Newcastle, London and Lancashire, albeit on a less frequent basis than the domestic games. This type of match, so far as Edinburgh was concerned, started ten years previously, and it was not long before players from the Saints were involved. The progressive rise in the standing of the club was mirrored by an increasing number of players called upon to represent Edinburgh. As will become apparent, professionalism in Scotland was not far around the corner. Once League football became established around the same time the 'inter-counties' quickly petered out. In the space of the 16 years from 1878 to 1894, when 73 matches of this type took place, 44 St Bernard's players represented Edinburgh. Only Hearts beat this total with 52. Hibs had 35, with Leith Athletic on 21, and the University on 20. The smaller clubs also contributed with the odd player from time to time.

Early Scottish international teams were composed entirely of players from clubs in the west of Scotland, due to the game being established earlier in that part of the country. From 1880 onwards their counterparts in the east were to receive recognition, but it was not until 1887 that the first St Bernard's players were chosen to represent their country.

Jamie Hutton

The Scotland team that beat Ireland 4-1 on 19 February 1887 at Hampden Park, Glasgow consisted of James Hutton and James Lowe at left half and inside left respectively. Lowe scored one of the goals. Thus these players jointly became St Bernard's first internationalists. At one time their Scottish caps were on display in Fisher's Bar at 1 Saunders Street, Stockbridge. This public house was demolished along with the rest of the street in

Jamie Lowe

the 1970s when there was a complete redevelopment.

By now St Bernard's had a very competitive fixture list with matches against many prominent clubs and they were also invited to take part in a football tournament held in conjunction with the Edinburgh International Exhibition of 1886. The Exhibition site was the Meadows and this great event lasted for six months with the closing ceremony taking place at the end of October. The football segment comprised of three separate matches with Third Lanark playing the Hibs at 2 pm on Thursday 7 October, followed by St Bernard's against the Rangers at 4 pm on the same day, with a reported 20,000 in attendance, not all necessarily at the matches of course! Unfortunately from the Saints point of view a silver cup was at stake in each match, and it was Hibs in winning 2-1 and Rangers beating the Saints 4-1, who received the silverware at the post-match reception. The following day Renton eased out the Hearts 2-1.

Once again top-class opposition in Preston North End were invited to Edinburgh at the end of the season. This time the Saints decided to take on their famous visitors with only a modicum of help from outwith their own membership in the shape of James McGhee the Hibs' centre forward. In front of a 3000 crowd Saints lost 0-5. The inevitable cup final defeat was sustained this time by 2-6 at the hands of Hearts in the second XI competition. In the third round of the Scottish Cup the Saints beat Armadale 5-2 at Powderhall. Even allowing for the fact that the game in general was played at a much slower pace than nowadays, this must have been a bit of a stroll for the Saints, as it is alleged James Hutton had time for a smoke! The St Bernard's Secretary was quick to contradict the accusation.

At the start of season 1887/88 Saints managed to tempt Robert Boyd from Mossend Swifts to the city to play for them. Mossend was a mining community just north of West Calder, and the Swifts were a power in the land, winning the Edinburgh Cup that very season and beating Saints 5-3 on the way. Boyd, like his teammates at the Swifts, was a miner and it was not uncommon to entice such a player away with the offer of an easier job. Boyd was a very good player who went on to win international caps for Scotland; he played only a few games for St Bernard's before returning to his village team. This was a blow for St Bernard's. Undoubtedly they could have done with Robert in the team in what turned out to be a disappointing season. Not only were no cup finals reached the club also suffered a disastrous 9-0 defeat in the fifth round of the Scottish Cup in Paisley, at the hands of Abercorn.

In these days the mode of travel to away games was by train and details in the press often instructed the team members to meet at the Waverley or Caledonian Railway Stations as appropriate. For the game against Rangers in Glasgow on 22 October, Lowe, Hutton and Donald Sutherland missed the train. Their sporting hosts allowed the Saints to borrow one of their players and the match was played 10-a-side. A 1-1 draw was perhaps not surprising with such goodwill around.

A popular pastime at this time was the five-a-side version of the game. Competitions were part of many of the athletic sports meetings. The Saints were particularly successful in these games winning their own sports in 1884, 1886 and 1887, while at South Queensferry those organised by the Bellstane Birds Football Club five times out of six. Typical of a combination that was successful at this time was George Heathcote, Sandy Robertson, Lindsay Waugh, George McBeth and James Wilson.

Another recreation that did not have the same impact was cricket, and the St Bernard's Cricket Club, a section of the football club, was dropped after three seasons in 1887 due to apathy amongst the members. At one time the football and the cricket seasons did not conflict and a club could accommodate both sports. However a clash emerged as the football season overlapped into May leading to the clubs catering exclusively for one sport.

The spring of 1888 saw some of the older players retire from the scene and original members George Heathcote and Andrew Arthur appear to have retired after the Abercorn Scottish Cup-tie defeat. Replacements were recruited from other clubs in the shape of James 'Curly' McIntosh a goalkeeper from Norton Park, an Abbeyhill team, and James Methven a full back from the same club. McIntosh replaced James Baillie in goal but the old custodian was far from finished and this great clubman started to show his versatility by appearing in various forward positions. Aided by their new players, the Saints set off on a winning run in the Scottish Cup, although this was halted in the fourth round when they came up against new opponents, the recently formed Celtic club from Glasgow. Despite their infancy, Celtic were quickly recognised as a power in the land, due to the fact that they recruited prominent players from other clubs at their outset, with Hibs and Renton in particular left to rue their losses. The Saints were obviously fully aware of the task that awaited them when the two teams met on 3 November 1988 at Powderhall before a crowd of 6000. To bolster their ranks, St Bernard's introduced two Edinburgh University players, Thomas P Blades and John E Knox, but were thwarted in their attempt to bring in a third by the name of Neilson, due to him being ineligible for the tie. This initiative proved to be fruitless, with the Celts advancing to the next round with a 4-1 win, then reaching the Final only to lose to Third

Lanark. It was not unusual for players from the University to turn out for St Bernard's and those bastions of the amateur game, Queens Park, the famous Glasgow club. We also find Queens Park players appearing for St Bernard's. Obviously there was a friendly association between the three clubs fostered through the athletic connection.

A famous club at the time was the Corinthians, a team of amateur players recruited from the public schools and the universities in England. Many of their members represented England in the early international matches, sometimes providing the full team. They did this on two occasions against Wales and players such as G O Smith and C B Fry were famous household names then, in the same way as David Beckham and Alan Shearer are today. They were renowned for undertaking tours to promote the game, not only in the United Kingdom, but much further afield, including Brazil and South Africa. Starting in 1886 Queens Park played annual matches against the Corinthians and this continued right through until 1938. Possibly through the connection with Queens Park the Saints arranged to play the Corinthians at Powderhall on Friday, 4 January 1889. Faced with such formidable opposition in front of a large holiday crowd, not for the first time in their history, the Saints decided to strengthen up. In defence they introduced Adams (Hearts), Ellis (Mossend Swifts) and McQueen of the Champfleurie club near Linlithgow, while augmenting the forward line with Buchanan (Cambuslang), Laing (Leith Athletic) and McGhee of the Hibs, all to no avail with the visitors running out 5-0 winners. This match proved to be the start of a series of matches between the two clubs that ran until 1900, not as long as the Queens Park series, but certainly far more enduring than any other Scottish club had with the Corinthians.

George Guild

In 1939 at a Supporters' Club function held in the Grand Restaurant to celebrate the 60th Anniversary of the Football Club, Tom Lamb, an old official and an ex-President, was to remark: 'In my active time we were looked upon as the second best club in Scotland. If not on account of play, the Club had a standing, and if a good team came to Scotland we had to play them'. If the Saints were regarded as the second best club, one has to presume that it was Queens Park that Mr Lamb regarded as the best.

Another first occurred on Saturday, 9 March 1889 at neutral Easter Road in the final of the Edinburgh Second XI Cup – Saints won their first cup! A crowd of 2000 turned up to see them largely dominate the first half with a goal from Forbes and two from Irving, giving them a 3-0 lead. Predictably the young Hearts fought back in the second half and scored twice. Another was disallowed, which was the subject of an unsuccessful protest from the Hearts, but the wee Saints held out for a historic win. *The Scotsman* reported that there was some rowdyism after the game was finished, but the large number of policemen who were present quickly quelled it. No doubt this did not distract the victory celebrations in Stockbridge that night. The best-known player in the St Bernard's team that day was the right back George 'Doddy' Guild. A native of Arbroath, 'Doddy' was a master at Heriot's School and played for the Saints for six years including many appearances in the first team. Although a fine footballer he is probably better known for his contribution as a bowler and batsman in the Heriot's FP cricket team of the early 1890s.

    Having used guest players to good effect on previous occasions, one cannot but think that the Saints went over the score for the Rosebery Charity Cup competition that season. Also, it would be interesting to know what the regular playing members of the club thought about losing their places in the quest to annex this particular cup. It was of course within the rules covering the charity competition. Three games were required to eliminate Leith Athletic in the semi-final. Whether it was St Bernard's or Third Lanark who won this tie, is open to question, as no fewer than six members of the Third's team, who had themselves won the Scottish Cup in February, turned out for the Saints including the whole forward line. Another player, by the name of Love, from the same Glasgow club also played, along with Buchanan of Cambuslang and McGhee of the Hibs. Only goalkeeper McIntosh and right back Methven were true Saints. In the final, Mossend Swifts from West Calder provided the opposition. St Bernard's continued with the same 'select', other than Forbes who replaced Johnston at inside left. The first game on 15 May at Tynecastle ended 1-1, but in the replay a week later, with the same team, the Saints went down by 4-3 to provide the Swifts with their one and only Rosebery triumph. To round off the season at Powderhall, the English Cup Holders, Preston North End, beat another reinforced Saints XI by 3-1. The committee was certainly not backward in bringing good class opposition to the city.

Chapter 3
The Logie Green Days

In October 1888 the Lord Provost's Committee submitted a recommendation to the Town Council, that the sports ground at Powderhall, belonging to the city, be taken over from the present tenant and converted into a public park. This was tantamount to a notice to quit. It became imperative that Mr W M Lapsley the good friend of St Bernard's, who had made the ground available to them, would have to secure a new site if he wished to continue his sporting attractions. He still held the lease of Pitt Street Baths and the Royal Gymnasium Grounds, which had been used by the St Bernard's second XI that season. He was fortunate in acquiring a long lease for the ground adjacent to the old Powderhall, and on 28 December 1889 the new Powderhall Grounds were opened. This was the enclosure which subsequently became Powderhall Stadium, and was home of the world famous Powderhall Sprint, Greyhound Racing and Speedway. This sporting venue lasted for over 100 years, but sadly within the past few years has been sold and redeveloped for housing.

While the old Powderhall had served the Saints well, one drawback with any shared arrangement is the availability of dates; with many pedestrian meetings being promoted at the time, clashes did occur. With this in mind the committee of St Bernard's sought out a ground of their own where they could operate with independence.

They secured a plot of land west of Beaverbank Place, known as Dickson's Nursery, on which they took a lease of ten years from the Heriot's Trust. This was redeveloped over a period of six months into a football ground. The ground was named Logie Green after the nearby mansionhouse of the same name. The ground was located where the row of tenements now stand in Logie Green Road.

Lord Provost Boyd opened Logie Green on Saturday, 24 August 1889 before a crowd of 4000 and Third Lanark, with whom they were described as having an ancient bond of union, provided the opposition. Could the bond have been the Volunteer Movement, which Third Lanark definitely branched from and St Bernard's might have originated, been the link? Anyway a 5-1 win for the 'first foots' from Glasgow was not the best of starts for the Saints. Results that first season at the new ground turned out to be a bit of a disaster with many defeats. This must have been disappointing for the club's supporters, who could to some degree console themselves with some new facilities on offer.

The club had a membership of 500, which included quite a number of the junior Dunrobin FC, and the good-sized pavilion situated at the north end of the ground contained a large clubroom. This was open every evening where the members could read all of the sporting papers. A piano and draughts and dominoes were also available. On the social scene the club held their first Annual Soiree that season in April 1890 at the Albion Hall in Stockbridge. The previous December a full house had turned up at the monthly smoker, with some people turned away, to see Jamie Hutton presented with a gold watch and chain. Not long before, those other stalwarts, George Heathcote and Jamie Lowe had received silver watches at other functions. Despite the success of these friendly occasions the relationship between the club's committee, and the support, was perhaps not so affable. The *Edinburgh Evening News* of Monday 2 December 1889 contained the gist of a letter from 'An Indignant St Bernard'. This was to the effect, that apparently the committee of the Logie Green club considered members to be "a load of dummies", and the writer promised a 'warm time' for the committee at the next General Meeting. Team selection was at the root of this particular complaint. The season saw a number of changes in the playing personnel also, with the introduction of the three Foyers brothers from Lanarkshire and Combe Hall from nearby Newhaven. Full back James Methven remained, as did Hutton and Lowe the club's internationalists. Towards the end of the season the stalwart James Baillie reappeared in goal. A sad note saw the death in April of John Foyers, one of the Foyers brothers. On the administration side, long time and highly-respected official William T Robertson resigned as Treasurer.

William T Robertson

The legalisation of professionalism in 1885 in England meant problems for the still amateur Scotland with an escalating increase in the flow of players to the south. It was now not only the best players who were moving to the top clubs but lesser-known clubs were now attracting Scots. St Bernard's were affected more than most by this development with Grimsby Town in particular, fishing to good effect around the Water of Leith and ending up with half of their team composed of ex-Saints. In a short space of time Reid, Ross, Sutherland, Riddoch and McBeth had all joined the 'Mariners'. The exodus did not stop there however, and to compensate for the losses St Bernard's themselves had to look elsewhere for replacements. They found the clubs in the mining towns of West Lothian, for instance, a ready source of fresh talent.

Needless to say the clubs in these communities did not take too kindly to losing their best players. There is the story of a delegation of St Bernard's officials going to Broxburn by pony and trap to interview Willie Wardrop, Bobby Marr and Tom Chambers.

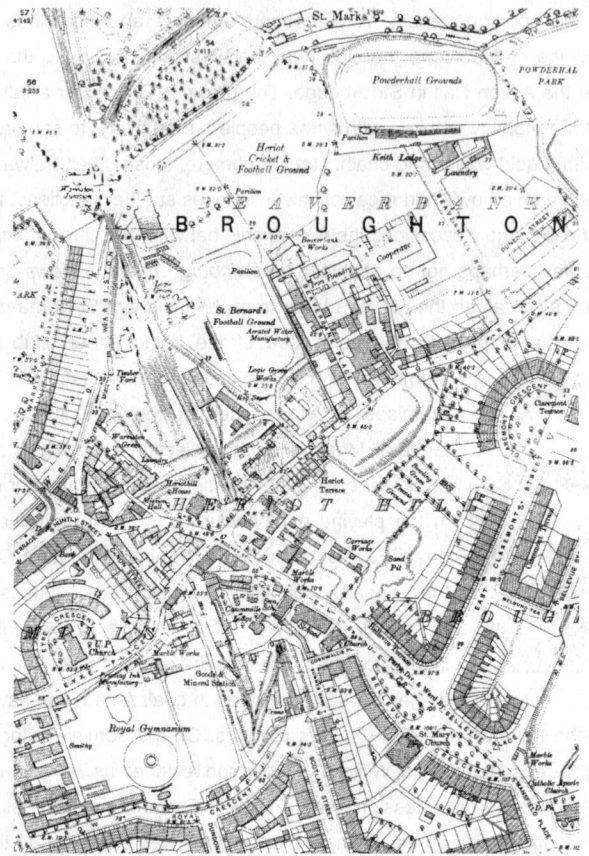

The Logie Green ground is shown at the centre of this map where Logie Green Road is now situated. Other venues used by the club at the Powderhall Grounds and the Royal Gymnasium are also seen. Powderhall Park at the top of the map was Old Powderhall and the Heriot cricket and football ground was to become New Logie Green making five grounds in all used by the Saints in the area.

The vehicle was left in the charge of a small boy who had accompanied the party while they visited the players. Some supporters of the local team got wind of what was happening and managed to persuade the boy that the officials had decided to stay the night. He immediately set off back to Edinburgh with the trap and was well out of reach when the hoax was discovered. Much against their will the Saints' officials did spend the night in Broxburn. On occasions officials visiting outlying areas would telegraph back to Edinburgh if they had been successful in signing someone. This was fraught with danger of course, in the event of the locals finding out about it while the official was still in town, but was overcome by sending a coded message. Otherwise no one knows what might have happened!

St Bernard's made their first ever visit to London and played the Corinthians at Kennington Oval the famous cricket ground, in front of a crowd of 5000, losing by 2-0. Another initiative saw the Saints take on the Scottish International team at Logie Green in a match billed to test the strength of Edinburgh football. Needless to say only four regular Saints players took the field, assisted by four from Leith Athletic, two from Norton Park and McMahon of the Hibs. A crowd of 1500 saw the locals go down by 5-3.

The Saints were one of 14 prominent clubs invited by Renton Football Club to attend a meeting at Holton's Commercial Hotel in Glassford Street in Glasgow on 20 March 1890. This was to discuss the question of forming a league in Scotland, similar to that which had recently been established south of the border. The other clubs were Abercorn, Cambuslang, Celtic, Clyde, Cowlairs, Dumbarton, Hearts, Queens Park, Rangers, Renton, St Mirren, Third Lanark and Vale of Leven. Tom Lamb represented St Bernard's, but some mystery surrounds why they alone, of the twelve clubs represented, did not join. Clyde and Queens Park declined to attend. The initial minutes of the Scottish League would probably have shed light on the matter had they not gone astray.

If the first season at Logie Green had been a bit disappointing, the following season was to become a nightmare. Things started off promisingly enough, with the Saints accepting an invitation to take part in the football tournament of the Second Edinburgh International Exhibition, held at Meggatland. Their opponents were Leith Athletic, a club formed in 1887, who were quickly establishing themselves and could quite rightly be regarded as one of the 'big four' in the capital, along with the Hibs, Hearts and the Saints. The *Edinburgh Evening Dispatch* put up a silver cup for this contest, one of four such matches staged at this successful event. The club from Leith acquired the cup by winning 3-1 in front of a 7500 crowd. If the reader is wondering what type of person supported St Bernard's at this time the *Scottish Sport* can perhaps shed some light on the subject, its reporter stated: " that from the small glance he had of the crowd he put them down as a decided high class (alias up-ish) set (St Bernard's people may take this as a compliment)"!

Tom Lamb

On the first Saturday of September, the Saints met the Adventurers in the first round of the Scottish Cup at home. Their opponents were one of a number of 'secondary' senior clubs to be found in the city, and hailed from the

Gorgie area. As expected St Bernard's strolled into the next round scoring seven goals in the process without reply. What followed shook the game in Scotland.

The Adventurers lodged a protest with the Scottish Football Association alleging professionalism against St Bernard's. This on the grounds that their left back, James Ross, had been induced to join the club from Dunfermline Athletic that season, by promise of remuneration and by paying him a weekly wage. Football in Scotland was of course still strictly amateur at this stage. Ominous rumours had been circulating about St Bernard's dealings with their players, but nobody had expected the Adventurers, or any other club for that matter, to take such an extreme step. It was also felt that the source of the protest was the Fife club. They were aggrieved at failing to retain Ross' services, and the Adventurers were frowned on for their involvement. St Bernard's of course denied the charges.

The Professional Committee of the SFA considered the matter on 19 September 1890. The protest was sustained, with St Bernard's being declared guilty of professionalism. Both the club and Ross would be suspended until 31 October and three officials, Alexander S McIntosh (secretary), W Murray (treasurer) and Thomas Paton would be prohibited from taking any active part in connection with football in Scotland until the same date. The upshot of this was that the Saints were withdrawn from the Scottish Cup and the Edinburgh Shield and could not play any recognised club during the term of the suspension. A sentence of six weeks seemed light when a player crossing the border as a professional would have been given a twelve-month suspension, even if he only played in one match down south, and the Professional Committee took some criticism for double standards. It was also alleged that every club in Scotland was saturated with professionalism and the SFA knew it!

In a surprise move, as a means of circumventing the ban and to keep the team playing, a new club 'Edinburgh Saints' was formed with the utmost haste. Application was formally made for the use of Logie Green and membership tickets of the new club were sold at a nominal figure to the members of St Bernard's who had season tickets. The club was admitted to the East of Scotland Football Association.

The Scottish Football Association would have none of it however and adjudged St Bernard's and 'Edinburgh Saints' to be the same club. This really set the 'cat amongst the pigeons' as they say, and both St Bernard's and Renton, who had played Edinburgh Saints at Logie Green on Saturday, 27 September 1890, were suspended by the SFA for a year. This meant that the Renton club, who had been the prime movers in creating the Scottish League, was also expelled from that competition. So incensed were they that they brought an action in the Court of Session against the SFA and were subsequently successful.

Thomas Paton on receiving a business posting to London with his legal firm employers resigned as Match Secretary. Around 1903 he was to move to Bradford and in his capacity as an accountant is given credit for saving Bradford City when they ran into financial difficulties shortly after their formation.

To fill the void left by the suspended St Bernard's another new club was formed called Edinburgh Northern and this received the approval of the SFA. They played at Logie Green and to all intents and purposes, although not officially, were St Bernard's by another name. However, they could not use any of the players who had represented 'Edinburgh Saints' in the ill-fated Renton match, because they were suspended. In effect they relied on the players from the former St Bernard's second XI and could also call on veterans James Baillie and James Lowe both of whom had missed the Renton match. The Northern did not play their first match until 6 December, drawing up a reasonable fixture list, but they were unable to play any of the top teams or enter any cup competitions at such a late stage. The last match in the short season was played against Leith Athletic on 2 May 1891.

The suspension of St Bernard's by the SFA had been lifted a few days earlier but insufficient time was available to reinstate the St Bernard's name before that match. However players James Methven, George Murdoch, Jack Dorkin and James McNab, all of whom had been affected by the ban, returned that day much to the satisfaction of their followers. Other team members Combe Hall and John McMillan had gone to England when the ban had taken effect, the former making particularly good use of his time there by picking up a FA Cup Winners Medal that season with Blackburn Rovers. Hearts second XI and Renton along with others, helped out with fixtures for the resurrected Saints in the final month in what had been a disastrous season – things could only get better!

League football had established itself in Scotland the previous season with the formation of the Scottish League with the Saints on the sidelines. The great difficulty that now presented itself, for any non-league club, was in obtaining enough suitable fixtures with clubs already involved in the league as these produced the good gates. St Bernard's were unable to join the Scottish League, but their application to get involved in the newly-formed Scottish Alliance, which was effectively a Scottish 'Second Division', was approved and things were very much getting back on an even keel. The Alliance was to all intents and purposes a west of Scotland league and being the only team from the east it lacked local derbies in so far as the Saints were concerned.

After a slow start to the league campaign, in which the first two matches were lost, the Saints settled down to spend a large part of the season in the top two or three positions. In the end however it was Linthouse a club from the Govan area of Glasgow that won the title of champions. This is how the top of the league table looked at the end of the season.

Scottish Alliance League 1891/92	P	W	D	L	F	A	Pts
Linthouse	22	15	03	04	89	49	33
Kilmarnock	22	13	03	06	76	49	29
Morton	22	12	03	07	67	66	27
St Bernard's	22	11	04	07	63	45	26
Northern	22	09	04	09	76	70	22

A team representing the Alliance took on the Scottish League in an Inter League match at Cathkin Park, Glasgow, but lost 4-3. Left back Robert Foyers was the only player from the club to play in that game.

St Bernard's fought through the preliminary rounds of the Scottish Cup only to meet Rangers; one of the exempted clubs, in the first round proper. They lost by 5-1. This was the first time that preliminary rounds had been introduced involving the Scottish League clubs along with one or two others being exempted until the first round proper. For the first time for several seasons Saints reached the finals of both the Edinburgh Cup and the Second XI equivalent where they met the corresponding teams of the Hearts. Both were lost, the respective scores being 0-2 and 2-4. The advent of league football now meant that these cups were beginning to lose their appeal to the public.

St Bernard's were also members of the Scottish Second XI Association from time to time and that season met the reserves of Leith Athletic in the first round of the national competition. After a close contest the Saints lost after a replay with the Athletic going on to win the Cup and repeating the feat the following season.

On the player front neither James Hutton nor James Methven played for the Saints that season both moving to England. Hutton joined Stockton and Methven moved to Derby County. James Methven's stay at the County was a long and distinguished one covering 16 seasons, no less, up to 1907. His total appearances for that club still stand as a record to this day. He played in the FA Cup Finals of 1898, 1899 and 1903 for Derby, all of which were lost.

Whether other clubs made presentations to their players with little or no publicity, or whether St Bernard's were a bit unique in honouring their players in this fashion, I am not sure, but once again we find notice in the press of an award being made. This time, James Guthrie, a sergeant based at Glencorse Barracks, Penicuik, who played in the autumn of 1891 received a cigar case and silver matchbox on being posted elsewhere.

Season 1892/93 saw St Bernard's in the Scottish Alliance for a second season. It was their line-up for the friendly match against Morton at Logie Green in early August however that caused a stir in Edinburgh football circles. It contained three prominent Hearts players in Isaac Begbie, Harry Marshall and William Taylor, all Scottish internationalists, also Leith Athletic's best player James Blessington was included. He was destined to have a distinguished playing career principally with Celtic. Many were sceptical that the Logie Green club would hold on to this illustrious quartet and they were proven right, with only Marshall playing in the following match before they all returned to their normal clubs.

Even without these stars the Saints early season results were admirable and the team led the league table in the first few months. Not only that but a run in the Scottish Cup led to a 3-2 win over the Rangers in the third round at Logie Green in front of an 8000 crowd. This resulted in the Saints reaching the semi-final for the first time ever with a match at Parkhead against Celtic the following Saturday. This turned out to be a disappointment for the club, and the 500 supporters who travelled west by special train, the side going down 5-0. 'Old boy' Blessington scored two goals for the victors.

Earlier in the season a 'handsome and commodious' press box was opened in the grand-stand in time for the Cowlairs home league game. Mr Monteith an official of the club was given the credit for this enhancement, much welcomed by the journalists!

Results in the Alliance were better than the season before with Saints finishing as runners up. Morton, Port Glasgow Athletic, Ayr, East Stirling and Kings Park had all dropped out from the previous season to be replaced by Cowlairs, Vale of Leven and Cambuslang.

The leading positions on the completed table were as follows: -

Scottish Alliance League 1892/93	P	W	D	L	F	A	Pts
Cowlairs	18	14	02	02	68	31	30
St Bernard's	**18**	**11**	**01**	**06**	**60**	**40**	**23**
Linthouse	18	11	01	06	52	46	23
Airdrie	18	10	02	06	62	48	22
Thistle	18	09	01	08	49	44	19

An interesting addition to the playing staff towards the end of the season was Walter Arnott the distinguished Queens Park full back. This famous internationalist, considered by many as the greatest full back of his time, was approaching the veteran stage but nevertheless was a decided acquisition for the club. Indicative of his standing, even then, was his selection for the international match against England on 1 April 1893, and, although listed as representing the Queens Park club he had in fact started playing for St Bernard's by then. Even a year later, and listed as representing the Saints this time, he was selected to play against Ireland. Injury however, prevented him taking his place on the day. One player who did win a cap at this time was Walter's full back partner Robert Foyers who played against Wales at Wrexham in 1893.

In the Edinburgh Cup Final Hearts beat the Saints 3-1 in February but it was the Rosebery Charity Cup Final between the same sides that caused much interest, and not a little controversy. The game was played at the end of the season at the new Powderhall, normally an athletics venue and rarely being used to stage football matches. Additionally the organisers seriously underestimated the interest in the game, and the arrangements were to be found wanting when a crowd of 10,000 turned up. The gates had been opened too late and chaotic scenes developed as spectators struggled to get into the ground. The Hearts team had turned up early, but St Bernard's, not for the first time did not, and their players eventually had to climb barriers to get in.

Saints used some guests, the Queens Park right wing of Thomas Waddell and William Gulliland were brought in, together with James Oswald the old Third Lanark centre forward who had been playing in England with Notts County. The undignified entry to the ground obviously did not affect the Saints players as they started well and built up a 3-0 lead by half time. In the second half the Hearts adopted a more physical approach and the match ended 3-3. The referee attracted some poor press comment for his mishandling of the game. St Bernard's decided to take matters further and lodged a protest with the Charity Committee on the grounds that the ball had not crossed the line for Hearts' second goal. Unfortunately charity was not forthcoming and the Committee ruled that they could not overturn the referee's decision in awarding the goal. Saints immediately intimated their withdrawal from the competition, and would not be swayed to change their minds, thereby ruling out a replay. The cup was awarded to Hearts. The real losers however were the charities as they would have benefited from the undoubted large proceeds that a second game would have generated.

Walter Arnott

Despite the controversy, the relationship between the two clubs was not so bad and Hearts provided the opposition three days later at Logie Green, in a match arranged as a benefit for the popular James Baillie, who had finally decided to hang up his boots.

St Bernard's made application for admission to the Scottish League for 1893/94 and were admitted along with Dundee, which coincided with the introduction of professionalism in Scotland in May 1893. Abercorn were the club to drop out. When the matter was discussed at the Scottish League's AGM on 12 June 1893 great emphasis was put on the standard of the various applicants' grounds and the conduct of their supporters. St Bernard's came up trumps on both counts. It was not necessarily the size of the support that was the issue that concerned the League authorities but their conduct, plus the unruly behaviour of the Abercorn support the previous season counted against that club. So well done the patrons of Logie Green! The good results in the Alliance and the win over the Rangers in the Cup obviously did no harm either.

This was a major step for the club. The Alliance League had served its purpose, especially after the disastrous 1890/91 season, when it might have been difficult to re-establish relations with other clubs with regard to fixtures. The geographical nature of that competition however, with the distinct lack of local derbies, affected the club's finances.

The Scottish League was a different kettle of fish altogether. Not only would the Saints be playing all the top clubs in Scotland, other than Queens Park, who refrained from joining the League until 1900, but the matches against fellow Edinburgh clubs Hearts and Leith Athletic would produce good gates. Hibs were still in the process of a revival after being inactive for about two years from February 1891. However they also had applied to join the League, but had been turned down as their ground was not deemed suitable. The season started well, and by the beginning of November the Saints, under the captaincy of Walter Arnott, were lying second in the League behind Celtic, just in time for their annual visit to London to meet the Corinthians. These trips were undoubtedly good fun. On this occasion the team also played against Oxford University. A tour of the colleges was part of the itinerary, with left-winger Barney Crossan adopting the disguise of a professor adding to the merriment. A year previously one of the Saints is reported to have fallen asleep whilst playing at Aldershot against the Highland Light Infantry! The hospitality in London must have been good! In fact a few years later a player was to remark if for nothing else it was worth joining St Bernard's for the London trips alone.

Everything in the garden was rosy until Celtic were encountered in the third round of the Scottish Cup at Parkhead. An 8-1 defeat was not the result the club was

James McNab

looking for, but as was commonplace at the time Saints lodged a protest. As part of an experiment with artificial lighting the Celtic pitch had wires hanging over it to support lights. St Bernard's protested that the play had been interfered with when the ball struck the wires. Considering the margin of defeat and the fact that the wires had been touched only on a few occasions there seemed scant grounds for complaint. The club later withdrew the protest.

New players that season included goalkeeper John Lindsay, the Scottish internationalist, who had made his name with the famous Renton team, George Murdoch, an old player of the club, who was returning after a spell with Third Lanark and James Oswald, another internationalist, coming back to Scotland after service with Notts County. Robert Foyers retained his position in the Scottish international team for the match against Wales. Not so fortunate were Walter Arnott and James Oswald, who were selected for the Irish and Welsh matches respectively but had to call off due to injury. Oswald recovered in time to take his place in the Scottish League team against the Football League at Goodison Park, Liverpool. Once again good service was recognised with James McNab receiving a purse of gold sovereigns from Tom Lamb, the club President.

The St Bernard's Sports meeting always popular, continued, but it was noticeable that the event was changing in nature. In the early days it was as much a fete day for the residents in the north of the city but was now run on more professional lines.

The first season in the Scottish League was a great success and the club's finishing position of third was never to be bettered by them.

Mention of season 1893/94 would not be complete without bringing up the subject of the second XI. In all 32 matches were played by the Wee Saints, 22 of these were won, 5 were drawn and only 5 lost. This was to be by far, their best season ever and reaching the fifth round of the Scottish Second XI Cup represented their best ever performance in that particular competition. The narrow 3-4 defeat in the Edinburgh Second XI Cup Final was also commendable given that the young Hearts won the Scottish version as well beating the Saint's conquerors, St Mirren in the final, played incidentally at Logie Green. Details of the complete season are given in the statistics section of this publication.

This is how the positions at the top of the table looked at the end of the season.

Scottish League Division 1 1893/94	P	W	D	L	F	A	Pts
Celtic	18	14	1	3	53	32	29
Hearts	18	11	4	3	46	32	26
St Bernard's	18	11	1	6	53	39	23
Rangers	18	8	4	6	44	30	20
Dumbarton	18	7	5	6	32	35	19

Encouraged by the success of the previous season, 1894/95 season started on a most progressive note with the provision of a new stand for the supporters. This replaced the old structure on the same site and provided accommodation for some 1200 people, with 700 or so more on terracing in front of it. Rather interestingly the club did not meet the cost of construction of £200 but a number of members did so on an individual basis, Lord Wolmer and a Mr Mitchell Thomson both made generous contributions. Two years later this 'grandstand committee' would be in a position to hand over the stand to the guarantors of the club free of any debt. It is more than probable in any case that the club itself would not have been able to fund the construction. The architect was a Mr Pearson of 24 Castle Street, whilst Messrs Marr & Co, joiners and contractors of Henderson Row, carried out the building work. It was considered that Logie Green would now have the capacity to accommodate 15,000 spectators.

On the playing front there were not too many changes from the team that saw out the prior campaign. Notable absentees were Walter Arnott and James McNab, both former captains. James Sneddon, who had been playing a back up role with city rivals Leith Athletic, replaced John Lindsay in goal. Robert Foyers switching from the left side, with William Cowan replacing him, covering Arnott's role at right back. Otherwise it was very much the same players who had finished the last term.

It is indicative of the reputation of Walter Arnott that on attending a match early that season he received a standing ovation from the patrons in the grandstand.

The advent of professionalism, and the leagues, had brought about a great deal of change in a short space of time. Clubs now had different priorities. The local cups, once the main competitions, were no longer as important, and at the AGM of the East of Scotland Football Association held in May 1894, Hearts, Hibs and the Saints all resigned their membership. As a result they did not play for the East of Scotland Shield or the City Cup that season or the next.

A new competition was the Edinburgh League, played in the last three months of the season, between the four leading clubs in the city. In essence the ten strong Scottish League provided clubs with 18 matches in a season. This programme, apart from the odd re-arranged game played after the New Year, was virtually over by Christmas time. League clubs became involved with Scottish Cup ties towards the turn of the year but it still left gaps to be filled in the fixture list and the Edinburgh League was seen as a better alternative to meaningless friendlies.

Councillor Hay formally opened the new stand on 11 August 1894 with St Bernard's beating Hearts 3-2 in a friendly. On the previous Saturday the Saints had opened Beechwood Park the new ground of Leith Athletic, situated near Easter Road.

The first two Scottish League matches of season 1894/95 provided a formidable challenge for the club, with Celtic and Rangers to be met on successive Saturdays. Saints lost both, but on a less savoury note we find that ashes were thrown at the Rangers' players. Manchester was visited for the first time for a friendly with Newton Heath FC prior to that club becoming Manchester United. A win there by 5-2 set the Saints up for a good run of results in the League. On the last Saturday of November Airdrie were beaten 4-2 in the first round of the Scottish Cup at Logie Green. The following weekend saw St Bernard's in London where Woolwich Arsenal were beaten 2-1. In present-day terms wins at Manchester United and Arsenal in the same season by any club would be looked on very favourably! Just before Christmas the Saints eased past Kilmarnock 3-1 at Logie Green in the second round of the Scottish Cup and thus qualified to meet Clyde. This game was much delayed due to bad weather and did not take place until 23 February. It had been delayed for ten weeks and for many years it held the record for the greatest number of postponements of a tie in the Scottish Cup.

Before it was played tragedy struck the club with the deaths of two players. In January 1895, John Inglis, a member of the second XI passed away, followed a month later by William Cowan, the regular left back in the first team. He was only 23 years of age. Cowan had been injured when struck by the handle of a crane he had been operating. He died a fortnight later. He lay in a coma and his post mortem diagnosed a compound fracture of the skull.

It was against this background that Tom Robertson offered his services to the club. This Scottish internationalist was a prominent player for Queens Park and was well known to the Saints, having also played for Cowlairs. His playing days were coming to an end. Subsequently he was to become a prominent referee and the President of the Scottish League from 1919/21.

Tom Robertson was not a direct replacement in the team for Cowan, but played his usual role of centre half, with captain William Baird moving from that position to right back this meant the versatile Robert Foyers switching to the left. The match against Clyde in the third round was duly played and won and St Bernard's moved on to the semi-final, only after the almost inevitable protest by the opposition had been considered. This time Clyde made two protests, one against James Oswald and the other against Barney Crossan. Both complaints were on the grounds of eligibility, it being alleged that they had taken part in minor games for other clubs. These were dismissed by the SFA, so the Saints met city rivals Hearts on 9 March 1895 at Tynecastle for a place in the final.

Things were not running smoothly for the Saints. Whilst they were able to turn out an unchanged defence for the match at Tynecastle, the forward line was presenting problems. Out through injury were John Wilson, their small but tricky right-winger, but more important was the loss of James Oswald the star centre forward. Whilst the vastly experienced Bobby Laing was drafted in to replace Wilson, someone to take the place of Oswald was more difficult. Over the years it had not been unknown for the Saints' committee to turn to a player from another club to fill a gap. Very often the connection with Queens Park came to their aid. Their players were of course amateur and therefore not bound by professional registration rules. On this occasion they looked to England and called on the services of James W Murison the amateur centre forward of Cambridge University. Another position that had been causing trouble, with regular left-winger Joseph Brady out from early in the season, was also now resolved by the acquisition in January of James Cleland from the Glasgow junior team Minerva.

Although this was the club's second appearance in the semi-final of the national competition it was undoubtedly its biggest match to date. A crowd of 15,000 created a ground record for Tynecastle showing the extent of local interest. Despite the efforts of Hearts in taking the precaution of strengthening the low paling which surrounded the pitch, some of the spectators streamed onto the park under the pressure of the crowd when it gave way. Order was soon restored. St Bernard's started the match brightly, but gradually the Hearts team that was to finish the season as League champions came more and more into the game. A closely contested game finished goal-less.

The inclusion of Tom Robertson did not weaken the side, although James Murison was found somewhat lacking. This was caused perhaps by a difficult train journey from the south that saw him struggle to make the kick off in time after disembarking at Polmont near Falkirk by mistake. Anyone can slip up but this error of judgement did not affect Murison in later life. He went on to become Chief Justice of the Strait's Settlements (Malaysia) from 1925 to 1933 and received the title Sir James William Murison. However he was replaced in the replay. Combe Hall who hailed from Newhaven had been a player for the Saints at the time when they were suspended for professionalism in 1890. He left then to join Blackburn Rovers and was a member of their FA Cup winning team of 1891. He was back in town and attended a club dance. His transfer from Blackburn followed immediately and he filled the centre forward position.

The replay took place the following Saturday at Logie Green, where special arrangements had been made by the St Bernard's committee to accommodate the very large crowd anticipated. New turnstiles were installed to ease access to the ground and the grandstand. Additional banking and terracing led to the claim that the ground now had the largest capacity of any in the city. The Saints fielded an unchanged team save for the inclusion of Hall. After listing a pool of fifteen players Hearts too showed only one change with Baird taking the place of Chambers.

A crowd estimated at 18,000 turned up to see the game. St Bernard's lined up as follows: Sneddon; Foyers and Baird; McManus, Robertson and Murdoch; Laing, Paton, Hall, Crossan and Cleland. The Hearts' team was Fairbairn; Battles and Mirk; Begbie, Russell and Hogg; McLaren, Baird, Michael, Walker and Scott.

After a goalless first half, during which both sides missed chances, the deadlock was broken in the second half when the Saints were awarded a free kick some thirty yards from goal. From this George Murdoch shot the ball into goal with terrific force where it glanced off the head of Combe Hall past the stranded Fairbairn. *The Scotsman* described the reaction to the goal as follows: 'sticks, hats and handkerchiefs being flourished in the air amid deafening cheers'. As would be expected the Hearts fought back but to no avail as the St Bernard's defence stood firm. The whistle sounded for the end of the game with the score 1-0 and the Saints were in the final. Surely more joyful scenes were never seen in the area as the Saints' supporters spilled out of the ground into Broughton Road and Rodney Street after first invading the pitch to mob their heroes.

Hearts had been the favourites to win the tie but may have underestimated their opponents. Few begrudged the Saints their success. In the final their opponents would be old friends Renton, who were not the force of earlier years but had rather surprisingly beaten Dundee 3-0 in the second replay of the other semi-final.

Saints under trainer James Wilson had prepared well for the semi-final and were to do so for the final itself. Except for Tom Robertson the team spent some time at Burntisland across the Firth of Forth from Granton. Wilson a native of Broxburn was undoubtedly a good trainer. He subsequently moved to Rangers and was also to be responsible later for the Scottish International side.

The Scottish Cup Final was played at Ibrox Park, Glasgow on 20 April 1895. Before the game the Saints had some good news and some bad news. The good news was that James Oswald their international centre forward would be in the line up. The bad news was that William Baird their captain was out. After injury he was unsure of lasting the 90 minutes and George Murdoch was given the captaincy. Combe Hall, who might have expected to be the one omitted, filled in at left back. Using their friendly relationship with the Corinthians a last minute attempt had been made to use L V Lodge of Cambridge University in that position. Like many in the Corinthians side at that time he was also an English internationalist but he declined the invitation.

The crowd of 12,000 included a contingent of 1000 from Edinburgh who travelled through in a special train from the Waverley Station. Saints lined up as follows: James Sneddon; Robert Foyers and Combe Hall; George Murdoch, Tom Robertson and Patrick McManus; Bobby Laing, Danny Paton, James Oswald, Bernard Crossan and James Clelland. The Renton team was Dickie; Ritchie and A McCall; Tait, McColl and Glen; McLean, Murray, Pryce, Gilfillan and Duncan. St Bernard's if anything were slight favourites to win. After all they held a mid table position in the Scottish League Division 1 whereas Renton only occupied a similar position in Division 2. League position of course can never be taken as a barometer for form in the Cup, and in Renton's favour was the Glasgow venue where the bulk of the crowd would be on their side. Murdoch won the toss and the team soon displayed good form. Just as it seemed they might have difficulty in turning this into goals, James Clelland struck twice in a three-minute spell. Both goals emanated from good work on the right wing. The first was a header and the second was a shot. Another ten minutes had elapsed before Renton managed to reduce the deficit to one with Gilfillan the scorer. The referee dismissed Saints protest that the ball had entered by the side net. At half time the score was 2-1 in favour of the Saints.

Twenty minutes from the end Renton upped the pace as they tried to save the game, but the St Bernard's defence stuck to its task, with goalkeeper James Sneddon in good form. Final score was St Bernard's 2 Renton 1.

'After the match the teams dined together in the Alexandra Hotel, Glasgow, where the Cup was presented to the winners, Mr W M Lapsley as president of the club taking the custody of it.' The report in *The Scotsman* goes on to say 'at the station there was a scene of much enthusiasm on the departure of both the special train and of that bearing the team and officials, while at the Waverley Station on the arrival of the team in Edinburgh, the scene was one to be remembered. Proceeding afterwards to the Hotel Metropole, Hanover Street, the team, officials and a number of supporters, further toasted the club on its success.'

St Bernard's Football Club

Standing: James Wilson (Trainer), Tom Robertson, James Oswald, Barney Crossan, James Sneddon and William Baird.
Seated: Bob Laing, Patrick McManus, James Murdoch, Combe Hall and Robert Foyers.
At Front: Robert Paton and James Clelland.

On arrival Mr Lapsley, the Club President, had sprinted to the Waverley Bridge hugging the Cup and jumped into a horse drawn carriage to take him to the hotel. The team members were carried shoulder high to their carriages for the short journey to Hanover Street. There is little doubt similar celebrations were held in Stockbridge, Canonmills, the main areas for support, and elsewhere in the city. The party in the Metropole broke up just before midnight. It was widely recognised that St Bernard's were worthy winners. The cup winners' medals were not presented on the day but at a function shortly afterwards; each player also received a gold scarf pin in the form of a replica of the cup. The merchants of the north of Edinburgh in recognition of the team's success presented these extra mementos.

It then fell for the Cup to be put on display in the window of old official William T Robertson's tobacco shop at 33 Deanhaugh Street in Stockbridge. Although taking part in many finals this was only the second cup to be won by the Saints and the very first by the first eleven!

At the time of writing St Bernard's are the only club with a one hundred percent record of success in Scottish Cup Finals. Played one, won one!

It was a very good season for Edinburgh with Hearts winning the League Championship, Hibs winning the Second Division, and Hearts the Scottish Second XI Cup – a clean sweep of all the national competitions at that time.

After their Scottish Cup win, the Saints had a very disappointing finish to the season, losing all six of the remaining matches. It had been reported that both Foyers and Oswald had been at loggerheads with the club committee during the season and both moved on. This unrest may have had a bearing on performances. Foyers went to Newcastle United with Oswald joining Rangers.

After a reasonable start to season 1895/96, things took a turn for the worse in late September, with 0-5 reverses at the hands of Hearts and Clyde in the League in successive matches. In search of a solution, the committee started switching the players from one position to another, to no avail. They were now near the bottom of the League and supporters expressed their discontent at the position, through the columns of the press, calling on changes in the committee if they could not do better.

Saints finished joint sixth in the Scottish League as some other teams also had an equally poor season as they adapted to the infant professional game. In the Scottish Cup the Saints beat Clackmannan and Annbank in the first two rounds. The latter were the winners of the inaugural Scottish Qualifying Cup and were only beaten 1-0 at Logie Green. A sterner test awaited them in round three, against Queens Park at Hampden. Tom Robertson was still helping out. However he could not assist the Saints in this match, as he was still a member of the Glasgow club, whose rules forbad its members playing against them in Scottish Cup ties. Saints won 3-2, a result that was not entirely expected. So much so that when the news came through to Logie Green play was suspended in the junior match between Claremont and Musselburgh Fern. On the journey back from Hampden to the centre of Glasgow a wheel came off the St Bernard's break. This mishap was more than compensated for by the reception afforded the team when they got back to the capital. A large crowd was on hand to welcome them at the Caledonian Station.

A repeat of the previous season's semi-final against the Hearts, again at Tynecastle, resulted. The training preparations were held in East Lothian with St Bernard's spending some time at North Berwick with Hearts opting for Aberlady. A crowd of 15,000 turned up on the day, many arriving early for fear that the ground could not accommodate everyone wishing to see the match. Tom Robertson returned to the fold with the further assistance from Queens Park of internationalist Bob Smellie at left back. In all Saints showed six changes of personnel from the corresponding game the previous year, with the Hearts showing a more settled line up with only two changes. This is how the teams lined up: Hearts: Fairbairn; McCartney and Mirk; Begbie, Russell and Hogg; McLaren, Baird, Michael, King and Walker. St Bernard's: John Russell; Duncan McLean and Robert Smellie; John Kinross, Tom Robertson and George Murdoch; John Wilson, Danny Paton, Bobby Laing, Isaac Wark and Combe Hall.

George Murdoch led out a St Bernard's team intent on repeating the success of the previous season, but the Saints did not play well. Very often semi-final cup-ties produce disappointing games with nerves getting the better of the players and so it proved on this occasion. Hearts had the better of the game but could not score. It very much looked as if another replay was on the cards at Logie Green, when Michael the centre forward of Hearts netted in 87 minutes. This proved to be the only goal, and although disappointed the Saints readily acknowledged that Hearts had been the better team.

Across the city at Easter Road Hibs had been locked in battle with Renton the beaten finalists from the previous season. A win for the 'Greens' by 2-1 ensured an all Edinburgh final for the first, and to date, the only time.

Up until then all the finals had been played in Glasgow but sensibly it was decided, that with two local teams involved in the game, this should be played in the capital. In terms of neutrality two venues presented themselves, Logie Green and Mr Lapsley's Powderhall. On a count of 8 votes to 6, Logie Green was given the nod by the SFA, although doubts had been expressed as to the Saints' ground having the capacity to house such an important event. Hearts went on to win the cup that season by beating the Hibs 3-1 in front of 17,034 spectators. This still remains the only time that the Scottish Cup Final has been played outside of Glasgow.

Saints finished the season in very unconvincing style indeed without a win, drawing three, and losing ten of the remaining matches.

In the lead up to season 1896/97 a split developed between the clubs in the city. Hearts apparently wanted St Bernard's replaced in the East of Scotland League by Dundee. Leith Athletic supported the Hearts, but the Hibs, in taking the side of the Saints, resigned from the League in protest. Relations, for various reasons, were strained and all four sides opted out of the East of Scotland Football Association. St Bernard's were re-admitted in late August. On a cheerful note Tom Robertson received a very much-deserved gold watch for his services to the club.

In an endeavour to boost their fortunes on the pitch, a batch of new players, mainly forwards, was recruited. Some of these men were returning to Scotland after having played in the Football League. Results were very mixed in the first half of the season although things took on a brighter aspect for a while during Christmas and New Year. After beating Abercorn 6-0 in a league match, a week later on Boxing Day, also at Logie Green, the Rangers were beaten 3-2 in the league. The improved form continued into the first round of the Scottish Cup, which saw the respected Queens Park eliminated with a 2-1 scoreline. St Mirren followed suit in the second round by 5-0, and hopes were raised, that despite their otherwise indifferent form, the Saints might be on course to a third Scottish Cup semi-final in three seasons. In fact there was even talk in some sections of the sporting press of the Saints going all the way and winning the final.

In the quarter-finals they were to meet a Dumbarton side languishing at the bottom of the Second Division, albeit away from home.

To the disappointment of their followers the team could not get a result at Boghead, losing 2-0 to a side who surprised everyone by going on to become runners up that season.

Peace must have been restored amongst the local clubs, as the East of Scotland League did proceed that season in much the same format as usual, with the four city teams participating, and not only included Dundee for the first time, but also East Stirlingshire.

The East of Scotland League was not a particularly successful competition, which took place between the years 1894 and 1907. Sometimes the full programme of matches was not completed, and sometimes matches would be carried forward to the following season. It was not uncommon for a club to concede ground advantage and play both matches against a particular club away from home. It is not surprising therefore, that against such a haphazard situation, a shortish life span evolved.

Aberdeen, Falkirk and Raith Rovers were also to be involved in subsequent seasons. However the 1896/97 season's league was completed and as follows:

East of Scotland League 1896/97	P	W	L	D	F	A	Pts
Hearts	10	6	1	3	28	14	15
Hibs	10	6	4	0	26	18	12
Dundee	10	5	3	2	20	13	12
St Bernard's	10	4	6	0	18	16	8
Leith Athletic	10	3	5	2	14	18	8
East Stirlingshire	10	2	6	1	11	35	5

Since the early 1880s, after Hibs had won the Edinburgh Cup outright, a Shield was put up for competition, this became known as the East of Scotland Shield and is still played for today.

Season 1896/97 was the only occasion that St Bernard's won the trophy, or to be more exact, their combination team did. Many clubs had combination elevens at this time and in fact a Scottish Football Combination League existed made up of second elevens. St Bernard's did apply to join but were unsuccessful. I have been unable to confirm the source of the term 'combination' in a football context. More than likely it refers to reserve teams which were composed of a combination of amateur players and those professionals attached to the club who were not in the first eleven at any given time. Certainly the composition of the teams would seem to bear this out. The term 'combination' did not last for long.

After disposing of Polton Vale, Trinity, Peebles Rovers and Broxburn Shamrock in the earlier rounds, by an impressive collective total of 22 goals scored and only 3 conceded, the Combination Eleven met Cowdenbeath for the custody of the Shield at Tynecastle. The first game on 6 March 1897 was drawn 2-2; the replay the following Saturday, this time in Dunfermline, resulted in a 3-2 win for the Saints. For the record the team was: Rutherford; Duncan and Kinross; Wark, Lowe and Murdoch; Wilson, Brady, Provan, Neilson and Henderson. The same players played in both of the games with Neilson and Henderson switching positions in the first encounter. Names that stand out in the line up were George Murdoch, captain of the Scottish Cup winning team, and the right wing of John Wilson and Joseph Brady, both of whom it will be recalled were unfortunate in missing out on Scottish Cup winners medals through injury.

Another famous trophy that Saints won for the first and only time, that same season, was the King Cup. The Cup had been donated by Percival King, the Edinburgh sports outfitter, and is still played for today by teams in the East of Scotland FA. Once again it was the Combination Eleven that brought the silverware to the club. The road to the final involved beating Adventurers, Peebles Rovers, Clackmannan and Lochgelly United before Polton Vale were met. The Vale came from Loanhead. They were enjoying a successful time, and this was their third successive appearance in the final, having won the cup two years previously. The final was played at the neutral venue of Penicuik, with the Saints eleven not dissimilar to that which had won the East of Scotland Shield, although not reckoned to be as strong. It lined up as follows, Rutherford; Duncan and Reece; Brodie, Lowe and Murdoch; Wilson, Brady, Neilson, McGraw and Henderson. Spurred on by the crowd, the Vale dominated the first half, then established a two-goal lead which could easily have been three, had the Saints' goalkeeper not saved a penalty on the stroke of half time.

After the break St Bernard's came more into it, pulled a goal back, then equalised with the very last kick of the game. The partisan crowd was incensed and attacked the referee. The St Bernard's officials ran to his aid together with three policemen on duty and managed to take him off to safety.

The replay was ordered for Easter Road. Polton Vale refused to agree on the terms imposed by the East of Scotland FA and the cup was awarded to St Bernard's.

At the start of April 1897 the club made a big effort to raise funds by holding a bazaar in the Masonic Hall in George Street. With a view to making it an attraction the hall was fitted up as an Indian Village. The objective was to raise sufficient funds to place the club on a satisfactory financial basis with a view ultimately to the purchase of Logie Green, then leased from the Heriot Trust. The bazaar achieved its objective and around £600 of debt was cleared. The recipient of a gold medal this time was a William Moncrieff who had been instrumental in making the event a success.

On a sadder note that same month it was reported that Mr W M Lapsley, the president of the club, had had an arm amputated following an accident at Kinross.

In an endeavour to curtail costs, the Saints decided to scrap their reserve team at the start of season 1897/98, thus saving an expenditure of £300. Most of the players from the previous season's first team were retained and some new faces added. Results for the two seasons since the Scottish Cup success had been disappointing to say the least, but the club were hopeful that this trend could be reversed. In the event things got worse, and the final league position showed a drop from seventh to ninth, in second last place above Clyde. Automatic promotion and relegation were not in place at this time, although a club or clubs finishing at the bottom of the table did come up for re-election. They could be voted out by their fellow members. Fortunately this fate did not befall Saints and both they and Clyde kept their places in the top league.

Little or no solace was to be found in the Scottish Cup either. After beating Dumbarton 3-1 at Boghead in a first round replay, the next round paired Saints with old friends Queens Park. The two teams had met each other in the Cup in both of the previous two seasons with St Bernard's winning on each occasion. This time the Glasgow club made no mistake, scoring five goals without reply, and at Logie Green! The famous R S McColl scored two of them. One comfort for the Saints' treasurer was the size of the crowd. A much above average 9000 attended the match. This figure was not really surprising as the Queens Park club was always a popular visitor to the city.

One of the Stockbridge junior teams, the North Western FC, made use of Logie Green that season on the days when the Saints were away from home.

After a year out, Saints re-introduced the second XI for 1898/99, this to be their last ever season. Over the years, on occasion, the team was entered for the Scottish Second Eleven Cup – the national competition for reserve teams, but had a poor record in it. Unlike their great rivals, and a club of a similar standing, Leith Athletic who triumphed twice, it was a trophy St Bernard's never won.

Hopes were high that the form of the first XI would improve with the introduction of younger players. In his preview of the season the reporter of the *Evening News* opinioned his liking for the intended line up. Things certainly improved, to the extent that not so many heavy defeats were encountered, although still too many games were lost, albeit by small margins. However the final league position was only improved by one place. Celtic ended any Scottish Cup hopes by winning 3-0 at Parkhead in the second round. There was no doubt that the team contained good players; perhaps they were too young, and perhaps there were not enough of them. Of that team Duncan McNicol, Peter Turner and James Tennant were all subsequently to be transferred to Arsenal. These players were the first of several St Bernard's men to go to the Gunners over the years. Full backs Alexander Kay and Alexander Wood were both to play for Sheffield United. Markie Bell and Robert Houston became members of Hearts' Scottish Cup winning team of 1901. Donald Cameron was to go to Rangers.

Alexander Kay

The playing side was not the only concern at Logie Green as the *Evening News* report of 20 April 1899 explains: '*St Bernard's Club to be carried on.*'

The St Bernard's Football Club held a special general meeting in the pavilion at Logie Green last evening when Mr W M Lapsley presided over a large attendance of members. The business was principally the nomination of office bearers for the next year. The difficulty in securing a ground to substitute Logie Green and the heavy liabilities upon the club, were the main topics of consideration. The chairman, after the minutes of last meeting had been approved, reported at length on the efforts made by the committee in charge of securing a new ground. When the Heriot Trust had agreed to refuse the extension of the lease of Logie Green, the committee made an offer for the vacant ground joining the Apostolic Church at Broughton, also owned by the Trust. This would have proved a very suitable ground for the club. The surrounding inhabitants however had raised objections and these proved too much for them. They next sought to secure the old Gymnasium Ground at Pitt Street, now occasionally let to a carnival company, with an offer also made for a field close to that of the Rugby Union at Inverleith. Both of these were refused. They then learned of a piece of ground near Powderhall. This proved difficult as the existing tenant's lease did not expire until November and even then it would require a considerable sum to secure it. In view of the heavy burden already on the club, the committee, before incurring any further responsibility, decided to bring the matter before the members (Applause). The financial statement, submitted by Mr Macdonald, showed that income amounted to £1843 and the expenditure to £1868 leaving a deficit of £25. This was an improvement on the previous year when there was a deficit of £95. The club's liabilities amounted to over £900. The question was then put forward whether the club should be carried on or not. It was intimated that several members of committee, and others who had advanced money, had intimated that such sums need not be reckoned as liabilities (Applause). Mr Lapsley stated that rather than see the St Bernard's beaten for a ground, he would place Powderhall at their disposal (Loud Applause). Mr Kinsey then moved that the club should be carried on, and when this was put to the meeting, it was carried unanimously. The following office bearers were nominated: President: W M Lapsley, Vice-President: Mr J Oliver, Secretaries: Messrs Louis Gumley and T Robertson, Treasurer: Mr A Somerville, Committee: Messrs W Glen, J McNab, R Macdonald, R B Martin, A McIntosh, W J Kinsey, W Baird and J E Swan. From that list, Mr Gumley withdrew his name from the position of Secretary, which left a contest for the members of committee, there being eight nominated for only six places. The question of turning the team into an amateur one was not considered, although it was indicated that some members would be in favour of floating it as a limited liability company.'

The club was fortunate in obtaining the use of Powderhall but of course it was not on a free basis but a business arrangement, as it was required to pay a rent. As a result of this Mr Lapsley felt it necessary to resign as President of St Bernard's so as to avoid any possible conflict of interest.

Other locations for a new ground had been looked at including a piece of ground owned by the Fettes Trust at Comely Bank and another near Warriston Cemetery but both were considered unsuitable.

The days at old Logie Green were over and it was not long before work commenced in constructing Logie Green Road, which runs through the middle of the site of the old football ground. The whole area of Lower Broughton was subject to a spate of fresh building as the city expanded. Legal proceedings were to be taken against the club if the embankments were not removed and the Heriot's Trust eventually agreed to accept the sum of £50 in full for the obligations. In June 1899 the

Scottish Sport reported that all that remained was the beautiful grandstand that was falling due for auction.

Chapter 4
A brief stay at New Powderhall

St Bernard's provided the opposition at the formal opening of Dens Park, Dundee on the 19 August 1899. Dundee had previously played at Carolina Port. The match was a friendly and the Saints were chosen because of a bond formed between the two clubs, both joining Division 1 in the same season. Then in October Saints were the visitors at the opening of the new stand at Celtic Park, Glasgow. These occasions were happy events in what was otherwise to be a season of great disappointment. Eight of the first ten league matches were lost, and whilst a revival of sorts was made in the remaining part of the season, the short nature of the league programme meant that the damage was done. On 16 December 1899 a crucial match was played in Glasgow against Clyde, who had an even poorer record than the Saints. To have any hope of preserving their status in the top league a win was essential. It was with some relief that this was achieved with a 4-2 win. Mr Anderson a former secretary of the club presented the players with silver cigarette cases as a mark of his appreciation. The Saints finished in second bottom spot, level on points with St Mirren, but this time they were voted out of Division 1 albeit after a test match at Dens Park, Dundee lost 2-1 to the Paisley team. Even if they had won the test match it is very likely they would still have suffered the same fate so much so that the purpose of the test match is unclear. Not only were there problems on the playing side, more seriously the club was in a parlous financial state.

The move to Powderhall, while really the only alternative at the time, was not a success. For one thing the stadium, although able to accommodate a sizable crowd, was not really made for football but was a ground which had been constructed for athletics. Furthermore it was very close to the Water of Leith, which meant that it was not uncommon for the ball to be kicked into the river causing delays whilst it was retrieved. A bigger problem was the clash of dates with athletic meetings that had been approved before the arrangement with the Saints came into place. This meant that the team hardly had a home match before October. Even then the home match with Dundee on 7 October was played at Easter Road. Maybe the Saints should have tried to move there, as it was their only win in ten league matches! Still Powderhall was better than no ground at all. This must have been a very unsettling time with perhaps tensions coming to the surface with a spate of suspensions by the club of players for reasons undisclosed to the public. In a short space of time Robert Houston, Donald Cameron, Alex Hood and Thomas Wilkie were all disciplined by the club. The suspension of the latter was *sine die*, which meant without limit of time, but while it ended his career with St Bernard's he went on to play for Partick Thistle.

If St Bernard's were at a very low ebb, football in the Stockbridge area in general appears to have been in good heart with no less than five junior teams in the locality. All of these teams entered the Scottish Junior Cup and indeed formed a league of their own called the Northern Junior League. The clubs were the Rosebery, North Western, Claremont, Woodburn Athletic and the Thistle. Beneficial to their existence was the availability of nearby Inverleith Park, which had numerous pitches and which on occasion was a focal point for large crowds.

Doubts were expressed at the time as to Edinburgh's capability to sustain three professional sides in the top division. Events over the subsequent 100 years would tend to bear this out. While Hibs and Hearts have both had an almost unbroken tenure in the top echelon Saints never did regain their place, with Leith Athletic only making a very brief reappearance in the early 1930s. To further demonstrate how the Saints were beginning to drop out of the upper tier of Scottish football at this particular time an Inter-City League was formed without them although their omission from it enabled the East of Scotland League to continue. The clubs taking part were Hearts, Hibs, Rangers, Celtic, Third Lanark and Queens Park. Saints' demotion to the Second Division would prove to be a turning point for the worse in their fortunes.

On 3 April 1900 a special meeting of all interested parties was held in the Free Gardeners Hall in Picardy Place with 200 people in attendance. The club treasurer disclosed that the gross liabilities amounted to £680. Discussions involved how the club should continue from here with one faction of the audience advocating the formation of a limited liability company. A number of football clubs had already taken this step. It was also felt that it would not be easy to get guarantors to support the club given the recent difficulties. Some others offered to set up a syndicate scheme, whereby certain of the members would subscribe a cash sum each, and would take over the running of the club from the members. It was even hinted at, that the club should abandon running a professional team, and operate an amateur one instead. Within the next few weeks it was announced that the suggestion for a syndicate had prevailed, with the proposal for the limited company failing to gain sufficient support.

Exactly a month later at a meeting of creditors of the club held in Dowell's Rooms, the members of the syndicate made an offer of 6/8d in the £1, in settlement of all claims that was accepted.

It was with a much-changed team that Saints embarked on their first ever season in Division 2 in 1900/01, and their second at Powderhall. It seemed that St Bernard's had recruited well. Patronage came in the form of Lord Rosebery, who attended the first home league match against Port Glasgow Athletic along with two young sons one of them, Lord Dalmeny, a footballer at Eton, kicked off then seemed reluctant to leave the field. However there is no record of him ever wearing the Saints' colours! Conversely the same cannot be said of the St Bernard's team itself who in the next home game against Clyde wore the famous Rosebery racing colours of primrose and pink and continued to do so until 1904. The Saints were not alone in sporting his Lordship's colours on the football pitch. The Scottish international team five months earlier, in their 4-1 win over England at Celtic Park, and on other occasions at the start of last century, was similarly attired.

The Saints did not let their followers down and went on to win the league title that season. In fact in October they had the distinction of being top of both the Second Division and the East of Scotland League. See the complete table below.

Sandy Brown

One match to disappear from the fixture list was that against the Corinthians, and it must be assumed that this was done on economical grounds, the cost of going to London proving to be too high. Certainly criticism had been mounting within the support about this given the terrible state of the club's finances. That season, Tottenham Hotspur won the FA Cup with the assistance of old Saints' player Sandy Brown, who scored a total of 15 goals in the cup run, a record that still stands today. He left Saints in 1896 and played for Preston North End and Portsmouth before arriving at White Hart Lane.

Scottish League Division 2 1900/01	P	W	D	L	F	A	Pts
St Bernard's	18	11	4	3	42	26	26
Airdrieonians	18	11	1	6	43	32	23
Abercorn	18	9	3	6	37	33	21
Clyde	18	9	2	7	43	35	20
Port Glasgow Athletic	18	10	0	8	45	43	20
Ayr	18	9	0	9	32	34	18
East Stirlingshire	18	7	3	8	34	39	17
Hamilton Accies	18	4	4	10	41	49	12
Leith Athletic	18	5	2	11	22	32	12
Motherwell	18	4	3	11	26	42	11

The problem of not having a home ground, over which they had sole use, was still with them, but a solution was at hand. It was announced that the club would be moving back to the Royal Gymnasium the following season.

Chapter 5
Back at the Royal Gymnasium

Baillie Murray formally opened the new ground at the Gymnasium, over which a seven-year lease had been taken, on Monday, 19 August 1901, with a match against the Hearts in the East of Scotland League. This they lost 2-1. In addition to the football pitch, which ran in a north to south direction, a five-lane cinder running track was laid down. This led to St Bernard's acting as promoters of their own Pedestrian Race meetings – a more than useful source of income to subsidise the costs of running the football team. So successful were they at this that a year or two on a suggestion was made that they should confine themselves to these activities and dispense with the football! A stand, which measured 196 feet long, was erected on the east side of the ground and could accommodate 1250 people. The entrances to the ground were from Eyre Place and Fettes Row. This was a far better arrangement for the Saints and use of the pitch was again back in their own hands. As they had no reserve side, Edinburgh Rosebery FC played at the ground when the team was away. By their continued use of this facility the Rosebery became known as the 'Wee Saints'. Like St Bernard's it was another old club with a strong Stockbridge connection. During their time at the Gymnasium they were a particularly successful junior side winning most of the local competitions. When they were unable to obtain use of the Gymnasium they played at Inverleith Park.

Derby matches with Leith Athletic took on a new significance with the Athletic moving from the Lochend district to Logie Green. This was not the old St Bernard's ground that now had buildings on it and a road running through it, but a new ground on the site of the old Heriot's School cricket and football ground immediately next to and only separated by a fence from the Powderhall Grounds. In effect two Scottish League clubs were now playing in the Canonmills area with their grounds less than a quarter mile apart. Both clubs were to remain at these grounds up to the First World War.

It must have been a disappointment to the club that they could not regain their Division 1 status by virtue of winning the lower league, but automatic promotion and relegation was still several years distant. They were still able to attract good young players to the club even though they were unable to hold onto them for any length of time. The side of 1901/1902 contained four such players. At right back was Archie Annan who went to Sunderland and was in the Bristol City FA Cup final team of 1909. At left back was Robert McEwan a local lad signed from the Rosebery. He went south to join Bury. Another player to go to Lancashire was Willie Bow an inside left who joined Blackburn Rovers. Bill Morrison joined the club at the end of that season from West Calder.

He was also to move south after another two seasons to Fulham. He was in the Raith Rovers Scottish Cup Final team of 1913.

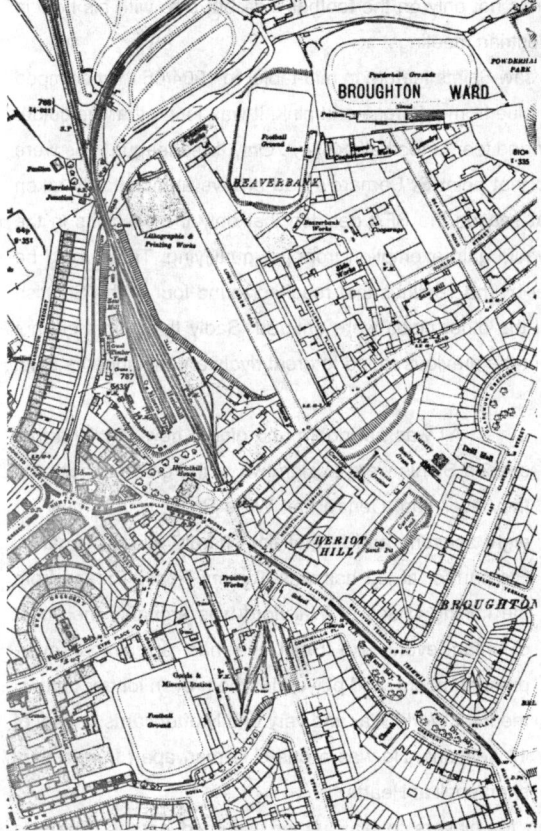

The St Bernard's Ground (the Royal Gymnasium) shown at the foot of the map with the Leith Athletic Ground (New Logie Green) next to Powderhall. Surely only the grounds of the two Dundee clubs have been nearer to each other.

To aid the Ibrox Disaster Fund the Edinburgh team that played Glasgow at Tynecastle that season and won 1-0 contained both McEwan and Bow. AJ Christie the famous Queens Park player also featured in a few matches whilst also playing some rugby for Daniel Stewarts College FP. One of the most famous Queens Park players of all time, R S McColl, guested for the Saints in a friendly at Greenock against Morton. Clearly, despite their new found lowly status, Saints had not entirely lost the entrepreneurial skills that were evident during their tenure of Logie Green, when many matches were arranged against top class opposition from England. An equally famous name, Vivian Woodward, the English international centre forward, was 'recruited' to play against the Hearts at home in an East of Scotland League match in May 1903.

The club received a serious blow at the end of February 1903 when W M Lapsley was killed in an accident. He and his wife had been travelling down Dundas Street in a cab, on their way to attend the Scotland versus Ireland rugby international at Inverleith, when the horse suddenly bolted. The efforts of Lapsley himself were unable to control the runaway animal on the steep incline after the coachman panicked and the cab crashed into a basement area at the junction with Great King Street. Lapsley was killed on impact and his wife was severely injured. He had always taken a great interest in the club and had been with them almost from the outset. His loss must have been felt greatly by St Bernard's not only on the football side but also with his help in organising the successful pedestrian meetings.

The next two seasons saw Saints feature in mid-table. In 1904/05 they slumped to bottom despite reverting to blue from primrose and pink. It was found that the colour pink could not stand 'the wear and tear of football activity'. Only three league wins were achieved in 22 games. Up to that point St Bernard's had always automatically taken part in the Scottish Cup. That season the SFA decided that only the 14 clubs in the Scottish League Division 1 would gain exemption from pre-qualifying. They would be joined in the first round proper by the 18 clubs that reached round four of the Scottish Qualifying Cup, into which all the other clubs were entered. Sadly the Saints did not even reach that stage, falling in the previous round to great rivals and neighbours Leith Athletic by 5-1.

Tommy Ross

All was not doom and gloom however, and that season Saints were to sign two of the greatest servants they ever had. Centre half Willie Smith was to play for eight seasons and in that time hardly missed a game. His partner at left half was Tommy Ross. Tommy from the mining village of Wallyford was arguably their best clubman ever. Like Smith he had an almost ever-present record, and played for them even longer up until the First World War and very briefly afterwards, a total of 11 seasons. He was a one-club man apart from a very short spell at Hearts.

It was not uncommon for players to play under assumed names. There is reason to believe that inside left 'Buchan', who played in the second half of that season, was in fact James McDonald who hailed from Peterhead, and who in subsequent seasons played under his own name. Certainly the name 'Buchan' does not appear in the list of professionals registered by St Bernard's with the SFA for that season, although he may have been an amateur. He was with the Saints for another two seasons before being transferred to Bradford City.

Season 1905/06 followed a pattern very similar to the previous one, although a more respectable position in the league was obtained. The Division 2 championship went to the Leith team, who again were responsible for Saints not qualifying for the

Scottish Cup. A 1-0 defeat in the second round of the preliminary competition did the damage. When Leith Athletic were formed into a limited company in 1905, the word 'Athletic' was dropped and they were simply known as Leith FC up until the First World War. Despite the change of name, most sources regard them as being one and the same club. At the end of the season Saints signed centre forward Sandy Hall from Peterhead. He only stayed for the following season before moving on to Newcastle United. He was one of a number of Aberdeenshire players to come to the Saints at this time. At New Year time, in 1905 and 1907, St Bernard's visited both Aberdeen and Peterhead to play matches, and more than likely it was the contacts made then that led to the arrival of these players.

Another cup competition was introduced in 1905, the Penman Cup. St Bernard's were one of 17 clubs from Fife, Clackmannan, Stirling, West Lothian and Edinburgh, who formed an association to administer this knock out contest for the cup presented by Mr George Penman of Cowdenbeath.

After their period in the doldrums, season 1906/07 turned out to be the best one for years for St Bernard's. Not only did the team win the Division 2 title but also they were beaten finalists in the Scottish Qualifying Cup. The team had a more settled look as all successful ones do. George Ramsay was a reliable goalkeeper who was in his first season with the club. The experienced full-back pairing of Peter Buchanan and Andrew Reid ably assisted him in defence. At half back Smith and Ross were still doing sterling work and were now assisted by Robert Findlay another Aberdonian. In attack they had Hall and McDonald both of whom were attracting the scouts from the clubs down south. Both were to move on in the close season.

The run in the Scottish Qualifying Cup started with a stutter at Broxburn before the local Shamrock were beaten with goals to spare in the replay at the Gymnasium. Another Broxburn side the Athletic suffered likewise in the next round. Victory in round three over Leith, who had won both Division 2 and the Qualifying Cup the year before, must have tasted particularly sweet after recent reverses at the hands of that club in the national competition. The Saints were on a roll and neither Arbroath, Forfar Athletic nor Johnstone from Renfrewshire in the subsequent rounds could prevent the Saints meeting Raith Rovers in the final at Tynecastle on 24 November 1906.

A crowd of 12,000 turned up to see if the Stockbridge club could add to their Scottish Cup success of 12 seasons previous. Up to that point no club had managed to win both cups. Not all the crowd was local, and it was estimated that 3000 travelled from Kirkcaldy to support the Rovers in four special trains. The Saints were almost at full strength and lined up as follows: George Ramsay; Peter Buchanan and Andrew

Reid; William Sloggie, William Smith and Robert Findlay; Alex Ritchie, Mungo Beveridge, Alex Hall, James McDonald and Robert Tait.

The Rovers had the better of the first half and after scoring early on added another just before half time. After the interval, with the wind now at their backs, the Saints came more into the game although the Kirkcaldy side were very dangerous on the break almost adding to their lead on several occasions. Twenty minutes into the half, outside left Tait managed to pull one back, much to the delight of the Stockbridge contingent in the crowd. If they were excited by this development, a minute later they were at 'fever height' according to the *Evening News* when Beveridge scored the equaliser. Spurred on by their supporters the Saints went for the winner but the Rovers defence held out.

The replay took place at Easter Road the following Saturday. Demonstrating a mode of transport of the time, an advert appeared in the *Evening News*, indicating that one four-in-hand carriage would leave Hamilton Place and another at Players' stables in Pitt Street, half an hour before the kick off. No matter how they travelled from Stockbridge the management of St Bernard's expressed their delight at the level of support for the team. The 12,000 gate at the first match at Tynecastle had been a record for a final. This record was beaten at the replay. Around 1000 more turned up with once again a good following from Fife.

Saints had the same line up while the Rovers showed one change. Again the Rovers went two up in the first half, but unlike the previous game, managed to add another just before the break. This proved to be too much of a deficit for a St Bernard's side that pulled one back through Robert Findlay near the end. In the closing minutes Saints even missed a penalty to effectively finish any chance of saving the game. Raith Rovers deserved their success and as the players were carried off shoulder high, the Trades Band from Kirkcaldy played 'See the Conquering Hero Comes'.

After the final it was St Bernard's who went from strength to strength winning the Division 2 title with the Rovers having a very poor campaign in the league. After a gap of two seasons Saints qualified for the Scottish Cup proper but went out in round 1 to old friends Renton after three games were needed to separate the sides.

The final positions in the league were:

Scottish League Division 2 1907/08	P	W	D	L	F	A	Pts
St Bernard's	22	14	4	4	41	24	32
Vale of Leven	22	13	1	8	54	35	27
Arthurlie	22	12	3	7	51	40	27
Dumbarton	22	11	3	8	52	35	25
Leith	22	10	4	8	40	35	24
Albion Rovers	22	10	3	9	43	36	23
Cowdenbeath	22	10	5	7	36	40	23
Ayr	22	7	6	9	34	38	20
Abercorn	22	5	7	10	29	47	17
Raith Rovers	22	6	4	12	40	48	16
East Stirlingshire	22	6	4	12	36	48	16
Ayr Parkhouse	22	5	2	15	33	63	12

The St Bernard's team that played for the greater part of season 1907/08 showed changes from the previous season. The defence had the settled formation of Ramsay, Buchanan and Reid, Findlay, Smith and Tommy Ross. The changes were in attack with a completely new set of forwards, recruited mainly of necessity to replace the players who had moved south. At outside right was Charles Murray who joined from Aberdeen East End with his inside partner Harry Simpson from Peterhead, who was only 18 years of age. James Simpson at centre forward was also from the same East End club in Aberdeen as Murray. In the Granite City they had formed that club's right wing. At inside left was young Peter Logan an Edinburgh boy from the Dalry district. The veteran of the youthful forward line was ex-Saint James Tennant at outside left. Seven years previously you will recall he had moved to Arsenal and was now back after a spell at Middlesbrough.

Once again the campaign in the Qualifying Cup held the attention of the followers of the Saints in the first half of the season. Home advantage in any cup-tie has always been desired. This particular season Saints had it made, as they say, with every game being played in Edinburgh. The Royal Garrison Artillery failed to fire in the first round and were defeated 5-0 then for the second year in succession Broxburn Athletic were beaten in the second. After a bye in the next round Abercorn, Galston and Hamilton Academicals were all defeated in the succeeding rounds. Raith Rovers had a more difficult run of games but still made the final again for a repeat of the previous year's final, again at Tynecastle, on Saturday, 30 November 1907.

The Saints team lined up as described already and by coincidence the defence of the Rovers team was along very similar lines, also to the previous season. Like Saints they also had new forwards. A large crowd crossed the Forth bringing the Kirkcaldy Trades Band with them once more. Edinburgh was proving to be a popular venue for the final. Once again the attendance of over 16,000 was a record for the competition. The involvement of two East of Scotland clubs had, of course, a part to play in this situation.

The game had not long started when centre forward Axford scored for the Rovers. St Bernard's reply was almost instantaneous. Harry Simpson was fouled in a scrimmage in front of goal straight from the kick off, and captain Peter Buchanan slotted home the resultant penalty kick, thus atoning for his miss a year earlier. The score remained level up to the interval. Rovers re-appeared in a changed strip of faded maroon and their performance from then on matched the state of their jerseys. In the second half St Bernard's had much the better of the play. They went into the lead through James Tennant. Another foul on Harry Simpson in the box, another penalty converted by Peter Buchanan and Saints were home and dry. The final score of 3-1 was the exact reverse of the last final and the Cup was on its way to the Gymnasium, via the Imperial Hotel in Leith Street where the presentation took place. In the Scottish Cup proper Saints put up a terrific fight against Queens Park. Three matches were required before the men from Hampden edged it 1-0.

In recognition of help received from the St Bernard's Swimming Club, in fundraising, St Bernard's showed their appreciation by presenting a cup for competition to the swimming club.

Peter Buchanan

Voted out of the East of Scotland League, which was all but dead anyway, the Saints made good use of the vacant dates in the second half of the season by embarking on a run in the Penman Cup. In the semi-final they met Raith Rovers at Stark's Park and beat them 2-1. The final was carried forward to the start of the following season. In Falkirk, on the last day of August 1908, Saints beat East Stirlingshire 1-0 to win the Penman Cup for the first and only time.

Nothing succeeds like success, and

the Saints were to make it a unique hat trick of cups in one season by annexing the Rosebery Charity Cup for the first time in May 1908. Who said St Bernard's could not win cups? This was their first win in five appearances in the final up to that point. In the semi-final against the Hibs at Easter Road they won on corners 2-1, after each side had scored a goal. In the final at the same venue Hearts were beaten 3-2 by a Saints' side showing two changes from that which had won the Qualifying Cup. Coming in at right half to replace Findlay was John Watson whilst taking the place of Murray at outside right was William Curran.

St Bernard's played very well that day and thoroughly merited their win. Goals by Curran and Logan built up a two-goal interval lead with Hearts pulling one back, before the almost inevitable Buchanan penalty virtually sealed it. Hearts scored again before the end to make the final score 3-2.

On the Wednesday before the Penman Cup Final in Falkirk, St Bernard's had the opportunity of winning a fourth cup when they lined up in the final of the East of Scotland Cup, more commonly known as the City Cup, at the Gymnasium. This was another final carried forward from season 1907/08. More or less the same clubs that competed in the East of Scotland Shield, also played for this Cup. Hibs and Hearts were however soon to drop out. In the years separating the two World Wars St Bernard's and Leith Athletic between them had a monopoly of winning it. On this occasion, however, the Saints were beaten only by the narrowest of margins of 2-1 by the Hearts.

Still on the subject of cups it was decided to do away with the East of Scotland League and to replace it with a North Eastern Cup, which took the form of a knock-out competition. Just up the Saints' street you might think given their cup successes at that time but, rather surprisingly, there was no St Bernard's entry. Whether this was by choice or otherwise is uncertain. They were of course in the Penman Cup competition whereas the clubs in the new competition namely, Leith Athletic, Hibs, Aberdeen, Hearts, Dundee and Falkirk were not involved.

Buoyed by all this success, it was decided 'to give the club back to the members', in a manner of speaking. It will be recalled, at the turn of the century, when the club almost folded, a private syndicate, at their own expense, took over the running from the members. It still remained in control, but to broaden the base of ownership again it was decided to form a limited company, in which the supporters could purchase shares and be more involved. On 1 September 1908 The St Bernard's Football Club and Athletic Club Limited was formally registered. The two types of share created were ordinary shares and vendors shares. The members of the private syndicate each received vendors shares in proportion to their share of the assets transferred to the limited company.

The first directors of the Company, all of whom had been in the private syndicate, were as follows:

John Mathieson, Printseller, 7 Dunrobin Place, Edinburgh	35
Walter Kemp, Commercial Traveller, 15 Bellevue Street, Edinburgh	35
Thomas James Gray, Storekeeper, 2 St David's Terrace, Edinburgh	35
George Alexander Pringle, Joiner, 69 Henderson Street, Leith	35
John Archibald Burns, Wholesale Stationer, 35 Jamaica Street, Edinburgh	35
James MacKerron, Fruit Merchant, 78 Temple Park Crescent, Edinburgh	50
Mark Slight Bookless, Mason, 9 Gladstone Terrace, Edinburgh	20
James Calder Mentiplay, Plumber, 85 Montgomery Street, Edinburgh	15
David Scotland Wemyss, Commercial Traveller, 26 Craighall Crescent, Leith	10
David Robert Blackwood, Wholesale Confectioner, 3 Heriothill Terrace, Edinburgh	10
William Gordon, Gas Meter Inspector, 5 Straiton Place, Portobello	10
Thomas Fraser, Teacher, 62 Braid Road, Edinburgh	10

Thomas J Gray   John Mathieson

Opposite each name is the number of vendors shares issued to each Director. From this we can determine that the club was valued at £300.

The object in forming the limited company, to raise further capital, was not a great success with only 300 Ordinary Shares being issued, mostly to the Directors!

The summer of 1908 saw Edinburgh host the Scottish National Exhibition held in Saughton Park. A football tournament was part of the events. St Bernard's was the only club from the capital to take part and Rangers, Queens Park and Dundee joined them. Hearts and Hibs declined to participate when satisfactory guarantees were not forthcoming from the organisers. The first match saw the Saints play Rangers and suffer a 1-0 defeat. Apart from games in the Second World War when Rangers 'A' took part in the North Eastern League, this was to be the last time the two clubs were to meet. The last ever game against Celtic had taken place in February 1904. The chances of meeting the Old Firm now were of course slim, while the club operated outwith Division 1, with only the possibility of being drawn against them in the Scottish Cup. The level of support these two clubs could attract, even then, meant a considerable financial windfall for a club like St Bernard's were they lucky enough to do so.

Harry Graham

The success of the previous season was not to be repeated. The challenge in the League petered out after a string of defeats in October, following an exit in round two of the Qualifying Cup, at the hands of Leith. October also saw the transfer of Peter Logan to Bradford City. The Yorkshire club was in the process of recruiting a number of Scots and Peter, along with James McDonald, who had left the Saints two years earlier for the same club, were both in the Bradford City team which beat Newcastle United to win the 1911 FA Cup Final.

As one player moved out so another moved in, and Harry Graham an inside right, was recruited from junior side Granton Oakvale. After little over a year he also was to move to Bradford City. Harry who had a very long and distinguished playing career, principally with Leicester City and the Hearts, was a qualified dentist and when his playing days were all but over he played a few matches for the Saints in 1925. Tom Paton it will be recalled was an old official of St Bernard's. He had become a prominent businessman in Bradford and more than likely it was due to this influence that these three players moved to the City. All of them were young and he was in a position to look after their interests, much in the same manner as players' agents do at the present time.

The City Cup was won at Logie Green when Leith were beaten 4-3 in the final. This cup success though, has to be put in perspective with the competition now devoid of both Hibs and Hearts for the first time.

Season 1909/10 saw Saints join Hibs, Hearts, Leith, Falkirk and Raith Rovers in the draw for a new cup, the Dunedin Cup, presented by a Mr Sharp, which kicked off the season. St Bernard's beat Hibs at the third attempt, and faced Raith Rovers, who had beaten Falkirk in the other semi, in the final at Tynecastle. An early goal from Harry Graham was all that separated the teams at the end of the day. The match referee was the same Tom Robertson who played for Saints in the Scottish Cup Final 14 years earlier by now a prominent official.

A creditable third position in the league was achieved but an early exit in the Qualifying Cup denied them entry to the Scottish Cup for the second season running. For the clubs that did not qualify for the Scottish Cup proper, the Scottish Consolation Cup had been introduced in 1908. Saints had entered the previous season but scratched to Bo'ness, when instructed to do so by the League along with other Second Division sides. A good run was achieved in this competition, with much excitement for the fans in the spring of 1910 but a fifth round defeat at Barrhead, by a narrow 2-1 scoreline saw their involvement come to an end. Their opponents, Arthurlie, went on to beat St Johnstone in the final. Sustaining interest beyond that point was the East of Scotland Shield, although Saints did not actually beat Hibs in the semi-final, due to the game being abandoned because of failing light with the score tied at 1-1. The Easter Road side withdrew from the competition without replaying it and the Saints met Hearts in the final. After 90 minutes the score was 1-1. Beforehand it had been decided corners would count in the event of a draw and Hearts' overwhelming advantage of 11-2 took the trophy to Gorgie. Near the end of the season Harry Graham moved to Bradford City and Harry Simpson went to Leicester Fosse.

St Bernard's versus Broxburn Athletic on Saturday 3 September 1910. This photograph is one of several taken on the day of the 1st Round Scottish Qualifying Cup tie and is a rare one of the pitch at the Gymnasium running in a south to north direction. When the Saints returned there in 1924 the pitch was moved 90 degrees to run west to east. The buildings of Eyre Crescent are seen in the background.

The continuing loss of good players, and the difficulty of trying to replace them with youngsters, had to have an effect sometime, and season 1910/11 emphasised the point being an indifferent one results wise. A run in the Qualifying Cup encouraged 600 supporters to travel by train to Falkirk for the fifth round match against East Stirling which was lost 2-0. The only other thing of any note was reaching the Rosebery Charity Cup final. Yet another player moved south – this time centre forward John Fleming to Newcastle United. He was the second centre forward to be transferred to the Tyneside club from the Saints in the space of four years following on Sandy Hall in 1907. Robert Grant, who was to give St Bernard's equally fine service up to the First World War, replaced George Ramsay in goal during the season.

After many years forming the backbone of the half back line, the Willie Smith and Tommy Ross partnership was broken up in season 1911/12, with the introduction of Willie Corstorphine from Hearts of Beath at centre half. Smith remained with the club that season, playing at inside right on a number of occasions, but rarely appearing in his normal position.

The Gymnasium ground at this time was proving to be a popular venue for important matches. It had of course a very central location, being only a few minutes walk downhill from the Waverley Station. No doubt the steep walk uphill seemed considerably longer if your team had been beaten! In April 1910 Ashfield and Arniston Rangers had fought out the semi-final of the Scottish Junior Cup at the Gymnasium with Ashfield winning 3-2. This was not the first time that the Saints had hosted such a match in the Junior Cup, as the 1895 semi between West Calder Wanderers and Glasgow Perthshire had been played at their Logie Green ground.

Saints' own involvement in the Qualifying Cup in 1911/12 was limited to two rounds; but they were honoured to host the final between Dunfermline Athletic and Dumbarton; a crowd of 10,500 attended. This must have been a bit of a tight squeeze in the small compact ground, where both ends of the track had to be taken in to accommodate the much larger than normal attendance. The Fifers won this one 1-0. The following season saw the final back again for the first staging of Abercorn against Arbroath. This time the teams finished level at 1-1 before moving on to Cowdenbeath, then Cathkin Park Glasgow, where the Paisley team prevailed.

A rare win over the Hearts by 1-0 in the Shield semi-final went some way to compensate for a poor start in the league. This left a run in the Scottish Consolation Cup as the only comfort to provide interest after the turn of the year. This was achieved to some extent, but for the third season in succession, in a national competition, the fifth round proved to be the stumbling block. It could not be said that the Saints went out without a fight, as it took three games to separate them and Cowdenbeath, before the Fife team won 2-0 at neutral Stark's Park, Kirkcaldy. The earlier win over the Hearts was in vain as Hibs beat the Saints 2-0 in the final of the Shield. Some consolation came when the City Cup was won for the second time. After they and opponents Peebles Rovers had tied at 1-1 in the replayed final at Tynecastle the Saints 'cornered' the trophy by 7-3.

A lack of consistency saw St Bernard's finish mid table in both season 1912/13 and 1913/14. That season however an old member of the club, resident in London, presented the Saints with a new set of blue and white hooped jerseys and these became the official colours.

In May 1913 St Bernard's made formal application to join the First Division. A copy of the letter was reproduced in the *Evening News* stating the sound financial position of the club, the good ground and team and the soundness of the Board of Directors. The Directors were of the opinion that the city could sustain a third side in the First Division as the Saints had a considerable following of their own which was not affected by Tynecastle or Easter Road. This was the only way open to the club to join the upper league, as there was no automatic promotion from the Second Division. The bid was unsuccessful.

John Ferguson

On 10 December 1913 the club held their third Annual Concert in the Royal Halls in Pitt Street, which saw inside right John Ferguson, presented with a gold chain and medal for his services to the club prior to his transfer to Third Lanark. John who was a student at the University at the time was highly popular. Even after his move to the Glasgow club he was the subject of several short-term transfers back to the Saints, as he was still eligible to play for them in the Consolation Cup that season. Sadly John was to be the first professional footballer to give his life for his country in the First World War. He was posthumously awarded the Victoria Cross.

Sad news in February 1914 was the death of George Drummond in Preston at the early age of 49. One of the first players to go to England from the Saints he was one of the Preston 'Invincibles'. He was trainer of the Falkirk side that won the Scottish Cup in 1913. The death of James Baillie was announced in March 1914. At a time when the best players were going south he always remained loyal to the Saints. When his playing days were over he became a referee. Not long before his death he was a director of the club for three years, truly a great St Bernard's man.

Starting in January 1914 the Saints set off on a run in the Scottish Consolation Cup. Victories over Bo'ness, Bathgate, Gala Fairydean, East Fife, Montrose and Vale of Leven saw them face St Johnstone in the final at Dens Park Dundee on Saturday, 18 April 1914. The Saints' line up that day was: Robert Grant; William Hodge and Andrew Amos; John Henderson, William Corstorphine and Tommy Ross; George Ross, John Ferguson, Thomas Hosie, Robert Hosie and Malcolm Goldie. Victory in the final and the Saints would become the first club to inscribe their name on all three national trophies – Scottish Cup, Qualifying Cup and Consolation Cup. The referee was Tom Robertson again.

The first match finished all square at 0-0, with all ten forwards on the park being heavily criticised for their poor attempts at scoring. The replay was a week later at the same ground with the Saints making a change at centre forward. As had happened sometimes in the past they turned to Hampden Park for assistance. The player introduced was Colin Buchan who had made 20 league appearances for Queens Park that season and he started the game very well. He came in for some heavy treatment, however, which reduced his effectiveness. St Johnstone scored a goal in each half but St Bernard's captain William Corstorphine's goal, in the very last minute, came too late to have any bearing on the final result. It was recognised that the Saints from Perth had deserved to win the Cup although the Edinburgh Saints had put up a good display, especially in the second game.

As we have seen St Bernard's were never prolific winners of cups. Disregarding the cups that were up for competition during the two World Wars, when football was in a very unstable state anyway, the Scottish Consolation Cup was really the only cup St Bernard's failed to win at least once.

Sandwiched between the Consolation Cup final matches was a midweek game for the Blenheim Cup. This was yet another new competition but exclusively played for by Leith and St Bernard's. Mr J McMenemy, the proprietor of the Queen's Hotel at the foot of Leith Walk, presented the trophy to the Port of Leith and the matches were conducted under the auspices of the Leith Burghs Association. Custody of the Cup was to be decided on the aggregate score over two legs, home and away. As both clubs were not now taking part in the Dunedin Cup the new contest filled the void caused by their exclusion.

World events were about to take centre stage. After the assassination of the Archduke Franz Ferdinand in Sarajevo, on 28 June 1914, the storm clouds of war began to gather over Europe although it was not until 4 August that Britain was involved. At the time, the general feeling was that the hostilities would be over fairly quickly. The football season 1914/15 went ahead as planned. On 4 December 1914 the

Evening Dispatch published a letter it had received from Jim Davie one of the St Bernard's players at the front: 'Just a line to thank you for the fags and cap which I very much appreciate. Talk about a rough game! This is it and it doesn't seem to be half time yet. I am telling you I won't be sorry when I hear the whistle go. We have Hamilton, late Dundee and Wilson, Dumbarton here, and I'll bet they would rather be shooting goals than shooting Germans. Tell the boys and T Brandon and committee I send my best regards, and wish them a successful season, as no doubt they wish us.'

It certainly was not 'half time' and the prediction of a swift conclusion proved to be very very wrong. As history shows, the bloodiest conflict known to man was the First World War, with enormous loss of life on both sides over a period of four years.

The Saints made a reasonable start to the league campaign while at the same time making steady progress in the Qualifying Cup. At the end of November with the war escalating it was reported that the directors of the club had given permission to Sir George McCrae to interview the players, with a view to enlisting. McCrae was in the process of forming his 'footballers' battalion', the 16th Royal Scots, in which players, notably from the Hearts were signed up. By the end of the year the Saints were in the final of the Qualifying Cup courtesy of victories over Duns, Peebles Rovers, Broxburn United, East Stirling and St Johnstone. In the final they faced Dykehead a club who hailed from Shotts in Lanarkshire. It was the first ever meeting of the two clubs. The Qualifying Cup was the only cup competition played under the auspices of the SFA, as the Scottish Cup was to be withheld that season and for the remainder of the war. The final was played at Ibrox on 2 January 1915 and the Saints' team that day was Robert Grant; John Hay and Alex Penman; George Bennett, Frank McGarrity and Tommy Ross; Willie Cox, David McDougall, Robert Couper, James Taylor and James Weir.

Saints were soon down as Dykehead scored twice in a five minute spell. Urged on by the veteran Tommy Ross they fought back with McDougall reducing the deficit. When Couper equalised the Saints had the upper hand and it seemed they would go on to win the game. However Dykehead finished strongly and the Gymnasium men were happy to hold out for the draw.

The replay was held a week later also in Glasgow but at Firhill, the home ground of Partick Thistle. Robert Couper the high scoring centre forward was injured and Saints adapted by switching David McDougall to fill the vacancy. Into the side came young Alex Ross, a brother of Tommy, to play his first ever game for the club. Otherwise the line up was unchanged. Once again the side from Shotts scored first, this time in the second half, as St Bernard's missed the influential Couper and young Ross struggled to find his feet. His brother Tommy played another grand game and from one of his promptings McDougall brought the sides level a few minutes later.

It needed a third game to separate the teams and this took place at Ibrox the following Saturday. Young Ross retained his place and it was McDougall who was left out with the return of the fit again Couper. After a goalless first half the Saints began to exert their authority and a good pass from Alex Ross set up Couper for the first goal. The Dykehead players began to lose the place a bit after this and when Cox and Couper added further goals it was all over.

After the success in the cup, the Saints went on a run of ten league wins out of 11 starts, the only defeat coming at Johnstone in Renfrewshire. Robert Couper scored in all these games bar the one against Dundee Hibs, which he missed through injury. In this spell he scored 17 goals in all. Such a run would often win a championship and it nearly did for the Saints that season when they finished level top, tying with Leith and Cowdenbeath, on 37 points each. A series of round robin matches were played to decide the championship. Unfortunately Saints lost both their games, 1-2 to Leith and 1-3 to Cowdenbeath whilst in the other game the Fife club beat Leith 1-0 to take the title.

If the Saints were disappointed by this set back it was not obvious. In the semi-final of the Rosebery Charity Cup they beat the Hearts 3-2, and in the final a week later on 8 May 1915, also at Tynecastle, they repeated the dose by accounting for Hibs by 4-3. This was the most recent Rosebery success since their initial win in 1908. The team in the final was Robert Grant; Andrew Amos and John Hay; George Bennett, Bill Morrison and Tommy Ross; Willie Cox, David McDougall, Robert Couper, Alex Ross and James Weir. The same group of players had accounted for Hearts in the semi-final, the only changes being positional with the inside forwards switched over. Bill Morrison was the same player who had left St Bernard's in 1904 to go to Fulham. He was now at the end of a distinguished career that had also taken in Glossop, Clyde, Raith Rovers, Falkirk and Morton.

Saints had won every game that season at the Gymnasium when the Hibs came visiting on Wednesday, 21 April in the East of Scotland Shield. This semi-final was the last home game of the season and a 2-0 win for the Hibs spoilt what would otherwise have been a 100% record.

St Bernard's Football Club

Scottish Qualifying Cup Winners 1915

Back Row: Tom Brandon (Trainer), Alexander Paterson (Treasurer), Robert Couper, David S Wemyss (President), Willie Cox, Robert Grant, Frank McGarrity, George R Lamont (Director), Walter Kemp (Director) and James Mentiplay (Hon Joint Secretary).
Seated: Robert Main (Hon Joint Secretary), David Clark (Director), Alex Ross, George Bennett, James Weir, Alex Penman, Archie Tavendale (Assistant Trainer) and Thomas R Mackenzie (Director).
At Front: Tommy Ross, David McDougall, James Taylor and John Hay.

The top of the league table showed as follows:

Scottish League Division 2 1914/15	P	W	D	L	F	A	Pts
Cowdenbeath	26	16	5	5	49	17	37
Leith	26	15	7	4	54	31	37
St Bernard's	26	18	1	7	66	34	37
East Stirlingshire	26	13	5	8	53	44	31
Clydebank	26	13	4	9	67	37	30

As the war intensified in Europe, the Scottish League decided to dispense with Division 2 for season 1915/16, and as it turned out for the remainder of the conflict. Division 1 continued for the whole duration of the hostilities. St Bernard's joined the

Eastern League along with some of their fellow second leaguers and clubs from the Central League. It was reported in the spring of 1915 that players Jim Davie, George Ross, James Hastie, Andrew Amos, George Prior, John French and William Wemyss had joined the 'colours' to serve their country, while James Taylor was on government work. Saints were still able to turn out a team that largely resembled that of the previous season. A prominent acquisition was Charlie Thomson the famous Hearts and Sunderland centre half. Charlie had also been an established internationalist for Scotland representing his country on no fewer than 21 occasions at a time when international matches were held far less frequently. He was now in the twilight of his career but still immensely popular, particularly with the youngsters in the Saints support with whom he made a great fuss, and who no doubt were delighted to see such a famous player in their team.

Saints did very well in the Eastern League. Only Armadale, who had won the Central League in the two previous seasons, stood between them and success in the form of silverware. The West Lothian club won the league and narrowly beat the Saints in the final of the Eastern League Cup with only the Blenheim Cup finding its way into the Gymnasium boardroom. The Scottish Qualifying Cup was also discontinued that season which meant that St Bernard's were to be the holders until it was played for again in 1919. Leith and St Bernard's were successful with applications to join the Gardener Cup Association. Clubs in West Lothian competed for this cup and that season it was played for on a round robin basis. Unfortunately the programme of matches involving Armadale, Bathgate and Broxburn United, as well as the two city clubs, was not completed.

The leading positions in the league were as follows:

Eastern League 1915/16	P	W	D	L	F	A	Pts
Armadale	21	17	2	2	52	17	36
St Bernard's	22	16	1	5	59	26	33
Cowdenbeath	22	12	3	7	38	20	27
Bathgate	22	12	2	8	45	30	26
East Fife	22	8	6	8	52	39	22
Broxburn United	22	9	4	9	29	29	22

Remaining fixture not completed

On a sad note one of the club's supporters by the name of Combe Rennie was knocked down by a bus and fatally injured in Broxburn after attending the Saints' match there early in the season. The fans rallied round in typical fashion by holding a collection for his widow. At the same time the press reported that former player Robert 'Scrappy' Gray had made a journey of 500 miles to Canada by pony and trap from the United States to join the colours of the Canadian Gordon Highlanders.

By the time season 1916/17 came round clearly it was becoming more difficult to run a club like St Bernard's because of the lack of available players with so many being drawn into the war effort. Leith pulled out that season with the Heriot's Trust writing off their arrears of rent. Often the team line up was not known until the very last minute. Some troops were still based in Edinburgh and from that source the Saints were able to obtain, amongst others, the services of young Warnie Cresswell a full back who was to obtain seven international caps with England after the war. At the time he was stationed at Redford Barracks. His club career in post war peacetime included South Shields, Sunderland and Everton with whom he won Division 1 twice and the FA Cup once. The St Bernard's team he played in finished third in the Eastern League. The top of the table showed:

Eastern League 1916/17	P	W	D	L	F	A	Pts
Cowdenbeath	18	11	5	2	45	19	27
East Fife	14	7	5	2	26	9	23
St Bernard's	18	10	2	6	37	23	22
Armadale	17	7	6	4	36	26	20
Dundee Hibs	17	6	3	8	29	33	15

Remaining fixtures not completed.
East Fife v Broxburn United not played following a dispute. East Fife awarded the points.

As there were so few league fixtures another competition the Saints took part in was the Loftus Cup. A Mr. Wallace from Dundee presented this now long forgotten cup in 1911 when it was contested for by Dundee Hibs, St Johnstone and winners Dunfermline Athletic in that first season, matches taking place between all three clubs on a home and away basis. Although it still continued before, during and, for a short spell, after the First World War the Fife club was the only winner and in the other seasons it was almost certainly abandoned as in 1916/17 when St Bernard's participated. That season it was a knock out competition but matches were still played on a home and away basis.

The Eastern League for 1917/18 shrunk to only seven clubs and did not include St Bernard's who by now had decided to cease operations. Many of the players were on active service. In an appreciative gesture full back John Hay was presented with a wristlet watch from officials and players prior to his departure. Tommy Ross was transferred to the Hearts.

The newspapers covering the period of the First World War make very depressing reading indeed as every issue contained long lists of those who had given their lives for their country. Needless to say St Bernard's were not unaffected, and both forward David McDougall and assistant trainer Archie Tavendale made the supreme sacrifice. Archie had also been with the Rosebery. Full back Alex Kay, who played for the Saints from 1898 to 1900, Fred Albert, the centre forward from 1911 to 1913, John Fleming, the centre forward from 1909 to 1911, Frank Lindlay, the outside left from 1916 to 1917 and John Ferguson, to whom reference has already been made, were other Saints known to have died in the conflict. For the remainder of the war the military authorities took over the Gymnasium and used it to store and repair heavy machinery. The continual movement of vehicles over the ground was to render it useless for sport.

Chapter 6
New Logie Green used for the Revival

St Bernard's did not go back to the Gymnasium when it was decided to resume operations for season 1919/20, due to the bad state of the ground. Fortunately they were able to obtain a lease over the new Logie Green, the ground that had been used by Leith until that club ceased operations during the war. Their initial offer of £30 per annum had been rejected by the Heriot's Trust but an increased one, of £40 for the first year, and £50 per annum for the remainder of a five-year lease, secured the ground. Another offer from Leith had been declined. Technically St Bernard's now had two grounds, as they still had the lease over the Gymnasium.

Having settled the ground issue the question of entering a league was addressed. The Second Division of the Scottish League was not re-formed immediately after the war. The Saints were accepted for the Eastern League, but along with some of the Fife clubs and the Stirlingshire and Clackmannanshire clubs, then opted for the Central League instead to reduce travel costs. Following these defections, the ten club Eastern League polarised north of the River Tay, along with three clubs from Fife. The Central League was 14 clubs strong and included four West Lothian clubs as well as those others who had decided against the Eastern League. The Saints and Hearts 'A' represented Edinburgh.

Andrew Amos

The directors appointed Jack Dalziel, who was well known in athletic circles, as trainer and groundsman. Andrew Amos from the pre-war team, who had been wounded at Loos, was appointed team captain. Another soldier, Angus Seed, who had assisted the Saints during the war while stationed with the Royal Fusiliers at Edinburgh Castle, was back. He had won the Military Medal in France. Saints also took the step for the first time of appointing a team manager. James Dawson who had played for Hearts and Liverpool took the role in a part-time capacity whilst continuing to play for the team.

The first Central League match to be played at their new home was on 16 August 1919. Saints got off to a good start when a team containing nine demobilised serviceman beat Armadale 4-1. Adam Archibald, who had been the Port of Leith's first winner of the Victoria Cross, kicked off proceedings. He was well known in junior circles and, when younger, had played trial games for St Bernard's.

Early season results were mixed. In the first round of the Qualifying Cup at Bathgate they suffered defeat by a solitary goal, which in normal circumstances would have been looked on with some dismay. That season we find the rather anomalous situation however of Saints entering the Qualifying Cup while already having a place in the Scottish Cup proper. This came about following the decision to exempt the 20 qualifiers, with the exception of Dumfries, from the 1914/15 version, through to the first round proper of the Scottish Cup. This reprieve came about because the Scottish Cup competition of 1914/15 was not held. Bathgate, incidentally, went on to win the Qualifying Cup.

The fortunes of the Saints and Bathgate seemed to be intertwined that season and another visit to West Lothian saw the Saints eliminated from the Central League Cup. Then after both clubs received byes in the first round of the Scottish Cup, they met at Logie Green in the second round where Saints made home advantage count in a 2-0 win. Saints form all season on their new home ground had been good. Great excitement was engendered when the third round brought a home tie against Albion Rovers, who were then in the Scottish League. So great was interest in the tie that a switch of ground was made to the adjoining Powderhall Stadium. The decision to change was fully vindicated when a vast crowd of 20,000 turned up to see the Saints battle hard for a 1-1 draw against their more illustrious opponents. Two factors probably contributed to there being a much bigger crowd than St Bernard's normally drew at the game: one was an immediate post-war boom in attendances and secondly the Saints had the city to themselves that day. The following Wednesday unfortunately the Saints lost the replay 4-1 at Coatbridge, despite the presence of Tommy Ross, who had been transferred back from the Hearts specifically for the game. Arguably St Bernard's greatest servant Tommy had played his last game for the club. Albion Rovers went on to make their only appearance in the final that season losing narrowly 3-2 to Kilmarnock.

St Bernard's managed to win the City Cup for a third time when they beat Broxburn United 4-0 in the final. At the end of that season Saints played a number of friendly matches. One of the matches was played at Bathgate Park, the home of the junior side Edinburgh Emmett. This ground, which had an ash pitch, was opened in August 1919. Situated in New Street, just to the east of the Waverley Station it was for many years the mecca for minor grade football in the city with matches taking place every night of the week. Attendances were good even allowing for the fact that Regent Road, perched high on the Calton Hill overlooking the ground, provided an excellent 'Jews' gallery' for those not willing to pay for admission. In the late 30s the site was acquired for a bus garage with the newly-opened New Meadowbank then becoming the focal point for the smaller clubs.

Although it was only Saints first season back, it did not take them long to unearth good players. Unfortunately as usual they found it impossible to hold on to them for any length of time. Building up a good team was always going to be difficult in these circumstances. Willie Henderson, a centre forward from Broxburn, quickly drew the scouts to Logie Green with his goal scoring feats. He was transferred to Airdrie on 27 May 1920 and later on joined Manchester United. Willie also played for the Hearts as well as other clubs. The other player to move south at the end of the season was goalkeeper Harry McNaughton who went to Liverpool.

The Central League as a competition was a success with the clubs able to draw healthy attendances. Perhaps unexpectedly the league would prove to be a threat to the Scottish League itself. This stemmed from the Central League not being affiliated to the Inter League Board and therefore not recognising that body's registration system. In other words the Central Leaguers were in a position, provided their finances allowed, to sign any player they wanted without having to notify or recompense his club. With the Central League clubs in a buoyant situation, players moved to them from the Scottish League. One of the most notable, was centre forward Andy Wilson who joined Dunfermline Athletic and was capped for Scotland whilst attached to the Fife club. Players of this calibre helped to swell the crowds. An old friend of mine Davie Walker once recollected that he had seen Andy play at Logie Green against St Bernard's. He recalled, with some relish I should add, that the Saints' full back Andy Amos had 'really got stuck in' to Wilson that day – obviously recognising the threat he posed!

St Bernard's themselves took advantage of the situation. Willie Frame of Clyde and Willie Henry, who had played for Manchester City and Rangers, formed a full back partnership. Willie Summers from Airdrie joined them at centre half. After a season Willie moved on to St Mirren, where he enjoyed a particularly good year in 1926, winning his only Scotland cap and collecting a Scottish Cup winners medal with the Paisley club into the bargain.

Saints did not have a good 1920/21 season. A first round exit at Armadale in the Qualifying Cup meant that they were denied any Scottish Cup action. The abandonment of the Scottish Consolation Cup after the war further served to deny them any chance of a run in a national competition. Some comfort was obtained when their name was inscribed on the City Cup, for a fourth time, courtesy of a 1-0 win over Leith Athletic in the final. Turning the clock back to the early days of the competition, the Saints brought back former players, Robert McLean and Willie Henderson from Airdrie, for the Rosebery Charity Cup. The move

Willie Henderson

paid off, with Henderson scoring twice to dismiss Hibs 3-1 in the semi-final at Easter Road. James Campbell, who had played for Scotland in 1913, joined the Saints after spells with Sheffield Wednesday and Huddersfield Town. He had been signed in time for the Hibs match and along with the Airdrie players played in the final at Tynecastle against the Hearts where Saints failed to find the net, losing by the narrow margin of a goal.

There were those in power in the Scottish League who thought that the threat posed by the Central League would quickly recede. They reasoned that the clubs in that league would find it difficult to maintain the higher wages demanded by the players who switched leagues. When the situation showed no sign of changing, it was decided to offer membership to the Central League clubs in a restored Division 2 of the Scottish League. This was done on the proviso that the players were returned to their clubs. A bargaining position was struck, that automatic promotion and relegation would operate between the two Divisions of the Scottish League and the deal was done. Membership of the Scottish League, also saw the former Central League clubs automatically included in the first round of the Scottish Cup, without the need to pre-qualify.

The resurrected second division bore a strong resemblance to the former Central League. Only the reserve teams of Hearts and Falkirk were not included. Johnstone and Vale of Leven joined from the Western League along with the Angus clubs, Arbroath and Forfar Athletic. What on the face of it appeared at first a reasonable deal for the ex-Central League clubs turned out otherwise. The loss of the star players saw the gates of the small clubs tumble and it was not too long before some of these clubs went to the wall. Few of them could have coped with the financial commitments that promotion would have brought. The big clubs had definitely won the day.

Whether clubs like St Bernard's would have prospered had the Central League remained in place is open to question. More than likely the post First World War boom in attendances would have subsided eventually as things returned to normal and the novelty of seeing games after a period of deprivation disappeared. Other factors such as high unemployment would also come into play. As it turned out post-war Britain did not become overnight a place fit for heroes to live in as some had predicted. Many of these clubs were located in areas of low population and would have found sustaining a first-class professional team difficult.

The first season back in Division 2 saw the Saints finish mid table, just as they had done in the two years spent in the Central League. The Scottish Cup had them drawn away at Alloa. The local Athletic were on a high at the time and that season romped away with the Division 2 title, finishing 13 points clear of their nearest challenger to claim the one promotion spot. A defeat by 3-1 from them was therefore hardly surprising. Players continued to be transferred to balance the books. Goalkeeper John Archibald moved to Newcastle United with Willie Cox, Alex Donachie and Abe Wilson of the forwards going to Hamilton Accies, Clydebank and Falkirk respectively.

Some younger officials joined the club at this time. They immediately implemented plans to smarten up the Logie Green ground. A new wall was erected at Warriston Road. This made Logie Green Road the only entrance to the ground and a new frontage set back from the road was erected there, which contained seven turnstiles. A further new turnstile at the stand enabled entry for an additional charge. The dressing rooms were also smartened up.

On the financial front changes were also under way. *The Scotsman* advertised a meeting to be held in the Wesleyan Halls, Hamilton Place on 9 December 1921 to consider the formation of a new public limited company. Nothing happened immediately in that direction. On 23 March 1922 the St Bernard's Football and Athletic Club Ltd, the private company formed in 1908, was placed in voluntary liquidation. It must be assumed that following this decision the club reverted to an unincorporated club on the same lines as when it was founded.

Being third from the bottom of the league in season 1922/23 must have been a disappointment for the committee whilst Queens Park who had just been relegated bounced back immediately as champions. Saints actually won their game against the 'Spiders' at Powderhall (used instead of Logie Green) and drew at Hampden Park, throwing the form book out of the window. These were the first ever meetings between the two clubs in the Scottish League. Also belying their poor league form, Saints put up a terrific fight against Dundee in the second round of the Scottish Cup. A 0-0 draw at Dens Park was an excellent result for the Saints. A crowd of 15,000 turned up for the replay on the following Wednesday with Powderhall being used again in view of the large attendance. Logie Green was also opened that day, but only to facilitate entry to the venue for the match. Unfortunately the Saints lost, albeit on a narrow 3-2 scoreline.

St Bernard's were to return to Powderhall for a third time, on 2 June 1923, for their last ever annual sports. This was the first sports since those held at the Marine Gardens just prior to the war. The meeting was conducted under professional auspices and attracted over 7000 spectators.

At this time it was rumoured that following the exercising of his option to purchase the Powderhall Grounds from Edinburgh Town Council, Mr F A Lumley had plans to create the enclosure into a Greater Powderhall. The sports cartoonist of the *Evening News* Tom Curr 'went to town' so to speak and depicted, in his weekly contribution, a colossal Hampden Park type oval emerging following the announcement. This giant stadium, which in the event did not happen, was to be the new home of St Bernard's. Other things were on the minds of the St Bernard's committee however, they still held the lease of the Gymnasium and moves were in hand to move back there.

St Bernard's league form in season 1923/24 was very poor as another third from bottom finish showed. The Scottish Cup was a different matter. They created one of the biggest shocks in the Scottish Cup that season when beating Raith Rovers in the third round at Kirkcaldy. The Raith team that was to finish fourth in Division 1 that season was star studded with none other than Alex James the leading light. Inside forward Alex was to become a member of the great Arsenal team of the early 1930s, which won the Football League in four seasons out of five, as well as an established Scottish internationalist. Also in the Raith team that day was Dave Morris at centre half. Shortly after the cup-tie he earned the first of six caps for Scotland. St Bernard's were given no chance at all of winning the tie especially at Stark's Park. Early indications were that the pundits who had predicted a big Raith win were to be proved right as the home team bombarded the St Bernard's goal. Every player played their part for the Saints but none more so than Tommy McAlpine who gave an inspired performance in goal. The Raith onslaught continued for the whole game. In a rare breakaway in the second half centre forward Archie Young seized his chance. He nipped in between Morris and Brown, the Raith goalkeeper, to score the only goal of the game. In the process he collided with a post, broke his arm and was carried off. Reduced to ten men St Bernard's held on for a memorable victory.

Aberdeen beat the Saints 3-0 at Pittodrie in the next round. Archie Young went into practice as a doctor in Eyre Place in premises next to the ground. He continued his association with the Saints by being on the committee of the Supporters' Club.

The decision was taken to move back to the Gymnasium in the 1924/25 season with the pitch in much the same situation as before, except that it would be turned round fully 90 degrees and a new stand would be built.

As all the work could not be completed in time for the start of the new season, an alternative venue needed to be found for home games. When an arrangement to play at Powderhall fell through the Saints' management were then successful in obtaining the use of Tynecastle on Saturdays. Hibs also required a temporary home whilst their new stand was under construction at Easter Road. Saints' application was in first however and Hibs had to settle for Friday evening use of the Hearts' ground until their own ground was available again. St Bernard's use of Tynecastle continued until mid November.

Chapter 7
Back home for the last time

St Bernard's moved back into the Gymnasium for the League match against Arthurlie on 15 November 1924, although once again the opening of a 'new' Saints' ground resulted in a defeat for the team, the Barrhead club returning home with the League points on the strength of a 1-0 win. Sir Patrick J Ford the local Member of Parliament for North Edinburgh performed the ceremonials and the Newhaven Brass Band provided the musical accompaniment. This match also saw the return of old favourite Harry Graham now very much in the twilight of his football career. As the grandstand was not yet completed it was necessary for the players to change in the neighbouring laundry until the water supply had been connected.

From the information that is available it appears that three separate organisations made up the reconstituted St Bernard's club. First of all there was the Royal Gymnasium Ground Company ('Ground Company') that purchased the ground. This was not a company constituted by one of the Company Acts but was a partnership of people associated with the club who took over the responsibility for the ground. It performed a role not too dissimilar to the old syndicate that had saved the club at the turn of the century, but without having overall control. This was still the responsibility of the St Bernard's Football Club ('Football Club') another unincorporated body run by the members. The third part of the set up was the St Bernard's Football Club Grand Stand Company Limited ('Grand Stand Company') that had been created to raise the capital necessary to finance the building of the new grandstand at the ground. There was of course an overlap of officials within the three bodies. The following table shows the position between the partners of the 'Ground Company' and the directors of the 'Grand Stand Company'. It is more than likely that the 'Football Club' had many of the same office bearers but no club records are available to consult.

The capital of the 'Grand Stand Company' was divided up into 100 Ordinary Shares of £1 each and 4400 Guaranteed Preference Shares of £1 each. As with the launch of the previous limited company back in 1908, the issue was under subscribed with only 2926 of the Guaranteed Preference Shares being taken up. The St Bernard's Football Club itself took up 700 of the shares although this may well have been of necessity. To meet the gap between the funding raised and the cost of the new stand, The Royal Bank of Scotland provided overdraft facilities of £2000, secured by a joint Guarantee given by the directors. The stand was duly completed and could accommodate around 1200 spectators. Those who know the site of the Gymnasium ground will realise that the pitch was located below the street level of Royal Crescent.

St Bernard's Partners and Directors	Ground	Stand
George Rankin Lamont, Merchant, 69 Trinity Road, Edinburgh	X	X
Walter Kemp, Provision Merchant, 15 Bellevue Street, Edinburgh	X	X
John Guthrie Fleming, Leather Merchant, 12 Barnton Terrace, Edinburgh	X	X
James Cooper, Coal Merchant, 23 Pitt Street, Edinburgh	X	
Harry Leith Stewart, Clerk, 12 Dalkeith Road, Edinburgh	X	X
Robert Muir Penman, Gentleman, 82 Polwarth Terrace, Edinburgh	X	X
David McLaren, Electrical Engineer, Granton Lodge, Edinburgh	X	
Robert D Tait, Leather Merchant, 15 Hope Park Terrace, Edinburgh	X	X
William Darlington, House Furnisher, 21 Pitt Street, Edinburgh	X	
David Clark, Publican, Gowanlee, Juniper Green	X	
Robert Murray, Fish Merchant, Main Street, Newhaven		X

In a somewhat unique arrangement, it was possible to enter the top of the stand at street level by means of a steel bridge constructed for that purpose. Today only the gates leading to the steel bridge remain opposite the bottom of Dundonald Street. Initially, after the stand was ready for occupancy in January 1925, reports indicate that it was filled to capacity. While on the face of it, this seems to be very encouraging, it should be mentioned that the new turnstiles at the stand had not yet been installed and as no extra admission fee could be charged it was freely available to everybody. This was only a temporary situation until the stand was fully completed.

Saints also appointed Thomas Heatlie of Broxburn United as the new Secretary/Manager but this appointment only lasted for the season.

In another development, on Christmas Eve 1924, former player Markie Bell formed the St Bernard's Supporters' Club. This was to prove of great assistance to the club and there is little doubt that its fund raising efforts over the years were vital to the football club, in fact, it was to be an ideal Christmas present. Its importance can be gauged by the introduction, the following year, of two of its members, namely John Miller and James Kirkwood, to the board of the football club.

Following changes to the laws of the game made by the International Board in 1924, it became possible to score a goal direct from a corner kick. The first club to take advantage of this change was St Bernard's. In their match at Coatbridge on 23 August against Albion Rovers, Tommy Alston scored in this manner, although it did not prove to be enough in a 2-1 defeat.

Playing wise, season 1924/25 was another poor one for the club and their final position in the league was only improved by one place, to fourth from bottom! Of concern to the directors at this time must have been the creation of a Third Division of the Scottish League. There was now a chance of dropping down a further division, as the Saints had been perilously close to bottom in the past two seasons! This prospect was soon to disappear but only because the Third Division itself proved to be not viable and collapsed. When the Saints were away from home Leith Amateurs FC were given permission to use the ground.

Just before they moved back to the Gymnasium, the club signed James Boyd from the junior club Petershill. A subsequent court action by the Glasgow club over the signing was dismissed. He played outside right, and it was not long before the scouts of other clubs were taking note of his performances. At the end of the season it was Newcastle United who won the race for his services. With the Tyneside club Boyd made two appearances in the team that won the Football League in 1926/27. A FA Cup winner's medal followed in 1932, with a solitary Scotland cap two years later.

The next season had no sooner kicked off, when the Saints had what surely must have been the most unusual sequence of results in their, or indeed any club's history. In the space of just over a week they beat Clerwood Amateurs 11-1 in the City Cup, Broxburn United 8-0 in the league, then lost 9-0 to the Hibs in the semi-final of the Shield! High scoring was to be a feature of the Scottish season with the Saints also amongst the goals on occasions. In other games they were on the receiving end, none more so than at Pittodrie in the first round of the Scottish Cup, when the Dons won 8-1.

A sad note was the unexpected death of Harry Stewart one of the group of younger directors who had taken over the running of the club after the war. He was fatally injured at Roseburn Terrace after being knocked down by a taxi cab after attending a match at Tynecastle. This tragedy bore similarities to that of W M Lapsley at the start of the century.

Peter Simpson

Saints moved up to seventh bottom of the league and discovered two good players in the process. Stephen Mitchell was a left back who signed from the Glasgow junior club St Rochs. Many clubs had been interested in him but he was considered to be too small for a defender. He played for St Bernard's for three seasons before moving to Northern Ireland where he played for Coleraine and Ballymena and was capped for the Irish League. The other player was Peter Simpson a local boy who came from Leith. His goal scoring exploits at centre forward were such that he was transferred within 18 months of joining the club. Initially he went to Kettering Town but it was with Crystal Palace, then in Division 3 (South) of the Football League, that he really made his name. In six seasons with the club he scored a total of 153 goals to become their record goal scorer. Season 1930/31 was particularly productive with 46 goals in 42 appearances.

By now the Supporters' Club had started running buses to away games leaving Fettes Row on match days. However this cost money and the resourceful youth of Stockbridge found another way of travelling to see their team, when it was not too far from home. An old supporter by the name of Pym Simpson recalled an occasion when he and his friends hired bicycles from a shop in Raeburn Place and cycled to Broxburn to see the Saints. This was all very well but the time spent on the trip far exceeded the length of the hire. To avoid confrontation with the shopkeeper on return the bikes were left along the road from the premises whilst a hasty retreat was made!

In an article in the *Evening News,* editor Walter McPhail commented very favourably on a visit he had made to the Gymnasium. In particular, he was impressed by the number of old photographs on display in the pavilion, which had brought back many happy memories. Sadly it is very possible these disappeared when the stand was vandalised as the ground lay empty during the Second World War. On good authority it is said some dozen photographs with some cups and medals of St Bernard's used to be on display in Clark's Bar in Dundas Street after the Second World War but their present whereabouts are unknown. It could be the residue of photographs from the stand found their way there. This pub was closely identified with the Saints, its owner David Clark, also being a director of the Saints. It is said the public rooms to the rear of this pub were used for meetings of the club committee.

The start of season 1926/27 saw the introduction of two players that were to figure prominently over the forthcoming years. From Lanark United they signed Willie Brown. Initially a left half, Willie played for the Saints for nine seasons, moving to left back when Stephen Mitchell moved on. After retiring he became the trainer of the team as well as acting as groundsman. Tommy Robertson was the other player, an inside forward who signed from Edinburgh Emmett and spent six seasons with the Saints. Unlike Brown, whose service was unbroken, Robertson was with the club on three separate occasions. His time at the Gymnasium was interrupted by spells spent at Middlesbrough and Tynecastle.

It was to be another season of inconsistency, and the only consolation, albeit small, was their position of eighth from bottom place in the league. This represented an improvement of one position. The defence was very settled but the same could not be said of the forward line where changes, both positionally and in personnel, were plentiful. This was particularly the case at centre forward, where many players were tried after the departure of Peter Simpson in December.

The playing performance the following season continued in a similar vein. A fourth from bottom placing in the league was not what their faithful supporters wanted. A positive development however saw Leith Athletic, regarded as their chief rivals, back in the same league. Like St Bernard's the port club had reformed back in 1919 but had played in the Western League and the Scottish Alliance before taking part in the ill-fated Division 3 of the Scottish League. The rivalry between the two clubs ensured good attendances and they would now meet on a more regular basis. Indeed the derbies again would be very local, just like the old days, with the Athletic back, for a short time at least, at nearby Logie Green, after brief sojourns at Chancelot Park and Wardie Park since reforming. Two players came to the fore that were to serve Saints well over a number of seasons. Willie Drummond played for St Bernard's for eight seasons and was truly 'Mr Versatile', appearing in every position, including goalkeeper, except outside left. He was the son of a Hearts' director. Donald Eadie was another stalwart for the club who spent eight seasons at the Gymnasium. His appearances were restricted to the forward line, where he was very effective at centre forward and on either wing, and was a prolific goal scorer.

It was around this time that the club adopted a change in their policy of recruiting players. Hitherto they had been in the market for any players that became available, regardless of where they came from, although generally from the central belt of Scotland. This of course could result in the recruitment of a player domiciled some distance from Edinburgh. If he could not travel to the city on training nights, he would be entrusted to train on his own or with his local club. Saints realised that this was a far from satisfactory arrangement and embarked on a policy of acquiring more local players. From Newtongrange Star they recruited James Gilchrist, Thomas Moffat, and Robert Barton, all miners. At the same time they signed R L Small the amateur goalkeeper of Edinburgh University who was selected to represent Scotland in the amateur international against England in 1929. This made him the first St Bernard's player to represent his country since Donald Cameron in 1900. Small was at that time studying to be a minister at New College. Almost immediately the changes paid dividends, and the Saints finished

Willie Forrest

a very creditable sixth in the league, ten points behind champions Dundee United. It had been a much better season by far and the team was now competing. Few heavy defeats were sustained but still players moved on. Left half Willie Forrest and outside left Willie Walker both went to Middlesbrough. Later Forrest became manager, then a director of Darlington.

The Golden Jubilee of the club was celebrated in the Wesleyan Hall, Hamilton Place with a Soiree and Concert run by the Supporters' Club. This proved to be a highly successful event presided over by Mr Walter McPhail the Editor of the *Evening News*. Reminiscences were exchanged and a good time seems to have been had by one and all.

At the end of the season Saints lost 4-0 to Murrayfield Amateurs in the semi final of the City Cup and on the face of it this would appear to have been a bit of a disaster for the professional St Bernard's. Murrayfield Amateurs, however, were probably the best amateur side ever to come from the city. That season they won the first of three successive Scottish Amateur Cups to add to a previous win in 1926. In 1939 they were to become five times winners of the famous trophy. Murrayfield Amateurs also added the Scottish Qualifying Cup that season beating Thornhill by no less than 8-1 in the final. Perhaps a defeat by that side was no great disgrace, although the Saints management would no doubt view it differently. Presiding over this period of change had been Mr David S Gordon, a former player with Hibs, who was really the first non-playing manager of the club. He was appointed in 1925 and resigned in 1928.

In August 1929 St Bernard's started to issue programmes and were to do so for the remainder of their existence. These consisted of eight pages and were very basic; in fact very similar to those issued by other Scottish clubs at the time. The notes of the first issue, for the match against Dunfermline Athletic, announced that the outlook for the coming season was very bright. Unfortunately this proved to be optimistic and the Saints could not build on the progress of the previous season. They dropped eight positions in the league to finish fourteenth. To make matters worse Leith Athletic, now playing at the Marine Gardens, finished as champions!

Cover of St Bernard's first programme published on Saturday 10 August 1929.

Goalkeeper Leonard Small left the Saints in September, which necessitated that Willie Drummond replace him in goal. Although he played for just over a season, Leonard Small is one of the best-remembered Saints. This is because of his distinguished career as a Church of Scotland minister. In 1966 he became Moderator of the General Assembly and as far as is known, he is the only St Bernard's player to have written an autobiography. The aptly named *The Holy Goalie* was published in 1993 but deals almost exclusively with his time as a minister.

For the game against Bo'ness, at the Gymnasium on 28 December 1929, the Saints' players wore black armbands as a token of respect for George Murdoch, the captain of the Scottish Cup winning team, who had died in Australia.

For five seasons, since the famous victory in Kirkcaldy, St Bernard's had not generated any excitement in the Scottish Cup due to early exits from the competition. After beating fellow Division 2 team Third Lanark in the first round, the draw paired them with Hearts in the next round. This was the first meeting of the two clubs in the Scottish Cup since the semi-final of 1896 and the match was played at Tynecastle before a crowd of 27,000. Saints had forfeited ground advantage for the resultant financial benefit although there were those amongst their support who disapproved, and thought that they would have increased their chances of winning by playing at the Gymnasium. They may have had some justification as the Saints put up a great show

Centre pages of the club's first programme on Saturday 10 August 1929.

and held Hearts to a 0-0 draw. Not only that but some Saints' supporters always maintained that the team was robbed of a win that day. It is alleged a shot from 'Sodier' Imrie, their popular outside left, entered the goal but rebounded back into play after striking the metal stanchion at the back. The referee did not give the goal. On the following Wednesday at Tynecastle in the replay, in front of 22,000, the Saints went down by 5-1.

After a very shaky start, Saints finished strongly in the following season 1930/31. It was probably no coincidence that the change in fortune came about with the arrival in January of Ned Weir on loan from Falkirk. A left half, he was one of a number of players to give good service to the club during the 30s. He left St Bernard's in 1938 to join Clyde and along with another ex-Saints player Davie Noble, was a member of the Clyde Scottish Cup winning team of 1939. Weir also holds the rare distinction of playing international football for two countries. After leaving the Saints he played for both Northern Ireland and the Irish Republic in 1939. To top off a fine end to the season, the Saints won the Rosebery Charity Cup for the first time since 1915. Particularly pleasing must have been the fact that they beat both Hibs and Hearts to do it. Although it could hardly be classed as a major triumph, it surely showed that things were beginning to move forward in the right direction.

Leonard Small

In September 1930 St Bernard's had introduced greyhound racing to the Gymnasium with a view to increasing revenue and they were not alone with other football clubs doing likewise. This was disapproved of by the SFA in general, and the residents of the Royal Crescent neighbourhood in particular, who raised a petition with 300 signatures. The experiment, which was run on very primitive lines, did not last long with the wrong type of person being drawn to the area. A Glasgow syndicate ran it but problems such as stones being thrown at the dogs were encountered.

The very active Supporters' Club put forward a suggestion that the club should also run an amateur team to develop talent, probably as a result of the success being enjoyed at that time by the Murrayfield Amateurs club, but nothing came of it. One idea that did get off the ground was the establishment by the supporters of a refreshment kiosk at the top of the terracing opposite the stand. This was on an unprotected area with no cover and a handy facility to have on a cold day. A Mrs Reilly ran it as well as being very involved in other areas of the Supporters' Club activities.

In June 1931 ex-Saint Leonard Small married Miss Jean McGregor in Lothian Road Church. Along with a bouquet of pink roses Jean carried a lucky horseshoe of blue and white ribbon, which had been presented to Leonard by a supporter prior to an important game for the Saints. The Smalls were happily married for 48 years.

St Bernard's unfortunately did not have Ned Weir in their team for the 1931/32 season as he had returned to parent club Falkirk. He was to move back to the Saints however the following season. A very settled line up, which usually augurs well for success, was beginning to emerge. On the administration side Bob Innes, a retired referee, took over as Secretary/Manager of the club and was to serve right up until the Second World War. He was the first appointed to the post since the departure of David Gordon, the duties having been shared in the intervening five seasons by directors Walter Kemp and James Kirkwood. Two Edinburgh clubs provided the local derbies that season and did not include almost perpetual rivals Leith Athletic who were still clinging on to their, albeit brief, existence in Division 1. Hibs, who had been relegated, provided the rivalry, along with Edinburgh City who were newly elected to the Scottish League. The City were an all-amateur team created to be 'the Queens Park of the east'. The idea may have been sound in principle, as Edinburgh had a high proportion of academic and professional people in the city. In practice it did not work out and the club spent a miserable time in the Scottish League. In eight seasons, more often than not they finished bottom of Division 2. St Bernard's were particularly hard on them and emerged with a 100% record in their encounters, which included some large wins.

Not since 1900 had St Bernard's and the Hibs met in the League and the meetings with the team from Easter Road were eagerly awaited down Stockbridge way. An early season 3-0 win for the Saints in the Shield semi-final set the tone for the games between the two clubs. Saints followed this up with a 4-2 win in the first league meeting at Easter Road. It was this return fixture on New Year's Day that provided not a little controversy. For the record, the Saints won 1-0 thanks to a Donald Eadie goal. On the park, or rather ordered off it, went Willie Brown and Hibs' Jimmy Dobson, to be followed later by 'Ginger' Watson the centre half of the visitors. For three players to be sent off was unusual at the time and the Easter Road club were furious, threatening to take up matters further with the SFA. They eventually relented. The crowd that day was estimated at 27,000, which if accurate, would constitute a record for the ground. From old photographs, and descriptions of the Gymnasium in the 30s, this must have been a very tight squeeze. Some sources have quoted that the ground was capable of holding 40,000. This I very much doubt.

St Bernard's finished in fifth position in the League. The top places in the final table looked like this:

Scottish League Division 2 1931/32	P	W	D	L	F	A	Pts
East Stirlingshire	38	26	3	9	111	55	55
St Johnstone	38	24	7	7	102	52	55
Raith Rovers	38	20	6	12	83	65	46
Stenhousemuir	38	19	8	11	88	76	46
St Bernard's	38	19	7	12	81	62	45
Forfar Athletic	38	19	7	12	90	79	45
Hibernian	38	18	8	12	73	52	44

The Saints made it four wins out of four over the Hibs at the end of the season, when they beat them 3-0 at the Gymnasium in the semi-final of the City Cup. New players to figure prominently that season were Bobby Davidson and Donald Murray. Davidson was an inside forward who signed from Bowhill Rovers in Fife, a very good player but like so many before him he did not stay very long with St Bernard's. A number of prominent clubs were having him watched and eventually he signed for Arsenal. Before joining the Highbury club he was transferred to St Johnstone, with whom he earned a Scottish League cap. That he did not make the expected breakthrough with Arsenal is perhaps not surprising as he joined them when that club was at the zenith of its powers in the 1930s. Bobby played 12 league matches for Arsenal in season 1934/35, when they won their third championship in a row, scoring two goals. The Gunners' side at that time was full of internationalists and Bobby could not displace the great Alex James. Donald Murray was a centre forward who hailed from Peeblesshire who had spent an unsuccessful spell with Ayr United, and joined the Saints from his local side Peebles Rovers. At the Gymnasium he was a prolific goal scorer for five seasons, no doubt aided by playing in that successful Saints' side.

Not much is known about the people who scouted for the club but one suspects that more often than not it was the directors themselves who took up the duty of covering the minor matches looking for fresh talent. One non-official who undertook the task was a Louis Gordon who covered a lot of the central belt of Scotland on behalf of St Bernard's. He discovered many of the players in the 1930s that went on to bigger things bringing much needed revenue in the form of transfer fees.

Edinburgh local derbies were even more plentiful in Division 2 in season 1932/33 due to Leith Athletic being relegated from Division 1. Hibs won the championship that season, but the Saints, Leith, and Edinburgh City all finished in the lower half of the final table. On the 19 November in front of a 10,000 crowd at the Gymnasium the Easter Road side took revenge for the previous season and both league points, virtue of a 1-0 win. Later in the season Hibs won the return fixture 4-1. Leith Athletic though were struggling following their demotion, but still managed to win 1-0 at the Gymnasium and draw 1-1 at Marine Gardens. In an otherwise moderate season Saints did manage to have their name inscribed on the City Cup for the ninth time. In the final they beat Penicuik Athletic from the Edinburgh & District League 6-0, but only after the first game had been drawn 1-1.

Inconsistency was at the root of St Bernard's problems. A good result could be obtained, one week against one of the top teams, only to lose the following week to moderate opposition. If they could have eradicated this fault they would have been in a position to challenge for the championship. Unfortunately this was not to be solved in season 1933/34 either, when another mid table finish fully highlighted the deficiency. A 3-0 win over Murrayfield Amateurs in the final of the City Cup was scant consolation to the loyal band of supporters. Leith Athletic, by no means a good team that year, were particularly severe on the Saints, taking all the league points, as well as winning the Blenheim Cup on aggregate over the two legs. One result that must have surprised not only the patrons of the Gymnasium, but also further afield, was the 10-1 demolition of newly-relegated Morton at the Gymnasium. As was customary Donald Murray was amongst the goals with a hat trick but it was newcomer Andy Brown who did most of the damage, going nap with five goals. Andy was transferred to Middlesbrough within two months. Given that St Bernard's home attendances were only around the 1000 mark, when other clubs of similar status were attracting more, it must have been difficult for the directors of the club to turn down any reasonable offer for a player. Whether Andy Brown would have gone on to do great things with the Saints is however, open to question. He did not play any first team games for the Teesside club. As a direct replacement, Jock Russell joined from Edina Juniors. Jock, from Livingston in West Lothian proved to be a great servant to the club. He played in quite a number of different positions in his time with the Saints, covering seven seasons and on the face of it, the Saints had done a good piece of business on this occasion! They did not have far to go for Jock as he was literally playing on their own doorstep. Edina Juniors had use of the Gymnasium at that time when the Saints were elsewhere.

Saints started season 1934/35 with almost the same squad of players that finished the previous season except for a fresh left wing partnership. The new players were Davie Noble, an inside forward, recruited from minor club Blackhall Athletic with John Hay as his partner on the wing from junior club Lanark United. A local derby is not the best fixture for the start of any season but fortunately for the Saints, the 1-0 defeat at home at the hands of Leith Athletic did not set the pattern for the remainder of the league programme. In fact it was quite the reverse. Finding the net was not to prove difficult that season. On 1 September they made the short journey over the Forth to Cowdenbeath and beat the home side 10-1! Other large wins with the odd reverse, saw St Bernard's finish in third position with more than 100 goals to their credit.

St Bernard's league record at the Gymnasium was good, the only defeats being the one against Leith Athletic and the other a 1-0 defeat by Morton. Home draws with Forfar Athletic, always a bit of a bogey team to the Saints, and Montrose were however poor results. Wins over these lowly placed clubs would have edged them even nearer the second promotion spot.

The final top table positions were:

Scottish League Division 2 1934/35	P	W	D	L	F	A	Pts
Third Lanark	34	23	6	5	94	43	52
Arbroath	34	23	4	7	78	42	50
St Bernard's	34	20	7	7	103	47	47
Dundee United	34	18	6	10	105	65	42
Stenhousemuir	34	17	5	12	86	80	39

The financial situation of the club was such that the pitch had to be hired out as much as possible to raise extra revenue. The local amateur and juvenile associations found it to be an ideal place to stage their finals and semi-finals due to the ground's location right in the middle of Edinburgh. It was from such a match that a famous Hibernian and Scotland internationalist literally made his first acquaintance with a senior pitch. A very young Lawrie Reilly was nominated to be the mascot for the night for a local team by the name of Raeburn. His duties involved running on to the pitch with a lucky horseshoe to present to the captain of the team. Unfortunately in the excitement of the occasion the young Reilly fell his full length on the turf much to the amusement of the assembled crowd!

Lawrie Reilly falls to good effect this time at Wembley Stadium in scoring for Scotland in the 3-1 win over England in 1949.

Hopes were high with a largely unchanged line up that Saints might do better the next season and clinch a promotion spot. Once again scoring goals was not a problem but the home record was not nearly so good. Five games were lost at the Gymnasium in the course of the season. This nullified a very good start away from home when five of the first six games were won by good margins and the other was drawn. In the event they finished in fifth place.

In cup competitions Saints showed up well. A 3-1 win over Leith Athletic in August saw the City Cup annexed for the tenth time. The first two early season attempts to settle the Shield semi-final against the Hibs ended in draws before the Saints edged it 3-2 at the third try the following April. The final against the Hearts also ended in deadlock. St Bernard's also reached the final of the Rosebery Charity Cup again beating Hibs in the semi-final. Hearts won both the final of this competition and also the Shield when it was replayed at the start of the following season.

The leading positions that season were:

Scottish League Division 2 1935/36	P	W	D	L	F	A	Pts
Falkirk	34	28	3	3	132	34	59
St Mirren	34	25	2	7	114	41	52
Morton	34	21	6	7	117	60	48
Alloa Athletic	34	19	6	9	65	51	44
St Bernard's	34	18	4	12	106	78	40

Perhaps it should be explained that at this time St Bernard's did not have a reserve team and ran on a very small pool of players. For example over the course of the season just finished only 15 professionals were registered with the SFA. That is a very small number when it is realised the figure also includes comings and goings! How did they cope? The team was very settled with a lack of injuries. Trialists could of course be introduced which covered any problems encountered. Amateurs could also be used but on the face of it St Bernard's did not use any in the season under review. The Saints also farmed out some promising players to other clubs usually in the East of Scotland League. They of course could be recalled but in practice most made only fleeting appearances and they were usually left to see the season out with their adopted clubs.

Season 1936/37 saw quite a number of changes in personnel. The last line of defence saw the introduction of T G Smith an amateur goalkeeper. He was a decided acquisition having already earned several amateur caps with Queens Park along with a Scottish League cap. He also played for Ayr United. The full back partnership of Charlie Fitzsimmons and Joe Allan stayed intact, but Ned Weir apart, there were changes at half back. At right half Fifer Jimmy Philp replaced Mick Langton and James Strathie took over from Dominic Marley at centre half. Forwards George Brooks and Davie Noble started the season but both moved together to Clyde at the end of September. Replacements came in the immediate recruitment of George Grant from Albion Rovers and Jimmy Pinkerton from Blackburn Rovers. Promising inside forward David Nelson who joined the club in December 1935 moved to Arsenal the following May. He was to stay at Highbury until 1946 but only made 32 first team appearances in that time. Youth was replaced by experience with the signing of Jimmy Johnston from Motherwell. Peter Flucker who could count both Hibs and Hearts amongst his previous clubs took over at centre forward from Donald Murray.

These changes certainly solved the problem of games lost at home and only champions Ayr United left the Gymnasium with full points that season. Yet again goals were plentiful and for the third season in a row the Saints topped the 100 mark. However it was not sufficient to gain a promotion spot. Saints finished in third place. A significant result was an 8-1 win at Forfar of all places on 12 September. The Athletic as examination of the statistics will show had been a 'thorn in the flesh' of the Saints for a number of seasons by defeating them when least expected. Consideration was being given to the possibility of running a reserve team in the East of Scotland League had promotion been obtained.

The top of the table looked like this:

Scottish League Division 2 1936/37	P	W	D	L	F	A	Pts
Ayr United	34	25	4	5	122	49	54
Morton	34	23	5	6	110	42	51
St Bernard's	34	22	4	8	100	51	48
Airdrieonians	34	18	8	8	85	60	44

Off the park one time secretary Louis Gumley had been elected Lord Provost of Edinburgh. He along with ex-Councillor Tom Lamb and the long-serving Tom Gray, both also former secretaries of the club, were spotted all sitting together in the Gymnasium stand at the Forfar Athletic match on 2 January 1937. Earlier in the season, George Allison, the famous manager of Arsenal had attended a home match.

The draw for the Scottish Cup threw up an interesting tie when the Saints were drawn away to the Hearts in Round 1. The match on Saturday, 30 January was played on atrocious ground conditions suffice that the *Evening News'* famous cartoonist Tom Curr captioned his Monday sketch on the match 'Tynecastle stages an Ice Carnival'. Saints were at full strength that day but when the referee blew for full time the home side had won the contest 3-1. Not that the hostilities were confined to the pitch. At half time both sets of supporters indulged in a no doubt lighthearted snowball fight.

The bank accounts of the club were maintained at The Royal Bank of Scotland, Castle Street, which was then based at the junction of Castle Street and Queen Street. As the writer was later to work in that particular office I was able to speak with the family of McDonald Lyon who had been Bank manager there for a period of 24 years up to 1946. The family explained that their father attended matches at the Gymnasium accompanied by another member of staff to collect the match drawings for depositing immediately thereafter in the safe at the branch, a customary practice for football clubs at the time. Apparently Mr Lyon thought the Saints to be pretty hopeless! Whether this was a fair assessment, or one provided by someone who was there under sufferance and would have preferred to be elsewhere we do not know!

Coronation Day in 1937 was on 12 May and the event was celebrated in Glasgow by the staging of a Charity Football Match at Hampden between Glasgow and Edinburgh. T G Smith, Ned Weir and George Grant represented St Bernard's in the Edinburgh line up. Since the introduction of professionalism matches of this type were only now played spasmodically and invariably for a charitable cause. One or two players, more often than not, came from St Bernard's. Others to represent the club in these inter-city encounters were James McEwan and Willie Bow (Ibrox Disaster Fund 1902), Willie Henderson (Sinclair Benefit 1920), Abe Wilson (Hearts War Memorial Fund 1921) and Joe Ramage, Stephen Mitchell, Hugh Walker and Peter Simpson (East of Scotland FA Benefit 1926). When the city entertained an international all-star select in April 1916 for the Belgian Relief Fund Tommy Ross played.

Changes in the line up for the 1937/38 season were minimal compared to the previous one. Jerry Kerr came in at full back to replace Charlie Fitzsimmons; Bill Aird was signed from Inverkeithing Juniors, he shared the centre half position with Jock Russell; Bobby Kemp played at either outside left and left half and Joe Dawson, who joined the club in the latter part of the previous season, continued at inside left. The Edina Juniors Club had a short life span and following their demise we find Leith Amateurs back using the vacant dates on a Saturday. An innovation saw the introduction of a public address system installed by the Standard Electrical Engineering Company of London in January.

After three seasons with high finishes in the league hopes were high in Stockbridge that the coming season might be the one that finally saw the Saints clinch promotion to Division 1. A 7-1 win at Tannadice in the first league game augmented the grounds for optimism. The following Wednesday heralded a depressing note with the death of former goalkeeper James Keenan in sad circumstances. He had been assisting Duns in a City Cup tie at Old Meadowbank against Leith Athletic when he suddenly collapsed and died. St Bernard's responded quickly and sent a team to the Berwickshire town the following week to play the local side in a match in aid of his dependents.

The home record was good with only three defeats. One of these was against Raith Rovers who were runaway winners of the division. The other defeats by bogy team Forfar Athletic, early in the season, and Kings Park at the end were against teams the Saints might have expected to beat and proved in the end to be very costly. For the third time in four seasons St Bernard's were only three points off the second promotion spot. So tantalisingly near yet so far! The top of the table showed as follows:

Scottish League Division 2 1937/38	P	W	D	L	F	A	Pts
Raith Rovers	34	27	5	2	142	54	59
Albion Rovers	34	20	8	6	97	50	48
Airdrieonians	34	21	5	8	100	53	47
St Bernard's	34	20	5	9	75	49	45

It was the Scottish Cup that was to provide the real interest. In the first round the Saints were drawn at home against Vale of Leithen from the East of Scotland League. Whilst many might have expected the Saints to score several goals against non-league opposition this did not materialise and a solitary goal saw them through. If the patrons of the Gymnasium were disappointed by the narrow win this was nothing compared with their counterparts at Tynecastle and Easter Road. Major shocks saw both Hearts and Hibs eliminated by Division 2 opposition. Hearts were beaten 3-1 by Dundee United at Tannadice. The biggest shock of all, however, was at Easter Road where perpetual strugglers Edinburgh City won 3-2. With Leith Athletic also going down at Dumfries this left St Bernard's and the City as the sole survivors from the capital. Just prior to the Vale game Ned Weir had been transferred to Clyde. In Bill Aird Saints had a ready-made replacement. Another home draw in the second round against Kings Park seemed on paper at least, well within Saints capabilities but once again they made heavy weather of it and could only draw at the Gymnasium. Edinburgh City had crashed out 9-2 at Kirkcaldy to leave the Saints as Edinburgh's only representatives in the competition. On the following Wednesday at Stirling three goals from George Grant helped to secure a 4-3 win in the replay. After a bye in the third round the draw for the fourth round saw the Saints paired with Motherwell at the Gymnasium. Since breaking the Rangers and Celtic monopoly by winning the Division 1 championship in 1931/32 Motherwell had remained a force in Scottish football and were usually to be found occupying a position near the top of the table. The draw created a great deal of excitement in the city, not to mention Stockbridge, and especially with the directors of St Bernard's, who saw the opportunity of a good gate with the city to themselves. In hindsight they made an error of judgment. The decision was taken to double the admission prices and remove the concessions. This was undoubtedly poor public relations at a time when money was scarce and backfired when only 3600 paid for admission. Many more could have been expected at the normal rates. A free view of a game could be obtained from the roofs of the surrounding buildings if one was inclined such was the situation of the ground. A 'great free gallery' was reported that day.

Fortunately this did not affect the play of the team who rose to the occasion in fine style. Motherwell scored first but Peter Flucker equalised within two minutes. In the second half Flucker was again involved when Saints took the lead. He shoulder charged the Motherwell goalkeeper, which was permissible at the time, who only partially cleared the ball. It fell to George Grant who scored. The visitors protested the legality of Flucker's action to no avail and when the same player scored five minutes from the end it was all over. Amid scenes of great jubilation Saints were in the semi-final for the first time in 42 years. Some even were seen singing their praises from the rooftops! Rangers, Kilmarnock and fellow second leaguers East Fife joined them. Tynecastle was chosen as the venue when the draw matched them with the club from Fife. This was St Bernard's fourth appearance at this stage of the competition. The draw could hardly be better for the Saints especially with the match taking place in Edinburgh. In the lead up to the game in addition to much enhanced coverage in the press the BBC had a special programme 'Fanfare' to cover the semi-finals in which the four teams were represented, captain Jerry Kerr representing the Saints.

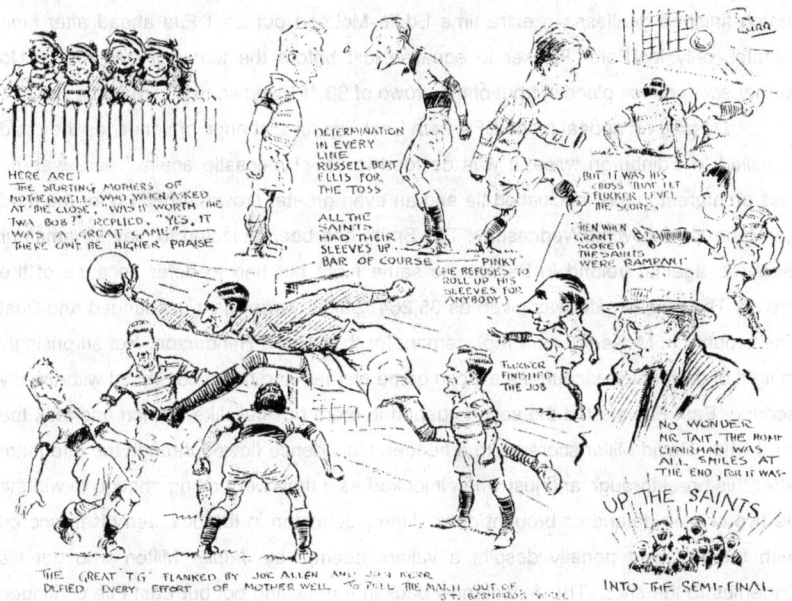

This is probably the best cartoon of many depicting a St Bernard's match drawn by Tom Curr for the 'Evening News'. He lived in East Claremont Street very near the ground and was heavily involved with the 46th Boys Brigade Company, the largest in Edinburgh, which was attached to Dublin Street Baptist Church. No doubt he was as pleased as anyone with the win over Motherwell in the Cup.

When the teams took the field on Saturday, 2 April 1938 there was fully 30,000 in the ground for a match that clearly had captured the appeal of the public. A large contingent had crossed the Forth to support their black and gold heroes. Amongst the good luck messages was one from Lord Provost Sir Louis Gumley who had attended the 1895 Final. Saints won the toss and elected to play towards the Gorgie Road end. Play was fairly even in the first half and this is reflected in the 1-1 scoreline at the break. Saints had taken the lead through Jimmy Johnston only for Andy Herd to equalise for the Methil team two minutes later. The second half continued in like fashion but without any further scoring. After the game it was announced that the attendance had been 34,200 and that the replay would be at the same venue on the following Wednesday.

By the time the second game came round it was known that the winners would face Kilmarnock in the final, the Ayrshire side having beaten Rangers 4-3 in the other semi. St Bernard's were unchanged but Henderson replaced the injured Duncan in the Fife line up. In the regulation 90 minutes Saints managed to hit the woodwork twice and East Fife had the ball in the net twice only to have the 'goals' disallowed, but the match finished goalless. In extra time Eddie McLeod put East Fife ahead after nine minutes only for Peter Flucker to equalise just before the teams turned round. No further scoring took place in front of the crowd of 30,185 and so to a third game.

Despite an appeal to the SFA from East Fife for a change of venue, as they had travelled to Edinburgh twice, it was decided to use Tynecastle again. There was no loss of interest in this fascinating tie and an even greater crowd turned up for the third game on the following Wednesday. T G Smith had been selected to play for amateur Scotland against Ireland in Belfast the same night but had to defer because of the replay. The official gate was given as 35,264. Saints were again unchanged and East Fife brought in McKerrell as a replacement for the injured Henderson. Not surprisingly in light of the earlier encounters a close game ensued and half time arrived without any scoring. East Fife started the second period in more businesslike fashion and took the lead when David Miller scored with a header. Confidence flowed through the Fife team after this breakthrough and just when it looked as if they were doing enough to win the tie two of their defenders brought down Jimmy Johnston in the box. Jerry Kerr scored with the resultant penalty despite a valiant attempt by James Milton who got his fingertips to the shot. The tie was now back in the melting pot but East Fife continued to play well. Six minutes from the end Danny McKerrell sent the black and gold contingent in the large crowd into ecstasy when he scored the winner. At the end of the game the supporters from Fife invaded the field to mob their team but for St Bernard's the cup dream was over. The team had not let anybody down and over the course of the three games, especially the first did have chances to win the tie but it was not to be. In contrast East Fife went on to make history as a Second Division club and win the Cup beating Kilmarnock after a replay.

There was certain discontent down Stockbridge way that East Fife had brought in Danny McKerrell the match winner on a loan agreement from Falkirk just two days before the second replay which undoubtedly strengthened the Fife team. However this was perfectly within the rules in being at the time and there was nothing that could be done about it.

By way of some consolation the Saints did win the Rosebery Charity Cup for the fourth and final time in their history when they beat Leith Athletic 4-0 in the final but with a tougher struggle than the score would suggest as all the goals came in extra time.

In a way St Bernard's could be described, as a 'patron saint' for minor football in the area such was the frequency, of some necessity it might be added, with which they lent out their ground to the local associations. While this brought in much needed income the heavy usage, sometimes matches were staged every night of the week, had its toll on the playing surface which did not have a close season to recover. Some aerial photographs taken in August at the start of a season show the goalmouths and a pathway right up the middle of the pitch to be completely devoid of grass. Obviously the Saints felt they could live with this so much so that in 1939 the Supporters' Club ran their own juvenile tournament over and above the others and were more than happy with the takings.

After the four seasons on the trot when promotion was all but achieved season 1938/39 showed a slight falling off with only a seventh place finish. Team wise there were not many changes but the loss for business reasons of goalkeeper T G Smith after only a few matches was a blow. His contribution to the successful run in the Scottish Cup the previous season should not be underestimated. The cup competitions did not bring much joy either with the only silverware to be adorning the Gymnasium boardroom at the end of the season, the City Cup won after beating Peebles Rovers 3-2 in the final. This minor success brought to 11 the number of Saints' wins in this particular competition. It was the record at the time and St Bernard's still currently hold the second highest number of wins after being overhauled by Berwick Rangers on 28. All of Berwick's successes have come since St Bernard's demise.

The City Cup was in fact the same trophy, put to a new use, as it had been used for the old Edinburgh Second XI Cup competition. The Saints' latest success was the last time it was played for before the outbreak of the Second World War and therefore the Saints held it for the duration of the hostilities. In 1946 workmen employed in the demolition of the Gymnasium Ground discovered it buried in the terracing! More than likely it had been stolen when the stand was vandalised and hidden for uplift at a later date. The Edinburgh Second XI trophy had of course been the first one ever won by St Bernard's back in 1889 and the words of James Baillie, who said if they ever won a trophy they would lose it on the way home, in a sense started to ring true!

On 18 February 1939 the popular Jimmy Johnston set a record when he scored all six goals in the 6-2 win over Forfar Athletic at the Gymnasium.

In the final amateur international before the Second World War Kenneth Shepherd the Saints' back up goalkeeper played against Ireland in a 1-1 draw. He was the last player from St Bernard's to represent his country following fellow amateurs Leonard Small and TG Smith, all goalkeepers.

Another milestone in the club's history, the 60th anniversary, was celebrated in the Grand Restaurant in South St Andrew Street with a Diamond Jubilee Dinner organised by the Supporters' Club. Followers had misgivings about the club's ambition but the directors at the Dinner said they were determined to get back to the First Division.

Jimmy Johnston

Despite the run of comparative success in the 1930s when the team was perpetual challengers for promotion from the Second Division St Bernard's never did seem to attract the crowds a club in that position would expect. They had a good ground judged by the standards of the time and it was very centrally situated. In the days before motorcars became affordable, and popular, public transport fulfilled the need and the ground was well served in this respect with vehicles passing virtually on all sides. Of course the club was perceived as 'second rate' whilst they remained in the Second Division, compared to Hearts and Hibs who both occupied positions in the First Division of the Scottish League. As the fixtures of these bigger clubs tended to alternate Saturday about, seldom did St Bernard's have the city to themselves. Another reason put forward in the press at the time was the close proximity of many of the local rugby clubs. There is much green belt to the north of the Canonmills and Stockbridge areas and here at the time were to be found the grounds of four prominent clubs. Seldom has club rugby attracted really big crowds but never the less it was an alternative on a Saturday for people living in the immediate area.

Although the political crises in Europe was worsening, following the rise of Nazi Germany, the 1939/40 football season kicked off as normal. The St Bernard's team line up was not much changed from that which had finished in the previous season. Results were mixed and the team was lying in tenth position when the league programme was stopped in light of war being declared on 3 September 1939 and a government ban imposed on organised football. The previous day before a good crowd newly-relegated Queens Park had been entertained at the Gymnasium. This was the first meeting between the clubs since season 1922/23 when Queens Park had spent one season in the Second Division. It was ironic that what was to be Saints' last ever Scottish League match, in normal peace time conditions, should be against a club with which they had had a very close relationship with in the early days. The match ended goalless. Afterwards it fell to Mr Robert D Tait the chairman of the club to bid his players 'au revoir' and asked them to keep in touch with the club and the fine supporters organisation who would keep them in mind in the event of an overseas posting. True to his promise presents were sent the following Christmas to those players serving in the Forces. Bob Innes resigned as secretary in early October. He had held the post for eight seasons and was in effect the manager of the club. Jack Reid was to take over for the remainder of the club's existence.

There now followed a period of some uncertainty as the impact of the war declaration and its repercussions took effect. There was still the possibility that the League programme might be resumed following a relaxation of the government imposed restrictions. It was at this point that Sir Louis Gumley suggested setting up three regional leagues to curtail the need for teams to travel further than necessary. In the end the League decided on two, an East and North East, and West split with sixteen clubs in each division. This meant that there was no place for Brechin City, Forfar Athletic, Montrose, East Stirlingshire and in Edinburgh, Leith Athletic and Edinburgh City. For Leith Athletic it could have read St Bernard's as it had been resolved only one of the smaller clubs in the city would be accommodated. In view of their poor record it was decided that Edinburgh City would drop out, but the Saints and Leith were really inseparable in terms of performance and it was St Bernard's who won the day on the strength of the toss of a coin!

Nearly all of the players who had contested the last Division 2 match against Queens Park were not now available although they still had the half back line of Philp, Flucker and Aird. Jim Philp, who normally worked in the pits, was shortly to contract double pneumonia but the Saints were able to employ him looking after the ground during his illness. The transfer of people round the country on war service meant that players were no longer able to play for their own clubs but could turn out as guests in the areas where they were based. In that season Saints were able to recruit goalkeeper Jock Wallace who had played down south for Blackpool and Derby County and full backs John Abbie and Robert Yorke from Partick Thistle and Ayr United respectively. Also assisting at full back was John Walker the brother of the famous Hearts' player Tommy Walker, who normally played for Belfast Celtic and whilst there had represented the Irish League. In at forward came George Hay, who had played for both Third Lanark and Queen of the South, Bill Theurer another Blackpool player, David Linton another old Partick Thistle man and the most famous of all, Jimmy Logie, who was to go on and star in the powerful Arsenal team of the post-war period.

At the outset results were quite good with draws recorded at Tynecastle and Pittodrie but a very bad run in March and April 1940 saw the Gymnasium men finish the season in thirteenth position out of 15, Cowdenbeath having dropped out of the League.

Generally speaking the new set up of East and West Leagues was not meeting with universal approval, with both Hearts and Hibs voicing concerns at the lack of involvement with the 'Old Firm', in particular, and other western clubs. This had a seriously detrimental effect on their finances and they were not prepared to stay with the same set up for another season. After much debate on the subject what emerged for season 1940/41 was a new league called the Southern League, which comprised of only 16 clubs drawn from East and West. As a result of the overall reduction in numbers from a total of 31, many clubs fell by the wayside. In effect what happened was the placement of Hibs, Hearts and Falkirk with the remaining clubs from the old West League after the withdrawal of Queen of the South, Kilmarnock and Ayr United. All the other clubs from the East and North East section were out of football for the season including St Bernard's. Attempts were made to obtain involvement for some of these clubs and the Saints amongst others were invited through to Stirling at the instigation of the Kings Park club to explore the possibility of a Midland League. Nothing came of this initiative, or from the invitations handed out to Leith Athletic, Edinburgh City and St Bernard's to join the Midlothian Junior League, which had lost a lot of clubs. The latter idea was not without some merit as it would have given football to the senior clubs and boosted the numbers in the junior league. The senior clubs felt, probably correctly, that it would affect their senior status and opted for no involvement. Edinburgh City were in fact able to continue by playing in the Lothian Amateur League.

In a sort of way St Bernard's did join the junior league for season 1940/41. A new club called Rosebery Juniors operating out of the Gymnasium joined Bathgate

George Heathcote Dingwall

Thistle, Bonnyrigg Rose Athletic, Armadale Thistle, Polkemmet Juniors, Haddington Athletic, Musselburgh Athletic and Winchburgh Juniors in the league. It is difficult to say what involvement St Bernard's did have with the new club. The old Edinburgh Rosebery, a Stockbridge club, had been a force in the junior game in the early years of the century and did have close connections with the Saints who allowed them the use of the Gymnasium but they were long defunct despite a short revival after the First World War. The Rosebery Juniors were also to use the ground and played in the St Bernard's colours of blue and white hoops. More than likely they had use of a strip from their hosts. The other link, and probably the strongest, was sponsorship of the team by the active St Bernard's Supporters' Club. Rosebery Juniors did not use any of the players from the St Bernard's team.

Rosebery Juniors only lasted until Christmas 1940 and like Musselburgh and Haddington were unable to finish the league programme. The remaining clubs in the area had to join up with Lanarkshire for the following season to make up a viable league such was the difficulty of running teams during the war emergency.

A North Eastern League was started for 1941/42 and St Bernard's were included. As the name implies it was some of the rejected clubs from the old East and North East League who formed it plus Rangers who entered their second eleven. The others were Aberdeen, Dundee United, East Fife, Dunfermline Athletic, Raith Rovers and old rivals Leith Athletic. The near neighbours of the Gymnasium and Logie Green days were to be closer than ever now with Leith Athletic ground sharing at the Gymnasium following the taking over of Meadowbank, the then home ground of Leith Athletic for Army use in August 1941. The *Evening Dispatch* reported that, following new soil and seeding work carried out by the supporters, the pitch was in good condition.

St Bernard's had to start again building a team from scratch after the season of inactivity. Goalkeeper James Matthews moved over from the defunct Rosebery Juniors to provide the only link with the two clubs and the only other familiar face was Jimmy Logie. Otherwise it was all new players and these were more than plentiful. The Saints never really had a settled line up and found it difficult to attract players. This was reflected in the results, which were poor. The 'Newman' listed for the match versus Dunfermline Athletic on 27 September 1941 was a Norwegian sailor. This was the only occasion as far as is known that a non-British player turned out for the Saints. The season was run in two periods – one from August up to November and the second from January to May. St Bernard's finished near the bottom of both. If anything at all could be taken out of the season it was a 2-0 win over Rangers Reserves at Ibrox.

Clearly things were at a low ebb in what was to be St Bernard's final season. One of the players who played in that team was George Dingwall who was only 16 years old at the time. He was a local boy and a grandson of George Heathcote, one of the founders of the club and the first captain. Thus we have a link with grandfather and grandson taking part in the very first and the very last matches of St Bernard's, as George played in the final match at Methil on 16 May 1942.

George was able to recall an occasion of a match at the Gymnasium that perhaps illustrates only too clearly how difficult things had become. No sooner had the teams kicked off than the Saints found themselves a goal down. It was obvious that the opposing right-winger had had acres of room to work in with nobody marking him, and the reason nobody was marking him was, the Saints had taken the field a man short! George who was sitting in the stand with some fellow reserves that day was hastily summoned to the home dressing room where sure enough an unused strip was still sitting on the peg.

To further illustrate the state of affairs, the last ever game against East Fife should have been played at the Gymnasium but it turned out that the Saints had already booked it out for a match between the 1st and 3rd Battalions of the Home Guard! It was switched to Bayview Park, Methil.

The attendances at the games of both St Bernard's and Leith Athletic that season were very poor indeed, with the admission monies drawn very often insufficient to meet the visiting team's guarantee. Against this background their fellow members voted them out off the League. It still seemed a harsh decision however involving two long-established clubs especially when their replacements were only the second elevens of Hearts and Hibs. If Dundee and St Johnstone, who were both inactive at the time, for example, had taken their places it might have made more sense. Both clubs appealed against the decision but to no avail.

When Hibs reserves were to drop out of the league after only one season an application by St Bernard's to rejoin was turned down.

In the August 1943 it was reported in the *Edinburgh Evening News* that the ground was about to be sold. This was confirmed a month later. It will be remembered that when the Saints had moved back to the Gymnasium in 1924 they had purchased the site by means of the Royal Gymnasium Ground Company. It was James Bowen & Sons who dealt in farm machinery who actually purchased the site. There was some optimism that the ground might still be available for football and the minor football associations were said to have made a substantial offer to the new owners but it came to nothing.

Optimistic noises were forthcoming that St Bernard's would continue after the war for definite and a committee was being formed. An advertisement appeared in the *Evening Dispatch* of 5 November 1943 intimating that a meeting of supporters and sympathisers was being held at the Gymnasium at 3 pm on the following Sunday. No report of this meeting appears although during the war coverage of sport in the press is understandably scant. Another year or so was to elapse when it was reiterated that the club would continue; a public company would be formed and a new ground was being sought in the Pilton/Comely Bank area. The club was reported to be 'in funds to the extent of £200 with full equipment'.

On 27 February 1945 the Saint Bernard's Football Club Grand Stand Company Ltd was wound up with the Secured and Ordinary creditors being repaid in full, with a dividend of 10/- (50p) for each £1 share held for the members. The principal creditor was The Royal Bank of Scotland, Castle Street Branch with a debt of £1493. The bank had provided the overdraft to meet the balance of the purchase price of constructing the grandstand after the share issue was undersubscribed at the outset.

The *Evening Dispatch* of 28 April 1945 brought the sad news that former player Sam Johnston was missing in Burma believed killed, to be followed two days later with a report that James Wood, who had played in the final season, had been killed in Western Europe. This brought to three the number of St Bernard's players who died in the conflict. Back in August 1943 Hugh Glass, who had played one match in the 1939/40 season, was believed to be drowned on duty for his country.

In July 1945 negotiations were proceeding with a view to merging Leith Athletic and St Bernard's. Neither club had a ground with the Gymnasium now sold, and Meadowbank not yet available again following use by the Army. The objective was to enter a combined Leith-St Bernard's team in a newly-formed Eastern League playing out off City Park on the Saturdays when Edinburgh City, who had entered the same league, were away from home. Before the decision to use City Park had been taken the enclosed Wood's Park ground in Portobello had come in for consideration. Other clubs in the league were Brechin City, Stirling Albion, East Stirling, Dundee 'A', Forfar Athletic, St Johnstone 'A' and Montrose. On the face of it, things were moving satisfactorily and a list of the opening fixtures was published showing the combined club to be away to East Stirlingshire on 25 August. However it was not to be, and on the eve of the season Leith-St Bernard's withdrew from the league. City Park was to cost too much to use and a very poor gate of less than 100 at an Edinburgh City match there, were reasons put forward for the change of heart. It was hinted that Meadowbank would be used the following season. In September 1945 the name 'Leith Athletic' appeared in the draw for the Victory Cup, their opponents to be Peebles Rovers. While they were to scratch from the competition this seemingly unilateral action taken by the Port club, however, cast doubts about the proposed amalgamation.

Six months later on, and it was thought that the merger was progressing with the St Bernard's directors being offered seats on the Leith board after taking up shares. The St Bernard's grandstand was sold to Leith Athletic for £2000 and re-erected at their Old Meadowbank ground. Other offers had been submitted by the newly-formed Stirling Albion and Birmingham City, but the Midlands club could not get the permit required by the immediate post-war transport restrictions to move it south.

On paper at least, St Bernard's still existed at the start of the 1946/47 season but were not included in the newly-formed Division C of the Scottish League because they did not have a home ground. The new division contained all of the previous seasons Eastern League clubs with the addition of Dundee United 'A' and, significantly, Leith Athletic. St Bernard's membership of the SFA entitled them to enter for the first post-war Scottish Qualifying Cup, that they duly did, being drawn away to border club Duns in round one. In the event they scratched. It was to be the end of the road for St Bernard's and at the SFA Council Meeting on Wednesday, 2 April 1947 their name was deleted from the membership.

Chapter 8
The Arsenal Stadium Mystery

This is strictly for the old film buffs. The above film was featured in cinemas just before the War and centred round a footballer who is poisoned during a match. Maybe this could be Romanov's next move for the Jambos just to keep the fans on their toes. You may of course wonder about the title and what has this to do with St Bernard's FC. Nothing really other than if you look closely at the cover you will see a small cigarette card sized photograph of Jimmy Logie, an Edinburgher by birth, who moved on to the Arsenal after a short spell at the Saints. The other even looser connection hinges on the word combination 'Stadium Mystery'.

The last chapter brought the whole St Bernard's story to a rather abrupt ending and many old fans must have wondered what had happened to their club and how the Stadium Committee had finally called a halt to this historically famous Edinburgh team. Many questions unfortunately will be left unanswered such as what happened to the Stadium Committee members and, somewhere in some forgotten archives, their statements, bringing some clarity to the unhappy ending. With no factual evidence their demise will still remain as something of a mystery.

However, although no rocket-scientist, the various facts and figures I have gathered over some considerable time seem to suggest that St Bernard's were no different to other clubs in the not so distant past, who had their problems i.e. Third Lanark who quickly fell foul of their entrepreneurial chairman Mr Hiddleston – another mystery with no real conclusion but much collusion. The almost takeover of the Hibees by Wallace Mercer and how all of a sudden were Hibs in such a precarious position and vulnerable to the Tynecastle Terror. Then only a few years ago there was the disappearance of Meadowbank Thistle followed by the appearance of new club Livingston. Bill Hunter chairman of both clubs could maybe throw some light on this change of name, stadium and location but to all intents and purposes really the same club!!

All of these and more are certainly mysteries to the general public and will remain so unless Hercule Poirot makes a come-back.

My personal view on the St Bernard's FC and Stadium mystery is that there is no such thing, only that the club folded due quite simply to market forces and the circumstances these placed them in.

There is no record of anyone who was extremely wealthy being involved with the club and the fact that the Directors took the unusual step of appointing two members of the Supporter's Club onto their Board in the 1920s surely bears out the vital contribution made by that organisation in raising funds against a background of poor attendances. In the city Hearts and Hibs have held the upper hand with the smaller League clubs like the Saints, Leith Athletic, Edinburgh City and Meadowbank Thistle unable to compete with them and failing to exist.

Some histories have cited the death of club director James Cooper during the War and the efforts made by his executors in taking action to recover monies he lent to the club as the reason for the winding up. This story lacks accuracy yet probably indicates that he had a major influence in their financial affairs. James Cooper did not die until December 1951.

He was a member of the group of 11 individuals who in 1924 formed the Royal Gymnasium Ground Company that purchased the ground for £2500. It was not the football club as such that made the acquisition. In 1944 the ground was sold for £4750 and Mr Cooper was still involved at that stage.

In the absence of a sight of any financial accounts for the club, it is impossible to tell, but it could be that he put up a large proportion of the initial purchase price as well as funding some of the running costs over the years. At the time the ground was sold, in addition to Mr Cooper only Robert Penman, David McLaren and Robert Tait remained of the original purchasers, the others having died or relinquished their positions. More significantly nobody had replaced them.

Against a background of the club not operating at all with the prospects looking anything but bright, and the remaining Directors not getting any younger, a decision to sell the ground was perhaps the sensible option. It could not have been an easy one as all of them had long standing connections and were committed to the Saints.

The loss of the ground, the key asset, meant that St Bernard's would have needed to start again after the War from scratch and as events showed this proved to be impossible.

So it is my view, that interesting as it may be to allude to a mystery, I personally subscribe to the view that the Saints died a natural death but certainly left their mark on the history of our famous game.

Chapter 9
Some Odds and Ends

In 1949 two football clubs were started in Stockbridge, which were to carry the St Bernard's name forward with distinction into the post senior club years.

St Bernard's First Class Juveniles, which catered for players under the age of 27, were members of the Scottish Juvenile Association until 1959 then became members of the Scottish Welfare FA until their demise in 1974. They were to be particularly successful in the Welfare set up being runners up in the Scottish Cup (Templeton Trophy) in 1960 after winning the Scottish Consolation Cup (Daily Record Trophy) in 1958 and again the following year.

The other club founded the same year was St Bernard's Boys Club who owe James Tulloch who lived in India Place the credit for their origin. The club in fact stemmed from the Edinburgh Academy Stockbridge Boys' Club, which had been founded in 1929 and had its own premises in Raeburn Place where the present Woolworth's store stands. At the time it was running four football teams in the local youth leagues but in the year in question had only two managers. This meant that two teams had to be abandoned and it was Mr Tulloch who came to the rescue when approached by the boys to run their team. Almost the whole of its existence has been spent in the ranks of the Scottish Secondary Juvenile Association (now the Scottish Youth

St Bernard's Under Age Juveniles – Scottish Cup winners 1961

FA). The most notable achievement was winning the national trophy at under 17 level, the Lord Weir Cup, in 1961. Typical of a team that season was Whitehead: Bedingfield and Locke: Wood, Cameron and Carnegie: McPherson, Duncan, McMorran, Aitchison and Nicolson with Hastie as reserve. St Bernard's BC teams have also appeared in two other Scottish Cup Finals. In 1975 and 2000 the under 12 and 21 teams respectively missed out at the final hurdle. The sons of James Tulloch have figured prominently in the club and in football in general most notably John and Stewart. A MBE was awarded to Stewart in 1994 for his services to youth football, which involved every post up to National Secretary of the Association of Scottish Youth Football Clubs. Many players have moved on to the higher grades from St Bernard's BC including Alex Cropley and Darren Jackson, both full Scottish internationalists. The club still survives at the present time having had a continuous existence for the past 60 years.

Alex Cropley

Darren Jackson

In 1950 the Duke of Buccleuch opened the King George V Memorial Recreation Ground at Eyre Place under the auspices of the National Playing Fields Association. This was built on the most northerly part of the old Gymnasium football ground and is still used by children as a play park. The whole site was essentially split in two with the remainder being taking over by Bowens for garage and other uses in connection with their farm machinery business. Since 1981 this particular part of the site has been taken over by The Royal Bank of Scotland and is used as a car park for its staff that work in buildings in Fettes Row.

By 1950 with all hope of the senior club being reformed having disappeared the St Bernard's FC Supporters' Club decided to wind up its affairs. Over the years they had had a major influence in the well being of the football club. In disbursing its funds the homes for the blind at Linburn and Newington each received £50 and £24 was sent to the Children's Shelter. The residual balance was used to purchase the St Bernard's Cup. This trophy is still played for annually by primary schools in the north side of the city at Warriston Recreation Ground in Inverleith Row. At the outset it was confined to the schools in the Stockbridge area, namely Dean, Canonmills, St Bernard's and Stockbridge itself but the disappearance over the years of all but the last named has seen an enlargement of the eligible area.

I have lived overlooking the Gymnasium ground all my life. The Saints were already out of existence at least in a playing sense when I was born in 1943. However I still have a recollection of the grandstand when I was very young before it was moved to Old Meadowbank in 1947. The supports for the steel bridge which led from Royal Crescent into the top of the stand lasted a bit longer. These of course provided a source of daring for the youth of the district and it was with some relief that the mothers of local 'trapeze artists' welcomed their removal. The only remnant of this entrance that remains are the gates in Royal Crescent.

When the grandstand was moved to Meadowbank ironically the Park family followed when my father took over a fruit shop at Parsons Green Terrace in 1949. After Leith Athletic gave up the ground in 1954 Murrayfield Amateurs used it for a spell and I used to go to the stand to see their matches. It was also used by the Edinburgh Monarchs Speedway but its life came to an end when the whole Meadowbank site was developed to house the 1970 British Commonwealth Games.

My grandfather was brought up in Stockbridge and although not a football fan used to say that he remembered when St Bernard's were the best team in Edinburgh, no doubt recalling the Scottish Cup success.

The only relative I had who used to go to the Gymnasium on a regular basis was my Uncle Joe who was a Hearts' supporter. When the Maroons were away and the Saints were at home he and his pals would be there. One of his friends was a man called Jimmy Graham who had a plumbing business at the top of Broughton Street and he was a real Saints die-hard. Jimmy had a very loud voice and was certainly not averse to expressing himself to anyone who he took a displeasure to, usually the referee. Being in a confined area Jimmy's voice was amplified by the echo coming off the wall at the back of the grandstand. Many's the time Uncle Joe, who was a quiet man himself, wished the terracing would have opened up and swallowed him as Jimmy bellowed forth and heads turned round to find out what all the noise was about. As practice for the Gymnasium Jimmy used to heckle at Speaker's Corner at the Mound on a Sunday.

In 1990 when the movement to fight off Wallace Mercer's takeover bid for the Hibs was under way a campaigner approached an old St Bernard's supporter to sign his petition. He looked at it and said: 'I am not going to sign that – nobody tried to save St Bernard's!'

To celebrate the centenary of St Bernard's winning the Scottish Cup an exhibition of memorabilia etc was on display in the Edinburgh Room of the Central Library in George IV Bridge in 1995. Visitors were invited to sign a book and add any comments to it. One of the entries was from a Mr Lowe who described himself as the son of James Lowe one of St Bernard's first internationalists. Given that Jamie Lowe had won his Scottish cap in 1887 this seemed highly improbable given the long time span. However it turned out to be correct, as the Mr Lowe who signed the book was 82 years old. He had been born when his father was 60 so it all fitted into place. The son was only nine when his father died in 1927.

One of my neighbours Freda Clark used to recall as a youngster she and her friends used to run around in the stand. One can imagine the reaction of the stand users to having a bunch of kinds making a nuisance of themselves while a match was in progress! Freda also remembered a shell-shocked veteran of the First World War called Willie who lived in Barony Street. He used to appear regularly at 15 Royal Crescent and sit on the steps asking everyone who passed by if a game was on that day. 'Not today Willie' was the usual reply.

Not long after my father bought the flat in Royal Crescent in 1938 one evening he was cleaning the windows just as the crowd was leaving the Gymnasium. One wag started singing the George Formby classic 'When I'm cleaning windows' much to the amusement of everybody.

As already mentioned elsewhere in the book some amount of consolation came St Bernard's way when they won the Rosebery Charity Cup in 1938 to make up for the disappointment of missing out on a Scottish Cup Final appearance. Joe Allan who was the right back gave his Rosebery medal to his wife Elizabeth. That was in 1938 the same year they were married. Elizabeth used it as a pendant on a neck chain and wore it always.

Stockbridge is very much a village within the city and at one time was very heavily populated. Things have moved on and while a 100 years ago it was not uncommon for families of six or more to live in a single house this is no longer the case and single occupancies are now very common. This coupled with the fact that whole streets, eg, Jamaica Street and India Place have disappeared or been redeveloped on a smaller scale means a much smaller population. However it still retains its own identity and a charm of its own. Raeburn Place is very much the 'High Street' and it is not without reason that the locals know Stockbridge as the 'Capital of Edinburgh'.

And so endeth our story. What had started off as an interest in the club who had played below the windows of my house and whose pitch area now serves as a car park for the Royal Bank became an obsession. Hundreds of visits to all the Edinburgh libraries, trawling through my now expansive collection of football books, wandering around the archives at the SFA Museum, questioning anyone with the most minute of football connections on whether they had any memorabilia, a granny that made the tea at half-time, a relation that played etc. gave me hours of satisfaction. All in all I worked on it for 24 years furthering my interest in the club by assisting the St Bernard's Boys Club on a secretarial basis for 14 years and this has been most rewarding.

APPENDIX 1

THE PLAYERS

Index

Column 1 – Player's name etc – names in **bold type** are players who represented their country.
Such appearances as a St Bernard's player are indicated in Column 6 by a number shown after the name of the country e.g. **Scotland appearances (1)**. Where a country is given without a number the player was capped when with one of his other clubs.

Column 2 – Player's normal playing position.
Abbreviations used ; G (Goalkeeper), RB (Right Back), LB (Left Back), FB (Full Back both right and left), RH (Right Half), CH (Centre Half), LH (Left Half), WH (Wing Half both right and left), OR (Outside Right), IR (Inside Right), CF (Centre Forward), IL (Inside Left), OL (Outside Left), IF (Inside Forward both right and left), F (Forward any position) and ? (Unknown usually applies to a signing who did not play at all).

Column 3 – Number of seasons player played for St Bernard's.

Column 4 – First season player played for St Bernard's.

Column 5 – Last season player played for St Bernard's.

Column 6 – Brief information traced about each player e.g. previous club(s) and later club(s).

A

Name	Pos		Seasons	Notes
Abbie, John L	OL	2	1939/40 1941/42	ex Partick Thistle. Crossgates Primrose
Adams	CF	1	1913/14	Fife Junior
Adams, Frank	OR	2	1893/94 1894/95	From Cowlairs. Returned to Cowlairs (19/9/1893)
Adams, James	**RH**	**3**	**1888/89 1897/98**	**From Hearts (20/1/1897) and Everton. died in USA on 24/4/1943. Scotland, Scottish League and Edinburgh. Scottish Cup Winner with Hearts 1891.**
Addison	G	1	1887/88	Arbroath
Adlem	CF	1	1939/40	Crystal Palace
Ainslie, Walter W	LB	2	1900/01 1901/02	from Vale of Leithen. To Mossend Swifts (4/10/1901). Sheffield Utd and Burslem Port Vale. Also Hearts
Aird, Hugh	IR	1	1914/15	Peebles Rovers (1922)
Aird, William	CH	5	1937/38 1941/42	from Inverkeithing Juniors. Member of Scottish Cup Semi-Final team 1938. To Greenock Morton (28/9/1940). To Dumbarton (9/6/1941). Also Bowhill Rovers. Scottish Southern League Cup Finalist with Morton 1942
Aitken, R	IL	5	1881/82 1887/88	'Mortonhall golfer and billiard player'
Albert, Frederick J	CF	2	1911/12 1912/13	from Corstorphine Rangers. To Canada. Killed in the First World War
Allan, Edward	RB	1	1902/03	from Bainfield
Allan, George Horsburgh	**CF**	**1**	**1895/96**	**Also regd. for Liverpool. Broxburn Shamrock, Leith Ath, Celtic, Vale of Avon, Linlithgow Ath and Bo'ness. died 9/10/1899. Scotland**
Allan, Joseph	OL	1	1897/98	law student from Inverness Caledonians. Played as 'Jackson'. Amateur player. Hearts 'A'.
Allan, Joseph 'Puggy'	LB	5	1934/35 1938/39	ex Dunfermline Ath and Leith Athletic. Member of Scottish Cup Semi-Final team 1938. To East Stirling
Allan, Robert	IL	1	1916/17	Dunfermline. Peebles Town Councillor died 1941.
Allan, Robert	RH	1	1924/25	Broxburn United
Allison, A	LH	1	1884/85	2nd XI Player
Allison, Alexander	RB	1	1926/27	Arbroath, Kettering and Chirnside United
Allison, John	IL	1	1924/25	To Stenhousemuir (12/12/1924)
Alston, Thomas	IL	1	1924/25	From Newtongrange Star. Gala Fairydean. Scored first ever goal from corner kick
Amos, Andrew	LB	4	1913/14 1919/20	from Wemyss Athletic. Played in Army football. Captain of St Bernards 1919/20. In Camerons WW1
Anderson	LB	1	1889/90	Kirkcaldy
Anderson, David L	CF	1	1922/23	From St Johnstone (29/31923) ex Hibs
Anderson, George 'Geordie'	CH	3	1888/89 1891/92	Leith Athletic and Edinburgh. Also Blackburn Rovers, New Brighton Tower and Blackpool.
Anderson, George	RB	1	1919/20	From Hibs (9/1/1920). To Hibs (6/2/1920)
Anderson, Samuel	IR	1	1922/23	Airdrie, Third Lanark and Nithsdale Wanderers. Also Hamilton Accies
Anderson, William	RB	4	1887/88 1891/92	Leith Athletic and Edinburgh.
Anderson, William	OR	1	1904/05	Musselburgh Fern
Angus	OL	1	1889/90	Dunrobin Athletic
Annan, 'Archie' J	RB	2	1900/01 1901/02	from West Calder. To Sunderland (29/4/1902). Bristol City, Sheffield Utd, West Lothian Albion and Bathgate. FA Cup Finalist with Bristol City 1909.
Archibald, John	G	2	1920/21 1921/22	To Newcastle Utd (27/4/1922). Also Albion Rovers, Reading, Grimsby Town, Darlington and Chelsea.
Arnott, Walter	**RB**	**2**	**1892/93 1893/94**	**Queens Park, Corinthians, Pollockshields Ath, Linfield Ath, Ashfield, Kilmarnock Ath, Ballina FC Third Lanark. Scottish Trialist 1893/94. Scotland and Glasgow. Captain of St Bernards 1893/94 Scottish Cup Winner with Queens Park 1884, 1886 and 1890. FA Cup Finalist with Queens Park 1884 and 1885. Had started playing for St Bernards when capped for Scotland on 1/4/1893 although club given as Queens Park.**

Name	Pos	Apps	Seasons	Notes
Arthur, Andrew 'Cutty'	IF	8	1879/80	Hearts. re-instated amateur. Edinburgh appearances (2).
Atherton, Thomas H	OR	1	1899/00	Dunfermline, Dundee, Hibernian,Tottenham Hotspur, Partick Thistle, Grimsby Town and Brentford Scottish League. Edinburgh Benburb and Dunfermline Juniors.

B

Name	Pos	Apps	Seasons	Notes
Baillie, T	IR	1	1891/92	Armadale and Bathgate Rovers. Hearts and Edinburgh.
Baillie, James 'Jem'	G	13	1880/81 1892/93	ex Raeburn. Also St James. Captain of St Bernards 1884/85 and 1885/86. Edinburgh appearances (9) and one with Edinburgh Northern. Prominent referee when the Scottish League started. Also played centre forward on occasions.
Baird, Alexander	CH	4	1899/00 1902/03	Vale of Clyde. To Port Glasgow Ath (14/2/1903)
Baird, David	OL	2	1889/90 1891/92	Hearts. Scotland, Scottish League and Edinburgh. Scottish Cup Winner with Hearts 1891, 1896 and 1901. Scottish League Championship with Hearts 1897. Finalist 1903.
Baird, William Urquhart	CH	8	1891/92 1898/99	Scottish Trialist 1892/93, 1893/94, 1896/97. Dundee. To Rangers (24/2/1899) and back (8/3/1899). President Yonkers Soccer FC 1913/14 (New York). Scotland appearances (1) and Scottish League (selected only). Edinburgh appearances (1). Captain of St Bernards 1894/95 and 1896/97.
Bald	IF	1	1920/21	Trialist from Glencraig Celtic
Ballantyne, J	HB	1	1892/93	Edinburgh University Dumfries and Galloway Students
Ballantyne, Robert	LH	2	1891/92 1892/93	Edinburgh University Dumfries and Galloway Students
Barbour, Thomas	IF	1	1896/97	2nd XI Player
Barclay	CH	1	1905/06	
Barclay, George	OR	1	1900/01	
Barclay, John	G	2	1898/99 1899/00	To Polton Vale (1/2/1900).
Barnett, R	CF	1	1884/85 1886/87	from Leith. Preston North End re-instated amateur to Saints. Edinburgh appearances (1).
Barrie, Alexander	RH	2	1901/02 1902/03	ex Celtic. Sunderland
Barton, Robert 'Bobby'	CH	3	1928/29 1930/31	ex Newtongrange Star. Penicuik Athletic. Captain of St Bernards 1928/29 and 1929/30
Bathgate, William	IR	2	1906/07 1907/08	Bonnyrigg Rose
Baxter, Alexander	CH	1	1890/01	Dunrobin and Edinburgh Northern
Baxter, William	IF	1	1893/94	Polton Vale and Burnley.
Beattie, John	LH	1	1924/25	From Dykehead (31/10/1924). Armadale
Begbie, Isaac	RH	2	1892/93 1900/01	To Hearts (4/8/1900). Dairy Albert, Leith Athletic and Bathgate. Scotland, Scottish League and Edinburgh Scottish Cup Winner with Hearts 1891 and 1896. Scottish League Championships with Hearts 1895 and 1897.
Bell, David	IL	2	1895/96 1896/97	Third Lanark.
Bell, John	CF	2	1889/90 1891/92	re-instated from Hyde. Returned to them later.
Bell, John	FB	1	1910/11	From Port Glasgow Ath (8/3/1911)
Bell, Mark Dickson	IR	3	1898/99 1900/01	Edinburgh Rosebery FC. To Hearts (1/11/1900). Southampton, Fulham and Clapton Orient. Scotland. Scottish Cup Winner with Hearts 1901.
Bell, Willie	FB	1	1888/89	Woodburn, Middlesbrough and Milton House. Scottish Junior Club Finalist with Woodburn 1887.
Bell, William B	RH	1	1933/34	
Bennett, George	RH	3	1914/15 1916/17	from Lochgelly, Hearts and St Johnstone.
Bennett, Walter	RB	1	1914/15	from East Fife (28/4/1915). To East Fife (8/19).
Bennett	RH	1	1889/90	'from the West'
Bernard, Alexander	RB	1	1924/25	Muirkirk

Name	Pos		Seasons	Notes
Beveridge, Mungo	IR	2	1905/06 1906/07	from Lochgelly. To Lochgelly Utd (28/3/1907). Dunfermline
Beveridge, William	LH	1	1898/99	Dunfermline Juniors
Birrell, William O	CH	1	1925/26	Dunfermline Ath, Cowdenbeath and Raith Rovers
Bishop, Andrew	OR	1	1889/90	ex Cowlairs. Edinburgh appearances (2).
Black	OL	1	1913/14	from Kilmarnock
Black	LH	2	1920/21 1921/22	ex Tranent
Black, James	IL	1	1912/13	Trialist from Selkirk.
Black, Alec	?	1	1892/93	Rangers and Barnsley.
Black, G	OL	1	1894/95	Junior International player from Dunfermline Juniors. Also played for Hearts.
Black, Robert	OL	1	1923/24	From Bathgate (14/9/1923) To Arbroath (8/12/1923)
Black, William N	OL	1	1906/07	Civil Service
Blackall, William	OR	2	1908/09 1909/10	To West Lothian Albion (13/10/1909)
Blackhall	IL	1	1916/17	Musselburgh Athletic
Blades, Thomas P	CH	1	1888/89	ex Edinburgh University. Edinburgh.
Blair, J	OL	1	1921/22	ex Hearts
Blessington, James	**IR**	**1**	**1892/93**	Hibs, Leith Hibs, Leith Athletic, Celtic, Preston North End, Derby County, Bristol City, Luton Town, Leicester Fosse, Belfast Celtic and Abertillery Town (Manager), Scotland, Scottish League and Edinburgh Scottish Cup Finalist with Celtic 1893 and 1894. Scottish League Championships with Celtic 1893,1894 and 1896.
Blythe, George	OR	1	1905/06	From Berwick Rangers and back (7/12/1905)
Bogie, Neil	CH	2	1903/04 1904/05	Ex Leith Thistle. Re-instated amateur
Bow, James	IL	1	1933/34	Gateshead 1936/37
Bow, William	IL	2	1901/02 1902/03	To Blackburn Rovers (19/8/1902). Burnley, Nelson, Darwin and Great Harwood. died 3/1/1929. Broxburn United (1901)
Boyd, James	**OR**	**1**	**1924/25**	Keppochhill School and Springburn Hibs. from Petershill To Newcastle Utd. Also Derby County, Bury, Dundee and Grimsby Town died 3/1991.Scotland. FA Cup Winner with Newcastle United 1932. Won English League Championship with Newcastle United 1927
Boyd, Robert	IL	1	1887/88	Mossend Swifts. Scotland and Edinburgh. Also Third Lanark, Leith and Middlesbrough. died 1930
Boyle, Joseph	OR	1	1927/28	Mid Calder Amateurs
Boyne, James	G	2	1926/27 1927/28	from Dunblane Rovers ex Hearts
Brady, Joseph	OL	1	1893/94 1897/98	Renton and Sheffield United. Scottish Trialist 1893/94. Re-instated amateur (13/8/1895). Edinburgh appearances (1).
Brebner, William	LB	1	1908/09	To Aberdeen Harp (2/1/1909)
Britton, James	IL	1	1888/89	Clyde
Brogan, James	IR	2	1920/21 1921/22	From Bathgate (5/10/1920)
Brooks, George	OR	3	1935/36 1938/39	ex Western United To Clyde (26/9/1936) Also Dunfermline Athletic, Kings Park and Falkirk From Clyde (5/1938) Dumbarton
Brown	CF	1	1890/91	to Southport Central.
Brown	IL	1	1901/02	Kirkcaldy
Brown	G	1	1896/97	Dunfermline Juniors international goalkeeper played under the nom de plume of 'Robertson'.
Brown, Alexander	**CF**	**1**	**1895/96**	Glenbuck FC, Preston North End, Portsmouth, Tottenham Hotspur, Middlesborough and Luton Town. Scotland. FA Cup Winner with Tottenham Hotspur 1901.(Scored in every round - record)
Brown, Andrew	IL	1	1933/34	To Middlesborough (14/12/1933). Raith Rovers

Name	Pos	Apps	Season	Notes
Brown, David	OR	2	1937/38 1938/39	from Restalrig United
Brown, James	IL	1	1895/96	To Kilsyth Wanderers (18/1/1896)
Brown, James	RH	4	1900/01 1903/04	From Rangers, Lochgelly Utd, Bo'ness, Hearts, Cowdenbeath and Dunfermline Ath.
Brown, James	CF	1	1907/08	To Uphall (18/4/1908) Bathgate
Brown, James	RH	1	1921/22	Motherwell
Brown, James	OL	1	1922/23	
Brown, John	IF	1	1907/08	Wallyford Violet and Bathgate
Brown, John B ' Jock '	CH	1	1926/27	To Bathgate (27/11/1926) Also Hearts, Portsmouth and Leith Athletic. Captain of St Bernards 1926/27
Brown, Thomas	IR	5	1899/00 1903/04	Leven Thistle. To Broxburn (26/9/1902) died in Colorado in 1936 after emigrating to San Francisco 34 years before.
Brown, William	RB	1	1912/13	from Leith (28/12/1912)
Brown, William	G	1	1919/20	From Raith Rovers (16/1/1920) To Raith Rovers (6/3/1920)
Brown, William	LH	9	1926/27 1934/35	from Lanark United ex Douglas Water Thistle died 3/4/1958
Brown, William	RH	2	1941/42 1942/43	Haddington Athletic To Hibs (11/4/1942) Reg cancelled (20/10/1942) Re-instated to Tranent Juniors
Brown, William	RB	1	1894/95	2nd XI Player
Brownlie,	OL	1	1909/10	
Bruce, Daniel	IL	1	1889/90	**Vale of Leven, Rangers, Notts County, Small Heath. Scotland Scottish Cup Finalist with Vale of Leven 1890. FA Cup Winner with Notts County 1894.**
Bruce, George	OL	1	1888/89	Scottish Junior Cup Finalist with Woodburn 1887.
Bruce, Robert	G	1	1924/25	From Stenhousemuir (30/10/1924)
Brunton	G	1	1899/00	
Bryce	CF	1	1895/96	
Bryce, J	?	1	1894/95	Played for Saints in the Third Lanark 5 a side Tournament (1894)
Bryce, Robert	LH	4	1879/80 1884/85	ex Edina. Accrington, Burnley. Edinburgh appearances (3).
Bryce, W	?	1	1894/95	Played for Saints in the Third Lanark 5 a side Tournament (1894)
Buchan	CH	1	1896/97	Royal Scots
Buchan	LB	1	1898/99	Edinburgh Harp. 2nd XI Player.
Buchan, Colin L	CF	2	1913/14 1914/15	from Peebles Rovers. Queens Park and Dundee. In Yeomanry WW1
Buchan, Thomas	IR	1	1939/40	Blackpool. Craig-Mer and Murrayfield Amateurs
Buchanan, James	RH	1	1889/90	Cambuslang
Buchanan, John	IF	2	1888/89 1889/90	Cambuslang. Scottish Cup Finalist with Cambuslang 1888.
Buchanan, Peter	RB	10	1897/98 1908/09	Callander Rob Roy and Derby County. From West Calder Swifts (1904). Adventurers. Captain of St Bernards 1906/07 and 1907/08.
Burgoyne, Thomas	OR	2	1925/26 1926/27	Kello Rovers and New Cumnock United
C				
Cairns	RB	1	1941/42	Haddington Athletic
Cairns, Andrew	LH	2	1897/98 1898/99	Leven Thistle. To Kirkcaldy (28/4/1899).
Cairns, David	OL	1	1910/11	To Broxburn Shamrock (19/4/1911)
Cairns, John	RB	1	1920/21	ex Penicuik
Calder, William	OR	1	1888/89 1889/90	Scottish Junior Cup Finalist with Woodburn 1887.
Caldwell	RH	1	1923/24	Edinburgh junior

Name	Pos	Apps	Seasons	Notes
Cameron	LH	1	1930/31	
Cameron, David	RH	1	1926/27	To Hearts (19/5/1927)
Cameron, Donald S	CF	2	1898/99	Dunfermline Juniors. Scottish Trialist 1898/99. To Rangers (9/4/1900) Scottish League appearances (1).
Cameron, Robert	CF	1	1906/07	Edinburgh Myrtle and Falkirk
Campbell, A	LB	1	1921/22	
Campbell, George	RB	1	1921/22	ex Leith Athletic
Campbell, James	LH	3	1920/21	ex Leith, Huddersfield Town and Sheffield Wednesday. died May 1925. Scotland. Captain of St Bernards 1920/21
Campbell, James	OL	2	1933/34	Reg cancelled (17/4/1933) Lochgelly and Hearts of Beath
Campbell, James	CH	2	1924/25	1925/26
Campbell, TF	RB	2	1901/02	1903/04 Queens Park and Edinburgh University
Campbell, William	OR	1	1894/95	2nd XI Player
Campbell, William	RB	1	1919/20	From Raith Rovers (20/1/1920)
Campbell, William S	OL	2	1886/87	1887/88 Marine Engineers in Shanghai. Edinburgh appearances (1).
Cannon	OL	1	1899/00	
Cannon, Alf	CF	2	1886/87	1888/89 Wolverhampton Wanderers. 2nd XI Player
Cannon, Charles	IR	2	1930/31	1931/32 from Manchester City
Cant	OL	1	1888/89	2nd XI Player
Cantley	IL	1	1884/85	2nd XI Player
Carr	LH	1	1901/02	
Cartmell	OR	1	1916/17	Huddersfield Town. To Hearts Sgt Royal Fusiliers. Blackpool and Swindon
Chalmers, Henry	OR	1	1887/88	Armadale and Edinburgh.
Chalmers, T		1	1893/94	Broxburn and Burnley
Chambers, Thomas	IR	3	1892/93	Hearts and Burnley.Scotland and Edinburgh. Scottish League Championship with Hearts 1895.
Charlton, Robert	OL	7	1879/80	1885/86 Became sports writer. Edinburgh appearances (4).
Childe	HB	2	1884/85	1888/89 2nd XI Player. to Grimsby Town
Christie, Alexander J	CH	6	1891/92	1901/02 Queens Park and Dunblane. Scotland. Scottish Cup Finalist with Queens Park 1900. Also played as 'Alexander' for the Saints' 1st and 2nd XIs. Played rugby also for Stewarts FP.
Christie, James	CH	1	1937/38	ex Hibs Reg cancelled (1/10/1937). Also Aldershot
Clark	IR	1	1902/03	
Clark	LH	1	1937/38	Clyde
Clark, David	OR	1	1930/31	from Cumbernauld Thistle Reg cancelled (13/11/1931)
Clark, George	CH	1	1903/04	To Beith (9/10/1903)
Clark, John	OR	1	1891/92	ex Edinburgh University. Hearts Trialist 1892
Clark, John	LH	1	1920/21	ex St Mirren
Clelland, James	OL	2	1894/95	1895/96 Loaned to Liverpool (April1895). Minerva, Abercorn and Third Lanark. Member of Scottish Cup winning team 1895
Clements, Robert	IL	1	1890/91	Leith Athletic. Scotland and Edinburgh
Cobban	OL	1	1912/13	Trialist from Vale of Grange
Collie, W	HB	2	1882/83	1883/84 ex Hanover. Club presented a gold pendant on departure to Australia April 1884.
Collier, Andrew	HB	1	1897/98	Kings Park
Collins	CF	1	1892/93	2nd XI Player
Collins, James	CF	1	1924/25	From Cowdenbeath (19/6/1924)To Alloa (16/10/1924) Lochgelly

Name	Pos		Season	Notes
Collins, Thomas	OR	1	1904/05	From Airdrieonians. Re-instated amateur.
Colthard	OR	2	1896/97 1898/99	Avenue juveniles and Dalry Primrose.
Colthard	IF	3	1887/88 1889/90	2nd XI Player
Common, John	RH	1	1925/26	From Wearside League Club. Also English League experience. To Chester le Street (9/3/1926)
Conner, Robert	OL	1	1904/05	From Partick Thistle. Re-instated amateur
Cook, Adam	IL	2	1919/20 1920/21	ex Galston. To Galston (19/8/1920)
Cooper	OR	1	1913/14	Dunfermline Ath
Corrigan, Edward	IL	3	1925/26 1927/28	From Ayr United (20/1/1926) From Dundee (22/1/1927) Also St Anthonys, Petershill and Celtic.
Corson, William	IF	2	1887/88 1890/91	from Ayrshire. Also Carlton cricketer. Edinburgh appearances (2).
Corstorphine, William	CH	4	1911/12 1914/15	from Hearts of Beath. Played as 'Anderson' as a trialist. Captain of St Bernards 1913/14.
Coupar, Robert	CF	4	1914/15 1919/20	Clyde and East Stirling ? Former Hearts' player.
Cousin, David	OL	1	1913/14	from Clackmannan and back (3/10/1913)
Cousin, James	OR	1	1913/14	Brother of David Cousins
Cowan	CF	1	1926/27	
Cowan, William	LB	3	1892/93 1894/95	from Leith Athletic (28/10/1893)
Cowe, Richard	OR	1	1913/14	Bonnyrigg Rose Athletic
Cox, Willie	CF	1	1884/85	Hibs
Cox, William E	RB	7	1913/14 1921/22	son of ex Hibs player. To Hamilton Accies (8/5/1922) Gainsborough
Craig	CF	1	1896/97	
Crawford, James	IR	1	1929/30	From Dumbarton ex Vale of Leven, Newtongrange Star and Hibs.
Cresswell, Warneford 'Warny'	RB	1	1916/17	South Shields, Sunderland, Everton, Hibs and Hearts. died 20/10/73. England and English League. Army footballer. FA Cup Winner with Everton 1933. Won English League Championships with Everton 1928 and 1932. ex 3 EVR. Original Saint
Creyk, John	G	1	1879/80	
Cringan, James A	CH	2	1939/40 1941/42	Ex Armadale Thistle and Bradford PA. Cardiff City
Crossan, Bernard 'Barney'	IL	3	1892/93 1894/95	Benburb. To Celtic (2/4/1896), Preston North End, Third Lanark. re-instated amateur 2/8/1898 died 1917. Member of Scottish Cup winning team 1895.
Crowe, James	IF	1	1885/86	ex West Calder. Edinburgh
Cumming, James	CH	1	1925/26	To Selkirk (21/4/1926)
Cummings, E	OL	1	1889/90	Alloa Athletic and RAF Leuchars Aeros.
Cunningham	CH	1	1895/96	Fair City Athletic
Cunningham, Archibald S	G	3	1934/35 1936/37	To Brechin City (24/11/1937). Lochgelly Albert, Perth North End and Newburgh Tayside
Curran, William	OR	2	1907/08 1908/09	Broxburn Athletic
Currie, Peter	OL	2	1911/12 1912/13	To Bradford City, Broxburn, Armadale and Dumbarton.
Cuthbertson, D	LB	2	1886/87 1887/88	ex Broxburn Thistle. Edinburgh.

D

Name	Pos		Season	Notes
Dailey	OL	1	1921/22	
Dally, HJ	IL	1	1941/42	Leith Wanderers ex Fife Junior signed amateur
Daly	?	1	1937/38	to Bonnyrigg Rose Ath
Davidson, Louis	IR	1	1905/06	From Broxburn (6/10/1905)
Davidson, Robert Fernie	RH	2	1934/35 1935/36	ex Dunnikier Juniors To Peebles Rovers (26/3/1936). Also Freuchie Rovers and Woodside Rangers

Name	Pos	Apps	Season	Notes
Davidson, Robert T	IR	2	1931/32	ex Prinslaw Utd and Bowhill Rovers To St Johnstone (16/3/1933) Also Arsenal, Coventry City, Hinkley Ath and Redditch Town. Scottish League. Won English League Championships with Arsenal 1935 and 1938.
Davie, J	CF	1	1941/42	
Davie, James	RH	1	1912/13	ex Hibs Also QPR and Brighton
Davy, Walter K	G	2	1904/05	also boxer. In Seaforth Highlanders WW1
Dawson	CH	1	1883/84	ex Middlesborough and Vale of Clyde.
Dawson, Alex F	IF	4	1938/39	2nd XI Player
Dawson, David	OL	1	1941/42	from Stoneyburn To Morton (25/7/1941)
Dawson, James M	CH	2	1919/20	1920/21 To Lochgelly Utd (18/10/1923) Also Raith Rovers and Dunfermline Athletic.
Dawson, Joseph	IL	3	1936/37	1938/39 late Liverpool and Hearts. ex East Fife. To Albion Rovers (20/1/1921). Also St Bernards player/manager.
Dee, Bobby	OR	1	1937/38	from Inverkeithing ex Cowdenbeath Reg cancelled (1/10/1938). Also Kelty Our Boys
Denholm	LH	1	1888/89	Subsequently official of Supporters Club. Breadalbane. Rep Rosebery Juniors EoS JFA 1940/41
Denholm	OL	2	1882/83	1883/84 2nd XI Player
Desson, W	IL	1	1925/26	from Moffat
Devine, James	IR	2	1899/00	1900/01 Leith Amateurs and Leith Athletic
Devlin, Henry	OL	1	1903/04	1904/05 from Cowdenbeath. To Millwall.
Dewar, George	OR	1	1887/88	from Shettleston Juniors
Dewar	RB	1	1909/10	Leith Athletic and Edinburgh.
Dick, Harry	RB	7	1937/38	1943/44 Leith Amateurs
Dickson, George P	OR	1	1927/28	ex Newtongrange Star Loaned to Gala Fairydean. Edina FC and Benford
Dickson, James	OL	1	1915/16	Musselburgh Bruntonians
Dickson, James	G	1	1919/20	to the Forces (8/1915)
Dingwall, George H	RH	3	1941/42	1943/44 To Raith Rovers (10/12/1919), Hearts 'A'
				ex Leith Wanderers Also Barony BC, Arsenal, Newtongrange Star, Airdrie, Dunfermline Ath and Hearts.
Dippie, William R H	OR	1	1928/29	Grandson of George Heathcote. Also Bellevue School
Dobbie	CF	1	1932/33	Bruce Peebles Amateurs (1939) Also Scottish Cricket International (1939) with Brunswick CC
Dobbie, James	IL	2	1922/23	1923/24 from Edinburgh Emmett
Dobie, Robert Tulloch	IR	4	1891/92	1896/97 To Bury (21/10/1896) and Leith Athletic. Edinburgh appearances (1).
Docherty, Frank	IR	1	1922/23	ex South Shields To Dykehead (10/10/1922) Junior Internationalist
Don, Daniel	CF	1	1923/24	Dunnikier Athletic Juniors.
Donachie, Alexander A	CF	2	1921/22	1922/23 ex Hamilton Accies. To Clydebank (19/12/1922) Also Carlisle Unted
Donaldson, Robert	RB	1	1924/25	From St Johnstone
Dorkin, Jack	CF	3	1888/89	1891/92 Leith Franklin CC and St George RFC. Went to Cork (1891). Also Southampton St Marys. Edinburgh appearances (2).
Dougal,	OL	1	1941/42	
Dougan, Patrick	IR	2	1910/11	1911/12 East Fife
Dougan, William	IR	2	1939/40	1941/42 ex Plymouth Argyle
Downie	IF	1	1895/96	A junior from Lanarkshire. 2nd XI Player.
Drummond, George	IF	2	1882/83	1883/84 ex St James. 'Preston North End also trainer PNE, Burnley and Falkirk. Died 14/2/1914 aged 49.
				One of the 'Preston Invincibles' of 1889. FA Cup Winner with Preston North End 1889. Finalist 1888.
				Won Football League Championships with Preston North End 1889 and 1890. Edinburgh appearances (3).
Drummond, James	CH	1	1915/16	To Lochgelly Utd (25/8/1916)

Name	Pos		Years	Debut	Notes
Drummond, William T	RB	8	1926/27	1933/34	54BB, Dalry Albert, Dalry Amateurs, Wallyford Bluebell, Leith Athletic, Montrose and Penicuik Ath. Son of a Hearts Director. Captain of St Bernards 1930/31
Duff	G	1	1884/85		Partick Thistle and Hearts
Duff, John	CF	3	1929/30	1931/32	Wemyss Athletic
Duffy, James	LB	1	1941/42	1943/44	Hearts of Beath. Brother of John Duffy To Hibs (11/8/1942)
Duffy, John	OL	3	1941/42	1943/44	Brother of James Duffy
Duke, William	IR	6	1924/25	1929/30	from Muirkirk Juniors ex Barnsley, Bradford and Swansea Town. Well known Craigentinny bowler.
Duncan, David	OL	2	1924/25	1925/26	From Newtongrange Star
Duncan, Stanley S	OR	1	1932/33		**Provisional signing from Eastern Hibs. Edinburgh City, Queens Park, Rosebery and Tranent Juniors. Hearts. Amateur Internationalist.**
Dunn	CF	1	1916/17		Brighton
Dunn, George K	RH	3	1930/31	1932/33	from Newcraighall. Portobello Thistle and Musselburgh Rose
Dunn, Jamie	IR	5	1879/80	1883/84	First Saint selected for Edinburgh but unable to play. Also South Western, Glasgow.
Dunn, John	OL	1	1923/24		To Leith Athletic (17/11/1923)
Dunsire, Andrew K	CF	1	1938/39		from Denbeath Star
Dunsmuir, Robert	LB	2	1923/24	1924/25	From Cowdenbeath (21/12/1923) ex Hearts To East Fife (29/11/1925)

E

Name	Pos		Years	Debut	Notes
Eadie, Donald	CF	8	1927/28	1934/35	from Wallyford Bluebell ex Oakbank. Also Cowdenbeath and Penicuik Athletic. Died 26/3/1980
Eadie, James	RH	1	1898/99		From Dunblane. To Dunblane (20/1/1899)
Early, Arthur	IL	1	1914/15		Dalkeith Thistle and Bonnyrigg Rose Athletic
Eddie, James	CF	1	1926/27		Hearts
Edgar, R	WH	1	1890/91		Dunrobin
Edmond, Thomas	IR	2	1897/98	1898/99	Prestonpans Athletic
Edwards	OL	1	1879/80		
Elliott, William	IR	1	1929/30		Reg cancelled (9/12/1929) Ex Leith Athletic
Ellis, Sandy	LB	1	1888/89		Mossend Swifts and Edinburgh. died 1938
Ellis, David	CF	1	1891/92		**Mossend Swifts, Hearts and Leith. Scotland and Edinburgh. died 1940**
Ellis, Jim	OR	1	1887/88		Mossend Swifts and Third Lanark. Edinburgh. died 1939
Elmore, George	IR	1	1915/16		To Broxburn Utd (22/10/1915) ex St Mirren and Partick Thistle.

F

Name	Pos		Years	Debut	Notes
Fairbairn	IL	1	1897/98		'did fairly well'!! Edinbugh Evening News in only game
Fairley	G	1	1901/02		To Broxburn. ex Seafield Ath
Fairley, James	LB	3	1908/09	1910/11	To Broxburn Utd (15/3/1924)
Fairley, Thomas	LH	1	1921/22	1923/24	ex Strathclyde. To Alloa Ath (11/9/1909)
Fairley, William	IL	2	1908/09	1909/10	from Tranent
Fairlie	IL	1	1913/14		Broxburn Thistle
Falconer, Douglas	CF	1	1941/42	1907/08	Preston North End and Black Watch
Faulds, Robert	OR	1	1912/13		Petershill

Name	Pos				Notes
Ferguson, David T	IR	3	1909/10	1911/12	signed 26/4/1910
Ferguson, J	CH	1	1889/90		ex Oakbank Thistle and Kinleith. Edinburgh.
Ferguson, John	IF	3	1911/12	1913/14	also Third Lanark. Killed in the First World War - posthumously awarded the Victoria Cross. 2nd Lt Scottish Rifles.
Ferguson	IR	1	1895/96		Dean Athletic
Findlay, Robert	RH	3	1906/07	1908/09	from Aberdeen District.
Finlay	OL	1	1880/81		ex Hanover
Finnerty	OL	1	1921/22		Trialist
Firth	OL	1	1916/17		Shepherds Bush
Fisher, James	CF	2	1896/97	1897/98	East Stirling. Scottish Trialist 1896/97. To Aston Villa (11/5/1897), Preston North End, Celtic, Fulham, Vale of Forth, Kings Park, Newton Heath and Vale of Leithen.
Fisher, Thomas	OR	1	1925/26		Kinghorn Thistle
Fisher, William	OR	1	1920/21		Ex Dundee and East Fife. To Lochgelly
Fitzgerald	IL	1	1939/40		Queens Park
Fitzsimmons, Charles C	RB	5	1932/33	1936/37	ex Partick Thistle
Fleming	CF	1	1932/33		
Fleming	LH	1	1888/89		2nd XI Player
Fleming, James	LH	1	1927/28		Hibs
Fleming, John	CF	2	1909/10	1910/11	To Newcastle Utd (20/4/1911). Tottenham Hotspur. died Belgium 18/8/17 (First World War)
Flucker, Peter	CF	4	1936/37	1939/40	Musselburgh Bruntonians, Hearts, Hibs, Arbroath and Queen of the South
Flucker, Thomas	IR	1	1914/15		Edinburgh and Leith Fish Trade
Flynn, J	OL	1	1937/38		On loan to Gala Fairydean To Bonnyrigg Rose Ath. Also Granton Rovers and Vale of Leithen
Forbes, John	CF	3	1888/89	1890/91	ex Hearts 2nd XI
Forbes, Gilbert	OR	2	1933/34	1934/35	Renfrew Juniors
Ford	?	1	1889/90		In Royal Scots team which won Surrey Senior Cup
Ford, Richard	CH	1	1923/24		To Bo'ness (2/4/1924) free transfer
Fordyce, Robert 'Bob'	LH	1	1924/25		ex Airdrie To Broxburn Utd (2/10/1924) Most capped Scottish bowling internationalist.
Forrest, Andrew	CF	2	1909/10	1910/11	To Duns (25/8/1910)
Forrest, Andrew	IL	1	1913/14	1914/15	To Peebles Rovers (1/8/1914)
Forrest, George	OR	1	1929/30		from York City
Forrest, Robert T	OL	1	1929/30	1930/31	Portobello Thistle and Edinburgh City
Forrest, William	LH	1	1928/29		Musselburgh Bruntonians Also Haddington and Tranent To Middlesborough (16/3/1929) Manager then Director of Darlington died 23/2/1965
Forsyth	G	1	1895/96		
Foyers, Andrew	LB	1	1889/90		Cambuslang, Clydesdale and Wishaw Thistle. Brother of John and Robert Foyers. Edinburgh appearances (2).
Foyers, John	CF	1	1889/90		Cambuslang. died c1/4/1890
Foyers, Robert 'Bobby'	**RB**	**6**	**1889/90**	**1896/97**	**ex Burnbank Swifts. Scottish Trialist 1892/93, 1893/94. To Newcastle Utd, Clyde. died 19/8/1942 aged 72 Scotland appearances (2). Member of Scottish Cup winning team 1895. Edinburgh appearances (10).**
					Scottish Alliance League appearance (1).
Frail, John	OR	2	1911/12	1912/13	from Lochgelly Utd (29/3/1912)
Frame, William	LB	1	1920/21		ex Clyde. To Clyde (11/12/1920)
Fraser, Tom	G	1	1883/84		The Club President pressed into emergency service in 1884.

Name				Pos			Notes
Fraser		1	1899/00	IL			a junior from Fife.
French, John D		2	1911/12	IL	1912/13		To Gala Fairydean (4/10/1912). In 9th Royal Scots WW1
Fyfe, Thomas			1893/94	G			Cowlairs
Fyfe, W		1	1884/85	OL			2nd XI Player
G							
Gair, Johnny		1	1884/85	FB			ex Edina. Also Hearts and Burnley. Edinburgh.
Galbraith, Alex		3	1897/98	RH	1899/00		To Vale of Leven (25/3/1898) and back (1/4/1898). To Vale of Leven (12/10/1899)
Galloway, George		4	1881/82	OR	1886/87		Vale of Leven. Scottish Cup Finalist with Vale of Leven 1885. Edinburgh appearances (3).
Gardiner, Harvey		1	1896/97	CH			Renton, Bolton Wanderers, Rangers and Wolverhampton Wanderers
Gardiner, James		1	1909/10	OR			Glencraig Celtic (Fife)
Garlich		4	1886/87	HB	1890/91		2nd XI Player
Gay, James McL		2	1920/21	LB	1924/25		from Perth Celtic. To Lochgelly Utd From East Fife (13/11/1924) Also Bathgate Ryle Athletic, Coventry City, Clapton Orient, Watford and Raith Rovers
Geddes, Robert		1	1921/22	IL			Peterhead junior
Geekie		1	1941/42	OL			Army
Gibb, Alexander		1	1910/11	F			Musselburgh Athletic
Giblin, Michael		3	1903/04	IR	1905/06		lived in Saunders Street, Stockbridge. Edinburgh Rosebery and Hearts
Gibson, Andrew		1	1905/06	CF			ex Brighton - appointed coach
Gibson, W		1	1887/88	G			Hearts
Gilbert		1	1941/42	LH			
Gilbert		1	1919/20	RB			Edinburgh Civil Service
Gilbert		1	1893/94	G			Balmoral Juniors (Edinburgh)
Gilchrist, James		5	1939/40	LB	1943/44		ex Newtongrange Star Portsmouth, Hearts and Berwick Rangers
Gilchrist, John		2	1928/29	RB	1929/30		ex Newtongrange Star
Gilchrist, Joseph D		1	1908/09	IL			Edinburgh player returned from South Africa
Gilhooley		2	1916/17	CH	1921/22		Celtic
Gillespie, George		**1**	**1887/88**	**G**			**Queens Park and Rangers. Scotland and Glasgow. Scottish Cup Winner with Queens Park 1886 and 1890. Finalist with Rangers 1877 and 1879.**
Gillies		1	1941/42	RH			
Gilmour		1	1906/07	OR			Edinburgh Junior trialist
Gilmour, Alexander		2	1925/26	OL	1926/27		Balgonia Scotia, Rosslyn, Raith Rovers and Dundee United
Gilmour, George		1	1912/13	OL			ex Hearts, Kirkcaldy and Raith Rovers.
Girdwood, G		4	1882/83	RB	1885/86		Hearts and Adventurers.
Glass, Hugh		1	1939/40	IL			Bonnyrigg Rose Ath and Arsenal. Killed in Second World War
Gloag, R		1	1889/90	CF			
Godfrey, Robert		2	1921/22	G			Scottish Schoolboy interntionalist 1913 with Second Division experience
Godsman, Adam		1	1898/99	CH			Inverness Clachnacuddin. To Clachnacuddin (3/3/1899). Also Derby County
Goldie, Malcolm		1	1913/14	OL			Clyde, Third Lanark and Clydebank. Moved to America
Goode		1	1897/98	G			'A western junior'
Goodfellow, George		1	1888/89	RB			2nd XI Player. Scottish Cup winner with Hearts 1890/91. Edinburgh. Died 8/8/1912

Name	Pos	Apps	Years	Notes
Gordon	IL	1	1934/35	from Musselburgh (27/12/1912)
Gordon, Allister E	?	1	1912/13	ex Hibs. To Leith Athletic (27/1/1922)
Gordon, David S	CH	1	1921/22	
Gordon, James E	**RH**	**1**	**1916/17**	**Rangers, Scottish International, Scottish League, Glasgow and Dunfermline Athletic**
Gordon, John	OR	1	1922/23	From Hibs To Leeds Utd (2/12/1922)
Gordon, Pat	?	1	1898/99	Dalry Primrose. Played for St Bernards 'A' v Armadale.
Gorman	CH	1	1920/21	
Gorman, Archibald	LH	1	1929/30	Trialist only with St Bernards Also Edinburgh City and Plymouth Argyle
Graham, Harry	IR	3	1908/09 1924/25	from Granton Oakvale. To Bradford City (15/4/1910). Birmingham, Raith Rovers, Hearts Leicester City and Reading. From Leicester City (1924/25). Scottish League and Edinburgh Scottish Cup Finalist with Raith Rovers 1913.
Graham, William	CF	1	1906/07	From St Mirren (25/4/1907)
Grant	OL	1	1907/08	Team trainer pressed into emergency service
Grant	CF	1	1921/22	Warrender Amateurs
Grant, Archibald W	RB	3	1902/03	1904/05 From West Calder (24/10/1902)
Grant, George	OR	2	1936/37	1937/38 from Albion Rovers ex Tranent Juniors' international To Clapton Orient Also Falkirk, Workington, Ballymena and Fauldhouse
Grant, James 'Puddin'	HB	4	1885/86	1888/89 from Leith Athletic. To Burnley. Edinburgh appearances (2).
Grant, James	OR	1	1900/01	1902/03 Edinburgh Renton. From Hibs (24/8/1901). To Dundee (21/11/1902)
Grant, Robert	G	6	1910/11	1915/16 West Lothian Albion, Armadale and Bo'ness (9/19) and Clackmannan.
Gray	OR	1	1914/15	
Gray, Robert	RH	1	1905/06	Grange Rovers
Gray, Robert C 'Scrappy'	CH	5	1898/99	1902/03 From Adventurers. Hearts.
Greenhorn, Thomas	G	1	1896/97	From Lochgelly United (13/4/1897) and back (4/5/1897)
Greig, Peter	RH	1	1904/05	Haddington Amateurs. Edinburgh Rosebery and East Stirling
Greig, Peter	IR	2	1913/14	1914/15 To Broxburn Utd (13/2/1915)
Groves, Willie 'Darlin'	**CF**	**1**	**1889/90**	**Celtic, Hibs Scotland, English League and Edinburgh. Scottish Cup Winner with Hibs 1887, Finalist 1896. Finalist with Celtic 1889. FA Cup Winner with West Bromich Albion 1892. Football League Championship with Aston Villa 1894.**
Guild, George ' Doddy '	RH	6	1884/85	1889/90 from Arbroath. Heriots FP CC. Schoolmaster at George Heriots School. Edinburgh appearances (5).
Guilliand, William	**OR**	**1**	**1892/93**	**Queens Park. Scotland and Glasgow. Scottish Cup Winner with Queens Park 1890 and 1893, Finalist 1892.**
Guthrie, James	LH	1	1891/92	soldier from Penicuik
Guthrie, James	IR	1	1905/06	Hearts 'A'

H

Name	Pos	Apps	Years	Notes
Hadley	LH	1	1941/42	
Haldane, David	IL	1	1941/42	
Hall, Alexander	RH	1	1890/91	Raith Rovers, Our Boys (Dundee), Fair City Athletic (Perth), Sheffield Wednesday and Hearts. Edinburgh.
Hall, Alexander N ('Sandy')	CF	2	1905/06	1906/07 From Peterhead (26/4/1906) To Newcastle Utd (16/4/1907) then Dundee. Dunfermline Athletic, Portsmouth. Galt FC (Canada).

Name	Pos				Notes
Hall, Combe	LB	4	1889/90	1895/96	resident of Newhaven (fisherman), Blackburn Rovers, Wanderers (SA) and Port Elizabeth (SA). Member of Scottish Cup winning team 1895. Also FA Cup winner with Blackburn Rovers 1891.
Hall, GA	**RB**	**1**	**1941/42**		**ex Edinburgh City. Scottish Amateurs**
Hamilton	RB	1	1905/06		
Hamilton, John	?	1	1894/95		To Bathgate (15/2/1895)
Hamilton, John	RB	1	1902/03		To Nithsdale Wanderers (11/11/1902) From Kilmarnock Rugby XI
Hamilton, T	IR	1	1902/03		
Hamilton, William	LH	3	1941/42	1943/44	Arsenal and Fulham.
Hanlon, Edward	RB	1	1909/10		To West Lothian Albion (13/10/1909) Recruited from same team
Hannah, James	**OL**	**1**	**1888/89**		**Third Lanark. Scotland. Scottish Cup Winner with Third Lanark 1889. Football League Championships with Sunderland 1892, 1893 and 1895**
Harrower, John	RB	3	1941/42	1943/44	Lochgelly Violet. To Dunfermline Ath (21/9/1942)
Harvey, James	RH	1	1925/26		To St Johnstone (19/4/1926) Also Falkirk, Clydebank and Dundee United
Harvey, Thomas	LH	1	1941/42		Celtic and Alloa Athletic
Hastie, James	RB	1	1914/15		In Gordon Highlanders WW1
Hay, William	LB	1	1899/00		London Caledonians
Hay, George	CF	1	1939/40		ex Queen of the South To Queen of the South (28/4/1940) Third Lanark and Newtongrange Star
Hay, John	RB	4	1914/15	1923/24	Wemyss Athletic. with Bathgate (9/1919). Also Bradford City. To Arbroath (4/12/1923)
Hay, John	OL	3	1934/35	1936/37	From Lanark United To Aldershot. Also senior experience in Ireland
Haywood, Norman	OR	1	1939/40		ex Watford ?, Raith Rovers, Queen of the South, Peebles Rovers and Millwall
Heathcote, George	RB	10	1879/80	1888/89	ex United RFC. Scorer at Grange CC for 20 years. died 22/11/1930. Captain of St Bernards 1878/79 until 1881/82 and also 1883/84. Edinburgh appearances (16).
Heggie, Charles W	**CF**	**2**	**1886/87**	**1887/88**	**ex Rangers. Glasgow South Western and Ailsa FC (Govan).Scotland, Edinburgh and Glasgow. became referee**
Henderson	IR	1	1889/90		ex Norton Park. Leith Athletic
Henderson	CF	1	1903/04		ex Queens Park
Henderson	CF	1	1896/97		Amateur player
Henderson, Thomas	RB	1	1901/02		Bathgate
Henderson, George B	CH	3	1921/22	1923/24	ex Kelty juvenile To Sunderland then Barnsley. Captain of St Bernards 1922/23
Henderson, JA	IR	3	1923/24	1925/26	'Cowdenbeath amateur'. Also Hearts
Henderson, James	OL	1	1902/03		from west. twin brother of William Henderson (1902/03)
Henderson, James	OL	1	1911/12		from Armadale Rangers
Henderson, John	RH	3	1911/12	1913/14	from Kelty Rangers. Manchester City, Cowdenbeath, Southend Utd, Cowdenbeath Hibs, Mid Rhondda, Gillingham and Dunfermline Ath
Henderson, Thomas	G	2	1900/01	1901/02	ex Hamilton. President Coltness Utd.
Henderson, Thomas	OR	1	1904/05		To Bo'ness (27/8/1904)
Henderson, William	OR	1	1902/03		from west. twin brother of James Henderson (1902/03)
Henderson, William	CF	2	1919/20	1920/21	From Broxburn. To Airdrieonians (27/5/1920). Also Manchester Utd, Preston North End, Clapton Orient, Hearts From Airdrie (7/5/1922) To Airdrie 25/5/1922 Morton, Torquay Utd and Exeter City
Henderson, William	OR	3	1928/29	1930/31	from Penicuik then Cardiff City. Reg cancelled (18/12/1930)
Hendry, Robert	OR	1	1923/24		To Broxburn Utd (16/8/1923)
Henry, William A	RB	1	1920/21		ex Manchester City. Also Blantyre Vics, Rangers, Falkirk and Leicester Fosse.

Name	Pos	#	Year	Year2	Notes
Herbste	OR	1	1916/17		Army
Herron	?	1	1902/03		for South Africa
Herron, James	RB	2	1907/08	1908/09	from Broxburn Thistle. Also Bo'ness
Heselwood, Charles J	CF	3	1902/03	1904/05	from North Western. Also St Bernards CC
Hickie, James	RB	1	1916/17		
Hill	OL	1	1889/90		
Hill, John	**LH**	**1**	**1888/89**		**Hearts. Scotland and Edinburgh. Scottish Cup Winner with Hearts 1891.**
Hilligan, Samuel	G	1	1927/28		Arthurlie, St Mirren, Bo'ness and Reading
Hislop	G	1	1900/01		from England
Hislop	RH	1	1890/91		Lugar Boswell
Hobbs	OR	1	1893/94		
Hodge, William	RB	1	1913/14		ex Brighton and Hove Albion
Hogg, George	LB	2	1890/91	1896/97	from Haddington
Hogg, Jas S	IL	2	1935/36	1936/37	prov signed 11/1935 from Loanhead West End loaned to Peebles Rovers
Holden, JC 'Jack'	LB	1	1884/85		ex Edinburgh University. Edinburgh.
Hood, Alexander R	LB	6	1899/00	1906/07	from Leith Athletic. To Hearts (3/11/1900). To Cowdenbeath (9/1/1904)
Hope	G	1	1906/07		
Hosie, Robert	IL	1	1913/14		from Third Lanark
Hosie, Thomas	CF	1	1913/14		from Bathgate (10/4/1914). Third Lanark
Hossack, Gordon	RH	2	1904/05	1905/06	Aberdeenshire
Houston	RH	1	1888/89		Woodburn
'Howard'	CF	1	1906/07		Out injured for two seasons before playing for St Bernards.
Houston, Robert	CF	4	1897/98	1900/01	Leven Thistle. To Kirkcaldy (28/4/1899). To Hearts (3/11/1900). Tottenham Hotspur. Scottish Cup winner with Hearts 1901. Also prominent golfer
Hume, William	RB	1	1931/32		from Falkirk
Hunter	LH	1	1903/04		Edinburgh University - from Ayrshire
Hunter, William	G	3	1894/95	1896/97	Mainly reserve goalkeeper whilst at the club
Hunter, William	CF	2	1904/05	1905/06	Re-instated amateur. To Airdrie. Rangers and Hamilton Accies. Scottish Cup Finalist with Hamilton Accies 1911.
Hutchison	G	1	1886/87		2nd XI Player
Hutton, Jamie	**HB**	**7**	**1884/85**	**1890/91**	**ex Northern. Scottish Trialist 1886/87,1889/90. to Stockton (8/91). Scotland appearances (1). Edinburgh appearances (11).**
Hyde, Peter N	CF	3	1908/09	1916/17	with Musselburgh 1912. Leith and Granton Oakvale. East Fife.
Igoe, John	RH	2	1933/34	1934/35	ex Charlton Athletic. Also Airdrie and Thames Association To Brechin City
Imrie	OL	1	1920/21		ex Bonnyrigg
Imrie, Hugh 'Sodier'	OL	3	1929/30	1931/32	ex Newtongrange Star. Dunfermline Athletic
Ireland	RH	1	1941/42		
Irving	IF	1	1888/89		

J

Name	Pos			Notes
Jack, Edward	CF	2	1895/96 1896/97	Shefield Utd. To Hearts (27/11/1896). Blackburn Rovers
Jack, William	RH	1	1910/11	Rosslyn Juniors
Jackson, Andrew	**HB**	**1**	**1886/87**	**Cambuslang. Scotland. Scottish Cup Finalist with Cambuslang 1888.**
Jackson, Charles	OL	3	1905/06 1907/08	lived at Marchmont, Edinburgh
Jacob	CH	1	1889/90	2nd XI Player
Jamieson, John	IR	1	1923/24	ex Halifax Town
Jamieson	G	1	1888/89	Norton Park
Jarvie, Alexander	OR	1	1897/98	Leven Thistle
Jenkinson	CF	4	1885/86 1888/89	
Johnson, James	RH	1	1934/35	Reg cancelled (5/9/1934)
Johnston	OL	1	1910/11	
Johnston, James W	IR	6	1936/37 1941/42	Tranent, Motherwell and Arbroath
Johnston, Robert	?	1	1920/21	From Hearts (17/11/1920)
Johnston, Samuel	OR	6	1938/39 1943/44	Bowhill Rovers
Johnston, Thomas	IR	1	1937/38	From Kelso Reg cancelled (22/2/1939) Also Peterborough United, Northampton Town, Nottingham Forest and Notts County
Johnston, Tom	IL	2	1887/88 1888/89	Managed Rotherham United, Grimsby Town, Huddersfield Town and York City.
Johnstone, Andrew	IR	1	1892/93	Armadale. Recipient of a benefit match in 1900 v Celtic following accident in the pit which left him blind.
Johnstone, AC 'Tony'	CH	1	1939/40	Southend Juniors (Edinburgh)
Johnstone, Cecil J	IL	2	1925/26 1926/27	Partick Thistle and Queens Park
Johnstone, JR	G	1	1931/32	To Leith Athletic (7/4/1927)
Johnstone, William	CF	1	1888/89	from Edinburgh City. Armadale
Johnstone, William	?	1	1906/07	Third Lanark
Johnstone, William	**IL**	**1**	**1888/89**	**Third Lanark. Scotland and Glasgow. Scottish Cup Winner with Third Lanark 1889.**
Johnstone, William G	CH	3	1901/02 1903/04	from Dumfries. To Bo'ness (29/4/1904) Rangers died 26/1/1968
'Jones'	RH	1	1921/22	Christie of Wemyss Athletic playing as trialist.
Joyce, Stephen	IR	1	1903/04	Kings Park

K

Name	Pos			Notes
Kane, Edward	RH	2	1923/24 1924/25	From Cowdenbeath (20/12/1923)
Kay, Alexander	RB	3	1898/99 1900/01	Dalry Primrose. To Partick Thistle (22/6/1900). Sheffield Utd. Killed in First World War
Keble	CH	1	1881/82 1886/87	Hearts
Keenan, James	G	5	1930/31 1934/35	Cameron Highlanders previously with Hibs. Collapsed and died playing for Duns at Meadowbank against Leith Athletic.
Kelling, Frederick	CH	1	1909/10	Won Paisley Charity Cup winners medal guesting for Albion Rovers (1934)
Kelly	CH	1	1899/00	Ex Bradford City. To Peebles Rovers (21/10/1909) Also Penicuik. Junior Internationalist
Kemp, Robert	LH	5	1937/38 1941/42	East Stirling and Stenhousemuir
Kennedy, J	HB	2	1886/87 1887/88	ex Bathgate Rovers

Name	Pos		Years	Notes
Kennedy, Robert	RH	5	1908/09 1916/17	Arniston Rangers. To Broxburn (28/12/1911). To Leith (27/11/1915). From Leith (8/12/1915) Fulham Bruntonians and Edinburgh Emmett. Lothian Road School, Glencairn, Kinleith Thistle and Dalkeith Thistle.
Kerr	IR	1	1889/90	Cowlairs
Kerr, John 'Jerry'	LB	2	1937/38 1938/39	Alloa Ath, Rangers, Armadale, Peebles Rovers and Motherwell. Manager Alloa Ath and Dundee United Captain of St Bernards 1937/38 and 1938/39
Kerr, Walter	G	1	1916/17	Leith Athletic and Raith Rovers (1917)
Kilgour	OL	4	1885/86 1888/89	
King, Alexander	CH	1	1900/01	From Dykehead (26/10/1900). Burnbank Juveniles, Wishaw Thistle, Darwin, Hearts and Celtic. Scotland and Scottish League. Scottish Cup Winner with Hearts 1896 and Celtic 1899. Scottish League Championship with Celtic 1898.
King, Alfred	OL	1	1931/32	ex Bristol Rovers and Tranmere Rovers
King, Robert	RH	4	1930/31 1933/34	from Bowhill Rovers. Montrose and Celtic
Kinghorn, Alexander	OR	1	1897/98	London Caledonians and Kings Park. Scottish Trialist 1897/98. Amateur from Grangemouth. Played for London v Sheffield 1898.
Kinross, J		1	1904/05	Bridge of Allan
Kinross, John	LB	3	1895/96 1897/98	To Kings Park (23/10/1897)
Kirkbride, John	RH	1	1923/24	ex Stenhousemuir, Armadale and South Shields
Kirkwood	OL	1	1888/89	Hibs
Kirkwood, James A	RH	1	1894/95	Third Lanark
Knox, HA	OR	1	1932/33	Murrayfield Amateurs and Northern Amateurs
Knox, John E	OR	1	1888/89	Edinburgh University. Edinburgh.
Kyle	IL	1	1926/27	Airdrie.

Name	Pos		Years	Notes
Lafferty, J	?	1	1892/93	Airdriehill and Aston Villa
Lafferty, Robert	OL	1	1894/95	Kilmarnock Athletic
Laidlaw, James T	IR	2	1926/27 1934/35	From Leith Athletic (15/2/1927). Also Dunfermline Ath and Musselburgh Bruntonians
Laidlaw, William	OL	1	1908/09	Dalry Albert and Dalkeith Thistle. To Kirkcaldy United
Laing, Robert Rae 'Bob'	IR	6	1887/88 1896/97	Leith Athletic. To Bury (17/10/1896) Scottish League and Edinburgh. Member of Scottish Cup winning team 1895.
Lamb	RH	1	1916/17	Army
Lamb, Michael	OR	1	1911/12	from Galashiels. Dundee Hibs and Broxburn
Lamb, Thomas	OL	3	1887/88 1889/90	Dalry Albert. Edinburgh appearances (1).
Lambert	OL	1	1916/17	
Landels, William	OL	1	1892/93 1893/94	2nd XI Player
Lang, James J	IF	2	1886/87 1887/88	Third Lanark and Clydesdale. Scotland and Glasgow. Scottish Cup Winner with Third Lanark 1878. Finalist with Clydesdale 1874.
Langton, Michael	RH	2	1935/36 1936/37	Hibs, Hearts and East Fife died 9/1/71 age 63 in Broxburn. Captain of St Bernards 1935/36
Lauder, Alexander	IL	1	1923/24	Partick Thistle and Stenhousemuir
Laverock, Herbert	OR	2	1892/93 1893/94	North Western
Law	IF	1	1894/95	Rob Roy
Law, Alexander G	IR	1	1906/07	To Bo'ness (7/5/1907)
Law, Thomas	LB	3	1921/22 1923/24	ex St Ninians Thistle. Captain of St Bernards 1921/22

Name	Pos	Apps	Season	Notes
Lawrence	IR	1	1883/84	2nd XI Player
Lawrence, William	OL	1	1922/23	ex Forth Rangers
Lawrie	LB	1	1920/21	ex Musselburgh Bruntonians
Lawrie, J	IL	2	1891/92 1892/93	Leith Athletic. 2nd XI Player
Lawson, David	IL	1	1919/20	
Lawson, William	OR	1	1911/12	ex Hibs, Bo'ness and Bristol Rovers.
Learmonth	IL	1	1894/95	2ndXI Player
Lee, Alexander 'Nancy'	OR	6	1897/98	Leith Athletic. To Broxburn (3/10/1902). Dalry Primrose, Dunrobin West End. Newtongrange Star
Lees, Andrew A	?	1	1922/23	Also Renfrew, Motherwell, Aberdeen, Swindon Town, Alloa Athletic, Lochgelly Utd, Queen of the South, Dykehead and Broxburn United
Leitch, William S	OR	1	1923/24	From Celtic on loan (15/11/1923) Also Irvine Meadow, Saltcoats Vics, Armadale, Ayr United and Kilmarnock. Scottish Cup Finalist with Celtic 1926
Lennie	OR	1	1909/10	Hearts' Tynecastle XI and Leith.
Leonard, Patrick	OL	1	1901/02	Manchester City
Libberton, James	G	2	1937/38 1938/39	loaned to Coldstream Also Penicuik Athletic
Lindley, Frank	OL	1	1916/17	Ex Dundee and Leith. Killed in the First World War
Lindsay	IL	1	1891/92	Trialist
Lindsay, John	G	1	1893/94	Renton and Accrington. Scotland. Scottish Cup Winner with Renton 1885 and 1888, Finalist 1886.
Linton	IL	1	1884/85	
Linton, David H	IL	1	1939/40	Partick Thistle and Dundee
Linton, Thomas	OL	1	1894/95	2nd XI Player
Logan	IL	1	1920/21	
Logan, Andrew	G	1	1909/10	brother of Peter Logan
Logan, D	OL	1	1909/10	ex Queens Park and Alloa.
Logan, J	OL	1	1910/11	Signed as an amateur
Logan, James H	CF	1	1904/05	to Bradford City (4/05) then Chesterfield.
Logan, Peter	IL	2	1907/08 1908/09	from Alva Rangers. To Bradford City (22/10/1908), died 1/4/1944 Edinburgh Schools Player and Dalry School FA Cup Winner with Bradford City 1911.
Logan, W	OL	1	1909/10	
Logie, James 'Jimmy'	IR	2	1939/40 1941/42	Lochore Welfare, Blackhall, Arsenal, Dunfermline Ath, Grimsby Town, Everton, Gravesend and Northfleet manager Scotland. FA Cup Winner with Arsenal 1950, Finalist 1952. In Arsenal Football League Championship winning sides of 1948 and 1953.
Loudon, Andrew	G	3	1930/31 1934/35	To Belfast Distillery. Glenboig St Josephs. Saved 3 penalties for Stranraer in 1937 Scottish Qualifying Cup Final
Love, William	RH	1	1888/89	Third Lanark
Low, John	OL	1	1920/21	From Dunfermline Ath (28/4/1921)
Lowe, Jamie	OL	10	1882/83 1891/92	ex Brunswick. Scottish Trialist 1886/87. Edinburgh appearances (16) and three with Brunswick. Captain of St Bernards 1887/88. Scotland appearances (1).
Lumsden, Robert	LH	1	1925/26	from the West Calder district
Lundie, James	RB	1	1884/85	Hibs. Scotland and Edinburgh. Scottish Cup Winner with Hibs 1887.
Lyall, Robert	IL	2	1902/03 1903/04	Vale of Grange
Lydon, Thomas	IR	1	1900/01	To Celtic (15/2/1901).

M

Name	Pos				Notes
Macfarlane, James L	FB	2	1929/30	1930/31	Leith Athletic and Vale of Leithen
Mackay, R A ' Bob '	IR	2	1885/86	1887/88	Lincoln City
Mackay, Thomas N	IR	1	1921/22		ex Hibs
Mackay, William	CF	3	1888/89	1890/91	ex Hearts. Northern. Raith Rovers. Edinburgh
Mackie	LB	1	1941/42		Fulham
Mackie, David	CF	1	1892/93		ex Mossend Swifts. Edinburgh appearances (1) and one with Mossend Swifts..
Maclachlan, Alastair S	OL	1	1931/32		from Dumbarton
MacLean, Thomas	IR	4	1915/16	1920/21	Loanhead Mayflower. To Bathgate (3/11/1920). Raith Rovers
Mailer	CF	1	1904/05		
Main, Robert	OR	1	1925/26		Shawfield Juniors, Dumbarton and Aberdeen
Malcolm, Andrew	IL	1	1913/14		from Clackmannan and back (10/4/1914)
Malcolm, Robert	IR	1	1922/23		Airdrie and Hearts
Mann, George	IF	1	1892/93		to East Stirlingshire then Blackburn Rovers.
Mark, George	OL	2	1900/01	1901/02	ex Bainfield
Marley, Dominic	CH	6	1930/31	1935/36	from Larkhall Thistle To Belfast Celtic. Quartier Celtic, Waterford and Kings Park. Captain of St Bernards 1931/32 to 1934/35.
Marr, Robert 'Bobby'	IL	1	1891/92		Broxburn and Burnley
Marshall, Harry 'Beef'	RH	1	1891/92		Hearts, Blackburn Rovers, Celtic, Raith Rovers, Clyde, Portobello Thistle, Alloa and Broxburn Athletic. died 1936 Scotland, Scottish League. Scottish Cup Winner with Celtic 1899 and 1900, Finalist 1902. Scottish League Championship with Hearts 1897. Edinburgh appearances (1).
Marshall, James L	OR	1	1926/27		From Hearts (30/12/1926)
Marshall, John	**OR**	**1**	**1888/89**		**Third Lanark. Scotland and Glasgow. Scottish Cup Winner with Third Lanark 1889.**
Marshall, Robert	OR	1	1932/33		Reg cancelled (8/2/1933) ex Hearts
Marshall, Robert G	OR	2	1905/06	1906/07	Liverpool - professional irrgularity
Marshall, Thomas	RH	1	1923/24		ex Ayr United
Marshalsey, William HG	RH	2	1930/31	1932/33	from Denbeath Star To Hearts (9/1/1931) Also Gala Fairydean, Duns and Cardiff City. Jed Artisans
Martin, Charles	RH	4	1893/94	1896/97	Re-instated amateur (13/8/1895)
Mason, William	G	1	1922/23		from Burnbank Athletic Junior Interntional To Hibs
Masterton, A	CH	1	1879/80		ex Hanover
Mather	CF	1	1901/02		
Mathieson, Robert	OR	3	1887/88	1889/90	ex Armadale and Edinburgh.
Mathieson, James A	G	1	1941/42		ex Queen of the South and Raith Rovers
Matthews, James	G	3	1941/42	1943/44	from Edinburgh Rosebery Also Dalkeith Thistle and Blairhall Colliery To Hibs (11/8/1942) Trans to Falkirk (30/8/1943). Scottish Southern League Cup Finalist with Falkirk 1943
Maxwell, Allan	CF	1	1897/98		ex Stoke, Cambuslang, Everton, Darwen and Third Lanark.
Maxwell, James	IR	1	1902/03		To Bathgate (13/12/1902)
Maxwell, William	LH	2	1899/00	1900/01	Linthouse

Name	Pos	#	Years	Notes
McAllister, Daniel	IR	1	1923/24	from Bathgate
McAllister, John	OR	2	1912/13 1913/14	from Bathgate (11/3/1913). Kilmarnock
McAlpine, Thomas	G	2	1923/24 1924/25	from Dunnikier Ath. To Hibs (8/11/1924)
McAulay, Hugh	RH	1	1889/90	Hibs
McAuslane, G	IF	3	1883/84 1885/86	ex Hanover. Edinburgh appearances (1).
McAvoy, Richard	HB	1	1921/22	St Mirren
McBeath, Alex	RH	1	1924/25	To Broxburn Utd (12/11/1924) Raith Rovers
McBeth, Alexander	LH	1	1916/17	Loanhead
McBeth, George	OR	4	1879/80 1882/83	Grimsby Town. Spent 8 years in Army in India - returned 1890. Played for Edinburgh Northern Joined his brother Robert in Burton on Trent in 1890. Edinburgh appearances (5).
McBeth, Robert	OL	2	1879/80 1883/84	Accrington and Grimsby Town. Owner of flourishing hotel business in Burton on Trent (1890).
McCaig	CH	1	1941/42	
McCaig, Alexander R	IL	1	1927/28	Larbert Central, Stenhousemuir, Falkirk, Alloa Athletic, Coventry City, Reading and Cowdenbeath
McCaig, James	IL	1	1929/30	from Edinburgh City
McCall, Archibald	LB	1	1891/92	Renton. Scotland and Scottish League. Scottish Cup Winner with Renton 1885 and 1888, Finalist 1886 and 1895.
McCall, James	IL	1	1891/92	Renton. Scotland and Scottish League. Scottish Cup Winner with Renton 1885 and 1888, Finalist 1886.
McCallum, Denis	OR	1	1932/33	Reg cancelled (16/9/1932) Also Dundee Utd, Celtic, Vale of Leven, St Patrick's Dumbarton, St Anthonys, Dumbarton, Clydebank, Nithsdale Wanderers, Glentoran, Bangor, Coleraine and Sligo Rovers.
McCartney, Robert	RB	1	1892/93	Leith Athletic and Edinburgh.
McColl	IF	1	1903/04	from Camelon
McColl, Robert S 'RS'	**CF**	**1**	**1901/02**	**Queens Park, Newcastle Utd and Rangers.Scotland, Scottish League and Glasgow Scottish Cup Finalist with Queens Park 1900 and Rangers 1905. Founder of the RS McColl retail outlets.**
McCracken, David	LB	2	1903/04 1904/05	ex Queens Park and Scottish Amateurs. To Greenock Morton.
McCulloch	OR	1	1920/21	ex Dundee
McCulloch, Michael J	IL	1	1925/26	To Cowdenbeath (4/3/1926) Also Falkirk, Hearts, Nelson, Chesterfield and Bournemouth. Native of Denny
McDermott, Charles M	LB	1	1941/42	Bradford City and Goole Town
McDonald	OL	1	1941/42	
McDonald	IR	1	1904/05	Norse Rovers
McDonald	OL	1	1915/16	ex Portobello Thistle
McDonald, George	LH	3	1891/92 1893/94	Dunrobin. To Hearts
McDonald, Hugh	CF	1	1898/99	Arniston Rangers. To Hearts of Beath (26/1/1899)
McDonald, James	OL	3	1890/91 1892/93	Brother of George McDonald (1891/92). Edinburgh appearances (1).
McDonald, James	IL	2	1905/06 1906/07	from Aberdeen area. To Bradford City (15/4/1907). Raith Rovers and Keighley Parkwood. died 8/1924 FA Cup Winner with Bradford City 1911. Played a number of matches for the Saints under the name of 'Buchan'.
McDonald, James	OR	1	1903/04	West Ham United
McDonald, JH	OL	1	1932/33	
McDougall, David B	IL	3	1914/15 1916/17	Bonnyrigg Junior. Killed in First World War
McEwan	RH	1	1885/86 1886/87	2nd XI Player
McEwan, Robert	LB	2	1901/02 1902/03	from Edinburgh Rosebery. To Bury. Rangers, Hearts, Chelsea, Dundee and Glossop.
McGarrity, Frank	CH	3	1914/15 1916/17	from Inverkeithing Utd. To Airdrieonians (13/11/1915) From Airdrieonians (21/4/1916)
McGrath, John	CF	1	1926/27	Motherwell

Name	Pos	Apps	Season	Notes
McGettigen, Neil	IL	4	1903/04	1906/07 From Severn Victoria
McGhee, James	**IF**	**1**	**1888/89**	**Hibs. Scotland and Edinburgh. Manager of Hearts. Scottish Cup Winner with Hibs 1887. Dykecar and Abercorn**
McGibbon, Donald A	IL	1	1922/23	'local lad' ex Rangers 'A'. Raith Rovers
McGirr, William	RH	1	1933/34	New Brighton, Leith Athletic and Cowdenbeath
McGlynn, GA	OL	1	1932/33	Ex Dundee Utd. Perthshire County CC. Amateur player from Dundee
McGregor	OR	1	1888/89	
McGregor, James	IR	1	1912/13	from Crieff Morrisonians. Also Dundee
McIlvenny, Harry	IL	2	1900/01	Burnley
McIlwraith, Francis	LB	1	1920/21	From Stevenson Utd (25/2/1921)
McInally, Arthur F	CH	1	1924/25	Celtic, St Mirren, Alloa, Clyde, St Mungo's Academy, Barrhead Bellmont, Kirkintilloch Rob Roy, St Mirren Juniors, Croy Celtic and Ayr United, Dumbarton Harp, Abercorn, Dunfermline Ath and Armadale. SL Div 2 Referee St Anthonys Secretary/Manager. Captain of St Bernards 1924/25
McInnes, Angus	OR	2	1896/97	1897/98 from Kings Park. To Burnley (12/3/1898) then Padiham. Also Dunblane.
McIntosh, James 'Curly'	G	3	1887/88	1889/90 ex Norton Park. Scottish Trialist 1889/90. To Leith Athletic (1890) Died 20/9/1942. Edinburgh appearances (4).
McIntosh, James	OL	1	1887/88	1889/90 Edinburgh appearances (1).
McKail, T	HB	5	1886/87	1892/93 2nd XI Player
McKay, John	G	4	1938/39	1941/42 from Kirkford Juniors To Raith Rovers. Aberdeen
McKay, Robert	OL	1	1905/06	Edinburgh junior
McKenna, James	IR	1	1901/02	Cambusing Hibernians
McKenzie	OR	1	1922/23	Trialist
McKenzie, George	IF	1	1882/83	ex Brunswick. Edinburgh.
McKenzie, John	CF	3	1898/99	1901/02 From Leith Athletic. Originally from Elgin. Off to London for employment (1900) ex Hearts re-instated amateur.
McKinnon, Archibald	OL	1	1888/89	Edinburgh appearances (1). Hearts and Raeburn
McKinnon, Duncan	IL	6	1880/81	1885/86 Falkirk. Re-instated amateur (4/8/1896). East Stirlingshire
McKinnon, Hugh	RB	1	1895/96	
McKinnon, William	**OR**	**1**	**1885/86**	**Dumbarton. Scotland. Scottish Cup Finalist with Dumbarton 1881.**
McKnight, John	IR	1	1895/96	To Lanemark (12/2/1896). Burnley, Darwin, Aston Villa and Hurlford
McKnight, John	CH	2	1926/27	1927/28 From Bathgate (2/12/1926) ex Queen of the South and Celtic
McLaren, James	**LH**	**2**	**1884/85**	**1887/88 Hibs and Celtic. Scotland, Glasgow and Edinburgh. Scottish Cup Winner with Hibs 1887. Celtic finalist 1889.**
McLean, Duncan	**RB**	**3**	**1895/96**	**1897/98 Scottish Trialist 1895/96, 1896/97, 1897/98. Renton Union, Renton, Liverpool and Everton. Scotland appearances (2). Won English League Championship with Everton 1891. Captain of St Bernards 1897/98**
McLean, James	G	1	1929/30	Cowdenbeath and Dalkeith Thistle
McLean, Robert	RH	2	1919/20	1920/21 From Airdrie (19/8/1920). To Airdrie (25/9/1920). Army (ASC)
McLean, Robert	RB	2	1921/22	1922/23 ex Livingston Utd. Alloa. To Cowdenbeath (14/4/23) Manager Doncaster Rovers
McLennan, Hugh	LB	5	1879/80	1883/84 London Scottish and Accrington
McLennan, J	LB	1	1879/80	a founder of London Caledonians. Accrington
McLennan, John	RH	1	1910/11	from Arniston Rangers
McLeod	RH	1	1916/17	from Prestonpans with KOSB
McLeod, Alexander	OR	1	1890/91	Leith Athletic
McLeod, Angus	LH	2	1923/24	1924/25 from Cowdenbeath (20/12/1923)
McLeod, Edward	RB	2	1919/20	1920/21 Falkirk. from Musselburgh To Broxburn

Name				Notes
McLeod, William		1	1889/90	LB Cowlairs. Scotland and Glasgow
McMahon, Alexander		1	1889/90 1890/91	IL Hibs and Celtic. Scotland, Scottish League, Edinburgh and Glasgow Scotttish Cup Winner with Celtic 1892, 1899 and 1900, Finalist 1893, 1894, 1901 and 1902. Scottish League Championships with Celtic 1893,1894, 1896 and 1898.
McManus, Patrick	RH	3	1893/94 1895/96	Mossend Swifts, Darlington, Hibernian, Celtic, West Bromich Albion, Warmley and Thames Ironworks. Member of Scottish Cup Winning team of 1895. Edinburgh.
McMillan, D	CH	2	1887/88 1888/89	ex Port Glasgow Ath.
McMillan, James A	IL	3	1895/96 1897/98	Everton. Scottish Trialist 1896/97. Scotland appearances (1). Derby County, Leicester Fosse, Small Heath, Bradford City and Glossop. died 4/11/1941. Edinburgh Saints
McMillan, John Stuart	IL	1	1890/91	To Abercorn (3/1/1910). ex Vale of Clyde
McMillan, Malcolm	OR	1	1909/10	Sunderland Albion
McMinn, John	CF	2	1887/88 1888/89	Had a trial spell at Stoke but returned to Saints.
McMurtie	IR	1	1887/88	
McNab	RH	1	1922/23	
McNab, Andrew	CH	1	1909/10	ex Glossop and Motherwell. To Broxburn (3/6/1910)
McNab, James	HB	6	1889/90 1894/95	Captain of St Bernards 1892/1893. Moved to Leith Athletic. Edinburgh appearances (2).
McNairn, William J	CF	1	1907/08	From Hamilton Accies (12/2/1908)
McNally	RH	1	1903/04	
McNamee, Francis	IR	1	1895/96	To New Brighton (9/11/1895)
McNaughton, Harry	G	1	1919/20	To Liverpool (6/7/1920)
McNaughton, John	CF	1	1882/83	ex Brunswick. died 1927. Also cricket umpire
McNeil, Alex 'Goudie'	OL	1	1896/97	Port Glasgow Ath and Abercorn. Left for the Cape (1899).
McNeil, Donald	RB	1	1895/96	Port Glasgow Athletic
McNeill, William J	LB	1	1904/05	Re-instated amateur. Myrtle Juniors
McNeill, James	OL	1	1926/27	From Lochgelly Utd (23/2/1927)
McNicol, Duncan	RB	2	1897/98 1898/99	ex Vale of Leven. To Woolwich Arsenal then Aberdeen. Captain of St Bernards 1898/99.
McPherson, James	RH	1	1889/90	Cowlairs
McPherson, Peter	CH	3	1935/36 1937/38	To Queen of the South (9/11/1937)
McQueen	G	2	1891/92 1892/93	2nd XI Player
McQueen, Matthew	RH	1	1889/90	Champfleurie, Bo'ness, Leith Ath, University, Hearts and Burntisland Th. Scotland, Edinburgh. Liverpool manager
McRitchie	IR	1	1922/23	'Trialist from the west with first league experience'
McRitchie, Robert	OL	2	1905/06 1906/07	Signed from Juvenile football
Meagher, James H	IL	2	1928/29 1931/32	ex Edinburgh Emmett. To Ayr United. Also Dundee,Dundee United,Raith Rovers and Newtongrange Star. Also in America
Meagher, John W	OL	1	1916/17	Army
Meikle, Thomas	OL	2	1902/03 1903/04	To West Calder Swifts (21/4/1904). Granton Oakvale
Mein, James ('Jimmy')	CF	1	1901/02	Edinburgh Rosebery and Adventurers Also St Bernards CC and Brunswick CC. Umpire at Grange CC until 1939.
Mercer	IR	1	1912/13	Broxburn (Trialist)
Merrie, Alexander	OR	1	1923/24	From St Mirren (4/31924) Also Saltcoats Vics, Nithsdale Wanderers, Alloa Athletic, Stenhousemuir, Portsmouth, Ayr United, Aberdeen, Hull City, Clyde, Crewe Alex, Brechin City, Aldershot, Exeter City, Workington, Cork City Gloucester City
Messer, Robert	OR	1	1915/16	East Fife. ex Leicester Fosse (10/11) and Bo'ness. Leeds City

Name	Pos	Apps	Season	Notes
Methven, James 'Logie'	FB	4	1887/88	1890/91 ex Norton Park. Derby County, died 25/9/1953. FA Cup Finalist with Derby County 1898,1899 and 1903. Captain of St Bernards 1889/90. Edinburgh appearances (2). Manager Derby County 1906/1922.
Middleton, Robert	HB	1	1894/95	from Dalry Primrose
Millar, AB	OL	1	1921/22	Edinburgh junior
Millar, B	OL	1	1921/22	
Millar, James	RB	2	1937/38	1938/39 from Vale of Leithen
Millar, William	CF	1	1905/06	From Renton (13/1/1906)
Miller, James	RH	1	1920/21	ex Airdrie To St Mirren
Miller, John	LB	1	1902/03	from Maxwelltown Volunteeers (15/8/1902) To Camelon (20/1/1903)
Miller, R	OR	1	1883/84	ex Hanover
Miller, Thomas	**RB**	**1**	**1919/20**	**ex Falkirk and Chelsea. To Bathgate. Scottish League. Served in Canadian Army in World War 1.**
Miller, William	CF	1	1902/03	
Mills	LB	3	1935/36	1937/38
Milne	LB	1	1895/96	1896/97 ex Arbroath
Milne, Edgar C	IL	2	1908/09	1909/10 Newtongrange Star , To Broxburn (18/3/1910)
Milroy, WG	LB	1	1888/89	Edinburgh University Dumfries and Galloway Students
Mitchell, Alexander	RB	2	1926/27	1927/28 From Broxburn United (26/4/1927) To Dunfermline Ath (4/7/1927)
Mitchell, James	CF	1	1935/36	ex St Johnstone To Peebles Rovers (20/2/1936 on loan) Also Kilmarnock
Mitchell, Stephen	**LB**	**3**	**1925/26**	**1927/28 From St Rochs Also Coleraine and Ballymena. Irish League and Edinburgh**
Moffat, Thomas	RH	3	1927/28	1929/30 from Newtongrange Star
Montgomery	CF	1	1900/01	
Montgomery, James	CF	1	1887/88	Hibs
Moonie	OR	1	1941/42	
Morgan, A	RB	1	1941/42	
Morgan, J	OR	1	1941/42	Leith Wanderers
Morrison, James	OL	1	1888/89	Third Lanark
Morrison, Simon	IL	1	1929/30	from Blackpool ex Musselburgh Bruntonians
Morrison, William	CH	4	1901/02	1914/15 From West Calder (16/4/1902). To Fulham. Glossop, Clyde, Raith Rovers, Falkirk and Greenock Morton. From Raith Rovers (15/4/1915). Scottish Cup Finalist with Raith Rovers 1913. Captain of St Bernards 1903/04
Morton, James	OR	5	1909/10	1916/17 from Bo'ness. ex Hibs and Newtongrange Star. To Broxburn Utd (8/13) then Barnsley and Bristol City.
Moultrie, J	OL	1	1893/94	Dunfermline Juniors
'Muir'	CF	1	1933/34	Trialist - Veitch of St Andrews Athletic
Muir,David	IL	1	1894/95	Queens Park and Rangers
Muir				Montrose
Muir, Daniel L	RB	3	1924/25	1926/27 from Armadale. to Dumbarton
Muir, Henry	LB	2	1911/12	1912/13 from Glencraig Celtic. Lochgelly. To Rangers (18/4/1913)
Muirhead, William	OL	1	1895/96	
Murdoch, Charles	RH	1	1907/08	Newcastle United
Murdoch, George	LH	7	1889/90	1896/97 Third Lanark. Scottish Trialist 1892/93, 1895/96. Re-instated (3/8/1897) died in Australia 28/12/1929. Captain of Scottish Cup Winning team of 1895. Also Lugar Boswell. Captain of St Bernards 1895/96 Edinburgh appearances (1).

Name	Pos			Notes
Murison, James W	CF	1	1894/95	Cambridge University and London Caledonians.
Murphy, John	CH	3	1941/42 1943/44	Hearts of Beath To Hibs (11/8/1942)
Murray	LH	1	1915/16	Loanhead international
Murray	CF	2	1912/13 1913/14	from west of Scotland
Murray	OR	1	1919/20	Kelty Rangers
Murray	CF	1	1898/99	from North of Scotland and an old University player.
Murray, Charles	OR	1	1907/08	From Aberdeen East End
Murray, Donald	CF	5	1931/32 1935/36	from Ayr United ex Peebles Rovers also Vale of Leithen. Clapton Orient trialist
Murray, Michael	OR	1	1923/24	from East Fife
Murray, William	LH	1	1919/20	From Falkirk (11/12/1919)

N

Name	Pos			Notes
Neal	IR	1	1912/13	from Fife
Neilson	OR	2	1903/04 1904/05	Musselburgh Fern
Neilson, James	IR	2	1896/97 1900/01	ex Kirkcaldy and Raith Rovers. Amateur player
Nelson, David	IR	2	1935/36 1936/37	from Douglas Water Thistle To Arsenal (26/5/1936) Also Fulham, Brentford, QPR, Crystal Palace and Ashford Town. Celtic loan 3/1/1942 Motherwell 1940
Nicol	CF	1	1920/21	Juvenile from Townhill, Fife
Nicol, W	?	1	1932/33	Lochgelly Utd ex Bournemouth
Nicol, William	IR	1	1930/31	Reg cancelled (19/11/1930)
Nicoll	CF	1	1889/90	Broxburn.
'Noble'	OL	1	1908/09	Trialist - Bert Menzies of Newtongrange Star.
Noble, David S	IL	3	1934/35 1936/37	ex Blackhall Ath To Clyde (26/9/1936). Scottish Cup Winner with Clyde 1939.
Notman	LH	1	1883/84	Glencairn and Edinburgh.

O

Name	Pos			Notes
Oates, James	LB	2	1903/04 1904/05	To Liverpool on business.
O'Brien, John	OR	1	1932/33	Hearts of Beath
O'Brien, Patrick G	RB	1	1895/96	Broxburn Shamrock, Hibernian, Middlesborough Ironopolis, Sheffield Utd and Newcastle Utd.
Oddy	RH	1	1916/17	Army and Staleybridge Rovers
O'Hara, John	RB	1	1891/92	ex Hibs
Oswald, John	IR	1	1888/89	Third Lanark, Burnley and West Manchester. Brother of James, Joseph and Willie Oswald.
Oswald, James 'Tinney'	**CF**	**4**	**1889/90 1894/95**	**Third Lanark, Rangers, Clydebank, Govanhill, Kilbirnie, and Notts County. Scottish Trialist 1893/94, 1894/95 with St B. Scotland appearances (1) and Scottish League (1). Glasgow. Member of Scottish Cup winning team of 1895. Scottish Cup Winner with Third Lanark 1889. FA Cup Finalist with Notts County 1891. Also earned Scotland caps with Third Lanark and Rangers.**
Oswald, Joseph	CH	1	1894/95	Played for Saints in the Third Lanark 5 a side Tournament (1894). Rangers and Morton.
Oswald, Willie	RH	1	1894/95	Played for Saints in the Third Lanark 5 a side Tournament (1894) A brother of James Oswald. Woodvale (Glasgow)

P

Name	Pos			Notes
Pace	LH	1	1889/90	Muirhouse Rovers

Name	Pos			Years	Notes
Paterson	CF	1		1932/33	
Paterson, John M	LH	2	1924/25	1925/26	From Hamilton Accies (29/1/1925)
Paterson, Lindsay	CF	2	1935/36	1936/37	from Western United
Paterson, Matthew	CH	1		1923/24	from Hibs (24/10/1923) Also Bellshill Athletic. Scottish Cup Finalist with Hibs 1914.
Paterson, Tommy	FB	1		1887/88	Broxburn Thistle
Paton, Daniel J F	IF	4	**1894/95**	**1897/98**	**Aston Villa. Scottish Trialist 1895/96, 1896/97. Scotland appearances (1).. Member of Scottish Cup winning team of 1895. Also Scottish Cup Finalist with Vale of Leven 1890. Clyde.**
Paton, Hugh	CF	1		1881/82	
Patrick, Robert R	CF	1		1927/28	Dalkeith Thistle and Dunfermline Athletic
Pattison, Andrew	IL	1		1911/12	from Wemyss Ath
Pearson	G	3	1881/82	1883/84	2nd XI Player and St James
Pearson, Thomas	RH	1		1916/17	St Mirren
Peden, Robert	CF	2	1895/96	1896/97	Newton Thistle and Motherwell
Penman, Alex R	LB	2	1914/15	1915/16	
Penman, William	RB	3	1910/11	1912/13	Lochgelly Utd
Penman, William	OL	1		1911/12	From Hearts (8/11/1923)
Peter, Martin R	OL	1		1924/25	From Hamilton Accies (27/11/1924)
Petrie, Thomas	OR	2	1888/89	1889/90	Re-instated amateur. Also Hyde and Middlesbrough. Scottish Junior Cup Finalist with Woodburn in 1887.
Pettigrew, Robert	CF	2	1922/23	1923/24	To Vale of Leven (22/2/1924)
Philip, Arthur	RB	2	1910/11	1911/12	Peterhead
Philip, James 'Bauldie '	FB	4	1890/91	1893/94	From a Stockbridge junior club. To Polton Vale (7/12/1893). Edinburgh appearances (1).
Phillips	OL	1		1893/94	2nd XI Player. To Hearts
Phillips	CF	1		1890/91	Milton Swifts. Left for Stoke
Phillips, Robert	CH	2	1898/99	1899/00	From North Western. To Lochgelly Utd (4/10/1899)
Phillips, William	OL	2	1893/94	1895/96	To Polton Vale (5/3/1896)
Philp, James M	RH	7	1935/36	1941/42	Crossgates Primrose. To Hearts (26/10/1940) To Hearts (9/6/1941) Also East Fife and Brechin City Scottish Cup Finalist with East Fife 1950. Scottish Southern League Cup Finalist with Hearts 1941. Scottish League Cup Winner with East Fife 1948 and 1950.
Pillar, Robert J	LB	4	1895/96	1898/99	Glenboig. Became a senior referee.
Pinkerton, James R	OL	2	1936/37	1937/38	Bute Athletic, Partick Thistle, Blackburn Rovers and Montrose
Potter, John	IR	1		1889/90	Broxburn
Pratt	IL	1		1887/88	2nd XI Player
Pray, John	RH	1		1903/04	from Bury. Rangers. FA Cup winner with Bury 1900
Pringle	IL	1		1887/88	Rangers
Prior, George	CF	4	1900/01	1906/07	Lochgelly Utd. To Sunderland (25/10/1901). Won English League Championship with Sunderland 1902. In Lothians and Borders Horse WW1
Provan, John	OR	3	1895/96	1897/98	West Calder and Burnley.
Pryde, David	OR	2	1934/35	1939/40	from Newtongrange Star To Peebles Rovers (24/1/1935) Also Arsenal, Margate, Torquay United. Bonnyrigg Rose Ath

R

Name	Pos		Season		Notes
Rae, James	LB	1	1888/89		Third Lanark. Scotland and Glasgow. Scottish Cup Winner with Third Lanark 1889.
Rae, John	IL	1	1899/00		from Kirkcaldy
Raeburn, James	RH	2	1926/27	1927/28	ex Raith Rovers Broxburn Utd, Tranent and Leith Benburb
Raiker, Thomas E	CH	1	1905/06		From Broxburn and back (26/5/1905)
Ramage	RB	1	1885/86		
Ramage, Andrew	OL	1	1904/05		Bridge of Allan
Ramage, Andrew	IL	2	1925/26	1928/29	Also Dundee, South Shields , Musselburgh Bruntonians and Penicuik
Ramage, James	CH	1	1924/25		From Newtongrange Star
Ramage, Joseph	G	1	1926/27		from Middlesborough 'A'
Ramage, Peter	?	1	1927/28		Bonnyrigg Rose
Ramsay, Andrew	OR	1	1941/42		ex Bonnyrigg Rose Ath
Ramsay, George W	G	6	1905/06	1910/11	ex Bonnyrigg Rose. Edinburgh Myrtle and Newtongrange Star
Ramsay, James	IR	1	1924/25		
Ramsay, John	IR	1	1921/22		Trialist with Hibs
Reed, Fred	RH	1	1916/17		ex West Bromwich Albion. Army
Regan, Robert H	OR	1	1939/40		Linlithgow Rose, Partick Thistle, Manchester City and Dundee
Reid	CF	1	1920/21		of Clackmannan Juniors
Reid, Andrew	FB	5	1904/05	1908/09	To St Mirren (8/6/1908). From Abergeldie, Aberdeenshire. Also Peterhead and Sunderland
Reid, Charles H	WH	2	1890/91	1891/92	from Piling
Reid, David	LH	1	1929/30		from Newtongrange Star
Reid, J	LH	1	1891/92		2nd XI Player
Reid, Jack ' Jake '	G	1	1883/84		Hearts and Edinburgh
Reid, Jack	OR	1	1924/25		Dunfermline and Hearts
Reid, Peter	CF	1	1913/14		from East Fife. To Nelson (14/1/1914)
Reid, William 'Lanky'	FB	2	1887/88	1888/89	To Grimsby Town
Riddle	OR	1	1932/33		
Riddoch, David	OR	5	1882/83	1886/87	Edina FC, Northern, Grimsby Town, Hearts and Berwick Rangers. Edinburgh appearances (1) and three with Hearts
Rintoul, Robert	CF	1	1921/22		Army and several English League clubs as an amateur. Beat the great Eric Liddell off 5 1/2yds at Hearts' Sports.
Ritchie, Alexander	OR	2	1906/07	1907/08	from Arniston Rangers. Trials Celtic and Hearts.
Ritchie, Alexander W	IL	1	1922/23		To Raith Rovers (29/5/23) Also Blackpool, Reading, Watford, Bournemouth and Third Lanark.
Ritchie, Archibald	HB	3	1886/87	1888/89	Went to China. Returned in 1893. Edinburgh appearances (1).
Ritchie, Harry	IR	2	1897/98	1898/99	Leven Thistle. Re-instated amateur (1899)
Ritchie, Robert G	RB	3	1899/00	1901/02	from Parkhead
Ritchie, Thomas	RB	2	1906/07	1907/08	To Uphall (17/10/1907). Arniston Rangers
Robb, Thomas G	G	1	1930/31		ex Edinburgh Waverley. Duns, Penicuik and Chirnside. Became a referee
Roberts, William	CH	2	1888/89	1889/90	Scottish Junior Cup Finalist with Woodburn in 1887. Bonnyrigg Rose and Edinburgh.
Robertson	RB	1	1904/05		
Robertson	IL	1	1896/97		Royal Scots
Robertson, Archibald	IL	1	1932/33		ex Airdrie. Kilsyth Rangers
Robertson, Eddie	CF	1	1883/84		2nd XI Player and St James

Name	Pos	Apps	Years	Notes
Robertson, G	IL	1	1921/22	2nd XI Player. Club presented gold pendant on departure to Australia in April 1884.
Robertson, J	IR	1	1883/84	from Kirkcudbright
Robertson, J	RH	1	1900/01	Newton Thistle, Stoke, Hibernian, Liverpool, Southampton and Brighton and Hove Albion.
Robertson, John T	?	1	1893/94	ex Polton Vale
Robertson, Peter	OR	1	1895/96	ex Hanover. Preston North End, Bootle and Arsenal (trainer). Soldier with South African Scottish Regiment.
Robertson, Sandy 'Pundy'	RH	4	1880/81 1883/84	Captain of St Bernards 1882/83. Edinburgh appearances (8). Died Germiston Hospital, South Africa 29/7/1927 aged 67.
Robertson, T	IL	2	1891/92 1892/93	
Robertson, T	CH	1	1893/94	Millwall Athletic
Robertson, Thomas	IL	6	1926/27 1932/33	Greenock Morton To Middlesborough (25/6/1927) ex Edinburgh Emmett To Hearts (30/3/1929) From Hearts (1930/31) in exchange for Marshalsay. Leith Celtic
Robertson, Tom	CH	2	1894/95 1895/96	Queens Park, Possil Bluebell, Glasgow Northern, Cowlairs and Aston Villa. died 28/1/1924 Scotland and Glasgow. Member of Scottish Cup winning team of 1895. Scottish Cup Winner with Queens Park 1890. Played in first game only of 1893 final with Queens Park. Finalist with Queens Park 1892.
Robertson, Tom	LH	4	1892/93 1898/99	Edinburgh and Stoke.
Robertson, William	LB	3	1891/92 1893/94	2nd XI Player
Robertson, William Tait	HB	1	1881/82	also Secretary. ex St Vincent RFC
Rodgers, John	CF	1	1910/11	from Vale of Grange. Also Leith Athletic
Rogers, George	OR	1	1914/15	Pumpherston Rangers
Rogers, William	RB	1	1936/37	ex Pumpherston Juniors. Motherwell
Ross	CH	1	1901/02	
Ross, Alexander	LH	2	1901/02 1902/03	West Calder
Ross, Alexander	IR	2	1914/15 1915/16	brother of Tommy Ross.
Ross, George	LH	4	1904/05 1909/10	To Peterhead (9/11/1906). To East Fife (8/10/1909)
Ross, George H	OR	2	1913/14 1919/20	'back after a long illness' (9/19). Tranent Juniors. In Royal Scots WW1
Ross, James	LB	1	1890/91	from Dunfermline - player involved in famous suspension case for professionalism. Died 12/1941 aged 76 Subsequently went to Sunderland Albion. Edinburgh.
Ross, James	IR	1	1923/24	Amiston Rangers (1927)
Ross, James Daniel	IF	1	1884/85	ex Northern. Preston North End, Liverpool, Burnley and Manchester City. Preston 'Invincible'. FA Cup Winner with Preston North End 1889, Finalist 1888. Won Football League Championships with Preston North End 1889 and 1890.
Ross, Thomas	LH	11	1906/07 1919/20	from Wallyford. To Hearts (1915/16). From Hearts (24/2/1920). To Hearts (1/3/1920). Wallyford Violet
Ross, William	FB	4	1886/87 1889/90	to Grimsby Town. Also Armadale. Captain of St Bernards 1886/87 and 1888/89. Scottish League and Edinburgh
Rusk, James	LH	1	1920/21 1921/22	ex Bathgate
Russell, David K	CH	1	1892/93	Hearts, Preston North End, Celtic and Broxburn. Scotland, Scottish League and Edinburgh Scottish Cup Winner with Hearts 1891 and 1896. Winner with Celtic 1900 and Finalist 1901. FA Cup winner with Preston North End 1889, Finalist 1888. In Preston North End Football League Championship winning sides of 1889 and 1890. In Scottish League Champoinship winning sides of Hearts 1895 and Celtic 1898.
Russell, James	RH	2	1895/96 1896/97	ex Grimsby Town Also Cambuslang. Scotland and Glasgow

Name		Pos		Years	Notes
Russell, John		G	3	1895/96	Newton Thistle Scottish Trialist 1896/97
Russell, John 'Jock'		IR	7	1933/34	from Edina Juniors To Leith Athletic (30/8/1939)) Also Berwick Rangers. Captain of St Bernards 1939/40 2nd XI Player
Rutherford, David		G	1	1896/97	
Rutherford, James		OR	1	1926/27	To Bathgate (11/12/1926) ex Third Lanark, Wemyss Ath, Peebles Rovers and Musselburgh Bruntonians.

S

Name	Pos		Years	Notes
Sanderson, James N	OL	1	1926/27	Norwood, Musselburgh Bruntonians and St Johnstone
Sanders, Sidney C	F	1	1916/17	Crystal Palace
Savage, Patrick	G	2	1920/21 1921/22	ex Cowdenbeath
Sayers, Alex	OR	1	1937/38	To Bo'ness Also Brechin City and Peebles Rovers. Also Broxburn Shamrock
Scoales, William	G	2	1888/89 1889/90	
Scobie	IR	2	1936/37 1937/38	Alnwick Town, Scremerston and Berwick Rangers
Scott	RB	1	1920/21	
Scott, Archibald	IL	2	1902/03 1903/04	from Glasgow
Scott, Forrest	RB	1	1907/08	from Bonnyrigg Rose Ath
Scott, Frank W	OR	4	1890/91 1893/94	Edinburgh Northern and Hearts. Edinburgh appearances (2).
Scott, Harry M	RB	1	1910/11	from Bonnyrigg Rose Ath. To Broxburn Ath (3/3/1911) Polworth and Hearts Tynecastle XI
Scott, J	IF	2	1890/91 1891/92	Edinburgh Northern
Scott, James	IR	1	1901/02	
Scott, James F	CF	1	1927/28	Corinthian midweek amateurs
Scott, R	IL	1	1902/03	
Scott, Walter	RB	2	1915/16 1916/17	from Raith Rovers (4/3/1916). Hearts
Scoular, Alexander	OR	1	1931/32	from Montrose. Armadale. Father of Jimmy Scoular (Newcastle United and Portsmouth)
Seed, Angus C	CH	2	1916/17 1919/20	Leicester Fosse. To Mid Rhonda (5/12/1919). also Seaham Harbour, Reading, and Workington. Everton (trial). Manager Barnsley FC (7/1942) died 7/3/1953. Army Military Medallist
Shand, J	IR	1	1889/90	Norton Park. 2nd XI Player
Sharkey	IL	1	1941/42	
Sharp	OR	1	1906/07	
Sharp, Alexander	OL	2	1894/95 1895/96	From Bathgate. Returned to Bathgate (14/11/1895)
Shepherd, Kenneth C	G	1	**1938/39**	**from Leith St Andrews On loan to Peebles Rovers Also Queens Park. Amateur Scotland appearances (1).**
Shirlaw, David	CF	1	1924/25	Dalkeith Thistle, Bathgate, Bristol City, Charlton Ath, Brentford and St Johnstone.
Shoolbread	HB	1	1887/88	
Shoolbread	HB	1	1881/82	
Sibbald, George	RH	1	1893/94	Broxburn Shamrock. To Leith Athletic then returned to Broxburn Shamrock. Edinburgh.
Simpson	LB	1	1897/98	
Simpson, Henry C	IR	4	1907/08 1915/16	From Peterhead. To Leicester Fosse (25/3/1910). Raith Rovers, Ayr Utd and East Stirling.
Simpson, James	CF	2	1907/08 1908/09	from Aberdeen
Simpson, Peter	CF	2	1925/26 1926/27	Leith Amateurs Kettering Town, Crystal Palace, West Ham United, Reading and Aldershot.Died March 1974 aged 69.
Sinclair, JW	IL	1	1921/22	
Skene, Dr Leslie H	G	1	**1900/01**	**Edinburgh University, Queens Park, Stenhousemuir, Fulham and Glentoran. Scotland and Scottish League. Selected to play for St Bernards in the 1901 Rosebery Charity Cup replay against the Hearts.**

Name	Pos	Apps	Season	Notes
Slavin	G	1	1916/17	Broxburn United
Sligo	G	1	1897/98	
Sloan, John	RB	1	1923/24	Coldstream
Sloggie, William	RH	2	1906/07 1907/08	ex Arniston Rangers. To Dunfermline Ath (5/11/1907)
Small, R Leonard	G	2	1928/29 1929/30	Amateur Scotland appearances (1). Also North Berwick High School, Edinburgh University, Bathgate.
Smeaton	CF	1	1893/94	Also played rugby for the St George RFC. Edinburgh Northern
Smellie	CH	1	1907/08	
Smellie, Robert	LB	2	1891/92 1895/96	Queens Park and Hamilton Accies. Scotland and Glasgow Scottish Cup Winner with Queens Park 1890 and 1893. Played in first game only of 1892 final.
Smith	IL	1	1941/42	
Smith	OL	1	1898/99	2nd XI Player
Smith	IR	1	1889/90	Muirhouse Rovers
Smith	IR	1	1921/22	
Smith, Andrew	FB	2	1908/09 1909/10	Newtongrange Star
Smith, Effingham	IL	1	1905/06	From Beith
Smith, Harold	?	1	1914/15	To Leith (5/5/1914)
Smith, James	G	1	1930/31	Reg cancelled (20/5/1930). St Johnstone
Smith, N	CH	1	1908/09	
Smith, TG	G	3	1936/37 1938/39	Queens Park, Ayr United and Corinthians. Amateur Scotland appearances (2) plus seven with Queens Park and two with Ayr United. Scottish League and Glasgow.
Smith, William	CH	8	1904/05 1911/12	Trainer Musselburgh Ath. Fisherrow Shop Assistants. died 10/4/40. Arniston Rangers and Newtongrange Star
Sneddon, James Jun	G	2	1894/95 1895/96	Broxburn and Leith Athletic. Member of Scottish Cup winning team of 1895. Scottish 2nd XI Cup winner with Leith Athletic in 1892 and 1893
Somerville	CF	1	1893/94	2nd XI Player
Speedie, James H	OR	1	1912/13	Hearts, Tranent Juniors amateur. Trialist with St Bernards. Killed in World War I
Speirs, James B	OR	1	1922/23	ex Armadale and Bo'ness
Stage, William	IR	1	1920/21	ex Hibs. Also Middlesborough, Bury, Burnley, Southampton, and Great Harwood. died 12/5/57
Stalker, R	CF	1	1906/07	Queens Park and Edinburgh Myrtle
Stanners, James	G	6	1901/02 1909/10	from Vale of Grange
Steel	CF	1	1922/23	
Steel, Robert	CF	2	1892/93 1893/94	ex Motherwell. To Motherwell (12/4/1894). Also Royal Albert
Stenhouse, Jim	IR			**Lochgelly Violet and St Mirren. St Bernards Trialist in 1938. Wartime Scottish Internationalist**
'Stevenson'	IR	1	1933/34	A prominent Midlothian junior
Stevenson, Jock	CH	1	1889/90	Arthurlie, Middlesbrough, Sunderland and Middlesbrough Ironapolis.
Stevenson, David	G	1	1920/21	ex Hibs
Stewart	RH	1	1941/42	
Stewart	CH	1	1889/90	ex Edinburgh University
Stewart	CF	1	1913/14	from Fife
Stewart, Andrew	OR	2	1895/96 1896/97	Queens Park and Third Lanark. Scotland and Glasgow
Stewart, David	LH	1	1893/94	Queens Park, Scotland and Glasgow.
Stewart, Henry J 'Smiler'	RB	3	1912/13 1914/15	Leith and Bury. from Tillicoultry. Kirkcaldy United

Name	Pos	Apps	Seasons		Notes
Stewart, WS	OL	1	1895/96		Queens Park
Stirling, James	RH	1	1922/23		Blantyre Victoria
Stoddart, George DT	G	1	1897/98		Army - played in England
Strachan, James G	OL	1	1908/09		To Broxburn (23/1/1909)
Strang	IL	1	1939/40		46th Boys Brigade (Canonmills)
Stratford, NR	RH	1	1916/17		Queens Park
Strathie, James W	CH	2	1936/37	1937/38	from Falkirk ex loan Kings Park To Luton Town (27/5/1937) Also Northampton Town and Corby Town
Stuart, Thomas	CF	2	1891/92	1892/93	ex Edinburgh Universty. Hearts trialist 1892
Summers, William	CH	1	1920/21		ex Airdrie. Also Burnbank Athletic, St Mirren, Bradford City and Newport County. Scotland Scottish Cup Winner with St Mirren 1926.
'Sutherland'	LH	1	1932/33		Trialist - T Clelland (Penicuik Athletic)
Sutherland, Donald	HB	4	1885/86	1888/89	to Grimsby Town. Edinburgh appearances (1).
Sutherland, Mal	IL	2	1890/91	1891/92	
Sutherland, Ian	CF	1	1920/21		Broomhill Juniors
Swanson, James	RB	1	1927/28		Leith Hawthorn, Portobello Thistle and Alloa Athletic
Sweeney, John	CH	2	1929/30	1930/31	from Hearts of Beath

T

Name	Pos	Apps	Seasons		Notes
Tait	IR	2	1932/33	1933/34	
Tait, Robert	OL	2	1905/06	1906/07	ex Leith Athletic
Tams, W	CF	1	1938/39		from Royal Scots Fusiliers Also Penicuik and Duns
Taylor	CH	1	1899/00		
Taylor	CH	1	1900/01		
Taylor, J	RH	2	1885/86	1886/87	
Taylor, James B	IL	2	1914/15	1919/20	from Tranent Juniors. Son of ex St Bernards player.
Taylor, John	IL	1	1915/16		late Leith and Hull City.
Taylor, Robert	LH	1	1920/21		Also Sauchie Utd, Alva Albion Rangers, Stenhousemuir, Third Lanark, Middlesborough, Southport, Connahs Quay, Shotton, Stafford Rangers and Bo'ness.
Taylor, William 'Cocky'	OR	4	1889/90	1892/93	Dalry Primrose, Hearts, Blackburn Rovers and Leith Athletic. Scotland and Edinburgh Scottish Cup Winner with Hearts 1891. Scottish League Championship with Hearts 1897.
Tennent	OL	1	1920/21		
Tennent, James	OL	5	1897/98	1908/09	Scottish Trialist 1898/99. To Woolwich Arsenal (19/5/1899) then Middlesborough. Linton Villa, Watford and Parkhead. From Middlesborough (1907/08). Scottish League appearances (1).
Tennent, Thomas	LH	1	1895/96		Wishaw Thistle. To Motherwell (27/12/1895)
Teviotdale	RH	1	1887/88		2nd XI Player
Theurer, William	OR	1	1939/40		ex Blackpool and Dalkeith Thistle. Hibs. Heriots School
Thomson	LH	1	1883/84		
Thomson	OR	1	1907/08		from Peterhead
Thomson	OL	1	1924/25		
Thomson	IL	1	1937/38		loaned to Duns
Thomson, Alexander	G	2	1896/97	1897/98	from St Ninians. To Kings Park (29/1/1898)

Name	Seasons	Apps	Pos	Notes
Thomson, Charles B	1915/16	1	CH	ex Hearts and Sunderland. died 6/2/1936. Scotland, Scottish League and Edinburgh Scottish Cup Winner with Hearts 1901 and 1906. Finalist 1903. FA Cup Finalist with Sunderland 1913. Scottish League Finalist with Sunderland 1913. In Sunderland Football League Championship winning team of 1913.
Thomson, F	1899/00	1	OR	Trialist
Thomson, George G	1928/29	1	OL	Ormiston Primrose, Raeburn, Ashton. 'Boyd' nephew of Charlie Thomson
Thomson, Hugh McL	1912/13	1	OL	from Partick Thistle. To Ayr United (21/9/1912)
Thomson, James	1904/05	2	OL	'not signed as amateur'
Thomson, William I	1912/13	2	IL	ex Raith Rovers and Arthurlie. To Vale of Leven.
Thornton, Peter	1913/14	1	LH	ex Bo'ness. Edinburgh.
Totten, Isaac	1887/88	3	CH	Parkhead
Turnbull	1898/99	1	LH	
'Turner'	1921/22	1	CF	Trialist- McAndrew of Glencraig Celtic.
Turner, Peter	1920/21	2	IL	Parkhead. To Woolwich Arsenal (4/5/1900) then Middlesborough. Luton Town, Watford and Leyton. Captain of St Bernards 1899/00. Scottish Trialist 1898/99.
	1898/99			

U

| Usher, James | 1912/13 | 1 | RB | Glencraig Celtic. To Broxburn Utd (22/10/1912) |

V

| Veitch, DD | 1941/42 | 1 | CH | ex Edinburgh City To East Fife |
| Veitch, James | 1908/09 | 2 | G | From Broxburn |

W

Waddell, Frank	1899/00	2	OR	from Glasgow Perthshire.
Waddell, John McA	1899/00	1	OL	from Moorepark
Waddell, Thomas S	1892/93	1	IR	Queens Park. Scotland and Glasgow. Scottish Cup Winner with Queens Park 1893, Finalist 1892.
Walker	1889/90	1	RH	2nd XI Player
Walker	1905/06	1	IL	
Walker, Hugh	1922/23	1	RH	'on month's trial from Third Lanark'
Walker, James	1926/27	1	IR	ex Arniston Rangers Barrow and Distillery
Walker, John C	1895/96	2	OR	ex Raith Rovers. Re-instated (3/8/1897). 2nd XI Player
	1939/40	1	LB	ex Belfast Celtic brother of Tommy Walker (Hearts) died 22/11/82 aged 72 Founded Gorgie Hearts FC Irish League
Walker, Peter	1901/02	2	CF	Peterhead
Walker, Robert	1939/40	5	CF	ex Edinburgh City, Hibs and Kings Park
Walker, William	1927/28	1	OL	To Middlesborough. Also Leith Rangers. Leith Athletic. Arbroath, Rosewell Rosedale and East Fife.
Wallace, John M	1939/40	1	G	Wallyford Bluebell. Raith Rovers, Blackpool, Derby County, Falkirk, Dumbarton and Leith Athletic
Walls, Alexander	1898/99	2	IL	from Newhaven.
Walls, Robert 'Rab'	1930/31	1	OR	Leith Emmett, Wemyss Athletic, Hearts, Hibs, Cowdenbeath and Aldershot. Also guested 1937/1938 Also Watford and Aberdeen
Ward	1912/13	1	IF	from Oban
Wardrop, William	1891/92	1	CH	ex Broxburn. Also Sunderland Albion. Edinburgh appearances (1) and one with Broxburn.

Name	Pos	Apps	Season	Season	Notes
Wark	CH	1	1900/01		
Wark, Issac	CH	3	1895/96	1897/98	Bathgate and West Calder
Waterston, John	LH	1	1889/90		Hearts and Edinburgh.
Watson	CF	1	1941/42		
Watson	RB	1	1920/21		
Watson, John W	IL	1	1929/30		Musselburgh Bruntonians
Watson, John W	RH	2	1907/08	1908/09	To Kirkcaldy Utd (24/3/1909). Edinburgh Rosebery
Watson, Peter	?	1	1911/12		from Broxburn (10/4/1912)
Watt	CF	1	1929/30		
Waugh, William Lindsay	LB	6	1879/80	1885/86	Hearts. Secretary EoS FA. Secretary of Hearts FC (XXXX). Edinburgh appearances (5).
Weightman, David	LH	2	1919/20	1920/21	ex East Fife To East Fife (13/10/1920)
Weir, Edward 'Ned'	**LH**	**7**	**1930/31**	**1937/38**	**Camelon Juniors,from Falkirk, To Clyde Also Player/coach Raith Rovers and Dunfermline Ath. Northern Ireland and Eire. Manager of Dundalk (1948) Scottish Cup Winner with Clyde 1939. Captain of St Bernards 1936/37**
Weir, James	OL	2	1914/15	1915/16	from Kilmarnock (30/5/1914) To Falkirk. Alloa Athletic. From Falkirk (26/10/1915)
Weir, John	G	2	1924/25	1925/26	Glenbuck
Welsh, George	OL	2	1919/20	1920/21	Local boy signed from Army football
Welsh, W	G	1	1927/28		
Wemyss, David S	OR	2	1903/04	1904/05	From Norse Rovers
Wemyss, George	LH	2	1912/13	1913/14	from Kirkliston Ath. To Broxburn Utd (13/3/1914). In Royal Scots WW1
White, James	RB	1	1888/89		Leith Athletic
White	IR	1	1895/96		
Whitehead, George	RB	1	1924/25		Dalkeith Th, Newtongrange Star, Hearts, Celtic, Motherwell, Royal Naval Division, Cowdenbeath and Falkirk. Raith Rovers and York City
Whitelaw, John	IL	1	1939/40		
Whyte, Albert	?	1	1919/20		
Whyte, Gordon	IL	1	1938/39		Henderson Thistle, Ormiston Primrose. Schoolboy internationalist. Died of an illness 1939
Wight, George	IF	4	1883/84	1886/87	ex Rose FC Hearts. Edinburgh appearances (3) and one with the Rose...
Wilkie, Alexander	OR	2	1909/10	1910/11	Kinleith Thistle, Broxburn and Cowdenbeath
Wilkie, John	CF	1	1941/42		ex Hearts of Beath To Morton (6/3/42) Brother of W Wilkie. Hearts and Craig-Mer
Wilkie, Thomas	**G**	**3**	**1897/98**	**1899/00**	**from Clyde. Suspended sine die by St Bernards (1899/00). Scottish League appearances (1), Queens Park**
Wilkie, W	OR	1	1941/42		ex New Brighton Brother of John Wilkie
Williams, Horace	CF	1	1923/24		from Sittingbourne. Reg cancelled by SFA Council (19/9/1923) ex Hibs. Also Army, Dundee, Mold, New Brighton, Blackpool, Peterborough United, Macclesfield Town, Caermarfon Town, Lovells Ath, Hereford United Died 1960.
Williamson	IR	1	1895/96		
Williamson	RH	1	1912/13		
Wilson	FB	1	1910/11		
Wilson, AB	IL	1	1921/22		Musselburgh Athletic (Trialist)
Wilson, Abe	IL	3	1920/21	1922/23	Arbroath
Wilson, George	RH	1	1895/96		From Falkirk (13/12/1922) 'on month's trial with Tottenham Hotspur' from Kelso. An ex rugby player.
Wilson, James	IL	6	1879/80	1885/86	Edinburgh appearances (1).
Wilson, John 'Titch'	**OR**	**4**	**1893/94**	**1896/97**	**Dunfermline Juniors. Scottish Trialist 1895/96. ESJFA. Scottish League appearances (1).**
Wilson, John	RB	1	1895/96		from Kelso. To New Brompton (15/10/1895), Lincoln City, Manchester City, Small Heath and Swindon Town.

Name	Pos		Years	Debut	Notes
Wilson, John	RH	2	1919/20	1920/21	From Raith Rovers
Wilson, John G	IR	1	1933/34		ex Plymouth Argyle
Wilson, William AR	RB	3	1910/11	1913/14	From Leith (9/2/1911). To Peebles Rovers (28/10/1911). From Peebles Rovers (1913/14)
Wimsett	OL	1	1921/22		
Winning	RH	1	1910/11		from Leith. Arniston Rangers
Winton	G	1	1885/86		Adventurers and Edinburgh.
Wood	RB	1	1905/06		
Wood, Alexander M 'Doctor'	LB	4	1896/97	1899/00	From Cowdenbeath. To Sheffield Utd (15/5/1900). Played in goal under the name of 'Tulloch'.
Wood, James	CH	3	1941/42	1943/44	from Haddington To Morton (11/4/1942) To Hearts (1/2/1943)
Woodward, Vivien J	**CF**	**1**	**1902/03**		**Tottenham Hotspur and Chelsea. England and English League. Chelmsford City**
Wright, Harry	OL	1	1903/04		To West Calder Swifts (21/10/1903)

Y

Name	Pos		Years	Debut	Notes
Yorke, Robert J	LB	1	1939/40		Ayr United, Aldershot, Dundee Utd and Hull City. Montrose
Yorston	FB	2	1911/12	1912/13	Penicuik (Trialist)
Young	LB	1	1898/99		2nd XI Player
Young	OL	1	1891/92		Gordon Highlander
Young, Archd C	CF	3	1923/24	1925/26	From Hamilton Accies (19/10/1923) ex Hibs Playing as an amateur (1925/26)
Young, W	CF	1	1881/82		

St Bernard's Football Club

APPENDIX 2

Team Line Ups

Key to abbreviations used in the team line ups section

General:
Where there is no entry in the competition column the game was a friendly.
The name of the opponents shown in block capitals indicates a St Bernard's home game.
A player's name in block capitals indicates a goal scorer.
Line Ups proceeded with the word 'from' indicate a selected line up only, the actual one not having been traced.
The numbers 1 and 2 after the abbreviations for a league game means Division 1 and Division 2 eg SL1 = Scottish League Division 1.
Numbers after a cup tie abbreviation shows the round of the cup played eg SCC3 = Scottish Consolation Cup Round 3.
Small letters 's' and 'f' after a cup tie abbreviation means the semi-final and final rounds of a cup eg CCf = City Cup final.
In Season 1899/00 the letter 'T' after the abbreviation 'SL' indicates the Scottish League test match played against St Mirren.
The letters 'po' after 'SL2' indicate the play off matches for the league title. (Season 1914/15)
Where '(n)' appears a neutral venue has been used for the game.
A * beside the score indicates an abandoned match.
Small letter 'c' shows a match decided on corners.
In 1932/33 the Bo'ness match marked '$' was expunged from the records.

Leagues:
CL = Central League (Seasons 1919/20 and 1920/21)
EL = Eastern League (Seasons 1915/16 and 1916/17)
ERL = Eastern Regional League (Season 1939/40)
ESL = Edinburgh/East of Scotland League
MJL = Midlothian Junior League (Rosebery Juniors 1940/41)
NEL = North Eastern League (Season 1941/42)
SA = Scottish Alliance League (Seasons 1891/92 and 1892/93)
SL = Scottish League

Cup competitions:
BC = Blenheim Cup (Note: '1l' and '2l' indicates first and second legs respectively)
CC = City Cup
CLC = Central League Cup (Seasons 1919/20 and 1920/21)
DC = Dunedin Cup
Disp = Edinburgh Evening Dispatch Trophy (Season 1890/91)
E 2nd XI C = Edinburgh Second XI Cup (Second XI only)
EC = Edinburgh Cup
EJC = East of Scotland Junior Cup (Rosebery Juniors 1940/41))
ELC = Eastern League Cup (Seasons 1915/16 and 1916/17)
ESS = East of Scotland Shield
ExT = Exhibition Trophy (Season 1886/87)
GC = Gardener Cup (Seasons 1915/16 and 1916/17)
KC = King Cup (Second XI only 1896/97))
LC = Loftus Cup (Season 1916/17)
NEC = North Eastern Cup (Season 1941/42)
PC = Penman Cup
S 2nd XI C = Scottish Second XI Cup (Second XI only)
SC = Scottish Cup
SCC = Scottish Consolation Cup
SJC = Scottish Junior Cup (Rosebery Juniors 1940/41)
SNE = Scottish National Exhibition Cup (Season 1908/09)
SQC = Scottish Qualifying Cup
StMC = St Michael's Cup (Rosebery Juniors 1940/41))

United / St Bernards   1875 / 1878

UNITED FC (Rugby Rules) 1875/76

1 06-Nov Kirkcaldy   1-0
2 04-Dec Cronstadt   1-0
3 10-Jan Comely Bank   3-0
4 17-Jan ST BERNARDS   0-0
5 19-Feb Cronstadt   3-0
6 16-Mar ST GEORGE   1-0

UNITED FC (Rugby Rules) 1876/77
1 09-Dec Kirkcaldy   1-0
2 23-Dec St Vincent   1-0

UNITED FC (Rugby Rules) 1877/78
1 01-Dec ST VINCENT   2-0
UNITED FC (Association Rules) 1877/78
1 02-Mar HEARTS   0-2
2 23-Mar BRUNSWICK   1-3   Return Game
3 06-Apr HANOVER   0-3   Return Game

ST BERNARDS FC (Rugby Rules) 1875/76
1 17-Jan United   0-0

ST BERNARDS FC (Rugby Rules) 1876/77
1 28-Oct Kirkcaldy   0-1

1879/80

#	Date		Opponent	Score							
1	06-Sep		Edina	0-1							
2	04-Oct	EC1	ROVERS	7-1							
3	11-Oct		Aberlady	8-0							
4	18-Oct		University	0-1	Anderson,A	Heathcote,G	Waugh,W	Wilson,J	Masterton,A	McBeth,G	Lamb,W	Dunn,J	McLennan,H	Laurieston,W	Paton,H
5	01-Nov		Brunswick	4-4	Anderson,A	Heathcote,G	Waugh,W	Wilson,J	Home,F	McBeth,G	Laurieston,W	Paton,H	McLennan,H	Dunn,J	Edwards
6	08-Nov	EC2	Hibernian	1-3	Anderson,A	Heathcote,G	Waugh,W	Home,F	Wilson,J	McBeth,G	Arthur,A	Dunn,J	McLennan,H	Laurieston,W	Paton,H
7	15-Nov		Rovers	4-0							
8	22-Nov		WAVERLEY	6-1							
9	29-Nov		CALEDONIAN	2-0							
10	20-Dec		HANOVER	3-2							
11	10-Jan		West Calder	3-0							
12	17-Jan		Hearts	2-3	Waugh	Heathcote	McLennan	Bryce	Wilson	Dunn	Charlton	Arthur	Laurieston	Paton	McBeth
13	07-Feb		Caledonian	0-1							
14	13-Mar		BRUNSWICK	2-0							
15	27-Mar		BUCCLEUCH	4-2							
16	10-Apr		ANCHOR	11-0							
17	24-Apr		EDINA	2-0							

1880/81

#	Date	Comp	Opponent	Score											
1	11-Sep	EC1	Rose	12-0											
2	25-Sep		HANOVER	5-3											
3	02-Oct		Glasgow Harmonic	6-3											
4	09-Oct		West Calder	6-0											
5	16-Oct		HANOVER	7-2											
6	23-Oct	EC2	Hearts	0-0	Baillie	Robertson	Waugh		Wilson	Bryce		Charlton	McLennan	Arthur	Dunn	McBeth	Finlay
7	30-Oct		Bathgate	9-0											
8	27-Nov		BUCCLEUCH	3-1											
9	04-Dec	EC3	CALEDONIAN	6-0											
10			Brunswick	3-2											
11	11-Jan		Hibernian	4-2	Baillie	Waugh		Heathcote	Wilson	Robertson	Bryce	McBeth	Arthur	Dunn	Finlay	Charlton
12	08-Jan	EC4	HANOVER	5-3											
13	15-Jan		WEST CALDER	9-1											
14	05-Feb		Shamrocks	2-0											
15	12-Feb		Perseverance	6-0											
16	19-Feb		HEARTS	2-1	Baillie	Heathcote	Waugh		Bryce	Robertson	Wilson	McBeth	Arthur	Finlay	Dunn	Charlton
17	05-Mar		Auburn	6-0											
18	12-Mar		Auburn	0-9?											
19	19-Mar	ECf	Hibernian	4-4	Baillie	Heathcote	Waugh		Wilson	Robertson	Bryce	Charlton	Dunn	McKinnon	Arthur	McBeth
20	02-Apr	ECf	Hibernian	0-1	Baillie	Waugh	Heathcote		Bryce	Thompson	Wilson	McBeth	McKinnon	Dunn	Arthur	Charlton
21	16-Apr		HEARTS	0-3	Baillie	Heathcote	Waugh		Wilson	Lamb	Bryce	Arthur	Charlton	Dunn	McKinnon	Shollbread
22	23-Apr		RAEBURN	8-0											
23	30-Apr		HANOVER	4-1											

1881/82

#	Date	Code	Opponent	Score											
1	03-Sep	ESS1	ZEBRAS	wo											
2	10-Sep	SC1	RAEBURN	17-0	Baillie	Heathcote	Waugh	Wilson	Robertson	Bryce	McBETH	Arthur	Dunn	McKinnon	Charlton
3	24-Sep		HEARTS	1-0	Lamb	Waugh	Heathcote	Bryce	Wilson	Robertson,J	Dunn	Robertson,A	Paton	Arthur	Charlton
4	01-Oct		KINLEITH	8-0	Pearson	Heathcote	Waugh	Robertson,A	Bryce	Wilson	Charlton	Dunn	Fyfe	McKinnon	Arthur
5	08-Oct	SC2	Rangers	1-6	Baillie	Heathcote	Waugh	Wilson	Robertson,WT	Bryce	ARTHUR	McBeth	Dunn	Charlton	McKinnon
6	15-Oct		Hibernian	1-2	Pearson	Heathcote	Waugh	Robertson	Lamb	Shoolbred	McBeth	Arthur	Davie	McKinnon	Charlton
7	22-Oct		ST MIRREN	1-3	Pearson	Heathcote	Waugh	Bryce	Shoolbred	Charlton	McKinnon	Dunn	Arthur	McBeth	Robertson
8	29-Oct		Third Lanark	0-4											
9				1-4											
10	05-Nov	ESS2	EDINA	9-0											
11	12-Nov		LENZIE	8-0	Fyfe	Heathcote	Lindsay	Bryce	Shoolbred	McBeth	Arthur	Dunn	Young	McKinnon	Charlton
12	19-Nov		ARBROATH	7-0	Fyfe	Heathcote	Waugh	Robertson	Bryce	McBeth	Arthur	Young	Dunn	McKinnon	Charlton
13	26-Nov		Brunswick	1-0											
14	03-Dec	ESS3	ROSE	12-0											
15	10-Dec	ESS4	HARP	11-0											
16	14-Jan		UNIVERSITY	3-2	Fyfe	Heathcote	McLennan	Robertson	Shoolbred	Galloway	Arthur	Dunn	Young	McKinnon	Fyfe,W
17	21-Jan		Dumbarton	0-5											
18	18-Feb		HANOVER	3-0											
19	25-Feb	ESSf	Hibernian (n)	2-4	Baillie	Heathcote	Waugh	Robertson,A	McKinnon	McBeth	Galloway	Arthur	Dunn	Young	Charlton
20	04-Mar		Arbroath	0-1	Pearson	Heathcote	Waugh	Robertson	Calder	McBeth	Arthur	McBeth	Dunn	Davie	Charlton
21	11-Mar		DUMBARTON	2-4	Baillie	Heathcote	Waugh	McKinnon	Robertson	Young	Galloway	Wilson	McBeth	Aitken	Charlton
22	06-Apr		PARTICK TH	5-2	Baillie	Waugh	McLennan	McKinnon	Davie	McBeth	Fyfe	Heathcote	Wilson	Aitken	Cowan
23	08-Apr		THIRD LANARK	6-2	Baillie	Heathcote	Waugh	McKinnon	Shoolbred	Charlton	Mosman	Wilson	Dunn	McBeth	Arthur
24	22-Apr		HANOVER	5-2	Baillie	McLennan	Waugh	Wilson	Keble	McKinnon	Charlton	Dunn	Heathcote	Arthur	Dunn
25	30-Apr		HIBERNIAN	5-0	Baillie	Heathcote	Waugh	McKinnon	Robertson	McBeth	Arthur	Dunn	Galloway	Young	Charlton

1882/83

#	Date	Code	Opponent	Score	Players
1	26-Aug		Vale of Leven	2-4	Baillie, Heathcote, Waugh, Robertson, McKinnon, McBeth, Drummond, Charlton, McNaughton, Wilson, Dunn
2	02-Sep		THIRD LANARK	2-1	Baillie, Waugh, Heathcote, Robertson, McKinnon, Charlton, Dunn, Wilson, McNaughton, Drummond, McBeth
3	09-Sep	SC1	Hearts	1-1	Baillie, Heathcote, Waugh, Robertson, McKinnon, McBeth, Galloway, DRUMMOND, McNaughton, CHARLTON, WILSON
4	16-Sep	SC1	HEARTS	3-4	
5	23-Sep	ESS1	TRAFALGAR	11-0	
6	30-Sep		University	4-1	
7	07-Oct		BRUNSWICK	10-2	Baillie, Heathcote, Waugh, McKinnon, Allison, McBeth, Drummond, Dunn, McNaughton, Wilson, Denholm
8	14-Oct		Muirhouse Rovers	9-0	
9	21-Oct		ST MIRREN	4-4	Baillie, Heathcote, McLennan, Robertson, McKinnon, McBeth, Drummond, Dunn, McNaughton, Wilson, Charlton
10	28-Oct		HAMILTON ACCIES	4-2	
11	04-Nov		ST BERNARDS 2XI	3-7	
12	11-Nov		EDINA	4-2	
13	18-Nov	ESS2	MUIRHOUSE Rovers	19-0	Baillie, Heathcote, Wilson, McKinnon, Robertson, McBeth, McKenzie, Galloway, McNaughton, Charlton, Lowe
14	25-Nov		Dumbarton	0-4	Pearson, Girdwood, McLennan, Robertson, Blaike, Lowe, Denholm, McKenzie, McNaughton, Galloway, Drummond
15	02-Dec	ESS3	Addiewell	8-0	from Baillie, Heathcote, Wilson, Robertson, McKinnon, McBeth, Drummond, McNaughton, McKenzie, Charlton and Lowe.
16	23-Dec		WANDERERS	8-0	
17	06-Jan		Third Lanark	?-?	
18	13-Jan		DUMBARTON	5-2	Baillie, Heathcote, Girdwood, Wilson, Drummond, McKinnon, McBeth, Galloway, McNaughton, Charlton, Lowe
19	20-Jan	ESS4	UNIVERSITY	1-2	from Baillie, Heathcote, Girdwood, Wilson, Drummond, McKinnon, McBeth, Galloway, McNaughton, Charlton and Lowe.
20	10-Feb		Hamilton Accies	0-2	
21	17-Feb		Hearts	3-1	Baillie, Heathcote, Girdwood, Wilson, McKinnon, Collie, Charlton, McKenzie, Lowe, Drummond, Galloway
22	10-Mar		EDINA	4-3	
23	24-Mar		EDINA	10-2	
24	31-Mar	RCCs	University (n)	5-3	Baillie, Heathcote, Charles, Robertson, Collie, McBeth, Lowe, Dunn, Drummond, Wilson, Charlton
25	14-Apr		Third Lanark	0-3	Baillie, Heathcote, Girdwood, McKinnon, Robertson, Aitken, Galloway, Drummond, Dunn, McBeth, Lowe
26	21-Apr	RCCf	HEARTS	0-2	Baillie, Heathcote, Charles, Drummond, Robertson, Charlton, Dunn, Wilson, Galloway, Lowe, McBeth
27	26-Apr		Hibernian	0-3	James, Heathcote, Ross,A, McKinnon, Ryan, Charlton, Wilson, McBeth, Drummond, Lowe, Riddoch
28	05-May		Hearts	1-4	from Baillie, Heathcote, Girdwood, Robertson, McKinnon, McBeth, Lowe, Blaike, Drummond, Wilson and Charlton.

1883/84

#	Date			Opponent	Score										
1	25-Aug			RANGERS	2-4	Baillie	Waugh	Heathcote	Collie	Robertson,A	Charlton	Wilson	Dunn	Drummond	Lowe	Riddoch
2	01-Sep			Third Lanark	3-3	Baillie	Heathcote	Girdwood	Collie	Robertson,A	Wilson	Charlton	Denholm	Drummond	Arthur	Lowe
3	15-Sep	SC1		Dunfermline	13-1	Baillie	Heathcote	Heathcote	Robertson	Collie	Wilson	Charlton	Denholm	Arthur	Lowe	McBeth
4	22-Sep	ESS1		ROSEBERY	22-0	from Baillie, Heathcote, Waugh, Robertson, Collie, Charlton, Wilson, Denholm, Arthur, Lowe and McBeth.										
5	29-Sep	ESS?		WEST CALDER	4-0	Baillie	Waugh	Heathcote	Collie	Robertson		Wilson	Denholm	Arthur	Lowe	McBeth,R
6	06-Oct			Hamilton Accies	5-0											
7	20-Oct	SC2		WEST BENHAR	7-0	Baillie	Heathcote	Waugh	Collie		Robertson,G	Charlton	Robertson,G	Arthur	Lowe	McBeth
8	27-Oct			St Mirren	3-5											
9	03-Nov	ESS2		Easter	5-1											
10	10-Nov	SC3		THORNLIEBANK	2-0	Baillie	Heathcote	Waugh	Collie	Drummond	Robertson,A	CHARLTON	ROBERTSON,J	Arthur	Riddoch	Lowe
11	17-Nov	ESS3		AVONDALE	4-2											
12	24-Nov			Hearts	2-0	from Baillie, Heathcote, Waugh, Robertson A, Collie, Lowe, Riddoch, Izzett, Arthur, McAuslane and Charlton.										
13	01-Dec	SC5		RANGERS	0-3	Baillie	Heathcote	Waugh	Robertson	Dawson	Charlton	McAuslane	Arthur	McBeth	Riddoch	Lowe
14	08-Dec			Hibernian	1-4	Baillie	Waugh	Heathcote	Calder	Collie	McAuslane	Lowe	Robertson,J	McBeth	Riddoch	Arthur
15	29-Dec			Accrington	2-3	Baillie	Heathcote	Girdwood	Collie	Robertson	McAuslane	Thomson	Lawrence	Robertson,E	Lowe	Riddoch
16	31-Dec			Blackburn Olympic	1-1	Baillie	Robertson	Girdwood	Robertson	Whyte	McAuslane	Thomson	McBeth	Robertson	Lowe	Drummond
17	01-Jan			Great Lever	0-6	Baillie	Girdwood	Heathcote	Collie	Whyte	McAuslane	Thomson	Drummond	Lawrence	Riddoch	Lowe
18	26-Jan			DUMBARTON	0-1	Baillie	Girdwood	Waugh	Collie	McLennan	Aitken	Thomson	Robertson,E	McAuslane	Riddoch	Lowe
19	02-Feb			HAMILTON Accies	3-2	Fraser	Heathcote	Waugh	Collie	McLennan	Wilson	Charlton	Robertson,E	Wight	Lowe	Riddoch
20	09-Feb			EDINA	4-2											
21	16-Feb			Dumbarton	0-8	Baillie	Allison	Kennedy	McLennan	Whyte	Thomson	Thomson	McAuslane	Robertson	Riddoch	Lowe
22	23-Feb	ESSs		WEST CALDER	7-4	from Pearson, Girdwood, Waugh, Collie, Whyte, Heathcote, McAuslane, Riddoch, Lowe, Baillie and Robertson E.										
23	01-Mar	ESSf	(n)	Hibernian	0-7	Pearson	Heathcote	Waugh	Allison	Whyte	McAuslane	McAuslane	Lawrence	Robertson,E	Baillie	Lowe
24	15-Mar			ARBROATH	2-1	from Baillie, Heathcote, Holden, Collie, Whyte, Riddoch, Lowe, Wight, Robertson E, Thomson and McAuslane.										
25	22-Mar	RCCs		HEARTS	4-2	Baillie	Heathcote	Waugh	Robertson	Collie	Wight	McAuslane	Drummond	Bryce	Lowe	McBeth
26	29-Mar			VALE OF LEVEN	2-1	Baillie	Heathcote	Waugh	Whyte	Robertson	Collie	Charlton	Lowe	Robertson	Wight	McAuslane
27	05-Apr			HEARTS	0-3	Baillie	Waugh	Whyte	McKinnon	Collie	Thomson	McAuslane	Wight	Arthur	Lowe	Riddoch
28	19-Apr			ST MIRREN	4-2	from Baillie, Heathcote, Waugh, Girdwood, Whyte, Lowe, Riddoch, Galloway, Robertson E, Wight and McAuslane.										
29	26-Apr	RCCf		HIBERNIAN	1-1	Baillie	Waugh	Heathcote	Robertson	Bryce	Lowe	McAuslane	Galloway	Wight	Drummond	McBeth
30	03-May	RCCf		PRESTON NE	2-3	Reid	Waugh	Heathcote	Aitken	Whyte	Lowe	Riddoch	McBeth	Baillie	Wight	McAuslane
31	14-May	RCCf		HIBERNIAN	0-1	Baillie	Waugh	Heathcote	Robertson	Bryce	Lowe	Riddoch	McBeth	Drummond	Wight	McAuslane

1884/85

#	Date	Opponent	Score											
1	30-Aug	Third Lanark	3-3	Baillie	Heathcote	Bryce	Robertson	White	Drummond	Barnett	White	Charlton		Lowe
2	06-Sep	BONESS	2-0	from Baillie, Heathcote, Holden, Bryce, Whyte, Drummond, Riddoch, Wight, Barnett, Lowe and McAuslane.
3	13-Sep	SC1	EDINA	6-0	from Baillie, Gair, Holden, Bryce, Whyte, Lowe, Riddoch, Barnett, Wilson, Wright and Charlton.
4	20-Sep		THIRD LANARK	3-1	Baillie	Gair	Holden	Heathcote	Bryce	Guild	Barnett	Riddoch		McAuslane	Arthur
5	27-Sep	ESS1	ADVENTURERS	9-0	from Baillie, Gair, Holden, Heathcote, Bryce, Guild, Barnett, Riddoch, Wight, Arthur and McAuslane.
6	04-Oct		HAMILTON ACCIES	2-0	from Baillie, Gair, Holden, Heathcote, Bryce, Guild, McAuslane, Wight, Arthur, Riddoch and Barnett.
7	11-Oct	ESS2	MUIRHOUSE ROVERS	3-2	from Baillie, Holden, Gair, Heathcote, Bryce, Guild, McAuslane, Wight, Arthur, Lowe and Barnett.
8	18-Oct		DUNDEE HARP	2-1	from Baillie, Gair, Waugh, Guild, Heathcote, Bryce, Riddoch, Lowe, Barnet, Wight and McAuslane.
9	25-Oct	SC3	West Benhar	1-5										
10	01-Nov		HEARTS	1-0	Baillie	Waugh	Gair	Heathcote	Guild	Barnett	Riddoch	Wight	Lorne		McAuslane
11	08-Nov		Hibernian	1-4	Baillie	Gair	Waugh	Heathcote	Guild	McAuslane	Lowe	Bryce	Wight	Riddoch	Barnett
12	15-Nov		ROYAL LYCEUM Theatre	7-0	from Baillie, Gair, Holden, Guild, Charlton, Bryce, Wight, Lowe, McAuslane, Riddoch and Barnet.
13	29-Nov	ESS3	Hearts	2-4	Baillie	Gair	Holden	Heathcote	Guild	McAuslane	Charlton	White	Bryce	Lowe	Riddoch
14	06-Dec		Arbroath	2-6										
15	13-Dec		ST JAMES	1-3	from Baillie, Gair, Holden, Heathcote, Guild, McAuslane, Childe, Bryce, Wight, Lowe and Riddoch.
16	20-Dec		West Calder	1-5										
17	03-Jan		BOLTON WANDERERS	0-7	Duff	Gair	Bryce	Heathcote	Guild	Ross	Allison	McAuslane	Wright	Baillie	Cantley
18	10-Jan		HEARTS	3-3	Heathcote	Gair	Heathcote	Guild	Childe	Guild	Lowe	Taylor	Wight	Allison	Linton
19	17-Jan		HIBERNIAN	0-4	Duff	Heathcote	Gair	Heathcote	Guild	Hutton	Taylor	Wight	Baillie	McIntosh
20	24-Jan		ARBROATH	2-1	Baillie	Heathcote	Gair	Heathcote	Hutton	Stuart	McIntosh	Lowe	Wight	Linton
21	31-Jan		UNIVERSITY	7-2	Baillie	Heathcote	Gair	Heathcote	Guild	Stuart	Hutton	Lowe	Wight	Allison	McAuslane
22	14-Feb		RANGERS	1-5	Baillie	Heathcote	Gair	Heathcote	Guild	Hutton	Hutton	Ross	Wight	Linton	?
23	21-Feb		GLENCAIRN	2-1	Butters	Heathcote	Gair	Hutton	Hutton	Ross	McIntosh	Lowe	Baillie	Wight	Fyfe, W
24	28-Feb		West Calder	2-2	from Baillie, Heathcote, Gair, Guild, Hutton, Lowe, McIntosh, Allison, Linton, Wight and McAuslane.
25	14-Mar		Hearts	2-1	Baillie	Heathcote	Gair	Heathcote	Guild	Hutton	McAuslane	Linton	McKinnon	Wight	McIntosh
26	04-Apr	RCCs	HIBERNIAN	0-4	Baillie	Heathcote	Gair	Guild	Hutton	McAuslane	Linton	Wight	Allison	Lowe
27	18-Apr		BATTLEFIELD	1-2	Baillie	Heathcote	Girdwood	Hutton	Childe	Guild	Lowe	McIntosh	Wight	Cantley	McAuslane
28	23-Apr		BLACKBURN ROVERS	2-0	Baillie	Heathcote	Girdwood	Hutton	Guild	Guild	Wight	Wight	McGhee	Cox	McIntosh	Lowe
29	09-May		Arbroath	0-1	Baillie	Lundie	McLaren								

1885/86

#	Date	Cup	Opponent	Score	1	2	3	4	5	6	7	8	9	10	11
1	22-Aug		Falkirk	4-5											
2	29-Aug		THIRD LANARK	2-3	Baillie	Heathcote	Girdwood	Guild	Hutton	Lowe	Riddoch	McAuslane	Taylor	Wight	McKinnon
3	05-Sep		PARTICK THISTLE	1-1	Baillie	Heathcote	Girdwood	Guild	Hutton	Lowe	Riddoch	McAuslane	Taylor	Wight	McIntosh
4	12-Sep	SC1	Hearts	2-5	Baillie	Heathcote	Girdwood	Hutton	Guild	Taylor,J	McIntosh	LOWE	RIDDOCH	Mackay,J	Wight,G
5	19-Sep		NORTON PARK	0-2	Baillie	Waugh,WL	Girdwood	Hutton	Guild	Taylor	Wight	LOWE	McIntosh	Keble	Lowe
6	26-Sep	SC1	HEARTS	0-1	Baillie	Girdwood	Waugh	Guild	Hutton	Taylor	Riddoch	Lowe	McIntosh	Aitken	McIntosh
7	03-Oct	ESS1	SARSFIELD	11-0	Waugh	Heathcote	Girdwood	Guild	Hutton	Taylor	Lowe	McIntosh	Baillie	Aitken	Wight
8	10-Oct		BATTLEFIELD	0-4											
9	22-Oct		Hibernian	1-5											
10	24-Oct	ESS2	PENICUIK Wanderers	6-0	Baillie	Heathcote	Girdwood	Hutton	Guild	Taylor	McIntosh	Riddoch	Lowe	Wight	Aitken
11	07-Nov		Hearts	2-3	Butters	Hutton	Heathcote	McEwan	Taylor	Lowe	Aitken	Wight	Baillie	Riddoch	McIntosh
12	14-Nov	ESS3	Broxburn Thistle	3-1											
13	21-Nov		WEST CALDER	5-0											
14	28-Nov		ARBROATH	Can											
15	05-Dec		UNIVERSITY	3-3											
16	12-Dec	ESS4	BROXBURN Shamrock	4-0											
17	19-Dec		Dunmore	0-1											
18	26-Dec		Boness	1-2	Baillie	Ramage	Ross	McEwan	Heathcote	Guild	Lowe	Thomson	Aitken	McIntosh	Riddoch
19	09-Jan		Franklin	4-1											
20	09-Jan		BONESS	7-0											
21	16-Jan		ARBROATH	8-1	Baillie	Heathcote	Girdwood	Guild	Taylor	Hutton	Wilson	Riddoch	Wight	Lowe	McIntosh
22	23-Jan	ESS5	LEITH THISTLE	6-0	Baillie	Heathcote	Girdwood	Hutton	Taylor	Guild	Wilson	Aitken	Lowe	McIntosh	Wight
23	30-Jan		BATTLEFIELD	2-2	Miller	Girdwood	Ramage	Taylor	Hutton	Riddoch	McIntosh	Bruce	Wight	Aitken	?
24	13-Feb		UNIVERSITY	5-0	Baillie	Girdwood	Heathcote	Guild	Hutton	Taylor	McIntosh	Riddoch	Lowe	Lowe	Wight
25	20-Feb	ESSf	HIBERNIAN	1-5	Baillie	Girdwood	Heathcote	Guild	Hutton	Wight	Wight	Crowe	Crowe	Riddoch	McIntosh
26	27-Mar		Cambuslang	1-6	from Baillie, Heathcote, Girdwood, Lowe, Hutton, Guild, McKay, McKinnon, McIntosh and Riddoch.										
27	03-Apr		Burntisland Thistle	2-3	Baillie	Heathcote	Girdwood	Hutton	Guild	McEwan	Wight	Riddoch	McIntosh	Bruce	
28	10-Apr		Partick Thistle	1-7	from Baillie, Heathcote, Girdwood, Hutton, Guild, Jenkinson, Lowe, McKinnon, McIntosh, Wight and McKay.										
29	15-Apr		OUR BOYS (Dundee)	1-2	Baillie	Girdwood	Heathcote	Guild	Hutton	Sutherland	Wight	Mackay	Grant	Lowe	McIntosh
30	17-Apr	RCCs	HEARTS	0-0	Baillie	Heathcote	Girdwood	Guild	Hutton	Jackson	McKinnon	Lowe	Heggie	Wight	Wilson
31	21-Apr		Fair City Athletic	3-1											
32	23-Apr		ROYAL OAK LEITH	3-3											
33	29-Apr	RCCs	HEARTS	1-4	Winton	Heathcote	Girdwood	Guild	Hutton	Jackson	Wilson	Wight	Mackay	Lowe	McKinnon

1886/87

#	Date	Code	Opponent	Score													
					from Baillie,	Heathcote,	Girdwood,	Lowe,	Taylor,	Hutton,	Guild,	Sutherland,	Riddoch,	Barnett,	Grant,	Arthur and Ross,W.	
1	14-Aug		Harp (Dundee)	1-3													
2	21-Aug		DUMBARTON	2-0	Baillie	Heathcote	Ross,J	Hutton	Guild	Kennedy	Barnett	Arthur	Lowe	Riddoch			
3	04-Sep		CAMBUSLANG	0-2	Baillie	Heathcote	Ross	Hutton	Guild	Kennedy	Barnett	Arthur	Lowe	Riddoch			
4	06-Sep		ACCRINGTON	3-3	Baillie	Heathcote	Ross,W	Guild	Hutton	Kennedy	Barnett	Arthur	Grant	Riddoch	Lowe		
5	11-Sep	SC1	BONESS	3-2	Baillie	HEATHCOTE	Ross,W	Hutton	Kennedy	Guild	ARTHUR	Barnett	Grant	Riddoch	Lowe		
6	18-Sep		HAMILTON ACCIES	4-0	Baillie	Heathcote	Ross	Sutherland	McEwan	Hutton	Grant	Arthur	BARNETT	Lowe			
7	25-Sep	ESS1	LEITH HARP	2-0	Baillie	Heathcote	Ross	Hutton	McEwan	Sutherland	Grant	Arthur	Barnett	Lowe			
8	02-Oct		NORTHERN (Glasgow)	1-1	Baillie	Heathcote	Ross	Guild	Hutton	Sutherland	McIntosh	Arthur	Barnett	Arthur	Grant		
9	07-Oct	ExT	Rangers	2-2	Baillie	Heathcote	Ross	Guild	Hutton	Sutherland	Grant	Arthur	Barnett	Lowe	Arthur		
10	09-Oct		POLLOCKSHIELDS ATH	1-4	Baillie	Ross	Heathcote	Guild	Hutton	Sutherland	Grant	Arthur	Barnett	Riddoch	Lowe		
11	16-Oct		HIBERNIAN	2-5	Hutchison	Baillie	Cuthbertson	Keble	Guild	Kilgour	Arthur	Wight	Heggie	Galloway	Baillie		
12	23-Oct	SC3	ARMADALE	5-2	Baillie	Heathcote	Ross	Sutherland	Guild	Hutton	Lowe	Riddoch	BARNETT	Grant	ARTHUR 3		
13	30-Oct	ESS2	SARSFIELD	5-1	Baillie	Heathcote	Ross	McEwan	Sutherland	Hutton	Grant	Arthur	Barnett	Riddoch	Lowe		
14	06-Nov		UNIVERSITY	5-0	Baillie	Heathcote	Ross	Hutton	Sutherland	Grant	Arthur	Campbell	Barnett	Lowe	Riddoch		
15	13-Nov	SC4	ERIN ROVERS	5-1	Baillie	Heathcote	Ross	GARLICH	Hutton	Sutherland	GRANT	Arthur	BARNETT	Arthur	LOWE 2		
16	20-Nov	ESS3	COWDENBEATH	6-0	Baillie	Heathcote	Ross	Hutton	Guild	Grant	Arthur	Sutherland	Barnett	Lowe			
17	27-Nov		Our Boys (Dundee)	5-2	from Baillie,	Cuthbertson,	Ross,W,	Hutton,	Guild,	Grant,	Arthur,	Sutherland,	Barnett,	Riddoch,	Galloway and Kilgour.		
18	04-Dec	SC5	Port Glasgow Athletic	2-6	Baillie	Heathcote	Ross	Cuthbertson,	Hutton	Sutherland	Grant	Riddoch	Lowe	BARNETT 2	Sutherland		
19	11-Dec		MOSSEND SWIFTS	0-2	Baillie	Ross	Cuthbertson	Guild	McIntosh	Grant	Arthur	Heggie	Barnett	Lowe	Arthur		
20																	
21																	
22	15-Jan		HEARTS	1-6	Baillie	Guild	Sutherland	Hutton	Grant	Lowe	Heggie	Riddoch	Campbell	Lowe		
23	22-Jan		FALKIRK	2-1	Baillie	Heathcote	Ross	Sutherland	Hutton	Kennedy	Sutherland	Campbell	Barnett	Arthur	Grant		
24	29-Jan		West Calder	3-2	Baillie	Ross	Grant	Kennedy	Hutton	Sutherland	Riddoch	Arthur	Barnett	Heggie	Campbell		
25	05-Feb	ESSs	Hibernian	2-4	Baillie	Heathcote	Ross	Kennedy	Kennedy	Grant	Lowe	Riddoch	Barnett	Heggie	Campbell		
26	12-Feb		RANGERS	0-2	Baillie	Heathcote	Ross	Hutton	Kennedy	Grant	Lowe	Barnett	Heggie	Campbell	Arthur		
27	19-Feb		Hearts	6-1	Baillie	Heathcote	Ross	Kennedy	Grant	Sutherland	Heggie	Campbell	Arthur	Barnett	Riddoch		
28	05-Mar		DUMBARTON ATHLETIC	1-0	Baillie	Heathcote	Ross	Guild	Kennedy	Grant	Heggie	Sutherland	Barnett	Arthur	Arthur		
29	19-Mar		Cambuslang	0-7	Baillie	Heathcote	Ross	Kennedy	Guild	Lowe	Grant	Riddoch	Barnett	Lowe	Campbell		
30	26-Mar	RCC	HIBERNIAN	2-2	Baillie	Heathcote	Ross	Kennedy	Grant	Hutton	Riddoch	Lowe	Arthur	Arthur	Heggie		
31	02-Apr		BATTLEFIELD	6-1	Baillie	Heathcote	Ross	Hutton	Grant	Kennedy	Hutton	Grant	Arthur	Arthur	Heggie		
32	08-Apr		Newcastle West End	3-1	Baillie	Heathcote	Ross	Grant	Kennedy	Hutton	Grant	Campbell	Arthur	Arthur	Heggie		
33	09-Apr		Sunderland	5-0	Baillie	Heathcote	Ross	Heathcote	Grant	Kennedy	Hutton	Heggie	Campbell	Riddoch	Arthur		
34																	
35	16-Apr		NORTHERN (Glasgow)	1-1	Baillie	Heathcote	Ross	Kennedy	Hutton	Grant	Hutton	Grant	Campbell	Arthur	Lowe	Heggie	
36	18-Apr	RCC	HIBERNIAN	2-2	Baillie	Heathcote	Ross	Hutton	Kennedy	Grant	Grant	Kennedy	Riddoch	Arthur	Heggie		
37	23-Apr		HEARTS	9-3	Baillie	Heathcote	Ross	Hutton	Grant	Kennedy	Kennedy	Lowe	Riddoch	Heggie	Arthur		
38	28-Apr	RCC	HIBERNIAN	1-6	Baillie	Heathcote	Ross	Kennedy	Hutton	Grant	Grant	Lowe	Campbell	Arthur	Heggie		
39	09-May		LEITH ASSOCIATION	3-1	Baillie	Heathcote	Hutton	Heathcote	Guild	Guild	Barnett	Barnett	Campbell	Arthur	McGhee		
40	13-May		PRESTON NORTH END	0-5	Baillie	Heathcote	Ross	Heathcote	Grant	Kennedy	Hutton	Campbell	Heggie	Arthur	Lowe		

1887/88

#	Date		Opponent	Score												
1	20-Aug		DUMBARTON	5-4	Gibson,W	Paterson,J	Heathcote	Grant,J		Sutherland	Shoolbread	Campbell	Mackay,R	Heggie,C	Lowe,J	Boyd,R
2	27-Aug		Arbroath	3-6	Addison	Shoolbread	Heathcote	Grant,J		McMillan	Lowe	Mackay	Campbell	Heggie	Arthur	Boyd
3	03-Sep	SC1	ARMADALE	3-2	McEwan	Heathcote	Paterson	Pearson		Guild	Grant	Boyd	LOWE	HEGGIE	Campbell	LAMB
4	10-Sep		NEWCASTLE WE	4-2	Baillie	Heathcote	Paterson	Grant		Guild	Grant	Lowe	Arthur	Heggie	Campbell	Corson
5	17-Sep	ESS1	LEITH WANDERERS	18-0	Baillie	Heathcote	Paterson	Hutton		Pearson	Ross	Lowe	Arthur	HEGGIE	Mackay	Corson
6	24-Sep	SC2	BROXBURN Shamrock	1-1	Baillie	Heathcote	Paterson	Hutton		Ross,W	Grant	Lowe	Arthur	HEGGIE 3	Campbell	Mackay
7	01-Oct	SC2	Broxburn Shamrock	4-1	Baillie	Heathcote	Paterson	Hutton		Guild	Grant	Lowe	Arthur	Corson	Campbell	Mackay + 1
8	08-Oct		COWLAIRS	1-1	Baillie	Heathcote	Paterson	Hutton		Guild	Hutton	Arthur	Heggie	Corson	Campbell	Mackay
9	15-Oct	(SC)	Dunfermline Athletic	2-1	from Baillie, Heathcote, Paterson, Hutton, Guild, Grant, Lowe, Heggie, Corson, Campbell and Montgomery.											
10	22-Oct		Rangers	1-1	Baillie	Heathcote	Paterson	Heathcote		Grant	?	Campbell	Corson	Montgomery	Pringle	Arthur
11	29-Oct	ESS2	Hearts	2-5	Baillie	Heathcote	Paterson	McMillan		Guild	Guild	Lowe	Corson	Montgomery	Campbell	Mackay
12	05-Nov		BELLSTANE BIRDS	6-1	Baillie	Heathcote	Paterson	Grant		Hutton	McMillan	Corson	Arthur	Heggie	Mackay	Campbell
13	12-Nov		ATHENIANS	5-1	Baillie	Heathcote	Hutton	Grant		Guild	Hutton	Campbell	Heggie	Arthur	Corson	Arthur
14	19-Nov		ST BERNARDS 1stXI	9-0	McMurtie	Anderson	Fleming	Garlick		Ritchie	Ross	Mathieson	Lamb	Jenkinson	Bruce	Kilgour
15			v St Bernards 2ndXI	0-9	Baillie	Paterson	Heathcote	Hutton		Guild	Grant	Corson	Arthur	Arthur	Mackay	Campbell
16	26-Nov	SC5	Abercorn	1-6												
17	03-Dec		East Stirling	6-1												
18	10-Dec		GLENCAIRN	1-0	Baillie	Paterson	Guild	Grant		Hutton	Arthur	Campbell	Mackay	Campbell	Pratt	Lowe
19	17-Dec		UNIVERSITY	0-4	Gillespie	Paterson	Methven	Sutherland		Guild	McEwan	Campbell	Heggie	McMinn	Lang	Other,AN
20	24-Dec		Partick Thistle	2-1	Baillie	Heathcote	Cuthbertson	Guild		Hutton	?	McEwan	Wilson	Heggie	Aitken	Pratt
21	31-Dec		LEITH ATHLETIC	1-2	Gibson	Heathcote	Paterson	Hutton		Guild	Campbell	Campbell	Arthur	Heggie	McMinn	Mackay
22	07-Jan		ADVENTURERS	2-2	Baillie	Paterson	Heathcote	Grant		Guild	Hutton	Campbell	McMinn	Heggie	Mackay	Corson
23	14-Jan		Broxburn Thistle	1-5												
24	21-Jan		Alloa Athletic	2-1	Baillie	Ross	Reid	Grant		Guild	Ritchie	McIntosh	Ellis	McMinn	Campbell	Garlick
25	04-Feb		UNIVERSITY	4-1	Baillie	Ross	Paterson	Ritchie		Guild	Ritchie	Grant	Heggie	McMinn	Reilly	Corson
26	11-Feb		West Calder	2-3	from Baillie, Paterson, Heathcote, Ritchie, Ross, Guild, McMinn, Heggie, Muir, McIntosh and Lowe											
27	25-Feb		Cambuslang	0-6	from Baillie, Paterson, Heathcote, Ross, Grant, Campbell, Heggie, Corson, McMinn and Lowe											
28	03-Mar		Leith Athletic	4-2	Baillie	Methven	Reid	Ritchie		Guild	Grant	Campbell	McMinn	Muir	Corson	Paterson
29	10-Mar		BURNTISLAND TH	5-1	Baillie	Methven	Reid	Ritchie		Guild	Hutton	Lowe	Paterson	McMinn	Grant	Baird
30	24-Mar		ARMADALE	1-3	from Baillie, Methven, Reid, Ritchie, Hutton, Grant, Campbell, Corson, Paterson, McMinn and Lowe.											
31	30-Mar		Northern	1-3	Baillie	Methven	Reid	Ritchie		Guild	Grant	McMinn	Baird	Paterson	Corson	Lowe
32	31-Mar		Newcastle West End	1-1	Baillie	Methven	Reid	Ritchie		Guild	Grant	McIntosh	McMinn	Paterson	Calder	Calder
33	02-Apr		Darlington	2-2	from Baillie, Reid, Methven, Ritchie, Guild, Grant, Lowe, Paterson, McMinn, Corson and AN Other.											
34	03-Apr		Middlesborough	1-5	Baillie	Reid	Methven	Grant		Roberts	Ritchie	Gould	McMinn	Paterson	Lowe	McIntosh
35	07-Apr		Sunderland	2-0	Baillie	Methven	Reid	Ritchie		Hutton	Grant	McMinn	Corson	Paterson	Johnston	Lowe
36	11-Apr		CAMBUSLANG	2-1	Baillie	Methven	Reid	Ritchie		Hutton	Thornton	Campbell	Corson	Paterson	Johnston	Lowe
37	14-Apr		HIBERNIAN	1-1	McIntosh	Mather	Ross	Ritchie		Thornton	Thornton	Chalmers	Baird	Paterson	Johnston	Laing
38	18-Apr		Albion Rovers	0-1	Baillie	Ross	Reid	Ritchie		Thornton	Guild	Baird	Dewar	Paterson	Johnston	Laing
39	21-Apr	RCC	HEARTS	3-5	Baillie	Reid	Methven	Cuthbertson		Ritchie	Hutton	Dewar	Campbell	Paterson	Johnston	Lowe
40	24-Apr		Mossend Swifts (n)	1-1	McIntosh	Methven	Reid	Ritchie		Hutton	Ritchie	Baird	Boase	Paterson	Johnston	Lowe
41	28-Apr		LEITH ATHLETIC	0-4	McIntosh	Methven	Reid	Ritchie		Ross	Corson	Corson	McMurtie	Paterson	Lowe	Johnston
42	05-May		Hibernian	6-1	McIntosh	Methven	Reid	Hutton		Teviotdale	Guild	Sutherland	Campbell	Baillie	McLaren	Lowe
43	18-May		PARTICK THISTLE	3-0	McIntosh	Methven	Reid	Ritchie			Sutherland	Guild	Campbell	Corson	Arthur	McIntosh,J
44	16-Jun		CAMERON Highlders													
			Burntisland Thistle	?-?												

1888/89

No	Comp	Date	Opponent	Score	1	2	3	4	5	6	7	8	9	10	11	12
1		18-Aug	RENTON	1-4	McIntosh	Methven	Reid	Hutton	Ross	Ritchie	Calder	Lowe	Johnston	McMinn	Sutherland	Baillie
2		22-Aug	LEITH HARP	3-1	McIntosh	Methven	Reid	Grant	Ross	Ritchie	Lowe	Johnston	Arthur	Cannon	McMinn	Baillie
3		25-Aug	LINTHOUSE	3-3	McIntosh	Methven	Reid	Ross	Ritchie	McKail	Baillie	McMinn	Cannon	Adams	Lowe	
4	SC1	01-Sep	LEITH ATHLETIC	7-1	McIntosh	Ross	Reid	Hutton	Mackay	Hutton	BAILLIE 2	McMinn	JOHNSTON	LOWE 2	McKINNON 2	
5		08-Sep	Hearts	1-0	McIntosh	Ross	Reid	Ritchie	Grant	Hutton	Lowe	McMinn	Baillie	Johnston	Lowe	
6		15-Sep	Abercorn	5-3	McIntosh	Ross	Reid	Ross	Grant	Ritchie	Lowe	Johnston	Corson	Baillie	McMinn	
7	ESS1	22-Sep	SUNDERLAND ALBION	2-3	McIntosh	Ross	Reid	Hutton	Grant	Ritchie	Methven	Johnston	Corson	Baillie	McMinn	
8		27-Sep	HEARTS	1-1	McIntosh	Reid	Ross	Reid	Grant	Ritchie	Lowe	Methven	Corson	Baillie	McMinn	
9	SC2	29-Sep	NORTON PARK	3-1	McIntosh	Reid	Ross	Reid	Ross	Ritchie	Heathcote	LOWE	JOHNSTON	Corson	METHVEN	
10	ESS1	06-Oct	Hearts	1-2	McIntosh	Reid	Ross	Reid	Ross	Ritchie	Grant	McMinn	McMinn	Corson	Lowe	
11		13-Oct	Kirkcaldy Wanderers	2-1	McIntosh	Reid	Ross	Reid	Ross	Hutton	Heathcote	Lowe	Johnston	Arthur	LAMB	CORSON
12	SC3	20-Oct	CAMBUSLANG	2-3	McIntosh	Reid	Ross	Reid	Ross	Ritchie	Methven	Corson	Grant	Dorkin	Lowe	Johnston
13		27-Oct	NORTHERN	0-1	McIntosh	Reid	Reid	Reid	Ross	Ritchie	Ritchie	Baillie	Johnston	Dorkin	Grant	Kirkwood
14	SC4	03-Nov	CELTIC	1-1	McIntosh	Reid	Ross	Reid	Ross	Ritchie	Blades	Corson	Dorkin	Dorkin	Baillie	Lowe
15		10-Nov	ST BERNARDS 1st XI	2-1	from Baillie, Reid, Methven, Greenshields, Kennedy, Hutton, Lowe, Laing, Arthur, Lamb and Corson.											
			ST BERNARDS 2nd XI		from Scoales, Guild, Heathcote, Fleming, Garlick, McKail, Colthard, Cant, Dorkin, Forbes and Mathieson.											
16		17-Nov	QUEEN of South Wands	3-2	McIntosh	Ross	Methven	Ross	Ritchie	Grant	Hutton	Buchanan	McGhee	Lamb	Irving	
17		01-Dec	Cowlairs	1-4	Thomson	Ross	Methven	Ross	Ritchie	Grant	Hill	Corson	Forbes	Irving	Lowe	
18		08-Dec	Leith Athletic	1-1	McIntosh	Ross	Methven	Ross	Hutton	Grant	Irving	McGhee	Baillie	Cant		
19		15-Dec	ROYAL Scots Aldershot	8-0	McIntosh	Ross	Methven	Methven	Grant	Grant	McKail	Corson	Dorkin	Irving	Forbes	
20		22-Dec	HIBERNIAN	2-1	McIntosh	Ross	Methven	Methven	Grant	Hutton	McKail	Lowe	Dorkin	Dorkin	Corson	Irving
21		29-Dec	Arbroath	2-6	from McIntosh, Ross, Methven, Guild, Grant, McKail, Corson, Irving, Dorkin, Forbes and Lowe.											
22		04-Jan	CORINTHIANS	0-5	McIntosh	Adams	Methven	Ellis	McQueen	Grant	Hutton	Lowe	Buchanan	Laing	McGhee	Corson
23		05-Jan	Queen of South Wands	2-3	McIntosh	Ross	Methven	Guild	McKail	McMillan	Hutton	Lamb	Arthur	Baillie	Forbes	Lowe
24		12-Jan	Mossend Swifts	0-7	McIntosh	Ross	Methven	Ross	Forbes	Grant	McKail	Corson	Irving	Baillie	Lowe	Lamb
25		19-Jan	UNIVERSITY	10-2	McIntosh	Ross	Guild	Guild	Methven	Mackay	Guild	Corson	Baillie	Dorkin	Taylor	Taylor
26		26-Jan	Kirkcaldy Wanderers	4-0	McIntosh	Ross	Ross	McKail	Irving	Guild	Taylor	Corson	Dorkin	Dorkin	Ritchie	Baillie
27		02-Feb	Hibernian	3-3	McIntosh	Guild	Methven	Hutton	Grant	Denholm	Hutton	Corson	Mackay	Colthard	Baillie	Lowe
28		09-Feb	Cambuslang	2-1	McIntosh	Ross	Methven	Ross	Grant	Fleming	Fleming	Corson	Mackay	Mackay	Ritchie	Forbes
29		16-Feb	ST BERNARDS 1st XI	0-2	McIntosh	Guild	Girdwood	Anderson	McMillan	Fleming	Hutton	McGregor	Baillie	?	Mathieson	Lowe
			v St Bernards 2nd XI													
30		23-Feb	Partick Thistle	4-2	Scoales	Methven	Goodfellow	Guild	Ross	McKail	Ritchie	Colthard	Cant	Mackay	McEwan	Irving
31		02-Mar	Alloa Athletic	0-2	McIntosh	Methven	Guild	Ross	McKail	McMillan	Fleming	Petrie	Baillie	McEwan	Forbes	Lowe
32		09-Mar	QUEENS PARK	3-8	from McIntosh, Heathcote, Methven, Grant, Hutton, Ross, Petrie, Lowe, Corson, Baillie and AN Other. Lowe and Grant dnp											
33		16-Mar	LEITH ATHLETIC	2-3	McIntosh	White	Goodfellow	Methven	Ross	Grant	Hutton	Corson	Petrie	Irving	Baillie	Laing
34		30-Mar	HEARTS	0-1	McIntosh	Methven	Goodfellow	Methven	Milroy,WG	Grant	McGhee	Petrie	Petrie	Lowe	Lowe	
35	RCC	06-Apr	Leith Athletic (n)	2-2	McIntosh	Methven	Methven	Methven	Grant	Buchanan	Marshall	Forbes	Corson	Oswald	Britton	Forbes
36		13-Apr	NEWCASTLE WE	1-2	McIntosh	Methven	Guild	Methven	Houston	Lowe	Buchanan	Petrie	Colthard	Irving	Oswald	Lowe
37	RCC	18-Apr	LEITH ATHLETIC	2-2	McIntosh	Methven	Goodfellow	Methven	Houston	McGhee	Buchanan	Hannah	Oswald	Johnstone	Irving	Bruce
38		23-Apr	Sunderland Albion	1-4	McIntosh	Methven	Goodfellow	Guild	Ross	McGhee	McGhee	Colthard	Oswald	Irving	Johnstone	Morrison
39		27-Apr	WISHAW THISTLE	0-4	McIntosh	Methven	Methven	Goodfellow	McKail	Ross	Ritchie	McGhee	Petrie	Colthard	Lowe	Heathcote
40	RCC	30-Apr	Leith Athletic (n)	5-1	McIntosh	Methven	Anderson	Methven	Rae	McGhee	Buchanan	Morrison	Petrie	Oswald	Irving	Lowe
41		04-May	Hibernian	1-3	McIntosh	Methven	Anderson	Methven	Rae	Rae	Roberts	Waterston	Petrie	Ross	Baillie	Hannah
42		11-May	BROXBURN	1-2	McIntosh	Methven	Methven	Methven	Rae	Goodfellow	Edgar	Waterston	McGhee	Oswald	Johnstone	McNab
43	RCC	15-May	Mossend Swifts (n)	1-1	McIntosh	Methven	Methven	Methven	Rae	Love	Love	Roberts	Waterston	Petrie	Fee	Irving
44	RCC	22-May	Mossend Swifts (n)	3-4	McIntosh	Methven	Methven	Methven	Rae	Love	McGhee	Edgar	McGhee	Morrison	Oswald	Hannah
45		27-May	PRESTON NE	1-3	Jamieson	Methven	Methven	Adams	Methven	McGhee	Waterston	McGhee	Lowe	Petrie	Bruce	Baird

1889/90

#	Date		Opponent	Score											
1	10-Aug	Trial	PRACTICE	?-?											
2	17-Aug	Trial	PRACTICE	?-?											
3	24-Aug		THIRD LANARK	1-5	McIntosh	Methven	Foyers	Ross,W	Hutton	Waterston	Fee	Petrie	Bell	Bruce	Buchanan
4	31-Aug		LEITH ATHLETIC	1-7	McIntosh	Methven	Foyers	Buchanan,A	Waterston,J	Hutton	Fee	Petrie	Bruce	Buchanan,J	Cummings
5	07-Sep	SC1	HEARTS	0-3	McIntosh	Methven	Foyers	Ross	Hutton	Waterston	Petrie	Cummings	Gloag	Lowe	Petrie
6	14-Sep	ESS1	ADVENTURERS	4-0	McIntosh	Foyers	Methven	Waterston	Hutton	Ross	Hall	Foyers	Gloag	Baillie	Hall
7	21-Sep		Falkirk	1-0	McIntosh	Methven	Foyers	Ross	Foyers,R	Lamb	Petrie	Gloag	Foyers,J	Lowe	Hall
8	28-Sep		Kirkcaldy Wands	5-2	McIntosh	Methven	Foyers,A	Ross	Aitken	Waterston	Lamb	Bell	Foyers,J	Bell	Hall
9	05-Oct	ESS2	HEARTS	0-3	McIntosh	Methven	Foyers,A	Ross	Hutton	Waterston	Bishop	Foyers,J	Foyers,R	Lowe	Hall
10	12-Oct		Hibernian	5-6	McIntosh	Methven	Foyers,A	Bennett	Hutton	Waterston	Bishop	Foyers,J	Foyers,R	Lamb	Lamb
11	19-Oct		CELTIC	0-3	McIntosh	Methven	Foyers,A	Bennett	Hutton	Waterston	Bishop	Foyers,J	Foyers,R	Hall	Hall
12	26-Oct		Leith Athletic	4-4	McIntosh	Methven	Foyers,A	Walker	Hutton	Waterston	Bishop	Foyers,J	Hall	Lowe	Lamb
13	02-Nov		Falkirk	3-4	McIntosh	Guild	Foyers	Bennett	Ferguson,J	Bell	Bishop	Foyers,J	Foyers,R	Lamb	Lowe
14	09-Nov		Clyde	2-3	Scoales	Methven	Foyers,A	Walker	Hutton	Angus	Angus	Foyers,R	Angus	Hall	Hall
15	16-Nov		University	2-0	McIntosh	Methven	Foyers,A	Bell	Stevenson	Waterston	Bishop	Foyers,R	Foyers,R	Lamb	Hall
16	30-Nov		MOSSEND Swifts	2-2	Jamieson	Methven	Foyers,A	Hutton	Waterston	Pace	Smith	Angus	Angus	Hall	Lamb
17	07-Dec		Hearts	1-4	McIntosh	Methven	Foyers,A	Walker	Murdoch	Hutton	Bishop	Foyers	Foyers,R	Hall	Angus
18	14-Dec		HIBERNIAN	7-5	McIntosh	Methven	Foyers,A	Foyers,R	Hutton	Waterston	Bishop	Angus	Mackay	Hall	Lamb
19	21-Dec		RENTON	3-0	McIntosh	Methven	Foyers,A	Hutton	Murdoch	Waterston	Bishop	Foyers,J	Mackay	Hall	Lamb
20	28-Dec		BATTLEFIELD	6-1	McIntosh	Methven	Foyers,A	Walker	Murdoch	Hutton	Foyers,R	Foyers,J	Mackay	Hall	Lamb
21	02-Jan		CORINTHIANS	1-1	McIntosh	Methven	Foyers,A	Foyers,R	Walker	Foyers,R	Walker	Foyers,J	Baillie	Hall	Lamb
22	04-Jan		Renton	0-1	McIntosh	Methven	Foyers,A	Murdoch	Foyers,R	Hutton	Bishop	Angus	Mackay	Hall	Lamb
23	18-Jan		HEARTS	2-5	McIntosh	Methven	Foyers,A	Walker	Mackay	Foyers,R	Foyers,J	Bishop	Forbes	Lamb,W	Paul
24	25-Jan		Cambuslang	1-4	Scoales	Adams	Foyers,A								
25	08-Feb		Corinthians	0-2	from McIntosh, Methven, Foyers,A, Foyers,R, Murdoch, Hutton, Bishop, McGhee,J, Mackay, Hall and Lamb.										
26	22-Feb		LINTHOUSE	3-2	Scoales	Methven	Foyers,A	Foyers,R	Murdoch	Walker	Bishop	Clark	Mackay	Hall	Lamb
27	01-Mar		CLYDE	3-3	Scoales	Methven	Foyers,A	Foyers,R	Stewart	Walker	Bishop	Clark	Forbes	Hill	Hill
28	08-Mar		Partick Thistle	3-5	Scoales	Methven	Foyers,A	Foyers,R	Hutton	Walker	Bishop	Potter	Nicoll	Hill	Hill
29	15-Mar		ARBROATH	4-4	Scoales	Methven	Foyers,A	Potter	Walker	Hutton	Bishop	Potter	Nicoll	Hill	Hill
30	22-Mar		FALKIRK	2-3	Scoales	Methven	Foyers,A	Walker	Guild	Potter	Bishop	Shand,J	Nicoll	Hill	Hill
31	29-Mar		LEITH ATHLETIC	1-4	Scoales	Methven	McLeod	McPherson,J	Murdoch	McGhee	Bishop	Foyers,R	Kerr	Potter	Hall
32	05-Apr	RCC	Hearts	1-6	McIntosh	Methven	Foyers	McQueen	McGhee	Hutton	Taylor	Laing	McMahon	Hall	Baird
33	12-Apr		NOTTS COUNTY	7-0	Baillie										
34	19-Apr		GLASGOW HIBS	?-?	from Baillie, Methven, Foyers, McNab, Murdoch, Hutton, Lamb, Hall, Foyers and two others.										
35	24-Apr		DUMBARTON	3-5	Baillie	Methven	Hutton	McAulay	Hislop	McGhee	Lowe	Henderson	Groves	Lamb	Shaw
36	03-May		Motherwell	4-1	Baillie	Methven	Anderson	Murdoch	Jacob	McNab	Lowe	Lowe	Baxter	Shand	Shand
37	09-May		BOLTON WANDS	1-2	Baillie	Methven	Anderson,W	McGhee	McQueen,M	Anderson,G	Hutton	McNab	McMahon	Hall	Baxter
38	16-May		SCOTLAND XI	3-5	Baillie	Methven	Anderson,W	McQueen,M	Anderson,G	Hutton	McNab	Laing	McMahon	Hall	Shand
39	21-May		SUNDERLAND	0-1	Baillie	Methven	Anderson,W	McQueen,M	Anderson,G	Hutton	McNab	Laing	McGhee	Hall	Hall

1881

Standing: Waugh, WT Robertson (Secretary), Baillie and S Robertson.
Seated: McKinnon, Wilson, Heathcote, Bryce, Charlton and Dunn.
At Front: G McBeth and Arthur.

1895

ST BERNARDS F.C (1894-95).
Winners of the Scottish Cup.
Back Row—JAMES OSWALD, G. M'LAREN, J. PATON (secy.), W. M. LAPSLEY (pres.), R. ANDERSON, H. WEIR, B. CROSSAN.
Seated—P. M'MANUS, J. ROBERTSON, G. MURDOCH, JAS. SNEDDON, R. FOYER.
In Front—R. LAING, D. PATON, JAS. CLELAND, C. HALL.

1895

Standing: James Wilson (Trainer), Pillar, Murdoch, McLean, Robertson, McKinnon, Russell and Wilson.
Seated: Clelland, Laing, Paton and Hall.

1899

St Bernard's in the dark jerseys – players' names unknown.

1890/91

ST BERNARDS FC

#	Date		Opponent	Score											
1	09-Aug		Raith Rovers	2-4	Robertson	Methven	Ross	Hislop	Murdoch	Hutton	Taylor	Clements	Phillips	HALL	McNab
2	13-Aug	Disp	Leith Athletic (n)	1-3	Baillie	Methven	Ross	Hall,A	Murdoch	Hutton	Taylor	Dorkin	Phillips	Hall,C	McNab
3	16-Aug		MOTHERWELL	3-1	Baillie	Robertson	Methven	Hutton	Reid	Phillips	Taylor	Dorkin	Baxter	Hall	McNab
4	23-Aug		Our Boys	4-5	Baillie	Methven	Ross	Reid	Murdoch	Hutton	Dorkin	Taylor	Phillips	Hall	McNab
5	30-Aug		HIBERNIAN	3-1	Baillie	Methven	Hutton	Murdoch	Reid	Hogg	Dorkin	Lowe	Baxter	Hall	McNab
6	06-Sep	SC1	ADVENTURERS	7-0	Baillie	Methven	Ross	Hutton	Murdoch	Hutton	LOWE	Hogg	Baxter	HALL 2	McNab
7	13-Sep		QUEENS PARK	2-2	Baillie	Methven	Ross	Ross	Murdoch	Hutton	Dorkin	Lowe	Baxter	Hall	McNab

EDINBURGH SAINTS FC

| 8 | 20-Sep | | Clackmannan | 5-2 | Baillie | Methven | Murdoch | Reid | Baxter | Hutton | Lowe | Corson | Hall | McMillan | McNab |
| 9 | 27-Sep | | Renton | 2-5 | Robertson | Methven | Fleming | Reid | Murdoch | Hutton | Williams | Corson | Hall | McMillan | McNab |

EDINBURGH NORTHERN FC

10	06-Dec		West Calder	2-0	from Baillie, Hogg, Sinclair, Jacobs, Lawrie, Scott,J, Scott,FW, Lowe, Smellie and Baxter										
11	13-Dec		BURNBANK SWIFTS	3-1	Baillie	Hall	Sinclair	Edgar	Govan	Lawrie	Lowe	Scott,J	Scott,FW	Baxter	Smellie
12	20-Dec		MOSSEND SWIFTS	1-4	Baillie	Hogg	Sinclair	Edgar	Govan	Lawrie	Lowe	Scott,FW	Scott,J	Baxter	Smellie
13	27-Dec		BROXBURN	7-3	Scoales	Sinclair	Hogg	Lawrie	Govan	Edgar	Scott,FW	Lowe,JW	Scott,J	Baxter	Smellie
14	03-Jan		ARMADALE	1-0	Baillie	Sinclair	Hogg	Lawrie	Govan	Edgar	Scott,FW	Lowe,JW	Scott,J	Baxter	Smellie
15	17-Jan		Broxburn	2-3	from Baillie, Sinclair, Hogg, Lawrie, Govan, Edgar, Scott,FW, Lowe, Baxter, Graham and Smellie.										
16	24-Jan		Leith Athletic	1-7	Hogg	Sinclair	Lawrie	Graham	Edgar	Scott,J	Lowe,J	Scott,FW	Baxter	Taylor	Smellie
17	07-Feb		Kirkcaldy Wanderers	3-3											
18	14-Feb		CAMERON Highlanders	2-1	Baillie	Philip	Hogg	Baxter	Robertson	Edgar	Couper	Lowe	Scott,J	Scott,FW	McDonald
19	21-Feb		LEITH HIBERNIAN	1-2	Johnston	Adam	Hogg	Philip	Robertson	Edgar	Scott,FW	Lowe	Neilson	Baxter	MacBeath
20	07-Mar		Lochgelly United	6-1	from Baillie, Adam, Hogg, Philip, Scott,J, Edgar, Scott, FW, Neilson, Smellie, Baxter and McDonald
21	14-Mar		WHITEFIELD	3-1	Baillie	'Swainbury'	Philip	Lawrie	Scott	Edgar	Hamilton	McDonald	Baxter	Scott	Smellie
22	21-Mar		UNIVERSITY	3-1	Baillie	Hogg	Philip	Lawrie	Scott	Edgar	Scott,FW	Baxter	McDonald	Hamilton	McDonald
23	28-Mar		Montrose	0-8	from Scoales, Philip, Hogg, Lawrie, Guild, Garrand, Scott, Lowe, Couper, Hamilton and McDonald.										
24	04-Apr		LEITH HIBERNIAN	4-4	Scoales	Philip	Hogg	McLean	Lawrie	Edgar	Scott	Couper	Smeaton	Hamilton	McDonald
25	11-Apr		CARRINGTON	0-0	Baillie	Philip	McLean	Lawrie	Baxter	Edgar	Couper	Lawrie	Smeaton	Hamilton	McDonald
26	18-Apr		KIRKCALDY	3-1	Baillie	Philip	McLean	Archibald	Baxter	Edgar	Smellie	Lowe	Hogg	Hamilton	McLeod
27	25-Apr		Hearts 2nd XI	1-4	Baillie	Philip	McLean	Lawrie	Reid	Edgar	Scott	Lowe	Hogg	Hamilton	McLeod
28	02-May		LEITH ATHLETIC	0-1	Baillie	Methven	Philip	Reid	Murdoch	Edgar	McLeod	Dorkin	Guthrie	Lowe	McNab

ST BERNARDS FC

29	09-May		HEARTS 2nd XI	2-4	from Baillie, Methven, Philip, Reid, Murdoch, Hutton, Dorkin, McLeod, Baxter, Sutherland and McNab.										
30	16-May		Armadale	0-2	McEwan	Methven	Methven	Philip	Edgar	Baxter	McNab	Hutton	McLeod	Hogg	Sutherland
31	21-May		RENTON	1-2	Baillie	Methven	Methven	Philip	Baxter	Murdoch	McLeod	Baxter	McLeod	Mackay	Sutherland
32	23-May		Thistle	0-4	McEwan	Methven	Methven	Philip	Baxter	Baxter	McLeod	Murdoch	Edgar	Lowe	McNab

1891/92

#	Date		Opponent	Score											
1	08-Aug	SA	KINGS PARK	2-4	Baillie	Philip	O'Hara	McNab	Wardrop	Ballantyne	Clark	Mackay	SUTHERLAND	Marr	McDONALD
2	15-Aug	SA	Ayr	2-6	Baillie	Hogg	Hogg	McNab	Wardrop	Edgar	Scott	Clark	Mackay	Sutherland	McDonald
3	18-Aug		HEARTS	3-3	Baillie	Philip	Hogg	McNab	Wardrop	Guthrie	Clark	Scott,F	Mackay	Marr	Sutherland
4	22-Aug	SA	EAST STIRLING	4-1	Baillie	Philip	Hogg	McNab	Wardrop	Edgar	'Williams'	SCOTT	MACKAY 3	MARR	Sutherland
5	29-Aug	SA	Airdrie	3-3	Baillie	Philip	Hogg	McNab	Wardrop	Guthrie	Clark	Scott	Sutherland	MARR	McDonald
6	05-Sep	SC1	Adventurers	5-0	Baillie	PHILIP	WARDROP	Guthrie	McNab	Guthrie	CLARK	Scott	LOWE	MARR	Sutherland
7	12-Sep	SA	Linthouse	2-1	Baillie	Philip	Foyers,R	McNab	Wardrop	Guthrie	CLARK	SCOTT	WILLIAMS	'Williams'	Sutherland
8	19-Sep	SA	KILMARNOCK	3-2	Baillie	Philip	Foyers,R	McNab	Wardrop	Guthrie	CLARK	SCOTT	'Williams'	SUTHERLAND	McDonald
9	26-Sep	SC2	DUNIPACE	7-1	Baillie	Foyers	'James'	WARDROP	WARDROP	Guthrie	LOWE	SCOTT	DORKIN 2	SUTHERLAND 2	SMELLIE
10	03-Oct		Vale of Gala	15-0	from McEwan, James, Scott, McNab, Reid, Guthrie, Clark, Scott, Dorkin, Sutherland and Lowe.										
11	10-Oct	SA	Morton	1-3	Baillie	Philip	Foyers	Philip	Wardrop	Guthrie	Clark	Scott	Dorkin	SUTHERLAND	McDonald
12	17-Oct	SC3	KIRKINTILLOCH Ath	5-1	Baillie	Philip	Foyers	McNab	Wardrop	Guthrie	CLARK 2	Stuart	Stuart	Sutherland	McDONALD 3
13	24-Oct	SA	East Stirling	3-3	Baillie	Philip	Foyers	McNab	Wardrop	Guthrie	CLARK	SCOTT	Stuart	Sutherland	McDonald
14	31-Oct		MOSSEND SWIFTS	6-4	Baillie	Philip	Foyers	McNab	Wardrop	Stuart	Clark	Guthrie	Guthrie	Sutherland	McDonald
15	07-Nov	SA	Partick Thistle	7-0	Baillie	Philip	Foyers	McNab	Wardrop	Guthrie	CLARK 2	SCOTT	STUART 2	McDONALD	SUTHERLAND
16	14-Nov	SA	AYR	2-2	Baillie	Philip	Foyers	McNab	Wardrop	Guthrie	Clark	LOWE	Stuart	Sutherland	McDONALD
17	21-Nov		Corinthians	3-5	from Baillie, Philip, Foyers, Reid, Guthrie, Clark, Scott, Stuart, Sutherland and McDonald.										
18	28-Nov	SC5	Rangers	1-5	Baillie	Philip	Foyers	Reid	Baird	McNab	Clark	Stuart	Stuart	Sutherland	McDonald
19	05-Dec		AIRDRIE	3-2	Baillie	Philip	Foyers	Philip	Wardrop	McNab	Clark	Stuart	Stuart	Sutherland	Baxter
20	12-Dec	ESS1	RAITH ROVERS	3-2	Baillie	Foyers	McNab	Guthrie	BAIRD	Scott,J	CLARK	Clark	Stuart	CHRISTIE 2	Sutherland
21	19-Dec	SA	GLASGOW Northern	4-1	Baillie	Philip	Foyers	McNab	BAIRD	Guthrie	CLARK	Clark	Stuart	Lawrie	McDONALD
22	26-Dec	SA	Kings Park	2-0	Baillie	Philip	Foyers	McNab	Baird	Guthrie	Sutherland	Reid	STUART	Christie	McDonald
23	02-Jan		CORINTHIANS	2-1	Baillie	Foyers	Foyers	McNab	Baird	Reid,J	McDonald	Sutherland	Stuart	Christie	Scott
24	09-Jan	ESSs	BATHGATE Rovers	4-1	Baillie	Philip	Foyers	McNab	Wardrop	Baird	Sutherland	Sutherland	Baxter	Scott	McDonald
25	16-Jan		Leith Athletic	1-3	Baillie	Foyers	Philip	Reid	McNab	McNab	McDonald	Reid	Stuart	Christie	Scott
26	23-Jan		BURNBANK Swifts	7-2	Baillie	Robertson	Philip	Foyers	Baird	Edgar	Clark	Christie	Christie	Christie	Sutherland
27	30-Jan	SA	GLASGOW Th	6-0	Baillie	Foyers	Foyers	Baird	Robertson	McNab	CLARK 2	Christie	STUART	SUTHERLAND 2	McDonald
28	06-Feb	SA	Port Glasgow Ath	2-4	Baillie	Philip	Foyers	McNab	Robertson	McNab	Clark	Christie	Stuart	Sutherland	McDONALD
29	13-Feb		LEITH ATHLETIC	0-2	Baillie	Philip	Foyers	McNab	Wardrop	Wardrop	Scott	Christie	Stuart	Sutherland	McDonald
30	20-Feb		Johnstone Wands	3-7	from Baillie, Philip, Foyers, McNab, Wardrop, Baird, Scott, Christie, Stuart, Sutherland and McDonald.										
31	27-Feb	ESSf	HEARTS	0-2	Baillie	Philip	Foyers	McNab	Baird	McDonald,G	Sutherland	Christie	Hogg	McDonald	Scott
32	05-Mar	SA	Glasgow Thistle	2-1	Baillie	Philip	Foyers	McNab	Baird	McDonald,J	Sutherland	Scott	HOGG	ROBERTSON	Sutherland
33	12-Mar	SA	PORT Glasgow Ath	4-2	McQueen	Philip	Robertson,T	McNab	Baird	Turner	McDONALD,J	SCOTT 2	Sutherland	Hume	Young
34	19-Mar	SA	PARTICK THISTLE	3-1	Baillie	Philip	Foyers	McNab	Baird	McDonald,G	McDONALD,J	Scott	SCOTT 2	Robertson,T	Young
35	26-Mar	SA	LINTHOUSE	3-3	Baillie	Foyers	Robertson,F	McNab	Baird	McDonald,G	McDONALD,J	Scott	Ellis,D	CHRISTIE	SUTHERLAND
36	02-Apr	SA	MORTON	1-1	Baillie	Foyers	Foyers	McNab	Baird	Marshall	McDONALD,J	Baillie	Philip	Christie	Sutherland
37	09-Apr	SA	Kilmarnock	0-1	Baillie	Philip	Foyers	McDonald,G	Baird	Marshall	McDonald,J	Scott	Baird	LINDSAY	SUTHERLAND
38	16-Apr	SA	AIRDRIE	4-1	Baillie	Philip	Foyers	McNab	Baird	Marshall	McDONALD,J 2	Baillie	Stuart	McNab	Sutherland
39	23-Apr		Leith Athletic	1-2	Baillie	Philip	FOYERS	McNab	Baird	Marshall	Scott	Scott	McDonald,G	Christie	Robertson
40	30-Apr	SA	Glasgow Northern	2-4	Baillie	Philip	Foyers	McDonald	Baird	Marshall	McDONALD 2	Anderson	Hogg	Lindsay	Sutherland
41	16-May		HEARTS	1-3	Baillie	Philip	Foyers	McNab	Baird	Marshall	Scott	Scott	McDonald,G	McNab	
42	21-May	RCCs	LEITH ATHLETIC	1-3	Baillie	Adams	Anderson,W	Begbie	Anderson,G	Marshall	McLeod	Scott	Laing	Blessington	Baird
43	23-May		GLASGOW Lge	1-2											

1992/93

#	Date		Opponent	Score											
1	04-Aug		Penicuik Athletic	5-2	Baillie	Philip	Cowan	Begbie	Baird	McNab	Dobie	Foyers	Russell	Blessington	Taylor
2	06-Aug		MORTON	5-0	Baillie	Philip	Cowan	McNAB	Baird	McDonald	Scott	Dobie	RUSSELL	Robertson	CHRISTIE
3	13-Aug	SA	Cowlairs	3-7	Baillie	Foyers	PHILIP	Murdoch	Baird	McNab	Scott	ROBERTSON	JOHNSTONE	Mackie	DOBIE 2
4	20-Aug	SA	LINTHOUSE	5-1	Baillie	Philip		Foyers	Baird	McNab	SCOTT 2	CHAMBERS	MANN	MANN	Dobie
5	27-Aug	SA	Partick Thistle	4-3	Baillie	Philip		Foyers	Baird	McNab	SCOTT 2	CHAMBERS	MACKIE	MANN 2	DOBIE
6	03-Sep	SA	CAMBUSLANG	7-0	Baillie	Philip		Foyers	Baird	McNab	SCOTT 2	ROBERTSON	MACKIE	Mann	Crossan
7	10-Sep	SA	COWLAIRS	2-3	Baillie	'Jones'		Foyers	Baird	McNab	SCOTT 2	Mann	MACKIE	DOBIE	CROSSAN
8	17-Sep	SA	AIRDRIE	4-2	Baillie	Philip		Foyers	Baird	McNab	Scott	Johnstone	Mackie	Dobie	CROSSAN
9	24-Sep	SA	Kilmarnock	3-1	Baillie	Philip		Foyers	Baird	McNab	Scott	Johnstone	Mackie	Dobie	Crossan
10	01-Oct	SA	Linthouse	1-3	Baillie	Philip		Foyers	Baird	McNab	Scott	Dobie	Mackie	Stuart	Crossan
11	08-Oct		Kings Park	5-3	Baillie	Philip		Foyers	Baird	McNab	SCOTT	JOHNSTONE	MACKIE 2	STUART 2	CROSSAN
12	15-Oct	SA	GLASGOW THISTLE	7-3	Baillie	Philip		Robertson	Baird	McNab	SCOTT	JOHNSTONE	Stuart	Dobie	CROSSAN 2
13	22-Oct	SA	Vale of Leven	3-1	Baillie	Philip		Robertson	Baird	McNab	Scott	Johnstone	Mackie	Stuart	Crossan
14	29-Oct	SA	ALBION ROVERS	3-0	Baillie	Foyers		Robertson,T, McNab, Baird, Murdoch, Scott, Johnstone, Mackie, Stuart, Dobie and Crossan.							
15	05-Nov		Corinthians	2-5	from Baillie, Philip, Robertson,T, McNab, Baird, Murdoch, Scott, Johnstone, Mackie, Stuart, Dobie and Crossan.										
16	07-Nov		HLI Aldershot	2-3	Baillie	Philip		Robertson	Murdoch	McNab	Crossan	Dobie	Mackie	Johnstone	Scott
17	12-Nov	SA	Cambuslang	3-1											
18	26-Nov	SC1	QUEEN of South W	3-2	Baillie	Philip		Foyers	McNab	Murdoch	SCOTT	Johnstone	MACKIE 3	DOBIE	Crossan
19	03-Dec		St Mirren	1-1	McQueen	Philip		Robertson	McNab	McCartney	Scott	McDonald	Collins	Dobie	Crossan
20	17-Dec	SC2	Royal Albert	5-2	Baillie	Philip		Foyers	McNab	Murdoch	SCOTT 2	Johnstone	MACKIE	Dobie	CROSSAN
21	24-Dec	SC2	ROYAL ALBERT	4-0	Baillie	Philip		Foyers	McNab	Murdoch	Scott	Johnstone	MACKIE	Dobie	CROSSAN
22	31-Dec		AYR	4-3	Baillie	Robertson,W		Foyers	McNab	Murdoch	Scott	Johnstone	Mackie	Dobie	Crossan
23	02-Jan		COWLAIRS	2-2	Baillie	Philip		Foyers	McNab	'Urquhart'	Scott	Johnstone	Mackie	Dobie	Crossan
24	04-Jan		CORINTHIANS	2-0	Baillie	Philip		Foyers	McNab	Robertson,T	Scott	Johnstone	Mackie	Dobie	Crossan
25	14-Jan		LEITH ATHLETIC	5-4	Baillie	Philip		Foyers	McNab	Robertson,T	Scott	Laverock	Mackie	Dobie	Crossan
26	21-Jan	ESS	LEITH ATHLETIC	3-2	Baillie	Philip		Foyers	McNab	Murdoch	Scott	LAVEROCK	JOHNSTONE	DOBIE	Laverock
27	28-Jan	SC3	RANGERS	0-5	Baillie	Philip		Foyers	McNab	Murdoch	Scott	Johnstone	Mackie	Dobie	Crossan
28	04-Feb	SCs	Celtic	3-1	Baillie	Philip		Foyers	McNab	Murdoch	Scott	Johnstone	Mackie	Dobie	Crossan
29	18-Feb	ESS	Raith Rovers	4-6	Baillie	Philip		Foyers	McNab	Murdoch	Scott	Johnstone	Mackie	Dobie	Crossan
30	25-Feb	ESSs	Hearts	0-6	from Baillie, Arnott, Foyers, McNab, McDonald, Murdoch, Johnstone, Laverock, Collins, Dobie and Crossan.										
31	04-Mar		GLASGOW Northern	7-0	Baillie	Arnott		Philip	McNab	McDONALD	SCOTT	LAVEROCK 2	COLLINS	DOBIE	CROSSAN
32	11-Mar		Everton	0-5	Baillie	Philip		Foyers	McNab	Murdoch	Scott	Laverock	Collins	Dobie	Crossan
33	18-Mar	SA	PARTICK THISTLE	0-0	Baillie	Arnott		Philip	McNab	Johnstone	Scott	Laverock	Crossan	Dobie	Landels
34	25-Mar	SA	Glasgow Thistle	2-5	Baillie	Arnott		Arnott	McNab	McDonald	SCOTT 2	Johnstone	STEEL	DOBIE	Crossan
35	01-Apr	SA	KILMARNOCK	5-0	Baillie	Arnott		Foyers	McNab	McDonald	SCOTT	Johnstone	STEEL	Dobie	Crossan
36	08-Apr	SA	GLASGOW Northern	2-2	Baillie	Arnott		Laverock	McNab	McDonald	SCOTT	JOHNSTONE	Steel	Dobie	Crossan
37	15-Apr	SA	Airdrie	2-2	Baillie	Robertson		Foyers	McNab	McDonald	Scott	JOHNSTONE 2	Steel	Dobie	Crossan
38	17-Apr		Arbroath	3-2	Baillie	Philip		McCartney	Chalmers	McDonald	SCOTT 2	JOHNSTONE	Johnstone	Dobie	Crossan
39	18-Apr		WOLVerhampton W	0-3	Baillie	McCartney		Foyers	McNab	McDonald	Scott	Murdoch	Laing	Dobie	Laverock
40	22-Apr	SA	VALE OF LEVEN	2-1	Baillie	McCartney		McCartney	McNab	McDonald	Scott	Johnstone	'Small'	Dobie	Crossan
41	29-Apr		LEITH ATHLETIC	0-3											
42	04-May	SA	SCOTLAND	0-1	Baillie	McQueen		Arnott	McNab	McNab	Scott	Steel	Mackie	Dobie	Crossan
43	06-May		Glasgow Northern												
44	08-May		Hearts	3-3	Baillie	Arnott		Arnott	McNab	McNab	Scott	Waddell	Oswald	Dobie	Crossan
45	13-May	RCCs	Broxburn	(n) 4-2											
46	27-May	RCCf	Hearts	(n) 2-2	Baillie	Baird		Philip	Gallagher	McDonald	Cleghorn	Scott	Laing	Dobie	Landels
47	30-May		HEARTS												

1893/94

#	Date	Opponent	Comp	Score											
1	05-Aug	Hearts		0-4	Lindsay	Arnott	Foyers	McNab	Baird	Murdoch	Adams	Steel	Oswald	Dobie	Crossan
2	12-Aug	LEITH ATHLETIC		2-1	Lindsay	Arnott	Foyers	Murdoch	Baird	Sibbald	McNab	Steel	Oswald	Crossan	Adams
3	19-Aug	Third Lanark	SL1	3-5	Lindsay	Arnott	Foyers	Sibbald	Baird	McDonald	SCOTT 2	STEEL	Oswald	Crossan	Brady
4	26-Aug	RANGERS	SL1	0-0	Lindsay	Arnott	Foyers	Sibbald	Baird	Murdoch	Scott	Dobie	OSWALD 2	CROSSAN	BRADY
5	02-Sep	Dumbarton	SL1	5-1	Lindsay	Arnott	Foyers	Sibbald	Baird	MURDOCH	McNab	McNAB 2	Smeaton	Crossan	BRADY
6	09-Sep	St Mirren	SL1	3-1	Lindsay	ARNOTT	Foyers	Sibbald	McDonald	Murdoch	Laverock	Steel	Oswald	Dobie	Brady
7	16-Sep	RAITH ROVERS		4-0	Fyfe	Philip	Robertson	Martin	McDonald	Murdoch	Scott	McNab	Smeaton	CROSSAN	Brady
8	18-Sep	Leith Athletic	SL1	2-4	Lindsay	Arnott	Foyers	Sibbald	Baird	Murdoch	Scott	McNab	Oswald	Crossan	Brady
9	23-Sep	RENTON	SL1	4-2	Lindsay	Arnott	Foyers	Sibbald	McNab	Murdoch	Scott	McNAB	OSWALD	CROSSAN	BRADY
10	30-Sep	Dundee	SL1	3-1	Lindsay	Arnott	FOYERS	Sibbald	Baird	Murdoch	Laverock	STEEL	OSWALD	CROSSAN	Brady
11	07-Oct	HEARTS	SL1	1-2	Lindsay	Arnott	Foyers	Sibbald	McNab	Murdoch	Scott	Laing	Oswald	Crossan	Brady
12	14-Oct	Celtic	SL1	2-5	Lindsay	Arnott	Foyers	Sibbald	Baird	McNab	Johnstone	Laing	OSWALD 4	CROSSAN	BRADY
13	21-Oct	THIRD LANARK	SL1	6-2	Lindsay	Robertson,W	FOYERS	Sibbald	Baird	Murdoch	Scott	Laing	Oswald	Crossan	Brady
14	28-Oct	Renton	SL1	1-0	Lindsay	Arnott	Foyers	Sibbald	Baird	McNab	Johnstone	LAING	OSWALD	CROSSAN	Brady
15	04-Nov	DUMBARTON	SL1	2-1	Lindsay	Arnott	Arnott	Sibbald	Baird	McNab	McNab	LAING	Johnstone	Crossan	Brady
16	11-Nov	Corinthians		3-2	Lindsay	Foyers	Foyers	Murdoch	Baird	Steel	Hobbs	McNab	Laing	Crossan	Brady
17	13-Nov	Oxford University		1-1	Lindsay	Arnott	Foyers	Murdoch	Robertson	Sibbald	Wilson	McNab	Laing	Crossan	BRADY
18	18-Nov	Leith Athletic		0-1	Lindsay	Arnott	Foyers	Sibbald	Baird	Murdoch	Wilson	McNab	Laing	Landels	Brady
19	25-Nov	Kilmarnock	SC1	3-1	Lindsay	Arnott	Foyers	Sibbald	Baird	Murdoch	Wilson	McNAB	Laing	Crossan	Brady
20	02-Dec	Queens Park		0-6	Lindsay	Arnott	Foyers	Sibbald	Baird	Murdoch	Wilson	McNab	Laing	Landels	BRADY
21	09-Dec	Leith Athletic (n)	ESS	2-3	Lindsay	Arnott	Foyers	Sibbald	Baird	Murdoch	Wilson	McNab	Laing	Landels	Phillips
22	16-Dec	Dumbarton	SC2	3-1	Lindsay	Arnott	Foyers	Sibbald	Baird	Murdoch	WILSON	SCOTT 2	Laing	Scott	Wilson
23	23-Dec	HIBERNIAN		0-3	Lindsay	Arnott	Foyers	Baird	Sibbald	Murdoch	Phillips	Crossan	Steel	Crossan	Brady
24	30-Dec	CASUALS		4-0	Lindsay	Arnott	Foyers	Sibbald	Baird	Murdoch	Wilson	Laing	Steel	Crossan	Brady
25	02-Jan	CORINTHIANS		4-0	Lindsay	Arnott	Foyers	Sibbald	Baird	Murdoch	Wilson	McNab	Steel	Crossan	Brady
26	13-Jan	Celtic	SC3	1-8	Lindsay	Arnott	Foyers	Sibbald	Baird	Murdoch	Wilson	Laing	OSWALD	CROSSAN	BRADY
27	20-Jan	CELTIC		1-2	Lindsay	'Frost,J'	Foyers	Sibbald	Baird	Murdoch	Wilson	LAING	Laing	Crossan	Brady
28	27-Jan	DUNDEE	SL1	3-5	Lindsay	Arnott	Foyers	McNab	Baird	Murdoch	Wilson	LAING	OSWALD	CROSSAN	Brady
29	03-Feb	RENTON	SL1	2-0	Lindsay	Arnott	Foyers	McNab	Baird	Murdoch	Wilson	Laing	Somerville	Crossan	Brady
30	17-Feb	Hibernian		2-4	Lindsay	Cowan	Arnott	McNab	Baird	Sibbald	Wilson	LAVEROCK	Oswald	Crossan	Brady
31	24-Feb	Wishaw Thistle		6-5	Lindsay	Arnott	Foyers	McNab	Baird	Murdoch	Wilson	Laing	Oswald	Crossan	Brady
32	10-Mar	LEITH ATHLETIC	SL1	3-2	Lindsay	Arnott	Foyers	McNab	Baird	Sibbald	Wilson	Laing	Oswald	CROSSAN 2	Brady
33	17-Mar	Aberdeen		8-1	from Lindsay, Arnott, Foyers, McNab, Baird, Murdoch, Wilson, Laing, Oswald, Crossan and Brady										
34	24-Mar	Leith Athletic (n)	CC	2-1	Lindsay	Robertson	Foyers	McNab	Baird	Murdoch	Wilson	Laing	Oswald	Crossan	Brady
35	31-Mar	ST MIRREN	SL1	8-3	Lindsay	Foyers	Foyers	McNAB	Baird	Murdoch	WILSON 2	LAING	Oswald	CROSSAN	BRADY 3
36	07-Apr	Hearts	SL1	4-2	Lindsay	Foyers	Foyers	McNab	Baird	Murdoch	WILSON	Laing	Oswald	Crossan	Brady
37	14-Apr	DUMBARTON		1-1	Arnott	Foyers	Arnott	McNab	Baird	Murdoch	Wilson	Laing	Oswald	Crossan	Brady
38	16-Apr	SUNDERLAND		2-4	Lindsay	Foyers	Cowan	McNab	Baird	Murdoch	Wilson	Laing	Oswald	Crossan	Brady
39	18-Apr	Rangers	SL1	2-1*	Lindsay	Foyers	Cowan	McNab	McDonald	Murdoch	Wilson	Laing	Somerville	Crossan	Brady
40	21-Apr	HEARTS		0-3	Lindsay	Foyers	Cowan	McDonald	Baird	Murdoch	Wilson	Laverock	Laing	Crossan	Moultrie
41	28-Apr	DERBY COUNTY		2-6	'Ross'	Foyers	Cowan	McNab	Baird	Murdoch	Wilson	Laing	Oswald	Crossan	Brady
42	02-May	Rangers	SL1	2-1	Lindsay	Foyers	Cowan	McNab	Baird	Murdoch	WILSON	LAING	Oswald	Crossan	Brady
43	05-May	Hibernian (n)	CCf	1-1	Lindsay	Foyers	Cowan	McNab	Baird	Murdoch	Wilson	Laing	Oswald	Crossan	Brady
44	09-May	Hibernian (n)	CCf	1-4	Lindsay	Foyers	Cowan	McNab	Baird	Murdoch	Wilson	LAING	Oswald	Crossan	Brady
45	16-May	Hibernian (n)	RCCs	1-2	Lindsay	Foyers	Cowan	McManus	Baird	Stewart	Wilson	Baxter	Oswald	Crossan	Brady
46	19-May	East Stirling		5-1	Lindsay	Foyers	Cowan	McManus	Baird	Robertson	Wilson	Laing	Oswald	Crossan	Brady

1894/95

#	Date	Comp	Opponent	Score												
1	02-Aug		BLACK WATCH	1-0	Sneddon	Foyers	Cowan	McManus	Murdoch	Robertson	Wilson	Pratt	Laing	Paton	Crossan
2	04-Aug		Leith Athletic	3-0	Sneddon	Foyers	Cowan	Oswald,W	McManus	Murdoch	Wilson	Laing	Oswald	Paton	Crossan
3	11-Aug		HEARTS	3-2	Sneddon	Foyers	Cowan	Martin	Baird	Murdoch	Wilson	Laing	Oswald	Paton	Crossan
4	18-Aug	SL1	CELtic	2-5	Sneddon	Foyers	Cowan	Martin	Baird	Murdoch	Wilson	Laing	OSWALD	Paton	Crossan
5	25-Aug	SL1	RANGERS	1-4	Sneddon	Foyers	Cowan	McManus	Baird	Murdoch	Wilson	PATON	Oswald	Crossan	Brady
6	01-Sep		Newton Heath	5-2	Sneddon	Foyers	Cowan	Martin	Baird	Murdoch	Wilson	Laing	Oswald	McManus	Brady
7	08-Sep	SL1	Clyde	4-1	Sneddon	Foyers	Cowan	McManus	MURDOCH	WILSON	Laing	Oswald	CROSSAN	Brady
8	15-Sep	SL1	Dumbarton	4-3	Sneddon	Foyers	Cowan	McManus	Baird	Murdoch	Wilson	Laing	OSWALD 2	Crossan	BRADY
9	17-Sep	SL1	LEITH ATHLETIC	6-3	Sneddon	Foyers	Cowan	McManus	Baird	Murdoch	WILSON	Laing	OSWALD 2	PATON	BRADY 2
10	22-Sep	SL1	CLYDE	0-3	Sneddon	Brown	Cowan	McManus	Baird	Murdoch	Wilson	Laing	Oswald	Paton	Crossan
11	29-Sep	SL1	Dundee	2-2	Sneddon	Foyers	Cowan	McManus	Baird	Murdoch	WILSON	Laing	OSWALD	CROSSAN	Paton
12	06-Oct	SL1	Hearts	3-4	Sneddon	Foyers	Cowan	McManus	Baird	Murdoch	Wilson	LAING	OSWALD	LEARMONTH	Crossan
13	13-Oct	SL1	Leith Athletic	2-0	Sneddon	Foyers	Cowan	McManus	Baird	Murdoch	WILSON	Laing	OSWALD	Crossan	Lafferty
14	20-Oct	SL1	THIRD LANARK	2-4	Sneddon	Foyers	Cowan	McManus	Murdoch	Baird	WILSON 2	LAING	OSWALD	Crossan	Sharp
15	27-Oct	ESL	Leith Athletic	5-2	Sneddon	Foyers	Cowan	McManus	Baird	Murdoch	Wilson	Laing	Oswald	Lafferty	Sharp
16	03-Nov	SL1	ST MIRREN	2-0	Sneddon	Foyers	Cowan	McManus	Kirkwood	McManus	Wilson	Laing	OSWALD	Crossan	SHARP
17	10-Nov	SL1	CELTIC	0-2	Sneddon	Foyers	Cowan	McManus	Baird	Kirkwood	Wilson	Lafferty	Oswald	Crossan	Sharp
18	24-Nov	SC1	AIRDRIE	4-2	Sneddon	Kirkwood	Cowan	McManus	Murdoch	MURDOCH	WILSON	LAING	Oswald	Crossan	PATON
19	03-Dec		Woolwich Arsenal	2-1	Sneddon	Cowan	Foyers	McManus	Kirkwood	Kirkwood	Wilson	Laing	Oswald	Sharp	Crossan
20	04-Dec		Corinthians	1-2	Sneddon	Cowan	Foyers	Murdoch	Baird	McManus	Sharp	Crossan	Laing	Paton	Wilson
21	08-Dec	SL1	DUNDEE	2-0	Sneddon	Foyers	Cowan	McManus	McManus	Wilson	MURDOCH	PATON	Oswald	Lafferty	Sharp
22	15-Dec	SC2	KILMARNOCK	3-1	Sneddon	Foyers	Cowan	McManus	Baird	Murdoch	WILSON 2	LAING	Oswald	Paton	Linton
23	22-Dec	SL1	DUMBARTON	5-0	Sneddon	Foyers	Cowan	McManus	BAIRD	MURDOCH	WILSON	Paton	OSWALD	LAING	Sharp
24	29-Dec		Raith Rovers	4-2	Sneddon	Foyers	Cowan	McManus	Baird	Murdoch	Wilson	Paton	Oswald	Laing	Clelland
25	02-Jan		CORINTHIANS	0-0	Sneddon	Foyers	Cowan	Kirkwood	BAIRD	McManus	Wilson	Paton	Oswald	Crossan	Clelland
26	05-Jan		Third Lanark	0-6	Sneddon	Baird	Robertson	Christie	McManus	Laing	Lafferty	Paton	Crossan	Clelland
27	02-Feb		Clyde	6-2	Sneddon	Foyers	Bard	Foyers	Murdoch	McManus	Wilson	Paton	Oswald	Crossan	Clelland
28	09-Feb		CELTIC	4-0	Sneddon	Foyers	Hall	Foyers	Robertson	Robertson	Laing	Paton	Oswald	Crossan	Black
29	23-Feb	SC3	Clyde	2-1	Sneddon	Baird	Foyers	McManus	Robertson	Murdoch	Wilson	Paton	Adams	CROSSAN	CLELLAND
30	02-Mar		HIBERNIAN	1-2	Sneddon	Baird	Foyers	McManus	Robertson	Murdoch	Laing	Paton	Murieson	Crossan	Clelland
31	09-Mar	SCs	Hearts	0-0	Sneddon	Baird	Foyers	McManus	Robertson	Murdoch	Laing	Paton	HALL	Crossan	Clelland
32	16-Mar	SCs	Hearts	1-0	Sneddon	Hall	Baird	McManus	Robertson	Murdoch	Laing	Paton	OSWALD	Laing	Sharp
33	23-Mar		St Mirren	1-0	Sneddon	Hall	Foyers	McManus	Middleton	Linton	Paton	Crossan	Oswald	Crossan	Clelland
34	30-Mar	ESL	HIBERNIAN	1-5	Sneddon	Hall	Foyers	Middleton	Christie	Robertson	Lafferty	Campbell	Paton	Laing	Sharp
35	06-Apr	SL1	HEARTS	0-3	Sneddon	Hall	Hall	Murdoch	Robertson	Middleton	Campbell	Paton	Laing	Crossan	Clelland
36	15-Apr	ESL	Hibernian	1-1	Sneddon	Hall	Foyers	Hall	Robertson	McManus	Laing	Paton	Oswald	Crossan	Clelland
37	20-Apr	SCf	Renton (n)	2-1	Sneddon	Foyers	Hall	Murdoch	Robertson	McManus	Laing	Paton	Oswald	Crossan	CLELLAND 2
38	27-Apr	SL1	Rangers	1-2	Hunter	Hall	Foyers	McManus	Robertson	Murdoch	Laing	PATON	Oswald	Crossan	Sharp
39	04-May	ESL	HEARTS	0-5	Sneddon	Hall	Foyers	McManus	Robertson	Murdoch	Wilson	Paton	Oswald	Crossan	Clelland
40	11-May	SL1	Third Lanark	0-4	Sneddon	Baird	Foyers	McManus	Robertson	McManus	Wilson	Paton	Oswald	Hall	Sharp
41	15-May	RCC	Hearts	3-7	Sneddon	Baird	Foyers	McManus	Robertson	Murdoch	Campbell	Paton	Laing	Muir	Clelland
42	18-May	ESL	LEITH ATHLETIC (n)	0-2	Hunter	Baird	Foyers	McManus	Robertson	Murdoch	Laing	Paton	Oswald	Hall	Clelland
43	25-May	ESL	Hearts	0-6	from Snedden, Baird, Foyers, McManus, Robertson, Murdoch, Paton, Muir, Hall, Clelland and Sharp

1895/96

#	Date	Comp	Opponent	Score											
1	03-Aug		LEITH ATHLETIC	6-5	Baird	Sneddon	Kinross	Wark	McKinnon	Murdoch	Wilson	McNamee	McKnight	Clelland	Hall
2	10-Aug		Hearts	1-4	Wilson	Sneddon	Kinross	McKinnon	Baird	Murdoch	McNamee	Paton	McKnight	Brown	Hall
3	17-Aug	SL1	DUNDEE	4-2	Wilson	Sneddon	Kinross	Murdoch	McKinnon	Tennant	Wilson	Paton	Laing	BROWN	Hall
4	24-Aug	SL1	St Mirren	3-1	Wilson	Sneddon	Kinross	Murdoch	Baird	Tennant	Wilson	PATON	Laing	Brown	HALL 2
5	31-Aug	SL1	Third Lanark	0-0	Murdoch	Sneddon	Kinross	Tennant	Baird	McKinnon	Wilson	Paton	Laing	Brown	Hall
6	07-Sep	SL1	DUMBARTON	4-3	Murdoch	Sneddon	Kinross	Wark	Baird	McKinnon	Wilson	Paton	Laing	BROWN 2	CLELLAND 2
7	14-Sep	SL1	RANGERS	3-4	Wilson	Sneddon	Kinross	Murdoch	McKinnon	Tennant	WILSON 2	Paton	McKnight	BROWN	Clelland
8	16-Sep	SL1	CELTIC	3-0	Wilson	Sneddon	Kinross	Murdoch	Baird	Tennant	WILSON	PATON	McKnight	BROWN	Clelland
9	21-Sep	SL1	HEARTS	0-5	Wilson	Sneddon	Kinross	Murdoch	Baird	Tennant	Wilson	Paton	Brown	BROWN	Clelland
10	28-Sep		Clyde	0-5	McKinnon	Sneddon	MILNE	Murdoch	Baird	Tennant	Paton	McKnight	Brown	Hall	Clelland
11	05-Oct	SL1	Dundee	1-4	Hunter	Hunter	Milne	Murdoch	Wark	Tennant	Wilson	Paton	McKnight	Brown	Hall
12	12-Oct	SL1	Rangers	0-2	Hunter	McLean	Milne	Murdoch	Wark	Tennant	Wilson	Paton	Laing	Brown	Hall
13	19-Oct	SL1	HIBERNIAN	2-5	Russell	McLean	Milne	Murdoch	'Urquhart'	Tennant	WILSON	Paton	LAING	Brown	Clelland
14	26-Oct	SL1	Dumbarton	3-4	Russell	McLean	Kinross	Hall	Wark	Tennant	WILSON	Paton	LAING	Brown	CLELLAND
15	02-Nov		Leith Athletic	1-2	Russell	McLean	Pillar	Wilson	Robertson	Laing	White	McKinnon	Paton	Downie
16	09-Nov	SL1	ST MIRREN	4-3	Russell	McLean	Pillar	Wilson,G	Robertson,T	WILSON,J 3	Paton	Laing	LAING	Hall
17	16-Nov		Corinthians	0-2	Russell	McLean	Pillar	McKinnon	Robertson	Tennant	Wilson	Paton	Laing	Brown	Hall
18	18-Nov		Sheffield Wednesday	0-1	Russell	McLean	Pillar	Murdoch	McKinnon	Tennant	Wilson	Paton	Laing	Wark	Clelland
19	23-Nov		Queens Park	1-1	Russell	McLean	Pillar	Russell	McManus	Murdoch	Wilson	Paton	LAING	Wark	Hall
20	30-Nov	SL1	Hibernian	3-2	Russell	McLean	Pillar	Russell	Robertson	Murdoch	WILSON	PATON	Laing	BROWN	Muirhead
21	07-Dec	SL1	Celtic	1-2	Russell	McLean	Pillar	Russell	Robertson	Murdoch	WILSON	Paton	Laing	Brown	Hall
22	14-Dec	SL1	Hearts	0-6	Russell	McLean	Pillar	Wilson	Robertson	Murdoch	WILSON	Paton	Laing	Brown	Muirhead
23	28-Dec		CLYDE	2-2	Russell	McLean	Pillar	McManus	Robertson	Russell	Laing	Paton	Laing	Wark	Muirhead
24	02-Jan		Hibernian	2-1	Russell	McLean	Smellie	Wilson	Robertson	Murdoch	Laing	Paton	Brown	Wark	Muirhead
25	02-Jan		CORINTHIANS	3-1	Russell	McLean	Pillar	Wilson,G	ROBERTSON	Murdoch	WILSON,J 2	PATON	Brown	Wark	MUIRHEAD 2
26	11-Jan	SC1	CLACKMANNAN	8-1	Russell	McLean	Smellie	Russell	ROBERTSON	Murdoch	WILSON	PATON	LAING	Wark	Muirhead
27	18-Jan		Stoke	2-3	Russell	McLean	Smellie	Russell	Robertson	Murdoch	WILSON	PATON	LAING	Wark	Muirhead
28	25-Jan	SC2	ANNBANK	2-0	Russell	McLean	Kinross	Russell	Robertson	Murdoch	WILSON	PATON	LAING	Wark	Muirhead
29	01-Feb	SL1	THIRD LANARK	4-1	Russell	McLean	Pillar	Russell	KINROSS	MURDOCH	WILSON	PATON	LAING	Wark	Hall
30	08-Feb	SC3	Queens Park	3-2	Russell	McLean	Pillar	McManus	Kinross	MURDOCH	Brady	Paton	Laing	Wark	Brady
31	15-Feb	SL1	CLYDE	1-4	Russell	McLean	Pillar	Baird	Robertson	Murdoch	Wilson	Hall	Brown	Wark	Muirhead
32	22-Feb	SCs	Hearts	0-1	Russell	McLean	Smellie	Kinross	Robertson	Russell	Wilson	Paton	Laing	Wark	Cunningham
33	29-Feb	ESL	Hibernian	0-5	Russell	McLean	Pillar	Kinross	Robertson	Murdoch	Wilson	Paton	Brown	Muirhead	Cunningham
34	07-Mar	ESL	HEARTS	1-2	Russell	Baird	Pillar	Kinross	Wark	Russell	Laing	Hall	Brown	Wark	Muirhead
35	14-Mar		Dundee	0-4	Russell	McLean	Pillar	Robertson	Kinross	Wark	Wilson	Ferguson	Brown	Peden	Cunningham
36	21-Mar	ESL	CLYDE	2-3	Russell	McLean	Pillar	Smellie	Kinross	Murdoch	Wilson	Paton	Peden	Wark	Cunningham
37	28-Mar	ESL	HIBERNIAN	2-3	Russell	McLean	Pillar	Kinross	Robertson	Murdoch	Wilson	Paton	Peden	Brown	Wark
38	04-Apr	ESL	Hearts	2-4	Russell	McLean	Pillar	Kinross	Baird	Murdoch	Wilson	Paton	Peden	Brown	Wark
39	11-Apr		NOTTINGHAM Forest	2-2	Russell	McLean	Pillar	Russell	Baird	Murdoch	Stewart	Paton	Peden	Wark	Cunningham
40	18-Apr	ESL	LEITH ATHLETIC	1-1	Russell	McLean	Pillar	Kinross	Baird	Russell	Stewart	Paton	Peden	Wark	Ferguson
41	20-Apr		EVERTON	1-3	Russell	McLean	Pillar	Murdoch	Baird	Russell	Wilson	Stewart	Peden	Wark	Phillips
42	22-Feb		BOLTON Wanderers	2-2	Russell	McLean	Pillar	Murdoch	Baird	Robertson	Wilson	Williamson	Peden	Law	Phillips
43	25-Apr		East Stirling	1-6	Russell	McLean	Pillar	Kinross	Baird	Russell	Wilson	Paton	Laing	Ferguson	Phillips
44	09-May	ESL	Leith Athletic	0-3	Russell	McLean	Pillar	Murdoch	Baird	Russell	Robertson	Paton	Peden	Bell	Wilson
45	13-May	RCC	Leith Athletic (n)	0-5	Russell	McNeil	Pillar	Kinross	Robertson	Murdoch	Laing	Robertson	Jack	Bell	Wark
46	20-May		HIBERNIAN	0-5	Forsyth	Baird	Pillar	Low	McEwan	Russell	McGraw	Laing	Bryce	Martin	Wark

1896/97

#	Date	Comp	Opponent	Score	1	2	3	4	5	6	7	8	9	10	11
1	08-Aug		PRACTICE MATCH	?-?											
2	15-Aug	SL1	Clyde	2-1	Russell	McLean	Pillar	Kinross	BAIRD	Paton	Robertson	Paton	FISHER	Jack	McMillan	McNeil
3	22-Aug	SL1	Celtic	0-2	Russell	McLean	Pillar	Kinross	Baird	Paton	Robertson	Wilson	Paton	Fisher	McMillan	McNeil
4	29-Aug	SL1	THIRD LANARK	2-3	Russell	McLean	Pillar	Kinross	Baird	PROVAN	Robertson	Dobie	FISHER	Dobie	McNeil
5	05-Sep	SL1	CLYDE	4-1	Russell	McLean	Kinross	Stewart	Baird	Robertson	PROVAN 2	Dobie	McMILLAN	NEILSON
6	07-Sep		Newcastle United	3-1	Russell	McLean	Russell	Wark	Jack	Robertson	Provan	Paton	Fisher	McMillan	Dobie
7	12-Sep	SL1	CELTIC	1-2	Russell	McLean	Russell	Stewart	Baird	Robertson	Neilson	Paton	Fisher	McMillan	McNeil
8	19-Sep	SL1	Hibernian	0-2	Russell	McLean	Murdoch	Wark	Baird	Robertson	Neilson	Paton	Fisher	McMillan	McNeil
9	26-Sep	SL1	Dundee	1-4	Russell	McLean	Russell	Jack	Baird	Robertson	Neilson	Bell	Fisher	McMillan	McNEIL
10	03-Oct	SL1	HEARTS	2-5	Russell	McLean	'Alexander'	Wark	Baird	Robertson	NEILSON 2	Bell	Fisher	McMillan	McNeil
11	10-Oct	SL1	Abercorn	3-2	Russell	McLean	'Alexander'	Wark	Baird	Robertson	Neilson	Bell	PROVAN 2	McMillan	McNeil
12	17-Oct	SL1	HIBERNIAN	0-1	Russell	McLean	'Alexander'	Wark	Kinross	Robertson	Neilson	Bell	PROVAN 2	McMillan	McNeil
13	24-Oct	SL1	Corinthians	2-1	from Russell, McLean, Wood, Wark, Lowe, Robertson, Neilson, Peden, Provan, McMillan, McNeill, Wilson and Paton.
14	26-Oct		Millwall Athletic	0-0	from Russell, McLean, Wood, Wark, Lowe, Robertson, Neilson, Peden, Provan, McMillan, McNeill, Wilson and Paton.
15	27-Oct		Brentford	0-0	Russell	McLean	Wood	Robertson	Alexander	Wark	Wilson	Paton	McNeil	Wilson
16	31-Oct	SL1	ST MIRREN	0-2	Russell	McLean	Wood	Robertson	Wark	Wark	Provan	Peden	Henderson	McMillan	McNeil
17	07-Nov		Hearts	1-3	Hunter	McLean	Wood	Wark,	Baird	Robertson	Provan	Peden	Christie	McMILLAN	McNeil
18	14-Nov	SL1	DUNDEE	2-1	Russell	McLean	Wood	WARK	Smith	Robertson	Provan	Peden	Fisher	McMillan	McNEIL
19	21-Nov	SL1	St Mirren	0-4	Kinross	McLean	Wood	Wark,	Baird	Robertson	Wilson	Paton	Fisher	McMillan	McNeil
20	28-Nov	SL1	Third Lanark	3-2	Russell	McLean	Wood	Wark	Baird	Robertson	McNEIL	Paton	McMillan	CHRISTIE	Fisher
21	05-Dec		Dundee	2-3	Russell	McLean	Wood	Wark	Baird	Robertson	McNeil	Paton	Henderson	McMillan	Fisher
22	12-Dec		Hibernian	3-3	Russell	Baird	Wood	Wark	Robertson	McNeil	Paton	Provan	McMillan	Fisher
23	19-Dec	SL1	ABERCORN	6-0	Russell	McLean	Wood	Wark	BAIRD	Robertson	McNeil	PATON	PROVAN 3	McMillan	FISHER 2
24	26-Dec	SL1	RANGERS	3-2	Russell	McLean	Wood	Wark	Baird	Robertson	McNeil	PATON	PROVAN	McMillan	Fisher
25	01-Jan		Morton	2-5	Thomson	Pillar	Russell	Robertson	Wood	McNeil	Provan	Henderson	Fisher
26	02-Jan		CORINTHIANS	2-1	Russell	McLean	'Fraser'	Wark	Baird	Robertson	McNeil	PATON	Provan	Fisher	McMillan
27	09-Jan	SC1	QUEENS PARK	2-1	Russell	McLean	Kinross	Wark	Baird	Robertson	McNEIL	PATON	Provan	McMillan	Fisher
28	23-Jan		ST MIRREN	1-0	Russell	McLean	Kinross	Wark	Baird	Robertson	Wilson	PATON	Provan	McMillan	Fisher
29	30-Jan	SC2	ST MIRREN	5-0	Russell	McLEAN	Kinross	Wark	BAIRD	Robertson	McNeil	Paton	Provan	McMillan	FISHER
30	06-Feb	ESL	Hibernian	2-1	Russell	McLean	Kinross	Wark	Baird	Robertson	McNeil	Paton	Provan	McMillan	Fisher
31	13-Feb		Queens Park	4-4	Russell	Adams	Kinross	Wark	Lowe	Robertson	McNeil	Brady	Neilson	McMillan	Fisher
32	20-Feb	SL1	Rangers	2-3	Russell	McLean	Kinross	Wark	Baird	Robertson	McNeil	Paton	Provan	McMILLAN	FISHER
33	27-Feb	SC3	Dumbarton	0-2	Buxton	McLean	Kinross	Wark	Baird	Robertson	McNeil	Paton	Provan	Neilson	Fisher
34	06-Mar		HIBERNIAN	0-5	Russell	Adams	Wood	Middleton	Phillips	Robertson	Colthard	Paton	Provan	McLeod	McNeil
35	13-Mar		Derby County	2-6	Russell	Adams	McLean	Robertson	Baird	Wood	McNeil	Paton	'Normac'	Fisher	Colthard
36	20-Mar	ESL	Hearts	0-4	Russell	McLean	Wood	Wark	Kinross	Robertson	McNeil	McMillan	Fisher	Paton	Brady
37	27-Mar	ESL	Dundee	2-3	Russell	Adams	Wood	Adams	Lowe	Robertson	McNeil	Paton	Provan	Brady	Fisher
38	03-Apr	ESL	East Stirling	1-3	Robertson	McLean	Wood	Adams	Kinross	Robertson	Wilson	Paton	Provan	McMillan	Fisher
39	10-Apr		HEARTS	0-1	Russell	McLean	Wood	Adams	Robertson	Baird	Paton	Brady	Provan	McMillan	McNeil
40	17-Apr		Victoria United	1-2	Russell	McLean	Kinross	Kinross	Baird	Robertson	McNeil	Paton	Provan	McMillan	Fisher
41	19-Apr	ESL	Leith Athletic	1-3	Greenhorn	McLean	Wood	Adams	Buchan	Robertson	Kinross	Fisher	McMillan	McNeil
42	24-Apr	ESL	DUNDEE	2-1	Greenhorn	Foyers	Wood	Adams	Baird	Robertson	Kinross	Paton	Provan	McMILLAN	Fisher
43	01-May	ESL	HIBERNIAN	1-2	Thomson	Foyers	Wood	Adams	Baird	Robertson	Kinross	Paton	Craig	Chambers	McMillan
44	05-May	RCCs	Hearts (n)	1-1	Thomson	Foyers	Wood	Adams	Baird	Robertson	Kinross	Paton	Provan	Chambers	McMillan
45	06-May		Partick Thistle	0-2	Russell	McLean	Wood	Foyers	Baird	Lowe	Fisher	Steen	Craig	Hutton	Downie
46	07-May	RCCs	Hearts (n)	1-4	Thomson	Foyers	Wood	Adams	Baird	Robertson	McInnes	Paton	Chambers	McInnes	Fisher
47	08-May		EAST STIRLING	6-0	Thomson	McLean	Wood	Adams	Baird	Robertson	Brady	Paton	Provan	McInnes	Jackson
48	10-May	ESL	LEITH ATHLETIC	3-0	Russell	McLean	Wood	Adams	Baird	Robertson	Brady	Paton	Chambers	McInnes	Jackson
49	15-May		Port Glasgow Ath	0-0	Russell	McLean	Wood	Wood	Baird	Robertson	McNeil	Paton	Provan	Chambers	McInnes

1897/98

#	Date	Comp	Opponent	Score													
1	01-Sep	Trial	PROBABLES	6-0	Thomson	Pillar	Adams	Robertson	Baird	Buchanan	McInnes	Paton	Chambers	McMillan	Allan
2		Trial	v POSSIBLES	3-0	AN Other	Kinross	Wood	McGill	Galbraith	Robertson	Nickling	Provan	Maxwell	Ross	Law
3	02-Sep	SL1	HIBERNIAN	2-4	Kinross	Adams	Pillar	Buchanan	Baird	Robertson	McInnes	Maxwell	Provan	McMillan	Allan
4	04-Sep	SL1	RANGERS	4-2	Russell	Pillar	McLean	Buchanan	Baird	Galbraith	McInnes	Paton	CHAMBERS	McMillan	ALLAN
5	06-Sep	SL1	HEARTS	0-0	Russell	Pillar	Wood	Buchanan	Baird	Galbraith	McInnes	Maxwell	Robertson,T	McMillan	McGill
6	11-Sep	SL1	Dundee	1-2	Russell	Adams	McLean	Buchanan	Baird	Galbraith	Cathcart	Paton	Maxwell	Chambers	McMillan
7	13-Sep		EAST of Scot Lge	2-7	Thomson	Pillar	McLean	Buchanan	Adams	Galbraith	McInnes	Paton	CHAMBERS	McMillan	Tennant
8	18-Sep	SL1	St Mirren	0-2	Russell	Adams	Wood	Galbraith	Baird	Robertson	McInnes	PATON	CHAMBERS	McMillan	Allan
9	20-Sep	SL1	CELTIC	3-2	Russell	McLean	Wood	Wark	Buchanan	Robertson	McInnes	Paton	Chambers	McMillan	Allan
10	25-Sep	SL1	HIBERNIAN	2-4	Russell	Kinross	Wood	Wark	Baird	Buchanan	McInnes	PATON 2	MAXWELL	CHAMBERS	McMillan
11	02-Oct	SL1	Clyde	1-5	Russell	McNicol	Wood	Wark	Baird	Galbraith	Kinghorn	PATON	Maxwell	Chambers	Allan
12	09-Oct	SL1	Hearts	1-6	Thomson	McNicol	Wood	Buchanan	Baird	Robertson	Kinghorn	Paton	Provan	McMillan	McINNES
13	16-Oct	SL1	Hibernian	1-3	Thomson	Buchanan	Wood	Pillar	Baird	Galbraith	Kinghorn	CHAMBERS	Paton	McInnes	Allan
14	23-Oct	SL1	THIRD LANARK	5-3	Russell	McLean	Wood	Buchanan	Baird	Robertson	Provan	Chambers	'Brown'	'White'	Allan
15	27-Oct	SL1	ROYAL SCOTS	1-2	Russell	McLean	Wood	Buchanan	Baird	Galbraith	Kinghorn	Chambers	PROVAN	PATON	Allan
16	30-Oct	SL1	ST MIRREN	3-5	Russell	McLean	Wood	Buchanan	Baird	Wark	BRADY 2	Chambers	Provan	McMillan	Tennant
17	06-Nov	SL1	Partick Thistle	2-3	Goode	McNicol	Pillar	Buchanan	Baird	'McGilvray'	Wilson	Chambers	'Swanston'	McMillan	Tennant
18	20-Nov	SL1	Queens Park	1-5	Thomson	McNicol	Wood	Buchanan	Cairns	Robertson	Kinghorn	CHAMBERS	Houston	McMillan	Tennant
19	27-Nov	SL1	ROYAL SCOTS	4-0	Thomson	McLean	Wood	Buchanan	Baird	Robertson	Allan	White	McInnes	'Normac'	Tennant
20	04-Dec	SL1	PARTICK Thistle	9-1	'Newman'	McLean	Wood	Wark	Baird	Cairns	KINGHORN	McInnes	HOUSTON 2	Paton	TENNANT 2
21	11-Dec	SL1	DUNDEE	4-1	Sligo	McLean	Wood	Wark	Baird	Cairns	KINGHORN	McInnes	HOUSTON 2	Paton	Tennant
22	18-Dec	SL1	Celtic	1-5	Sligo	McLean	McNicol	Buchanan	Baird	Cairns	Kinghorn	McINNES	Houston	Paton	Tennant
23	25-Dec	SL1	Third Lanark	0-6	Tulloch	McLean	McNicol	Buchanan	BAIRD	Cairns	Jarvie	McInnes	Houston	Paton	Tennant
24	01-Jan	SL1	CLYDE	3-1	Wood	McNicol ?	Wood	Buchanan	Baird	Cairns	Jarvie	McInnes	Houston	Paton	TENNANT
25	03-Jan		CORINTHIANS	1-1	Wilkie	Pillar	Wood	Robertson	Baird	Cairns	Allan	McInnes	Chambers	Paton	Allan
26	08-Jan	SC1	DUMBARTON	1-1	Wilkie	McLean	Wood	Buchanan	Baird	Cairns	Chambers	McInnes	CHAMBERS	PATON	Tennant
27	15-Jan	SC1	Dumbarton	3-1	Wilkie	McLean	Wood	Robertson	Baird	Cairns	Chambers	McInnes	BUCHANAN 2	Paton	Tennant
28	22-Jan	SC2	QUEENS PARK	0-5	Wilkie	McLean	Wood	Robertson	Buchanan	Cairns	Jarvie	McInnes	Ritchie	Cairns	Houston
29	29-Jan	ESS	Raith Rovers	5-3	Stoddart	McNicol	Wood	Buchanan	Cairns	Robertson	Kinghorn	Paton	Houston	Paton	Tennant
30	05-Feb	ESL	LEITH Athletic	1-2	Wilkie	McNicol	Wood	Buchanan	Cairns	Robertson	Houston	Ritchie	Houston	Kinghorn	Tennant
31	12-Feb		Corinthians	2-0	Wilkie	McNicol	McLean	Buchanan	Baird	Robertson	Lee	Paton	Ritchie	Lee	Tennant
32	14-Feb		Brentford	3-0	Wilkie	McNicol	Wood	Buchanan	Baird	McLean	Kinghorn	Ritchie	Allan	Paton	Tennant
33	15-Feb		Tottenham	0-4	Wilkie	McNicol	Wood	Robertson	Baird	Cairns	Kinghorn	Ritchie	Houston	Lee	Allan
34	19-Feb	ESSs	Leith Athletic (n)	2-3	Stoddart	McNicol	Wood	Robertson	Baird	Cairns	Lee	Ritchie	Buchanan	Paton	Tennant
35	26-Feb	ESL	Dundee	2-2	Wilkie	McNicol	Wood	Buchanan	Baird	Cairns	Kinghorn	Ritchie	Houston	McInnes	Tennant
36	05-Mar	ESL	Hibernian	1-2	Wilkie	McLean	Wood	Galbraith	Baird	Cairns	Lee	Ritchie	Houston	McInnes	Tennant
37	12-Mar	ESL	HEARTS	2-1	Wilkie	McLean	Wood	McLean	Baird	Robertson	Lee	Ritchie	Cairns	Paton	Houston
38	19-Mar	SL1	Rangers	1-8	Wilkie	McNicol	Wood	McLean	Baird	Cairns	Lee	Ritchie	Houston	Paton	Tennant
39	02-Apr	ESL	Hearts	1-3	Wilkie	McNicol	Wood	McNicol	Baird	Cairns	Lee	Ritchie	Houston	Allan	Tennant
40	09-Apr	ESL	HIBERNIAN (n)	0-2	Wilkie	McLean	Wood	McLean	Baird	Cairns	Lee	Ritchie	Houston	Paton	Tennant
41	11-Apr	ESL	DUMBARTON	5-0	Wilson	Simpson	Buchanan	Baird	Galbraith	Dawson	'Colthard'	Allan	Allan	Lee	Allan
42	16-Apr	ESL	Leith Athletic	3-1	Wilkie	McNicol	Wood	Robertson	Galbraith	Cairns	Ritchie	Paton	Allan	Tennant	Houston
43	18-Apr	ESL	DUNDEE	1-1	Wilkie	Buchanan	Simpson	Cairns	Galbraith	Lee	Brown	Ritchie	Allan	McInnes	Houston
44	23-Apr		Hibernian	1-3	Stoddart	Buchanan	Simpson	Paton	Galbraith	Davidson	Brown	Ritchie	Cairns	Fairbairn	Houston
45	30-Apr		Morton	0-2	Wilkie	Buchanan	McNicol	Cairns	Baird	Newman	Lee	Brown	Houston	Paton	Tennant
46	07-May	RCCs	Hibernian (n)	1-1	Barclay	Pillar	Wood	Galbraith	Baird	Cairns	Houston	Edmond	'Normac'	Lee	Tennant
47	11-May	RCCs	Hibernian	1-4	Barclay	Pillar	Wood	Galbraith	Baird	Cairns	Houston	Brown	Cameron	Colthard	Tennant

1898/99

#	Date	Comp	Match	Score											
1	06-Aug	Trial	PROBABLES	4-1	Barclay	McNicol	Kay	Wood	Galbraith	Cairns	Newman	Lee	Beveridge	Ritchie	Houston	Turner	Tennant
1		Trial	v RESERVES	2-4	King	Kay	Robertson	Wilson			McIntosh	Crawford	Edmond	McDonald	Wallace	Bell
2	15-Aug		Hearts	2-0	Wilkie	McNicol	Kay	McNicol	Galbraith	Totten		Lee	Cairns	Ritchie	Houston	Turner	Tennant
3	20-Aug		LEITH ATHLETIC	0-1	Wilkie	Kay	McNicol	Galbraith	Totten		Cameron	Beveridge	Ritchie	Houston	Turner	Tennant
4	27-Aug		HIBERNIAN	3-4	Wilkie	Kay	McNicol	Galbraith	Totten		Lee	Cairns	Ritchie	McDonald	Turner	Tennant
5	30-Aug		East Stirling	1-1	Wilkie	Kay	Newman	'Alexander'	Totten		Lee	Cairns	Ritchie	Houston	Turner	Tennant
6	03-Sep	SL1	Dundee	3-0	Wilkie	Buchanan	McNicol	GALBRAITH	Totten		LEE 2	Beveridge	Ritchie	McDonald	TURNER	Tennant
7	10-Sep	SL1	Partick Thistle	1-3	Wilkie	McNicol	Wood	Buchanan	Totten		Lee	Galbraith	Cairns	CAIRNS	Ritchie	Lee
8	17-Sep	SL1	HEARTS	0-2	Wilkie	Buchanan	McNicol	Galbraith	Totten		Tennant	Cairns	Turner	McKenzie	Ritchie	TENNANT 2
9	19-Sep	SL1	RANGERS	3-4	Wilkie	Kay	McNicol	Galbraith	Totten		LEE	Cairns	Bell	McKenzie	Turner	Tennant
10	24-Sep	SL1	Hibernian	4-2	Wilkie	Kay	McNicol	Galbraith	Totten		LEE	Cairns	RITCHIE	McKenzie	Turner	Tennant
11	01-Oct	SL1	THIRD LANARK	0-1	Wilkie	Kay	McNicol	Galbraith	Totten		Lee	Cairns	Ritchie	McKenzie	Turner	TENNANT
12	08-Oct	SL1	Celtic	1-2	Barclay	McNicol	Totten	Baird			Lee	Galbraith	Ritchie	MCKENZIE	Turner	TENNANT
13	15-Oct	SL1	St Mirren	2-3	Wilkie	Kay	McNicol	Totten	Baird		Ritchie	Cairns	Bell	CAMERON	TURNER	Tennant
14	22-Oct	SL1	PARTICK THISTLE	1-3	Barclay	Kay	Wood	Buchanan	Totten		Lee	Beveridge	RITCHIE	CAMERON	Turner	Tennant
15	29-Oct	SL1	CELTIC	3-4	Wilkie	Kay	Wood	Eadie	Totten		Ritchie	Cairns	Ritchie	CAMERON	TURNER	TENNANT
16	05-Nov	SL1	Hearts	1-3	Barclay	Kay	Wood	Buchanan	Totten		LEE	Cairns	Ritchie	CAMERON	Turner	Tennant
17	12-Nov	SL1	HIBERNIAN	2-1	Wilkie	Kay	Wood	Galbraith	Baird		Lee	Cairns	Ritchie	CAMERON	TURNER	TENNANT
18	19-Nov	SL1	Clyde	1-1	Wilkie	Kay	Wood	Galbraith	Totten		LEE	Cairns	Ritchie	Cameron	TURNER	Tennant
19	26-Nov	SL1	Third Lanark	2-5	Wilkie	Kay	Wood	Galbraith	Totten		Lee	Cairns	Ritchie	Cameron	TURNER	TENNANT
20	03-Dec	SL1	Rangers	4-1	Wilkie	Kay	Wood	Galbraith	Baird		Ritchie	Cairns	RITCHIE 2	Cameron	TURNER	TENNANT
21	10-Dec	SL1	CLYDE	0-0	Wilkie	Kay	Wood	Galbraith	Totten		Lee	McNicol	RITCHIE 2	Cameron	Turner	Tennant
22	17-Dec	SL1	ST MIRREN	2-2	Wilkie	Kay	Young	Eadie	Baird		Beveridge	Robertson	Houston	McKenzie	Walls	Smith
23	24-Dec	SL1	DUNDEE	0-5	Wilkie	McNicol	Kay	Galbraith	Phillips		Bell	Cairns	Ritchie	Cameron	Turner	Smith
24	31-Dec	SL1	HEARTS	1-3	Barclay	Kay	Wood	Eadie	Totten		Bell	Cairns	Ritchie	Cameron	Walls	Beveridge
25	02-Jan		Leith Athletic	3-1	Barclay	McNicol	Wood	Galbraith	Phillips		Lee	Cairns	Ritchie	McKenzie	TURNER	TENNANT
26	03-Jan		CORINTHIANS	2-1	Wilkie	McNicol	Kay	Galbraith	Totten		Houston	Cairns	RITCHIE	CAMERON 3	TURNER	Tennant
27	07-Jan	ESL	HIBERNIAN	4-2	Wilkie	McNicol	Kay	Galbraith	Totten		Lee	Bell,M	Ritchie	Cameron	Turner	Beveridge
28	14-Jan	SC1	Boness	0-3	Wilkie	McNicol	Kay	Galbraith	Totten		Lee	Cairns	Ritchie	McKenzie	Turner	Tennant
29	21-Jan	SC1	BONESS	4-1	Wilkie	Wilkie	Kay	Galbraith	Gray		Ritchie	Cairns	Ritchie	Cameron	Turner	Houston
30	04-Feb	SC2	Celtic	1-1	Barclay	Wilkie	Kay	Galbraith	Gray		Robertson	Cairns	Ritchie	Cameron	Turner	Tennant
31	11-Feb		HEARTS	3-5	Wilkie	Kay	Wood	Totten			Lee	Cairns	Ritchie,Cameron,Turner and Cairns.			
32	18-Feb	ESSq	Hearts	4-4	Wilkie	Kay	Wood	Totten	Baird		Lee	Cairns	Ritchie	Cameron	Turner	Beveridge
33	25-Feb	ESL	Raith Rovers	1-4	Wilkie	Kay	McNicol	Godsman			Phillips	Gray	Ritchie	Cameron	Turner	Houston
34	11-Mar	ESL	Dundee	0-1	from Wilkie, Kay, McNicol, Totten, Baird, Galbraith, Bell, Ritchie, Cameron, Turner and Cairns.											
35	18-Mar	ESL	Hibernian	3-2	Barclay	McNicol	Wood	Totten			Lee	Robertson	Houston	Walls	Turner	Tennant
36	25-Mar	ESL	RAITH ROVERS	7-1	Wilkie	McNicol	Wood	Totten			Phillips	Gray	Ritchie	Walls	Turner	Tennant
37	01-Apr	ESL	DUNDEE	3-3	Wilkie	McNicol	Wood	Totten			Phillips	Gray	Ritchie	Walls	Turner	Tennant
38	08-Apr	ESL	HEARTS	0-2	Wilkie	McNicol	Wood	Galbraith			Lee	Gray	Houston	Walls	Turner	Tennant
39	15-Apr	ESL	LEITH ATHLETIC	1-1	Barclay	Kay	Wood	Totten			Lee	Gray	Ritchie	Walls	Turner	Tennant
40	17-Apr	ESL	Hearts	2-2	Wilkie	McNicol	Kay	Totten			Ritchie	Gray	Bell,M	McKenzie	Turner	Tennant
41	22-Apr	ESL	Leith Athletic (n)	1-2	Barclay	Kay	McNicol	Totten			Lee	Galbraith	Ritchie	Cameron	Turner	Tennant
42	29-Apr	RCC	ABERCORN	2-3												
43	03-May	ESL	Hibernian	1-2	from Wilkie, McNicol, Wood, Totten, Gray, McKenzie, Bell, Walls, Cameron, Turner and Tennant.											

1899/00

#	Date	Opponent	Lg	Score												
1	15-Aug	Raith Rovers		2-0	Barclay	Kay	Wood	Buchanan	Phillips	Gray	Cameron	Atherton	McKenzie	Walls	Bell	
2	16-Aug	HIBERNIAN		1-1	Wilkie	Kay	Ritchie	Buchanan	Totten	Galbraith	Waddell, F	Atherton	Cameron	Turner	Waddell, J	
3	19-Aug	Dundee		1-1	Wilkie	Kay	Ritchie	Buchanan	Totten	Galbraith	Waddell, F	Atherton	Cameron	Turner	Waddell, J	
4	23-Aug	Leith Athletic		1-0	Barclay	Kay	Wood	Buchanan	Gray	McKenzie	Waddell, F	Atherton	Bell	Walls	Hay	
5	26-Aug	Hearts	ESL	0-4	Wilkie	Kay	Ritchie	Buchanan	Totten	Galbraith	WADDELL,F	Atherton	Cameron	Turner	Waddell, J	
6	02-Sep	St Mirren	SL1	3-4	Wilkie	Kay	Wood	Buchanan	Totten	Galbraith	Waddell, F	Atherton	HOUSTON	Turner	Waddell, J	
7	09-Sep	HEARTS	SL1	2-4	Wilkie	Kay	Wood	Buchanan	Totten	Galbraith	WADDELL,F	Atherton	Houston	TURNER	Waddell, J	
8	16-Sep	Kilmarnock	SL1	1-2	Wilkie	Kay	Wood	Buchanan	Totten	Galbraith	WADDELL,F	Bell	Cameron	Turner	Bell	
9	23-Sep	Dundee	SL1	0-3	Wilkie	Kay	Wood	Buchanan	Phillips	Maxwell	Waddell, F	Atherton	Houston	Turner	Bell	
10	25-Sep	Aberdeen		3-1	Wilkie	Kay	Wood	Buchanan	Phillips	Maxwell	Waddell, F	Atherton	Cameron	Bell	Lee	
11	07-Oct	DUNDEE	SL1	2-0	Wilkie	Ritchie	Wood	Buchanan	Gray	Maxwell	Lee	BELL	Turner	Bell	WADDELL,J	
12	14-Oct	Hearts	SL1	0-5	Barclay	Kay	Wood	Buchanan	Gray	Maxwell	Lee	Bell	Waddell, F	Turner	Waddell, J	
13	21-Oct	Third Lanark	SL1	0-2	Barclay	Kay	Wood	Buchanan	Totten	Maxwell	Lee	Bell	Waddell, F	Turner	Smith	
14	28-Oct	Celtic	SL1	0-5	Barclay	Kay	Wood	Maxwell	Turner	Atherton	Atherton	Lee	Buchanan	Bell	Waddell	
15	04-Nov	KILMARNOCK	SL1	1-1	Barclay	Kay	Wood	Buchanan	Totten	McKenzie	THOMSON,F	Cameron	Houston	Turner	Bell	
16	11-Nov	HIBERNIAN	SL1	0-4	Barclay	Kay	Wood	Buchanan	Totten	McKenzie	Atherton	Cameron	Houston	Turner	Bell	
17	18-Nov	CLYDE	SL1	3-2	Barclay	Kay	Wood	Buchanan	Gray	McKenzie	Lee	CAMERON	Houston	Turner	BELL	
18	25-Nov	Rangers	SL1	3-4	Barclay	Kay	Wood	Buchanan	Gray	McKenzie	Lee	Houston	CAMERON 2	TURNER	Bell	
19	02-Dec	CELTIC	SL1	1-1	Hood	Kay	Wood	Buchanan	Gray	Maxwell	Lee	Houston	Cameron	TURNER	Bell	
20	09-Dec	THIRD LANARK	SL1	4-0	Hood	Ritchie	Wood	BUCHANAN	GRAY	McKenzie	LEE	Houston	CAMERON 2	TURNER	Bell	
21	16-Dec	Clyde	SL1	4-2	Hood	Ritchie	Wood	Buchanan	Gray	Maxwell	Lee	Walls	McKenzie	TURNER 2	Bell	
22	23-Dec	RANGERS	SL1	0-1*	Hood	Ritchie	Wood	Buchanan	Gray	McKenzie	Lee	Houston	Cameron	Turner	Bell	
23	25-Dec	Middlesborough		1-2	from Hood, Kay, Wood, Buchanan, Gray, McKenzie, Lee, Houston, Cameron, Turner and Bell.											
24	30-Dec	ST MIRREN	SL1	3-3	Hood	Kay	Ritchie	Buchanan	Totten	Maxwell	Lee	Houston	LEE 2	Turner	Bell	
25	01-Jan	Morton		1-6	Barclay	Kay	Wood	Buchanan	Totten	Maxwell	Lee	McDonald	CAMERON	McDonald, Jas	Bell	
26	03-Jan	CORINTHIANS		0-3	Hood	Ritchie	Wood	Maxwell	Ritchie	Gray	Maxwell	Lee	Houston	McKenzie	Fraser	
27	06-Jan	Hibernian	SL1	1-1	Hood	Ritchie	Wood	Buchanan	Totten	Gray	Maxwell	Lee	HOUSTON	McKenzie	Bell	
28	13-Jan	ARBROATH	SC1	1-0	Hood	Kay	Wood	McKenzie	Gray	Maxwell	Lee	Houston	Cameron	Turner	Bell	
29	20-Jan	Raith Rovers	ESL	1-1	Hood	Kay	Wood	Maxwell	Gray	Maxwell	Lee	Houston	Cameron	Turner	Bell	
30	27-Jan	Partick Thistle	SC2	1-2	Hood	Kay	Wood	Buchanan	Ritchie	Maxwell	Walls	Lee	CAMERON	Turner	Walls	
31	03-Feb	RANGERS	SL1	1-4	Hood	Ritchie	Wood	Maxwell	Gray	McKenzie	Lee	Bell	Cameron	Turner	Bell	
32	10-Feb	LEITH ATHLETIC		2-3	Hood	Ritchie	Wood	Buchanan	Maxwell	McKenzie	Bell	Brown	Cameron	Turner	Walls	
33	24-Feb	LEITH ATHLETIC	ESS1	3-0	Hood	Kay	Wood	Buchanan	Ritchie	McKenzie	Bell	Brown	Cameron	Brown	Bell	
34	03-Mar	LEITH ATHLETIC	ESL	1-0	Hood	Kay	Wood	Buchanan	Totten	Maxwell	Maxwell	Houston	Cameron	Turner	Bell	
35	10-Mar	RAITH ROVERS	ESL	6-1	Hood	Kay	Wood	Buchanan	Ritchie	Totten	Totten	Brown	Houston	Turner	Bell	
36	17-Mar	Hibernian	ESSs	2-2	Hood	Kay	Wood	Maxwell	Maxwell	Gray	Totten	Brown	Brown	Turner	Bell	
37	24-Mar	Hibernian	ESSs	2-2	Hood	Kay	Wood	Buchanan	Ritchie	Gray	Totten	Houston	Brown	Turner	Bell	
38	07-Apr	St Mirren (n)	SLT	1-2	Hood	Kay	Wood	Buchanan	Gray	Ritchie	Totten	Maxwell	Devine	Brown	Bell	
39	14-Apr	Dundee	ESL	1-2	Hood	Kay	Wood	Buchanan	Gray	Maxwell	Ritchie	Maxwell	Brown	Turner	Bell	
40	16-Apr	DUNDEE	ESL	0-2	Hood	Kay	Wood	Buchanan	Gray	Maxwell	Ritchie	Maxwell	Brown	Turner	Bell	
41	21-Apr	Leith Athletic	ESL	2-0	from Hood, Kay, Wood, Buchanan, Gray, Ritchie, Maxwell, Brown, Houston, Turner and Bell.											
42	23-Apr	HIBERNIAN (n)	ESL	1-2	Hood	Kay	Wood	Buchanan	Gray	Ritchie	Maxwell	Houston	Brown	Turner	Bell	
43	25-Apr	Hearts	RCC	0-4	Hood	Kay	Wood	Totten	Buchanan	Gray	Ritchie	Maxwell	Brown	Turner	Bell	
44	30-Apr	Hearts	ESL	3-1	Hood	Kay	Wood	Ritchie	Buchanan	Maxwell	Grant	Devine	Houston	Turner	Bell	
45	09-May	Cowdenbeath		4-1												
46	12-May	Partick Thistle	ESL	1-1	Hood	Kay	Ritchie	Buchanan	Gray	Baird	Maxwell	Devine	Houston	Rae	Cannon	
47	14-May	Hibernian	ESL	2-3	Brunton	Kay	Wood	Buchanan	Gray	Baird	Grant	Grant	Houston	Rae	Bell	
48	15-May	Raith Rovers	ESL	0-1	Hood	Robertson	McKenzie	Kay	Kelly	Maxwell	Brown	Brown	Main	Rae	Bell	
49	26-May	Celtic (n)	ESL	0-3	from Simpson, Annan, Ainslie, Nelson, Kelly, Baird, Grant, Devine, Maxwell, Simpson, Mein and Bell.											

1900/01

#	Date	Comp	Opponent	Score											
1	11-Aug	Trial	PRACTICE MATCH	?-?											
2	16-Aug	ESL	HEARTS	2-1	Annan	Ainslie	Baird	Gray	Ritchie	Grant	Prior	Maxwell	Devine	Prior	Lee
3	25-Aug	ESL	Leith Athletic	3-0	Annan	Ainslie	Robertson	Ritchie	Baird	Grant	Prior	Maxwell	Devine	Prior	Lee
4	27-Aug		HIBERNIAN	1-1	Annan	Ainslie	Buchanan	Maxwell	Miller	Lee	PRIOR 2	Forbes	Houston	Prior	Mein
5	01-Sep	SL2	PORT GLASGOW ATH	4-1	Annan	Ainslie	Buchanan	Ritchie	Baird	GRANT	PRIOR	HOUSTON	DEVINE	PRIOR	Bell
6	08-Sep	SL2	CLYDE	3-1	Annan	Ainslie	Buchanan	Maxwell	Maxwell	Grant	Prior	Houston	DEVINE	Prior	Bell
7	15-Sep	SL2	LEITH ATHLETIC	2-0	Annan	Ainslie	Buchanan	Gray	Maxwell	Grant	PRIOR	Houston	DEVINE	PRIOR	BELL
8	22-Sep	ESL	Dundee	1-3	Annan	Ainslie	Buchanan	Taylor	Gray	Baird	Prior	Maxwell	Devine	Prior	Bell
9	29-Sep	SL2	Hamilton Accies	3-2	Annan	Ainslie	Buchanan	Baird	Baird	Grant	PRIOR 2	Bell	Devine	Prior	Lee
10	06-Oct	SL2	Leith Athletic	2-1	Henderson	Ritchie	BUCHANAN	BAIRD	Maxwell	Grant	PRIOR	Houston	Devine	PRIOR	Bell
11	13-Oct	ESL	Airdrie	1-3	Henderson	Ritchie	Buchanan	BAIRD	Bell	Lee	Prior	Grant	Devine	Prior	Devine
12	20-Oct	SL2	Port Glasgow Athletic	2-3	Henderson	Ritchie	BUCHANAN 2	Gray	Maxwell	Grant	PRIOR 2	Maxwell	LYDON	Prior	Bell
13	27-Oct	SL2	Clyde	2-1	Henderson	Ainslie	Buchanan	Gray	Maxwell	Grant	PRIOR	King	Lydon	PRIOR 2	Bell
14	03-Nov	SL2	HAMILTON ACCIES	3-3	Henderson	Ainslie	Buchanan	Gray	Maxwell	GRANT	Prior	King	Lydon	Prior	Lee
15	10-Nov	SL2	ABERCORN	2-0	Henderson	Ritchie	Buchanan	Gray	Maxwell	GRANT	PRIOR	King	DEVINE	Prior	Lee
16	17-Nov	SL2	Ayr	0-1	Henderson	Ritchie	Buchanan	Lydon	Barclay	Grant	Prior	King	Barclay	PRIOR	Lee
17	24-Nov	SL2	MOTHERWELL	4-3	Henderson	Ritchie	MAXWELL	Buchanan	Baird	LEE	PRIOR	King	DEVINE	PRIOR	Mark
18	01-Dec	SL2	East Stirling	1-1	Annan	Ainslie	Buchanan	Ritchie	King	GRANT	Prior	McIlvenny	Devine	Prior	Mark
19	08-Dec	ESL	Dundee	1-3	Annan	Ainslie	Maxwell	Ritchie	King	Barclay	Prior	McIlvenny	Devine	Prior	Mark
20	15-Dec	SL2	Motherwell	2-2	Ritchie	Ainslie	Buchanan	Gray	King	Maxwell	Prior	McIlvenny	LEE	Prior	Mark
21	22-Dec	SL2	AIRDRIE	4-3	Annan	Ainslie	Maxwell	Ritchie	King	LEE 2	Prior	McILVENNY	Devine	PRIOR	Mark
22	25-Dec		Middlesborough	0-1											
23	29-Dec	SL2	Abercorn	1-1	Annan	Ritchie	Buchanan	Gray	Maxwell	Lee	Prior	McIlvenny	Devine	Prior	MARK
24	01-Jan		St Mirren	0-2	Henderson	Ainslie	Buchanan	Robertson	Lee	Grant	Prior	McIlvenny	Wark	Prior	Maxwell
25	05-Jan	ESL	Hearts	3-4	Annan	Ritchie	Buchanan	Wark	Baird	Grant	McIlvenny	Prior	DEVINE	DEVINE	Lee
26	12-Jan	SC1	PARTICK THISTLE	5-0	Annan	Ritchie	Buchanan	Gray	Baird	GRANT 3	PRIOR	McIlvenny	DEVINE	PRIOR	Mark
27	19-Jan	SL2	EAST STIRLING	5-0	Annan	Ritchie	Buchanan	Gray	Baird	GRANT	GRANT	McIlvenny	Devine	PRIOR 2	Lee
28	26-Jan	SC2	Morton	1-1*	Annan	Ritchie	Buchanan	Gray	Baird	Grant	PRIOR	McIlvenny	Devine	PRIOR	Mark
29	09-Feb	SC2	Morton	1-3	Annan	Ritchie	Maxwell	Gray	Baird	Grant	Grant	McIlvenny	Devine	Prior	Lee
30	16-Feb	ESS	WEST CALDER	4-1	Annan	Ritchie	Buchanan	Gray	Baird	Grant	Waddell	McIlvenny	Devine	Prior	Lee
31	02-Mar		LEITH ATHLETIC	1-1	Henderson	Ritchie	Maxwell	King	Baird	Grant	Robertson	King	Lee	Prior	Mark
32	09-Mar		Celtic	2-0	Annan	Ritchie	Buchanan	Gray	Baird	Grant	Prior	McIlvenny	Lee	Prior	Lee
33	16-Mar		Partick Thistle	1-0	Annan	Ritchie	Maxwell	King	Baird	Grant	Prior	McIlvenny	Lee	Prior	Mark
34	30-Mar	ESL	Raith Rovers	3-3	Annan	Ritchie	Buchanan	King	Baird	Grant	Prior	Neilson	Lee	Prior	Lee
35	06-Apr		Preston North End	2-2	Annan	Ritchie	Maxwell	King	Baird	Grant	Prior	McIlvenny	Lee	Prior	Mark
36	15-Apr	ESL	LEITH ATHLETIC	2-2	Annan	Ritchie	Maxwell	Gray	Baird	Grant	Prior	McIlvenny	Lee	Prior	Mark
37	24-Apr		Raith Rovers	2-2	Annan	Ritchie	Buchanan	King	Baird	Grant	Prior	Neilson	Lee	Prior	Lee
38	27-Apr	SL2	AYR	1-0	Annan	Ritchie	Buchanan	King	Baird	Grant	Prior	McIlvenny	DEVINE	Prior	Lee
39	29-Apr	ESL	Hibernian	1-2	Annan	Ritchie	King	Gray	Baird	Grant	Montgomery	King	Mark	Prior	James
40	06-May	ESSs	Hearts	0-4	Annan	Ritchie	Buchanan	Gray	Baird	Lee	Grant	McIlvenny	Devine	Grant	Mark
41	11-May		DUNDEE	1-0	Hislop	Ritchie	Brown	King	Baird	Grant	Prior	McIlvenny	Lee	Prior	Lee
42	20-May	RCCs	HEARTS	4-4*	Henderson	Ritchie	Ainslie	Taylor	Mark	Brown	Mark	McIlvenny	Mein		
43	25-May	RCCs	Hearts (n)	1-2	from Skene, Annan, Ritchie, Brown, Taylor, Baird, Mark, Lee, Prior, McIlvenny and 'Smith'.										

1901/02

#	Date		Comp	Opponent	Score	Baillie	Murdoch	Pillar	Phillips	?	McNab	Dobie	Lowe	Bryce	McIntosh	?
1	08-Aug			Old Hearts	0-0	Hood	Annan	Ritchie	Baird	Brown	Johnstone	Lee	McDonald	Prior	McIlvenny	Forsyth
2	10-Aug	Trial		PRACTICE Match	?-?											
3	15-Aug			Partick Thistle	1-1	Hood	Annan	Ritchie	Baird	Brown	Johnstone	Lee	'Forsyth'	Prior	McIlvenny	Lee
4	17-Aug		ESL	Lochgelly United	3-1											
5	19-Aug		ESL	HEARTS	1-2	Hood	Annan	Baird	'Gibson'	Brown	Johnstone	Mark	Mark	Prior	McIlvenny	Lee
6	24-Aug		SL2	Clyde	1-0	Hood	Annan	Ritchie	Barrie	BROWN	Johnstone	Grant	Brown	PRIOR 2	McIlvenny	LEE
7	31-Aug		SL2	AYR	4-1	Hood	Annan	Baird	Barrie	Johnstone	Baird	GRANT	Brown	Prior	McILVENNY	Lee
8	07-Sep		SL2	Partick Thistle	1-5	Hood	Annan	Baird	BARRIE	Johnstone	Baird	Grant	Lee	Prior	Bow	Mein
9	14-Sep		SL2	East Stirling	0-0	Hood	Annan	Baird	Barrie	Brown	Johnstone	Grant	Lee	Prior	Bow	Leonard
10	21-Sep		SL2	ABERCORN	1-1	Hood	Annan	Baird	Barrie	Brown	Johnstone	Grant	Scott	Prior	Bow	Leonard
11	28-Sep		SL2	Hamilton Accies	1-4	Hood	Annan	Ritchie	Barrie	CHRISTIE,AJ	Baird,A	GRANT	LEE	PRIOR	Bow	Leonard
12	05-Oct		SL2	PARTICK Thistle	2-0	Hood	Annan	Ritchie	Brown	Christie,AJ	Baird,A	Grant	McIlvenny	PRIOR	Bow	Leonard
13	12-Oct		SL2	AIRDRIE	2-1	Hood	Annan	Baird	Brown	Gray	Johnstone	Lee	McIlvenny	Mein	Bow	Leonard
14	19-Oct		SL2	Port Glasgow Ath	0-5	Hood	Annan	Baird	Barrie	Brown	Baird	Lee	McIlvenny	Grant	Bow	LEONARD
15	26-Oct		SL2	LEITH ATHLETIC	0-1	Hood	Annan	Ritchie	Buchanan	Barrie	Baird	Lee	McILVENNY 2	Mein	Bow	Leonard
16	02-Nov		SL2	MOTHERWELL	4-0	Hood	Annan	Ritchie	Buchanan	Christie,AJ	Gray	Greig	Scott	Scott	Bow	Johnstone
17	09-Nov		SL2	Dunfermline Ath	4-1	Hood	Annan	McEwan	Buchanan	Barrie	Baird	Lee	Scott	Mein	BOW	Leonard
18	16-Nov		SL2	HAMILTON Accies	0-1	Hood	Annan	Ritchie	Buchanan	Gray	BAIRD	Grant	Ross	McIlvenny	BOW	Leonard
19	30-Nov		SL2	PORT Glasgow Ath	2-1	Hood	Annan	Ritchie	Buchanan	Barrie	Baird	Grant	McKENNA	McIlvenny	BOW	Leonard
20	07-Dec		SL2	EAST STIRLING	4-0	Hood	Annan	Ritchie	Buchanan	Barrie	Baird	Lee	McKenna	McKENZIE 2	BOW 2	McIlvenny
21	21-Dec		SL2	CLYDE	2-3	from Hood, Annan, McEwan, Buchanan, Barrie, Baird, Lee, McKenna, McIlvenny and Johnstone.										
22	25-Dec			Middlesborough	1-2	Hood	Ritchie	McEwan	Barrie	Brown	Baird	Lee	Brown	McKenna	Bow	Johnstone
23	26-Dec			Grimsby Town	2-2	Hood	Annan	McEwan	Johnstone	Barrie	Baird	Lee	Johnstone	McColl	McIlvenny	Leonard
24	31-Dec			Morton	2-2	Hood	Ritchie	Bryson	Buchanan	Barrie	Gray	'Bell'	Johnstone	McKenzie	Brown	Leonard
25	01-Jan		ESL	Raith Rovers	0-1	Hood	Annan	McEwan	Buchanan	Barrie	Baird	Barrie	McIlvenny	McKenzie	Bow	Leonard
26	02-Jan		SL2	Ayr	1-0	Hood	Annan	Ritchie	Buchanan	Gray	Baird	Lee	McILVENNY	Walker	Bow	Leonard
27	11-Jan		SC1	MOTHERWELL	0-1	Hood	Annan	Ritchie	Buchanan	Barrie	Baird	Lee	Johnstone	Mather	Bow	Lee
28	18-Jan		SL2	Abercorn	0-1	Hood	Annan	Ritchie	Barrie	Brown,J	Baird	Brown,T	Grant	McKenzie	Bow	Lee
29	25-Jan		SC2	Falkirk	0-2	Hood	Ritchie	Annan	Barrie	Brown,J	Baird	BROWN	Lee	Walker	Bow	Grant
30	01-Feb		SL2	Leith Athletic	1-2	Hood	Annan	Ritchie	Barrie	McEwan	Baird	Brown,T	McIlvenny	Walker	Bow	Grant
31	08-Feb		ESL	Dundee	1-6	Hood	Annan	McEwan	Barrie	Brown,J	Baird	Brown,T	McIlvenny	Walker	Bow	Grant
32	22-Feb		ESS	Leith Athletic (n)	2-0	Hood	Ritchie	McEwan	Barrie	Brown	Baird	Brown,T	McIlvenny	Walker	Bow	Grant
33	01-Mar		SL2	Airdrie	1-3	Hood	Ritchie	Annan	Barrie	Brown	Baird	Lee	Brown,J	WALKER 2	Bow	Grant
34	08-Mar		SL2	ARTHURLIE	2-1	Fairley	Annan	McEwan	Barrie	Ritchie	Baird	Brown	McIlvenny	Walker	Bow	Grant
35	15-Mar		ESSs	Hibernian	0-3	Hood	Ritchie	McEwan	Lee	Johnstone	Baird	BROWN,T	McIlvenny	Walker	Bow	Grant
36	22-Mar		SL2	Motherwell	1-2	Hood	Annan									
37	28-Mar			Barrow	0-2											
38	29-Mar			Wigan United	0-3											
39	31-Mar			Burnley	1-0	Stanners	Annan	McEwan	Johnstone	Ross	Barrie	Walker	Lee	Brown	Baird	Bow
40	05-Apr		SL2	Arthurlie	3-0	Hood	Angus	McEwan	Lee	Barrie	Baird	Brown	Johnstone	Walker	Bow	Grant
41	12-Apr		ESL	Leith Athletic	1-2*	Stanners	Annan	McEwan	Lee	Barrie	'Anderson'	Brown	Johnstone	Walker	Bow	'Smith'
42	14-Apr		ESL	Hearts	0-1	Stanners	Annan	Baird	Smith	Barrie	Ross	Brown	Johnstone	Walker	Bow	Grant
43	21-Apr			SUNDERLAND	2-1	Stanners	Annan	McEwan	Lee	Barrie	Ross	Brown,T	Brown,J	McNallie	Bow	Grant
44	26-Apr		ESL	LEITH ATHLETIC	2-3	Stanners	Baird	McEwan	Lee	Barrie	Ross	Brown,J	Brown,J	Maxwell	Bow	Smith
45	28-Apr		ESL	HIBERNIAN	3-1	Stanners	Dodds	McEwan	Lee	Barrie	Ross	Grant	Gallagher	Brown	Bow	Ferguson
46	30-Apr			Broxburn	2-1	Stanners	Baird	McEwan	Lee	Johnstone	Ross	Campbell	Johnstone	Maxwell	Bow	Smith
47	03-May		ESL	DUNDEE	3-3	Stanners	Baird	McEwan	Barrie	Morrison	Ross	Grant	Brown	Maxwell	Barr	Lee
48	05-May		ESL	Raith Rovers	2-2	Stanners	Henderson	Dodds	Barrie	Smith	Johnstone	Campbell	Brown	Lyall	Bow	Lee
49	10-May			West Calder (n)	2-6	Stanners	Bird	Campbell	Barrie	Morrison	Ross	Smith	Bow	Maxwell	Grant	Johnstone
50	17-May			Hearts	0-2	Stanners	Campbell	McEwan	Barrie	Morrison	Ross	Brown,T	Johnstone	Maxwell	Bow	Lee
51	24-May		RCC	Bathgate		Anderson	Ross	Lee	Johnstone	Murphy	Gibson	Mitchell	Maxwell	Bow	Lee	

1907

Second Division Champions and finalists Scottish Qualifying Cup 1906/07

Back Row: A Grant (Trainer), R Martin, J Mathieson, D Blackwood, A Reid, T Gray (Hon Sec), T Ritchie, W Kemp and J Mentiplay.
Seated: G Prior, A Ritchie, W Sloggie, W Smith, P Buchanan (Capt), R Findlay, W Bathgate, J MacDonald and R Tait.
On Ground: G Ramsay and T Ross.

Photograph courtesy of SFA Museum

Winners of the Penman, Scottish Qualifying and Rosebery Cups 1907/08.
Back Row: A Grant (Trainer), M Bookless, T Gray (Hon Sec), J Mathieson (Vice President), J Mentiplay, and JA Burns.
Middle Row: P Hyde, W Laidlaw, J Herron, W Smith (with ball), A Reid and J Veitch.
Front Row: W Curran, T Ross, J Tennant, A Smith, R Findlay, W Watson and E Milne.
On Ground: G Ramsay, Penman Cup, Scottish Qualifying Cup, Rosebery Cup and H Simpson.
Absent: P Buchanan, J Simpson, C Murray and P Logan.
Photograph courtesy of the SFA Museum

1902/03

#	Date	Comp	Opponent	Score												
1	09-Aug	Trial	PRACTICE Match	?-?												
2	15-Aug	ESL	LEITH ATHLETIC	0-0	Stanners	McEwan	Baird	Morrison	Ross	Ritchie	Hamilton	Maxwell	Johnstone	Lee	
3	16-Aug	SL2	ABERCORN	4-1	Stanners	McEwan	Baird	Morrison	Ross	GRANT 2	Johnstone	Maxwell	BOW	LEE	
4	18-Aug	ESL	Hearts	0-3	Stanners	Hamilton,J	Baird	Morrison	Ross	Grant	Hamilton,T	Maxwell	Miller	Brown,J	
5	23-Aug	SL2	Falkirk	1-0	Stanners	Hamilton	Baird	Morrison	Johnstone	Grant	Brown,T	Brown,T	Maxwell	LEE	
6	30-Aug	SL2	LEITH ATHLETIC	0-1	Stanners	McEwan	Brown,J	Morrison	Johnstone	Grant	Maxwell	Brown,T	Miller	Lee	
7	01-Sep	ESL	Hibernian	1-4	Meikle	Wood	Baird	Morrison	Johnstone	Grant	Lyall	McNally	Miller,J	Lee	
8	06-Sep	SL2	Airdrie	0-1	Stanners	Hamilton	Baird	Morrison	Brown	ROSS	Johnstone	Miller	Lyall	Lee	
9	13-Sep	SL2	EAST STIRLING	3-1	Stanners	Hamilton	Baird	Morrison	ROSS	Grant	Johnstone	MILLER 2	Lyall	Lee	
10	20-Sep	SL2	Clyde	1-0	Stanners	HAMILTON	Baird	Morrison	Ross	Grant	Johnstone	Miller	Lyall	Lee	
11	27-Sep	SL2	Leith Athletic	0-1	Stanners	Hamilton	Baird	Morrison	Ross	Grant	Johnstone	Miller	Lyall	Lee	
12	04-Oct	SL2	AIRDRIE	0-1	Stanners	Hamilton	Lee	Morrison	Ross	Grant	Johnstone	Miller	Lyall	Lee	
13	11-Oct	SL2	Hamilton Accies	2-3	Stanners	Hamilton	Baird	Morrison	Ross	GRANT	Johnstone	Miller	LYALL	Walker	
14	18-Oct	SL2	FALKIRK	8-3	Stanners	Allan	McEWAN	Baird	Ross	Henderson,W	MILLER	WALKER 3	LYALL	HENDERSON,J	
15	25-Oct	SL2	Motherwell	3-4	Stanners	Grant	McEWAN	Baird	Ross	Henderson,W	MILLER	Anderson	Lyall	Henderson,J	
16	01-Nov	SL2	RAITH ROVERS	1-1	Stanners	Grant	McEwan	Baird	Ross	Henderson,W	MILLER	Walker	Lyall	Henderson,J	
17	08-Nov	SL2	Abercorn	5-3	Stanners	Grant	McEwan	Baird	Ross	Henderson,W	MILLER 2	WALKER 3	Johnstone	Henderson,W	
18	15-Nov	SL2	ARTHURLIE	2-2	Stanners	Grant	McEwan	Baird	Ross	Henderson,J	Miller	WALKER 2	Johnstone	Henderson,W	
19	22-Nov	SL2	East Stirling	1-4	Stanners	Grant	McEwan	Baird	Ross	Henderson,W	Miller	Walker	Johnstone	Henderson,W	
20	29-Nov	SL2	MOTHERWELL	1-2	Stanners	Grant	McEwan	Baird	Ross	Henderson,J	Miller	Walker	SCOTT	Henderson,W	
21	06-Dec	SL2	CLYDE	3-0	Stanners	Allan	McEwan	Grant	Johnstone	Henderson,W	BROWN	MILLER	Scott	HENDERSON,J	
22	13-Dec	SL2	Raith Rovers	2-1	Stanners	Allan	McEwan	Grant	Johnstone	HENDERSON,W	Brown	Miller	Scott	HENDERSON,J	
23	20-Dec	SL2	Arthurlie	2-1	Stanners	Allan	Brown	MORRISON	Johnstone	Henderson,W	Lyall	Miller	Scott	Henderson,J	
24	25-Dec	SL2	BLACK WATCH	3-2	Meikle	Allan	Grant	Morrison	Ross	Jenkins	Brown	Miller	Scott	Cox	
25	27-Dec	ESL	HIBERNIAN	2-3	Stanners	Allan	Grant	Morrison	Johnstone	Henderson	Brown	Miller	Scott	Glen	
26	03-Jan	SC1	Ayr	2-1	Stanners	Allan	Grant	Morrison	Gray	Henderson	Brown	Miller	Scott	Johnstone	
27	17-Jan	SC1	PORT Glasgow Ath	1-2	Stanners	Grant	Gray	Morrison	Johnstone	HENDERSON,W	Brown	Miller	Scott,R	Scott,A	
28	24-Jan	ESL	Dundee	0-4	Stanners	Allan	McEwan	Morrison	Baird	Henderson,W	Brown	Miller	Scott	Scott,R	
29	31-Jan	ESS	BATHGATE	5-0	Stanners	Allan	McEwan	Morrison	Baird	HENDERSON,W	Brown	Miller	Scott,A	Scott,A	
30	07-Feb	SL2	AYR	1-0*	Stanners	Allan	McEwan	Morrison	Johnstone	Henderson,W	Brown,J	Miller	Scott	Henderson,J	
31	14-Feb	SL2	AYR	2-0	Stanners	Allan	McEwan	Morrison	Johnstone	Henderson,J	Brown,J	MILLER 2	Scott	Henderson,W	
32	28-Feb	ESL	Leith Athletic	1-0	Stanners	Allan	McEwan	Morrison	Johnstone	Henderson	Brown	Miller	Scott	McFarlane	
33	14-Mar	ESL	East Stirling	2-2	Stanners	Allan	Morrison	Johnstone	Henderson	Brown	Dickson	Miller	Scott	Meikle	
34	21-Mar	SL2	Albion Rovers	2-1	Stanners	Allan	Morrison	Buchanan	Johnstone	Tait	Brown	Miller	Meikle	Johnstone	
35	28-Mar	SL2	Montrose	2-2	Stanners	Allan	Morrison	Grant	Johnstone	Meikle	Brown	Bell	Scott	Taylor	
36	04-Apr	SL2	HAMILTON Accies	2-1	Stanners	Morrison	Brown	Johnstone	HENDERSON	Allan	MILLER	Scott	Meikle		
37	10-Apr		Middlesbrough	0-3	from Stanners, Morrison, McEwan, Brown, Grant, Johnstone, Henderson, Dickson, Miller, Scott and Meikle.										
38	15-Apr		Boness	1-1	Stanners	Grant	McEwan	Bain	Marshall	Gibb	McPherson	Johnstone	Meikle	Smellie	
39	18-Apr	ESS	Leith Athletic	2-3	Stanners	Grant	McEwan	Brown	Morrison	Henderson,J	Henderson,W	Miller	Scott	Meikle	
40	20-Apr		SUNDERLAND	2-2	Stanners	Grant	McEwan	Brown	Morrison	Henderson,J	Henderson,W	Miller	Scott	Meikle	
41	25-Apr	ESL	DUNDEE	2-3	Stanners	Grant	McEwan	Brown	Morrison	'Jackson'	Johnstone	Meikle	Miller	Scott	'Smith'
42	02-May	ESL	HEARTS	1-1	Stanners	Grant	McEwan	Brown	Morrison	Johnstone	Henderson	Williams	Miller	Woodward	Scott
43	18-May	RCC	HIBERNIAN	1-2	Stanners	Grant	McEwan	Brown	Morrison	Johnstone	Brown	Clark	Miller	Meikle	Scott

1903/04

#	Date	Comp	Opponent	Score												
1	08-Aug	Trial	Practice Match	?												
2	15-Aug	SL2	Ayr	0-2	Stanners	Grant	Morrison	Brown,J	Clark	Johnstone	Nelson	Joyce	Heselwood	Scott	Meikle	
3	18-Aug		BLACK WATCH	3-0	Stanners	Meikle	Morrison	Bogie	Maxwell	Russel	Nelson	Joyce	Heselwood	Johnstone	McNally	
4	22-Aug	SL2	East Stirling	1-3	Stanners	Meikle	Morrison	Brown	Bogie	Johnstone	Nelson	Joyce	HESELWOOD	Clark	McColl	
5	27-Aug		W Calder Swifts	3-2												
6	29-Aug	SL2	ALBION ROVERS	2-1	Stanners	Grant	Morrison	Brown	Bogie	Clark	Nelson	Brown,T	Heselwood	Johnstone	MEIKLE 2	
7	05-Sep	SL2	LEITH ATHLETIC	1-2	Stanners	Grant	Bogie	Brown	Morrison	Johnstone	Nelson	Joyce	Heselwood	McColl	Wright	
8	12-Sep	SL2	Hamilton Accies	1-5	Hood	Grant	Oates	Brown	Morrison	Johnstone	Nelson	Joyce	BROWN,T	Scott	McColl	
9	19-Sep	SL2	AYR	1-1	Hood	Grant	Oates	Bogie	Morrison	Johnstone	Nelson	Joyce	HESELWOOD	Scott	McColl	
10	26-Sep	SL2	Albion Rovers	0-4	Stanners	Grant	Oates	Brown	Morrison	Johnstone	Wilson	McColl	Brown	Scott	Wright	
11	03-Oct	SL2	Ayr Parkhouse	2-1	Stanners	Grant	Morrison	Bogie	Morrison	Oates	Brown,T	JOYCE	Clark	Scott	Johnstone	
12	10-Oct	SL2	Raith Rovers	2-1	Stanners	Grant	Morrison	Brown	Pray	Oates	Brown,T	JOYCE	LYALL	Scott	McColl	
13	17-Oct	SL2	RAITH ROVERS	1-2	Stanners	Grant	Morrison	Pray	Brown	Oates	Brown,T	Johnstone	Lyall	SCOTT	McColl	
14	24-Oct	SL2	Falkirk	1-3	Stanners	Grant	Morrison	Pray	Brown	Oates	Nelson	Joyce	Heselwood	SCOTT	McColl	
15	31-Oct	SL2	ARTHURLIE	2-1	Stanners	Grant	Morrison	Pray	Morrison	Oates	NEILSON	Joyce	Heselwood	SCOTT	JOHNSTONE	
16	07-Nov	ESL	Hearts	0-2	Stanners	Grant	Oates	Pray	Morrison	Brown	McDonald	Joyce	Heselwood	Scott	Johnstone	
17	14-Nov	SL2	Leith Athletic	2-3	Stanners	Grant	Oates	Pray	Morrison	Brown	Lyall	JOYCE	Heselwood	Scott	Johnstone	
18	21-Nov	SL2	FALKIRK	1-3	Stanners	Grant	Oates	Bogie	Morrison	Johnstone	Meikle	Joyce	Heselwood	Scott	JOHNSTONE	
19	12-Dec	SL2	Arthurlie	2-1	Stanners	Grant	Oates	Bogie	Morrison	Johnstone	Meikle	BROWN	Henderson	McGettigen	Scott	
20	19-Dec	SL2	EAST STIRLING	1-1	Stanners	Grant	Oates	Pray	Morrison	Johnstone	MEIKLE	Brown	McGettigen	Joyce	Scott	
21	25-Dec	SL2	Grimsby Town	1-5	Stanners	Grant	Oates	Bogie	Morrison	Johnstone	Meikle	Joyce	Heselwood	McGettigen	Scott	
22	26-Dec	SL2	ABERCORN	4-2	Stanners	Grant	Oates	Bogie	Morrison	Johnstone	MEIKLE 2	McGettigen	Heselwood	McGettigen 2	Devlin	
23	01-Jan	SL2	HAMILTON Accies	0-1	Stanners	Grant	Oates	Brown	Morrison	Oates	Wemyss	Joyce	SCOTT 2	Scott	Devlin	
24	02-Jan	SL2	AYR Parkhouse	2-1	Stanners	Grant	Oates	Brown	Morrison	Oates	Wemyss	Johnstone	Scott	McGettigen	DEVLIN	
25	09-Jan	SC1	Clyde	2-1	Stanners	Grant	Oates	Bogie	Morrison	Oates	Wemyss	Joyce	Joyce	McGettigen	DEVLIN	
26	23-Jan	SC1	W CALDER Swifts	1-1	Stanners	Grant	McCracken	Brown	Morrison	Oates	Wemyss	Joyce	Scott	McGettigen	Devlin	
27	30-Jan	SC1	W Calder Swifts	3-3	Stanners	Grant	McCracken	Brown	Morrison	OATES	WEMYSS	Meikle	Scott	McGettigen	Devlin	
28	06-Feb	SC1	W Calder Swifts	2-0	Stanners	Grant	McCracken	Johnstone	Morrison	Oates	Wemyss	Scott	HESELWOOD	McGettigen	Devlin	
29	13-Feb	SC2	CELTIC	0-4	Stanners	McCracken	Grant	Johnstone	Morrison	Oates	Wemyss	Meikle	Gibson	McGettigen	Devlin	
30	20-Feb		Queens Park	1-3	Stanners	Grant	McCracken	Bogie	Morrison	Oates	Johnstone	Brown	Heselwood	McGettigen	Devlin	
31	27-Feb	ESSp	BONESS	3-0	Stanners	Grant	McCracken	Brown	Morrison	Oates	Wemyss	Giblin	Heselwood	McGettigen	Devlin	
32	05-Mar		Abercorn	2-0	Stanners	Grant	McCracken	Bogie	Morrison	Oates	WEMYSS	Giblin	Heselwood	McGettigen	Devlin	
33	12-Mar	SL2	CLYDE	1-4	Stanners	Grant	McCracken	Bogie	Morrison	Oates	Wemyss	Giblin	Heselwood	McGettigen	Devlin	
34	19-Mar		Boness	2-2	Stanners	Grant	Oates	Bogie	Morrison	McNally	Stewart	Johnstone	Giblin	McGettigen	Devlin	
35	26-Mar	ESL	Aberdeen	1-1	Stanners	Grant	McCracken	Bogie	Morrison	Oates	Wemyss	Johnstone	Heselwood	McGettigen	Devlin	
36	02-Apr	ESL	Leith Athletic	1-1	Stanners	Watson	McCracken	McNally	Morrison	Oates	Wemyss	Giblin	Bogie	McGettigen	Devlin	
37	09-Apr	ESL	Falkirk	1-2	Stanners	Grant	McCracken	Grant	Morrison	Oates	WEMYSS	Giblin	Bogie	McGettigen	Devlin	
38	16-Apr	ESL	Hibernian	2-1	Stanners	Grant	McCracken	Oates	Morrison	Bogie	Smith	Johnstone	Giblin	McGettigen	Devlin	
39	23-Apr	ESSs	HIBERNIAN	0-0	Stanners	Grant	Oates	Bogie	Morrison	Oates	Wemyss	Sanderson	Giblin	McGettigen	Devlin	
40	30-Apr		East Fife	3-0	Stanners	Grant	McCracken	Grant	Morrison	Bogie	Neilson	Giblin	Sanderson	McGettigen	Devlin	
41	07-May	ESL	LEITH Athletic	2-2	Stanners	Grant	McCracken	Bogie	Morrison	Oates	Wemyss	Giblin	Heselwood	McGettigen	Devlin	
42	14-May		Dalkeith Thistle	3-1												
43	14-May	ESSf	Hearts (n)	2-7	Stanners	Grant	McCracken	Bogie	Morrison	Oates	Wemyss	Giblin	Heselwood	McGettigen	Devlin	
44	21-May	RCCs	Hibernian (n)	0-2	Stanners	Campbell	'Smith'	Bogie	Oates	Hunter	Wemyss	Giblin	Heselwood	McGettigen	Devlin	

1904/05

#	Date	Opponent	Comp	Score	1	2	3	4	5	6	7	8	9	10	11
1	15-Aug	Dundee	ESL	1-2	Stanners	Oates	Buchanan	Hunter		Bogie	Greig	Scott	Greig	Wemyss	Giblin	Heselwood	McGettigen	Devlin
2	20-Aug	Hamilton Accies	SL2	0-4	Stanners	Buchanan		McNeil	Bogie	Greig	Oates	Hunter		Bogie	Heselwood	McGettigen	Devlin
3	24-Aug	East of Scotland Jnrs		?														
4	27-Aug	Falkirk	SL2	1-2	Stanners	Buchanan	Hunter	Greig	Bogie	Oates	Wemyss	Giblin	HESELWOOD	McGettigen	Devlin
5	31-Aug	BLACK WATCH	SQC1	2-1	Stanners	Buchanan	Hunter	Greig	Bogie	Oates	Wemyss	Giblin	HESELWOOD 2	McGettigen	Devlin
6	03-Sep	Arthurlie	SL2	1-1	Stanners	Buchanan	Hunter	McNeil	Greig	Bogie	Oates	NEILSON	Giblin	Heselwood	McGettigen	Devlin
7	05-Sep	Hibernian	ESL	1-1	McNeil	Oates		Greig	J Smith	Devlin	Scott	Giblin	Prior	McGettigen	Devlin
8	10-Sep	BLACK WATCH	SQC1	2-0	Stanners	BUCHANAN	Hunter	Oates	Smith	Greig	Oates	Neilson	Ramage	Heselwood	McGettigen	A Smith
9	17-Sep	West Calder Swifts	SQC2	1-1	Stanners	Buchanan	Hunter	Greig	Smith	Oates	Kinross	Ramage	Heselwood	McGettigen	Devlin
10	24-Sep	WEST CALDER SW	SQC2	3-1	Stanners	Buchanan	Hunter	Greig	Smith	Oates	Kinross	RAMAGE 3	Heselwood	McGettigen	Devlin
11	01-Oct	Leith Athletic	SQC3	1-5	Stanners	Buchanan	McNeil	Lyall	Smith	Oates	Hunter	WEMYSS	Giblin	Ramage	McGettigen	DEVLIN
12	08-Oct	AYR	SL2	2-1	Stanners	Buchanan	McNeil	Hunter	Smith	Oates	Hunter	Wemyss	Smith	RAMAGE	McGettigen	DEVLIN
13	15-Oct	ABERCORN	SL2	2-0	Stanners	Buchanan	McNeil	Hunter	Smith	Oates	Hunter	Wemyss	Smith	Ramage	Heselwood	DEVLIN
14	22-Oct	Albion Rovers	SL2	2-3	Stanners	Buchanan	McNeil	Hunter	Smith	HUNTER	Oates	Neilson	Ramage	Heselwood	McGettigen	Devlin
15	29-Oct	Raith Rovers	SL2	2-1	Stanners	Oates	McNeil	Hunter	Smith	Hunter	Oates	Wemyss	Smith	Ramage	Heselwood	DEVLIN
16	05-Nov	ALBION ROVERS	SL2	1-5	Stanners	McCracken	McNeil	Greig	Smith	Greig	Oates	Wemyss	Heselwood	Heselwood	McGettigen	McGettigen
17	12-Nov	RAITH ROVERS	SL2	0-4	Stanners	McCracken	McNeil	Greig	Smith	Oates	Smith	McNeil	McDonald	Anderson	Devlin	Connor
18	19-Nov	East Stirling	SL2	2-1	McNeil	Buchanan	McNeil	Greig	Smith	Oates	Smith	Greig	McGettigen	Anderson	Devlin	Connor
19	26-Nov	LEITH ATHLETIC	SL2	0-2	Stanners	Buchanan	McNeil	Greig	Smith	Smith	McCracken	McGettigen	Anderson	Hunter	Devlin	Ramage
20	03-Dec	Aberdeen	SL2	1-1*	Coghlan	Buchanan	Reid	Greig	Smith	Smith	McCracken	McGettigen	Anderson	Hunter	Devlin	Thomson
21	10-Dec	ARTHURLIE	SL2	2-3	Davy	Buchanan	McNeil	Greig	Smith	Smith	McCracken	McGettigen	WEMYSS	HUNTER	Devlin	Connor
22	17-Dec	Abercorn	SL2	2-3	Davy	Buchanan	McNeil	Greig	Smith	Smith	McCracken	WEMYSS	Anderson	HESELWOOD	CONNOR
23	24-Dec	ABERDEEN	SL2	0-3	Davy	Buchanan	McNeil	Greig	Smith	McNeil	McCracken	Wemyss	Heselwood	Hunter	Devlin	Connor
24	31-Dec	Leith Athletic	SL2	1-4	Stanners	BUCHANAN	McNeil	Greig	Smith	Greig	Collins	McGettigen	Hunter	Devlin	Connor
25	07-Jan	Aberdeen	ESL	1-6	Stanners	Grant	Lyall	Greig	Smith	McNeil	Wemyss	Heselwood	Anderson	Ramage
26	03-Jan	Peterhead		0-3	Stanners	Hay	Buchanan	Craig	Bogie	Greig	Collins	McGettigen	Heselwood	Anderson	Ramage
27	07-Jan	Ayr	SL2	1-5	Stanners	McNeil		McNeil	Smith	Greig	Hunter	Bogie	McGettigen	Hamilton	Devlin	HUNTER
28	14-Jan	Clyde	SL2	0-5	Davy	McNeil	Buchanan	McCracken.	Smith	Ross	Greig	McGettigen	DEVLIN	Hunter	Devlin	Ramage
29	21-Jan	Aberdeen	SL2	1-1	Davy	Robertson	Reid	Buchanan	Greig	Ross	Smith	Ross	Hunter	BUCHAN	McGettigen	Thomson
30	28-Jan	Falkirk	SL2	1-2	Davy	Reid	Buchanan	Reid	Smith	Ross	Smith	Ross	McGettigen	Giblin	Devlin
31	04-Feb	CLYDE	SL2	1-1	Davy	Buchanan	Reid	Buchanan	Smith	Smith	Ross	Smith	Ross	Devlin	Heselwood	Thomson
32	11-Feb	HIBERNIAN	ESSs	2-1*	Davy	Buchanan	McNeil	Reid	Smith	Ross	Smith	Ross	Giblin	Buchan	GREIG
33	18-Feb	EAST STIRLING	SL2	1-1	Stanners	Reid	Buchanan	Reid	Smith	GIBLIN	Ross	Devlin	Heselwood	Greig	Devlin
34	25-Feb	HAMILTON ACCIES	SL2	0-0	Stanners	Buchanan	Buchanan	Reid	Smith	Devlin	Ross	McGettigen	Heselwood	Greig	Ramage
35	04-Mar	HIBERNIAN	ESSs	4-1	Stanners	Buchanan	Buchanan	Reid	Smith	Wemyss	Ross	McGettigen	Giblin	Buchan	Greig
36	11-Mar	BO'NESS	CC	3-1	Stanners	Buchanan	Buchanan	Reid	Smith	Henderson,T	Ross	McGettigen	Giblin	Buchan	Henderson,W
37	18-Mar	Dundee	ESL	0-6	Stanners	Buchanan	Buchanan	Reid	Smith	Giblin	Ross	McGettigen	Hamilton	Buchan	Ramage
38	25-Mar	Hibernian	ESSs	1-1	Stanners	Buchanan	Buchanan	Reid	Smith	Giblin	Ross	McGettigen	'Hamilton'	'Hamilton'	Greig
39	01-Apr	Hibernian (n)	ESSs	1-3	Stanners	Buchanan	Buchanan	Reid	Smith	Wemyss	Ross	McGettigen	Giblin	Fisher	Johnstone
40	17-Apr	Leith Athletic	SL2	1-1	Stanners	Buchanan	Buchanan	Reid	Smith	Giblin	Ross	McGettigen	Hunter	Buchan	Devlin
41	22-Apr	FALKIRK	SL2	2-2	Stanners	Reid		McNeil	Smith	Wemyss	Ross	McGettigen	Hunter	Buchan	Jackson
42	24-Apr			4-0												
43	29-Apr	Dalkeith Thistle	ESL	1-4	Stanners	Buchanan	Reid	Smith	Ross	Giblin	Devlin	Hunter	Buchan	Jackson
44	03-May	Bonnyrigg District		0-0												
45	06-May	LEITH ATHLETIC	CCs	1-1	Grant	Buchanan	Reid	Hossack	Smith	Jackson	Ross	Hunter	Hunter	Jackson	Giblin
46	08-May	HEARTS	ESL	1-2	Grant	Buchanan	Reid	Hossack	Swan	Tait	Crawford	Ross	Steedman	'Urquhart'	Greig
47	10-May	Falkirk	SL2	0-2	Stanners	Innes	Buchanan	Hossack	Smith	Giblin	Ross	McGettigen	Hunter	Ford	Jackson
48	12-May	Leith Athletic (n)	CCs	1-1*	Stanners	Buchanan	Reid	Hossack	Smith	Jackson	Ross	McGettigen	Heselwood	Buchan	Ford
49	13-May	Hibernian	ESL	0-2	'Watson'	Muir	Reid	Hossack	Smith	Ross	Smith	Ross	McGettigen	Mailer	McDonald
50	20-May	Hearts	RCCs	1-2	Davy	Buchanan	Reid	Hossack	Raiker	Ross	Wemyss	Jackson	Smith	Buchan	Thomson

* lost on toss of coin

1905/06

#	Date	Lg	Opponent	Score											
1	12-Aug		Trial Match	?-?	Stanners	Buchanan	Reid	Hossack	Smith	Ross	Black	Guthrie	McDonald	Buchan	Thomson
2	15-Aug	ESL	Aberdeen	0-1	Stanners	BUCHANAN	Reid	Hossack	Smith	Ross	Gray	Guthrie	McDonald	McGettigen	Jackson
3	19-Aug	SL2	ALBION ROVERS	1-2	Stanners	Buchanan	Lyall	Crawford	Simpson	Ross	Johnstone	Guthrie	Prior	McGettigen	Tait
4	23-Aug		Broxburn	0-0	Hughes	Buchanan	Reid	Gray,R	Smith	Ross	Gray,R (Sen)	GUTHRIE	McDonald	McDONALD	McDonald
5	26-Aug	SL2	Vale of Leven	4-2	Stanners	Buchanan	Reid	Hossack	Smith	ROSS	GRAY	GUTHRIE	Prior	McDONALD	Jackson
6	02-Sep	SOC1	BATHGATE	2-2	Hughes	BUCHANAN	Reid	Hossack	Smith	Ross	Gray	Guthrie	GIBLIN	McDONALD	JACKSON
7	09-Sep	SL2	Hamilton Accies	4-0	Stanners	Buchanan	Reid	McGettigen	Smith	Ross	Gray	Guthrie	GIBLIN	McDonald	JACKSON
8	16-Sep	SL2	Cowdenbeath	2-2	Stanners	Buchanan	Reid	McGettigen	Smith	Ross	Giblin	Guthrie	Hunter	McDonald	Jackson
9	18-Sep		NEWCASTLE Utd	2-2	Stanners	Buchanan	Reid	McGettigen	Smith	Ross	Gray	McGettigen	Giblin	McDonald	Jackson
10	23-Sep	SOC2	LEITH	0-1	Stanners	Buchanan	Reid	Hossack	Smith	Ross	Gray	Guthrie	Giblin	McDonald	Jackson
11	30-Sep	SL2	Ayr	0-0	Stanners	Buchanan	Reid	Hossack	Smith	Ross	Gray	McGettigen	Guthrie	McGettigen	McKay
12	07-Oct	ESSs	Hearts	0-2	Stanners	Buchanan	Reid	Hossack	Smith	Ross	Prior	McGettigen	Guthrie	McGettigen	McKay
13	28-Oct	SL2	Albion Rovers	0-4	Stanners	Buchanan	Reid	Hossack	Smith	Ross	Gray	Guthrie	Giblin	McGettigen	McKay
14	04-Nov	SL2	East Stirling	1-1	Stanners	Buchanan	Reid	Hossack	Smith	Ross	Gray	BEVERIDGE	McDonald	Beveridge	McKay
15	11-Nov	SL2	HAMILTON Accies	4-0	Stanners	Buchanan	Reid	Hossack	Smith	Ross	Blythe	BEVERIDGE 3	McDONALD	McDONALD	McGettigen
16	25-Nov	SL2	CLYDE	0-0	Stanners	Buchanan	Reid	Hossack	Smith	Ross	Blythe	Guthrie	McDonald	Beveridge	JACKSON
17	02-Dec	SL2	EAST STIRLING	3-2	Stanners	Buchanan	Reid	Hossack	Smith	Ross	Marshall	BEVERIDGE	GUTHRIE	McDonald	McKay
18	09-Dec	SL2	AYR	5-1	Hood	Buchanan	Reid	HOSSACK	Smith	Ross	MARSHALL	BEVERIDGE 2	GUTHRIE	McDonald	McKay
19	16-Dec	SL2	Arthurlie	0-4	Stanners	Buchanan	Reid	McGETTIGEN	Smith	Ross	Tait	Beveridge	GUTHRIE 2	McDonald	McKay
20	23-Dec	SL2	Raith Rovers	3-4	Stanners	Buchanan	Reid	Hossack	Smith	Ross	Tait	Beveridge	GUTHRIE	McDonald	McKay
21	30-Dec	SL2	VALE OF LEVEN	3-0	Stanners	Buchanan	Reid	Tait	Smith	Ross	McGettigen	BEVERIDGE	GUTHRIE	McDONALD	McKay
22	01-Jan		Berwick Rangers	1-3											
23	02-Jan	ESL	Falkirk	2-3	Hood	Buchanan	Lyall	Tait	Smith	Ross	Millar	Beveridge	Gray	Walker	McKay
24	06-Jan	SL2	Clyde	0-2	Stanners	Buchanan	Reid	Tait	Smith	Ross	Lyall	Guthrie	Beveridge	McDonald	McGettigen
25	13-Jan	SL2	COWDENBEATH	1-0	Stanners	Buchanan	Reid	Lyall	Smith	Ross	Gray	Beveridge	McDONALD	Tait	Jackson
26	20-Jan	SL2	RAITH ROVERS	5-2	Stanners	Buchanan	Reid	Hossack	Smith	Ross	GRAY 2	BEVERIDGE 2	Giblin	McDonald	Tait
27	27-Jan	SL2	Abercorn	1-2	Stanners	Buchanan	Reid	Hossack	Smith	Ross	Giblin	Beveridge	Millar	McDonald	Gray
28	03-Feb	SL2	ABERCORN	1-0	Stanners	Reid	Buchanan	Hossack	Smith	Ross	GRAY	Beveridge	Millar	McDonald	Tait
29	10-Feb	SL2	ARTHURLIE	4-1	Stanners	Buchanan	Reid	Hossack	Smith	Ross	Giblin	BEVERIDGE 2	Gray	McDonald	TAIT 2
30	17-Feb		Newcastle Utd 'A'	2-5	from Stanners, Buchanan, Reid, Dickson, Smith, Ross, Giblin, Beveridge, Gray, McDonald and Tait.										
31	24-Feb	SL2	LEITH	2-5	Stanners	Buchanan	Reid	HOSSACK	Smith	Ross	Giblin	Beveridge	Gray	McDONALD	Tait
32	10-Mar	PC	Falkirk Amateurs	WO											
33	17-Mar	SL2	Leith	0-1	Stanners	Buchanan	Reid	HOSSACK	Smith	Ross	Gray	Beveridge	Giblin	McDonald	Tait
34	24-Mar	ESL	Dundee	0-2	Hood	Smith	Buchanan	Hossack	Smith	Ross	McKay	Guthrie	Millar	McDonald	McGettigen
35	31-Mar	SL2	Raith Rovers	1-1	Stanners	Buchanan	Reid	Hossack	Smith	Ross	Millar	Beveridge	Guthrie	McDonald	McRitchie
36	14-Apr	PC	Alloa Athletic	0-4	Stanners	Buchanan	Reid	Hossack	Smith	Ross	Giblin	Beveridge	Guthrie	McDonald	McRitchie
37	21-Apr	ESL	HIBERNIAN	0-0	Allan	Buchanan	Reid	Johnston	Smith	Ross	Brown	Guthrie	McDonald	Smith	McRitchie
38	23-Apr	CC	Leith (n)	0-1	Stanners	Buchanan	Reid	Hossack	Barclay	Beveridge	Smith	Smith	McDonald	McDonald	Thomson
39	26-Apr		Dalkeith & District	2-2	from 'McKay', Hume, Reid, Hossack, Smith, Ross, Tait, Beveridge, Giblin, McDonald and McRitchie.										
40	28-Apr		Falkirk	1-2	Hossack	Buchanan	Reid	Findlay	Smith	Ross	Tait	Beveridge	Giblin	McDonald	McRitchie
41	01-May	ESL	LEITH	2-0	Hood	Smith	Reid	Hossack	Tait	Ross	Giblin	Beveridge	Hall	McDonald	McRitchie
42	05-May	ESL	HEARTS	0-5	Hood	Ramsay	Reid	Hossack	Tait	Ross	Giblin	Beveridge	Hall	McDonald	McRitchie
43	14-May		Hibernian	1-1	Hood	Ramsay	Reid	Smith	Findlay	Ross	Marshall	Buchan	Thomson	McDonald	McRitchie
44	15-May		Adventurers	2-3											
45	26-May	RCCs	Hearts	1-3	Ramsay	Hamilton	Reid	Tait	Findlay	Ross	Thomson	Smith	Hall	Buchan	McRitchie

1906/07

#	Date	Comp	Opponent	Score	1	2	3	4	5	6	7	8	9	10	11
1	15-Aug		Airdrie	2-3	Ramsay	Reid	Thorburn	Weir	Smith	Tait	Ritchie	Beveridge	Hall	McDonald	McRitchie
2	18-Aug	SL2	DUMBARTON	3-0	Ramsay	Buchanan	Reid	Tait	Smith	Findlay	Ritchie	Beveridge	HALL 3	McDonald	McRitchie
3	21-Aug		Boness	0-3	Ross	Hamilton	Reid	Prior	Smith	Muir	Gibb	Beveridge	McGettigen	Miller	Robertson
4	25-Aug	SL2	Ayr	3-0	Hope	Buchanan	Dodds	Tait	Taylor	Findlay	Ritchie	BEVERIDGE	HALL 2	McDonald	McRitchie
5	29-Aug		Hibernian	1-1	Boyd	Reid	Reid	Tait	Smith	Prior	Ross	Beveridge	Hall	McDonald	White
6	01-Sep	SQC1	Broxburn Shamrock	4-0	Ramsay	Buchanan	Reid	Tait	Smith	Findlay	McRitchie	Beveridge	HALL	McDonald	BLACK
7	08-Sep	SQC1	BROXBURN Shamrock	3-1	Ramsay	Buchanan	Reid	Ross	Smith	Findlay	Marshall	BEVERIDGE	Hall	McDONALD 2	Black
8	15-Sep	SL2	East Stirling	4-0	Ramsay	Buchanan	Reid	Ross	Smith	Findlay	Marshall	Beveridge	HALL 2	McDonald	Black
9	17-Sep	ESS1	Hearts	1-5	Ramsay	Buchanan	Reid	Ross	Smith	Findlay	Marshall	Tait	HALL 2	McDonald	Black
10	22-Sep	SQC2	Broxburn Athletic	5-0	Ramsay	BUCHANAN	Beveridge	Ross	Smith	Findlay	Marshall	Beveridge	Hall	McDonald	Tait
11	29-Sep	SQC3	Leith	3-1	Ramsay	Buchanan	Reid	Ross	Smith	McRitchie	Marshall	Tait	McDONALD	McDonald	Black
12	06-Oct		AYR	2-1	Ramsay	BUCHANAN	Reid	Ross	SMITH	Findlay	Ritchie	Beveridge	TAIT	McDonald	Tait
13	13-Oct	SQC4	ARBROATH	2-1	Ramsay	Buchanan	Reid	Sloggie	Smith	Findlay	Ritchie	Beveridge	Law	McDonald	Tait
14	20-Oct		LEITH	2-1	Ramsay	Buchanan	Reid	Sloggie	Smith	Findlay	Ritchie	Beveridge	LAW 2	McDONALD	TAIT
15	27-Oct	SQC5	Forfar Athletic	5-0	Ramsay	Buchanan	Reid	Sloggie	Smith	Findlay	Ritchie	Beveridge	LAW 2	McDONALD	TAIT
16	03-Nov	SL2	VALE OF LEVEN	1-0	Ramsay	BUCHANAN	Reid	Sloggie	Smith	Findlay	Ritchie	Beveridge	Hall	McDonald	Tait
17	17-Nov	SQCs	JOHNSTONE	3-1	Ramsay	Buchanan	Reid	Sloggie	Smith	Findlay	RITCHIE	BEVERIDGE	Hall	McDONALD	TAIT
18	24-Nov	SQCf	RAITH ROVERS (n)	2-2	Ramsay	Buchanan	Reid	Sloggie	Smith	Findlay	Ritchie	Beveridge	Hall	McDonald	TAIT
19	01-Dec	SQCf	RAITH ROVERS (n)	1-3	Ramsay	Buchanan	Reid	Sloggie	Smith	FINDLAY	Ritchie	Beveridge	Hall	McDonald	Tait
20	08-Dec	SL2	ABERCORN	2-0	Ramsay	Buchanan	Reid	Sloggie	Smith	Findlay	RITCHIE	Law	HALL	McDonald	McRITCHIE
21	15-Dec	SL2	Leith	0-1	Ramsay	Buchanan	Reid	Sloggie	Smith	Laidlay	Ritchie	Beveridge	Tait	McDonald	McRitchie
22	22-Dec	SL2	ARTHURLIE	3-2	Ramsay	BUCHANAN	Reid	Sloggie	Tait	Findlay	Ritchie	TAIT	LAW	Hall	McRitchie
23	29-Dec		Hearts	2-3	Ramsay	Buchanan	Reid	Sloggie	Tait	McDonald	Irving	Ritchie	Hall	McDonald	McRitchie
24	31-Dec	ESL	Dundee	4-1	Reid	"Brown"	Reid	Sloggie	Smith	Findlay	Ritchie	Tait'	Hall	McDonald	McRitchie
25	01-Jan		Aberdeen 'A'	2-1	Ramsay	Sloggie	Reid	Sloggie	Smith	Tait	Ritchie	Law	Hall	McDonald	McRitchie
26	02-Jan		Petermead	1-5	Ramsay	Sloggie	Bathgate	Findlay	Smith	Ross	Ritchie	Law	HALL	McDonald	McRitchie
27	05-Jan	SL2	Arthurlie	3-0	Ramsay	Ritchie	Reid	Sloggie	Smith	Findlay	RITCHIE 2	BATHGATE	Tait	McDonald	TAIT
28	12-Jan	SC1	Ayr Parkhouse	3-1	Ramsay	Ritchie,T	Reid	Sloggie	Smith	Findlay	RITCHIE	Bathgate	Cameron	McDONALD	TAIT
29	19-Jan	SL2	ALBION ROVERS	2-1	Ramsay	Buchanan	Reid	Findlay	Smith	Ross	Ritchie	Bathgate	Cameron	McDonald	TAIT
30	26-Jan	SC1	Renton	1-1	Ramsay	Buchanan	Reid	Finlay	Smith	Ross	Ritchie	Bathgate	Cameron	McDonald	TAIT
31	02-Feb	SC1	RENTON	0-2	Ramsay	Ritchie	Reid	Ritchie	Smith	Ross	Ritchie	Bathgate	Smith	TAIT	McDONALD
32	09-Feb		RENTON (n)	2-3	Ramsay	Buchanan	Ritchie	Buchanan	Findlay	Ross	RITCHIE	Bathgate	Howard	McDonald	Tait
33	16-Feb	SL2	Cowdenbeath	0-0	Ramsay	Buchanan	Reid	Finlay	Smith	Ross	Ritchie	Bathgate	Howard	McDonald	Tait
34	23-Feb	SL2	Dumbarton	1-3	Ramsay	Buchanan	Reid	Finlay	Smith	Ross	Ritchie	Bathgate	Hall	McDonald	Hall
35	02-Mar	CCp	Abercorn	1-0	Ramsay	Buchanan	Reid	Finlay	SMITH	Ross	Ritchie	Bathgate	Hall	McDonald	Tait
36	09-Mar	SL2	BATHGATE	1-1	Ramsay	Buchanan	Reid	Finlay	Smith	Ross	Ritchie	Bathgate	Hall	McDonald	Tait
37	16-Mar	SL2	Vale of Leven	0-0	Ramsay	Buchanan	Reid	Finlay	Smith	Ross	Ritchie	Bathgate	Hall	McDonald	Tait
38	23-Mar	SL2	EAST STIRLING	3-5	Hood	RITCHIE	Lyall	Sloggie	Prior	McRitchie	Sharp	Cameron	HOWARD	Law	Jackson
39	30-Mar	SL2	Albion Rovers	1-0	Ramsay	Buchanan	Reid	Finlay	Smith	Ross	Ritchie	Bathgate	Hall	HOWARD	Tait
40	01-Apr	SL2	Raith Rovers	3-2	Ramsay	Buchanan	Reid	Finlay	Smith	Ross	Ritchie	Bathgate	HALL 2	McDonald	TAIT
41	06-Apr	PC1	AYR PARKHOUSE	2-0	Ramsay	Buchanan	Reid	Sloggie	Findlay	Ross	RITCHIE	Cameron	HOWARD	HOWARD	McRitchie
42	13-Apr	SL2	East Stirling	0-1											
43	20-Apr	SL2	RAITH ROVERS												
44	24-Apr	PC3	COWDENBEATH	1-2	Ramsay	Buchanan	Reid	Sloggie	Findlay	Ross	Glimour	Bathgate	Graham	Brown	Tait
45	27-Apr	ESL	Dunfermline Ath	2-0	from Ramsay, Ritchie, Reid, Sloggie, Smith, Ross, Ritchie, Bathgate, Brown, Tait and Ferguson.										
47	01-May		Dundee	3-1	Ramsay	Reid	Ritchie	Chatham	Smith	Ross	Grant	Cameron	Bathgate	Brown	AN Other
48	11-May	ESL	Amiston Rangers	0-2	Ramsay	Buchanan	Ritchie	Smith	Smith	Kennedy	Bathgate	Ritchie	Bathgate	Graham	Logan
49	15-May	RCCs	Wallyford Violet	2-2	Ramsay	Buchanan	Dugdale	Smith	Smith	Ross	Gilmour	Brown	Bathgate	Stalker	McRitchie
50	18-May	RCCs	LEITH c1-2 (n)	0-0	Ramsay	Buchanan	Reid	Findlay	Findlay	Ross	Brown	Bathgate	HOWARD	'McDonald'	'Ferguson'

1907/08

#	Date	League	Opponent	Venue	Score													
1	15-Aug	SL2	Broxburn		1-1	Ramsay	Herron	Reid	Kennedy	Smith	McDonald	Ritchie	Bathgate	Fraser	Fairlie	Fleming
2	17-Aug	SL2	Ayr		2-3	Ramsay	Buchanan	Reid	Bathgate	Smith	Ross	Ritchie	Brown	BROWN,J	LOGAN	Grant
3	24-Aug	SL2	COWDENBEATH		1-0	Ramsay	Buchanan	Reid	FINDLAY	Smith	Ross	Ritchie	Bathgate	Brown,J	Brown	Logan
4	31-Aug	SL2	Abercorn		1-2	Ramsay	Buchanan	Reid	Findlay	Smith	Ross	Ritchie	Bathgate	BROWN,J	Brown	Logan
5	07-Sep	SOC1	ROYAL Garrison Art		5-0	Ramsay	Scott	Reid	FINDLAY	Smith	Ross	Ritchie	BROWN 2	Brown,J	LOGAN	TENNANT
6	14-Sep	ESS	LEITH		0-1	Ramsay	Buchanan	Reid	Findlay	Smith	Ross	Bathgate	Brown	Brown,J	Logan	Tennant
7	16-Sep	SL2	Leith		0-1	Ramsay	Buchanan	Reid	Murdoch	Smith	Ross	Ritchie	Brown	Finday	Logan	Tennant
8	21-Sep	SOC2	BROXBURN Athletic		1-0	Ramsay	Buchanan	Reid	Murdoch	Finday	Ross	Bathgate	SMITH	SMITH 2	Brown,J	Tennant
9	28-Sep	SL2	Arthurlie		4-1	Ramsay	BUCHANAN	Reid	Murdoch	Finday	Ross	Ritchie	LOGAN 2	SMITH 2	Brown	Tennant
10	05-Oct	SL2	Leith		1-1	Ramsay	Buchanan	Reid	Ross	Finday	Murdoch	Ritchie	Logan	Smith	Brown,J	Tennant
11	12-Oct	SL2	Dumbarton		0-4	Ramsay	Buchanan	Reid	Findlay	Smith	Ross	Ritchie	Brown	Smith	Brown,J	Tennant
12	19-Oct	SOC4	ABERCORN		5-1	Ramsay	Buchanan	Reid	Findlay	Smith	Ross	MURRAY 2	Simpson,H	SIMPSON,J	LOGAN	TENNANT
13	26-Oct	SOC5	VALE OF LEVEN		2-1	Ramsay	Buchanan	Scott	Findlay	Smith	Ross	Murray	Simpson,H	Simpson,J	LOGAN	TENNANT
14	02-Nov	SL2	GALSTON		1-0	Ramsay	Buchanan	Reid	Findlay	Smith	Ross	Murray	Simpson,H	SIMPSON,J	Logan	TENNANT
15	09-Nov	SL2	East Stirling		0-2	Ramsay	Buchanan	Reid	Findlay	Smith	Ross	Murray	Simpson,H	Simpson,J	Brown	Ritchie
16	16-Nov	SOCs	HAMILTON ACCIES		3-1	Ramsay	BUCHANAN	Reid	Findlay	Smith	Ross	'Thomson'	Simpson,H	SIMPSON,J 2	Logan	Tennant
17	23-Nov	SL2	Cowdenbeath		1-0	Ramsay	Buchanan	Reid	Findlay	Smith	Ross	Murray	Simpson,H	SIMPSON,J	Logan	Tennant
18	30-Nov	SOCf	RAITH ROVERS (n)		3-1	Ramsay	BUCHANAN 2	Reid	Findlay	Smith	Ross	MURRAY	Simpson,H	Simpson,J	Logan	TENNANT
19	07-Dec	SL2	AYR		1-1	Ramsay	Buchanan	Reid	Findlay	Smith	Ross	Murray	Brown,John	Simpson,J	Logan	Tennant
20	14-Dec	SL2	Vale of Leven		0-0	Ramsay	Scott	Reid	Findlay	Smith	Ross	Murray	Brown	Simpson,J	Logan	Tennant
21	21-Dec	SL2	Raith Rovers		0-2	Ramsay	Buchanan	Reid	Findlay	Smith	Ross	Ritchie	Brown	Simpson,J	Logan	Tennant
22	28-Dec	SL2	EAST STIRLING		0-1	Ramsay	Buchanan	Reid	Findlay	Smith	Ross	Brown	Ritchie	Murray	Logan	Tennant
23	01-Jan		Everton		1-1	Ramsay	Buchanan	Reid	Findlay	Smith	Ross	Murray	Simpson,H	Simpson,J	Logan	Tennant
24	04-Jan	SL2	Ayr Parkhouse		1-2	Ramsay	Buchanan	'Reid'	Findlay	Smith	Ross	Murray	'Wilson'	Simpson	BROWN	Tennant
25	11-Jan	SL2	ALBION ROVERS		5-2	Ramsay	BUCHANAN	Reid	Findlay	Smith	Ross	MURRAY	Simpson,H	Simpson,J	LOGAN	Jackson
26	18-Jan	SL2	DUMBARTON		1-1	Ramsay	Buchanan	Reid	Findlay	Smith	Ross	BROWN,J 2	Simpson,H	Simpson,J	Logan	TENNANT
27	25-Jan	SC1	QUEENS PARK		1-1	Ramsay	Buchanan	Reid	Findlay	Smith	Ross	Murray	Brown,J	Simpson,J	Logan	TENNANT
28	01-Feb	SC1	Queens Park		1-1	Ramsay	BUCHANAN	Reid	Findlay	Smith	Ross	Murray	Simpson,H	Simpson,H	Logan	Tennant
29	05-Feb	SC1	Queens Park (n)		0-1	Ramsay	Scott	Reid	Findlay	Smith	Ross	Thomson	Simpson,H	Simpson,J	Logan	Tennant
30	08-Feb	SL2	AYR PARKHOUSE		3-2	Ramsay	Buchanan	Reid	Findlay	Smith	Ross	MURRAY 2	Simpson,H	Simpson,J	BROWN,J	Tennant
31	15-Feb	SL2	ABERCORN		2-2	Ramsay	Scott	Reid	FINDLAY	Smith	Ross	Murray	Simpson,H	Simpson,J	HENDERSON	Tennant
32	22-Feb	SL2	Albion Rovers		3-1	Ramsay	Buchanan	Reid	Findlay	Smellie	Ross	Simpson,J	Simpson,H	McNAIRN 2	Logan	TENNANT
33	29-Feb	SL2	RAITH ROVERS		2-3	Ramsay	Buchanan	Reid	Findlay	Smith	Ross	Simpson,J	Simpson,H	SIMPSON,H	Logan	Tennant
34	07-Mar	SL2	ARTHURLIE		1-0	Ramsay	Buchanan	Reid	Findlay	Smith	Ross	BROWN,J	Simpson,H	McNAIRN	Logan	Simpson,J
35	14-Mar	PC1	Hearts of Beath		3-0	Ramsay	Buchanan	Reid	Findlay	Smith	Ross	Miller	Simpson,H	Simpson,J	Logan	Tennant
36	28-Mar	PC3	Boness		1-1	Ramsay	Buchanan	Reid	Findlay	Smith	Ross	Simpson	Brown	Simpson,J	Logan	Tennant
37	04-Apr	PC3	BONESS		1-0	Wood	Buchanan	Reid	Lindsay	Smith	Ross	Murray	Brown	Brown	Logan	Tennant
38	11-Apr		Aberdeen		2-1	'Ramsay'	Buchanan	Reid	Lindsay	Bruce	Ross	Simpson,J	Simpson,H	Thomson	Dick	Milne
39	13-Apr		PEEBLES ROVERS		1-1	'Ramsay'	Buchanan	Reid	Watson	Smith	Ross	Simpson,J	Simpson,H	McNairn	Logan	Tennant
40	18-Apr	CC	Leith		2-2	Ramsay		Reid								
41	20-Apr		Dalkeith Thistle		2-3											
42	22-Apr	CC	Leith		2-0	Ramsay	Buchanan	Reid	Watson	Smith	Ross	Simpson,J	Simpson,H	McNairn	Logan	Tennant
43	25-Apr	PCs	Raith Rovers		2-1	Ramsay	Buchanan	Reid	Watson	Smith	Ross	Ritchie	Simpson,H	Simpson,J	Logan	Tennant
44	28-Apr	CCs	HIBERNIAN		0-0	Ramsay	Buchanan	Reid	Watson	Smith	Ross	McNairn	Simpson,H	Simpson,J	Logan	Tennant
45	29-Apr		Arniston Rangers		2-2											
46	30-Apr		Musselburgh & Dist		2-3											
47	02-May	RCCs	Hibernian		1-1*	Ramsay	Buchanan	Reid	Watson	Smith	Ross	Murray	Simpson,H	Simpson,J	Logan	Tennant
48	16-May	RCCf	Hearts (n)		3-2	Ramsay	Buchanan	Reid	Watson	Smith	Ross	Curran	Simpson,H	Simpson,J	Logan	Tennant

1908/09

#	Date			Opposition	Score												
1	05-Aug	SNEs		Rangers (n)	0-1	Ramsay	Herron	'Forsyth'	Watson	Smith	Ross	Shand	Simpson,H	Cameron	Logan	'Noble'	Tennant
2	15-Aug	SL2		COWDENBEATH	2-5	Ramsay	Buchanan	Herron	FINDLAY	Smith	Ross	Watson	Simpson,H	Simpson,J	LOGAN	'Noble'	Laidlaw
3	18-Aug			Penicuik Juniors	2-2												
4	22-Aug	SL2		Ayr	4-1	Ramsay	Buchanan	Herron	Watson	Smith	Findlay	BLACK 2	Simpson,H	SIMPSON,J 3	Logan		Tennant
5	26-Aug	CCf		HEARTS	1-2	Ramsay	Smith	Herron	Watson	Smith	Ross	Black	Simpson,H	Simpson,J	Logan		Laidlaw
6	29-Aug	SL2		DUMBARTON	4-2	Ramsay	Watson	Herron	Findlay	Smith	Ross	BLACK 2	Simpson,H	SIMPSON,J 2	Logan		Laidlaw
7	31-Aug	PCf		East Stirling	1-0	Ramsay	Watson	Herron	Findlay	Smith	Ross	Black	Simpson,H	Simpson,J	Logan		Tennant
8	02-Sep			HEARTS	2-2	Ramsay	Smith,A	Brown	Kennedy	Moffat	Dow	McIntosh	Forrester	Hynd	Mathieson		Strachan
9	05-Sep	SQC1		WEST Lothian Albion	5-1	Ramsay	Smith,A	Brebner	Watson	Smith	FINDLAY	Black	Simpson,H	SIMPSON,J 2	LOGAN		LAIDLAW
10	12-Sep	SL2		Leith	0-3	Ramsay	Smith,A	Watson	Findlay	Smith	Ross	Black	Simpson,H	Simpson,J	Logan		Laidlaw
11	19-Sep	SQC2		LEITH	0-1	Ramsay	Herron	Smith,A	Findlay	Smith	Ross	Black	Curran	Simpson,J	Logan		Curran
12	21-Sep	ESSs		HEARTS	1-4	Veitch	Herron	Watson	Findlay	Watson	Ross	Black	Simpson,H	Simpson,J	LOGAN		LAIDLAW
13	26-Sep	SL2		ABERCORN	2-1	Veitch	Herron	Smith,A	Findlay	Smith	Ross	Curran	SIMPSON,H	Simpson,J	LOGAN		LAIDLAW
14	03-Oct	SL2		Arthurlie	4-0	Veitch	Herron	Smith,A	Findlay	SMITH	Ross	Black	Simpson,H	Simpson,J	Logan		Laidlaw
15	10-Oct	SL2		AYR	0-0	Veitch	Buchanan	Smith,A	Findlay	Smith	Ross	Black	Simpson,H	Hyde	Simpson,J		Laidlaw
16	17-Oct	SL2		Albion Rovers	0-2	Veitch	Buchanan	Smith,A	Findlay	Smith	Ross	BLACK	Simpson,H	Hyde	Simpson,J		Laidlaw
17	24-Oct	SL2		Cowdenbeath	1-2	Veitch	Buchanan	Smith,A	Findlay	Smith	Ross	Black	Simpson,H	Hyde	Simpson,J		Laidlaw
18	31-Oct	SL2		Raith Rovers	1-4	Veitch	Buchanan	Smith,A	Watson	Smith	Ross	Black	Simpson,H	HYDE	Ross		Milne
19	07-Nov	SL2		ARTHURLIE	1-0	Veitch	Buchanan	'Reid'	Findlay	Smith	Findlay	Black	Simpson,H	HYDE	Watson		Milne
20	14-Nov	SL2		RAITH ROVERS	3-3	Veitch	Buchanan	Smith,A	Findlay	Smith	Ross	Black	Graham	HYDE 3	Simpson,H		Milne
21	21-Nov	SL2		ALBION ROVERS	1-1	Veitch	Buchanan	Smith,A	Findlay	Smith	Ross	Simpson,H	Graham	HYDE	Milne		Simpson
22	28-Nov	SL2		Dumbarton	0-1	Veitch	Buchanan	Smith,A	Watson	Smith	Ross	Black	GRAHAM	Hyde	Hyde		Simpson
23	05-Dec	SL2		LEITH	3-2	Veitch	Smith	Buchanan	FINDLAY	SMITH	Ross	Black	Simpson,J	Hyde	Hyde		Milne
24	12-Dec	SL2		Ayr Parkhouse	0-1	Ramsay	Buchanan	Smith,A	Watson	Smith	Ross	Black	Findlay	Hyde	Simpson,H		Milne
25	19-Dec	SL2		Vale of Leven	0-4	Ramsay	Buchanan	Smith,A	Findlay	Smith	Ross	Black	Graham	Hyde	Simpson		Milne
26	26-Dec	SL2		VALE OF LEVEN	0-2	Ramsay	Buchanan	Smith,A	Findlay	Smith	Ross	BLACK	Simpson,H	Hyde	Fairley		Milne
27	02-Jan	SL2		Abercorn	1-2	Ramsay	Herron	Smith,A	FINDLAY	SMITH	Ross	Black	Graham	Hyde	FAIRLEY		FAIRLEY
28	09-Jan	SL2		East Stirling	4-1	Ramsay	Herron	Smith	Watson	Smith	Ross	Black	Graham	Simpson	FAIRLEY		SIMPSON
29	23-Jan			St Mirren 'A'	4-1	Ramsay	Herron	SMITH	Findlay	Smith	Ross	Black	Graham	Simpson	Ferguson		Fairley
30	30-Jan	SL2		AYR Parkhouse	1-0	Ramsay	Herron	Smith	Watson	Smith	Ross	Black	Graham	Hyde	Simpson		Fairley
31	06-Feb	SL2		Kilmarnock 'A'	3-1	Ramsay	Herron	Smith	Findlay	Smith	Curran	Curran	Graham	Simpson	Gilchrist		Fairley
32	13-Feb	SL2		EAST STIRLING	2-0	Ramsay	Herron	Smith	Findlay	Smith	Ross	Curran	Graham	HYDE	Simpson		MILNE
33	20-Feb			Middlesborough	0-4	from Ramsay, Herron, Smith,A, Findlay, Smith, Ross, Curran, Simpson, Fairley and Milne.											
34	27-Feb			Peebles Rovers	2-2	Ramsay	Herron	Smith	Simpson	Smith	Gilchrist	Curran	Graham	Sinclair	Fairley		Milne
35	06-Mar	PC		Lochgelly United	1-2	Ramsay	Herron	Smith	Findlay	Smith	Ross	Curran	Graham	Hyde	Simpson		Milne
36	13-Mar	PC3		Alloa Athletic	2-2	Ramsay	Herron	Smith	Findlay	Smith	Ross	Curran	Graham	Hyde	Simpson		Milne
37	20-Mar	CC		BROXBURN Athletic	0-1	Ramsay	Buchanan	Smith	Simpson	Smith	Ross	Black	Graham	Hyde	Dewar		Milne
38	27-Mar			ARNISTON Rangers	2-1	Ramsay	Herron	Buchanan	Findlay	Smith	Hyde	Simpson	Graham	Hyde	Fairley		Milne
39	03-Apr	CC		Broxburn Athletic (n)	2-0	Allan	Smith	Reid	Findlay	Thomson	Ross	Black	Graham	Simpson	Fairley		Milne
40	10-Apr			Hearts 'A'	4-3	Ramsay	Smith	Fairley	Findlay	Smith	Ross	Curran	Graham	HYDE	Simpson		Milne
41	17-Apr	CCf		Leith	1-0												
42	22-Apr			Newtongrange Star	2-2												
43	28-Apr			Midlothian Jnr Lge	0-2												
44	01-May	RCCs		Leith (n)		Ramsay	Hanlon	Fairley	Smith,A	Smith,N	Ross	Black	Hyde	Hyde	Fairley		Logan

1909/10

#	Date	Comp	Opponent	Score											
1	16-Aug	DCs	Hibernian	1-1	Ramsay	Smith,A	Fairey	Kennedy	Kelling	Ross,T	McMillan	Graham	Ross,G	Simpson	Milne
2	21-Aug	SL2	East Stirling	1-3	Ramsay	Smith,A	Fairey	Kennedy	Kelling	Ross,T	McMillan	Graham	Ross,G	SIMPSON,H	Logan
3	23-Aug	DCs	HIBERNIAN	0-2*	Ramsay	Smith,A	Fairey	Kennedy	Smith	Ross,T	McMillan	Graham	Ross,G	Simpson,H	Logan
4	28-Aug	SL2	AYR	3-0	Ramsay	Smith,A	Fairey	Ross,G	Smith	Ross,T	LENNIE	GRAHAM	HYDE	Simpson,H	Logan
5	30-Aug	DCs	HIBERNIAN	1-0	Ramsay	Smith,A	Fairey	Kennedy	Smith	Ross,T	McMillan	Graham	Hyde	Simpson,H	Logan
6	01-Sep	DCf	RAITH ROVERS	1-0	Ramsay	Smith,A	Fairey	Ross,G	Smith	Ross,T	McMillan	Graham	Hyde	Simpson,H	Logan
7	04-Sep	SQC1	Broxburn Athletic	3-1	Ramsay	SMITH,A	Fairey	Kennedy	Smith	Ross,T	McMillan	Graham	HYDE	Graham	LOGAN
8	07-Sep		BradfordCity	1-2	Ramsay	Fairey	Smith,J	Kennedy	Smith.W	Kennedy	Milne	Simpson	Hyde	Graham	Gardiner
9	11-Sep	SL2	Cowdenbeath	0-3	Ramsay	Smith,A	Fairey	Ross,G	Smith	Ross,T	Gardiner	Graham	Hyde	Simpson	Milne
10	18-Sep	SOC2	KIRKCALDY Utd	0-1	Ramsay	Smith,A	Fairey	Kennedy	Smith	Ross,T	Gardiner	Graham	Hyde	Simpson	Logan
11	25-Sep	SL2	DUMBARTON	2-1	Ramsay	Smith,A	Fairey	Kennedy	Smith	Ross,T	Lennie	GRAHAM 2	Gardiner	Simpson	Logan
12	02-Oct	SL2	VALE OF LEVEN	6-1	Ramsay	Hanlon	Smith,A	Kennedy	Smith	Ross,T	Black	GRAHAM 2	Gardiner	SIMPSON 2	LOGAN 2
13	09-Oct	SL2	Ayr	0-3	Ramsay	Smith,A	Fairey	Kennedy	Smith	Ross,T	Hyde	Graham	Gardiner	SIMPSON	Logan
14	16-Oct	SL2	LEITH	1-1	Ramsay	Smith,A	Fairey	Kennedy	Smith	Ross,T	Hyde	Graham	Gardiner	SIMPSON	Milne
15	23-Oct	SL2	Albion Rovers	2-3	Ramsay	Smith,A	Fairey	Kennedy	Smith	Ross,T	LOGAN	GRAHAM	GARDINER	Simpson	Milne
16	30-Oct	SL2	Arthurlie	2-1	Ramsay	Smith,A	Fairey	Kennedy	Smith	Ross,T	Logan	GRAHAM	Gardiner	SIMPSON	Brownlie
17	06-Nov	SL2	Leith	1-0~	Ramsay	Smith,A	Fairey	Kennedy	Smith	Ross,T	Logan	Graham	Gardiner	SIMPSON	Milne
18	13-Nov	SL2	COWDENBEATH	1-0	Ramsay	Smith,A	Fairey	Kennedy	Smith	Ross,T	Logan	GRAHAM 2	Hyde	Simpson	LOGAN
19	20-Nov	SL2	Ayr Parkhouse	3-2	Ramsay	Smith,A	Fairey	Kennedy	Smith	Ross,T	Gardiner	GRAHAM	Gardiner	Simpson	Logan
20	27-Nov	SL2	Abercorn	3-3	Ramsay	Smith,A	Fairey	Kennedy	SMITH	Ross,T	Gardiner	GRAHAM	FLEMING	Simpson	Logan
21	04-Dec	SL2	Vale of Leven	2-1	Ramsay	Smith,A	Fairey	Kennedy	Smith	Ross,T	Gardiner	GRAHAM	FLEMING	Simpson	LOGAN 2
22	11-Dec	SL2	EAST STIRLING	6-2	Ramsay	Smith,A	Fairey	Kennedy	Smith	Ross,T	GARDINER	GRAHAM 3	FLEMING	SIMPSON	Logan
23	18-Dec	SL2	Leith	0-1	Ramsay	Smith,A	Fairey	Kennedy	Smith	Hyde	Wilkie	Graham	Fleming	Simpson	Logan
24	25-Dec	SL2	Raith Rovers	1-2	Ramsay	Smith,A	Fairey	Kennedy	Smith	Ross	WILKIE	Graham	Fleming	Simpson	Logan
25	01-Jan	SL2	ARTHURLIE	2-1	Ramsay	Smith,A	Fairey	Kennedy	Smith	Ross	Wilkie	Graham	FLEMING 2	Simpson	Logan
26	04-Jan		EAST of Scot FA	6-0	Ramsay	Johnson	Smith,A	Kennedy	Smith	Ross	Wilkie	Simpson,H	Fleming	Hyde	Campbell
27	08-Jan	SCC1	WEST Lothian Albion	3-0	Ramsay	Smith,A	Fairey	Kennedy	Smith	Ross	Wilkie	Graham	FLEMING 2	Simpson	LOGAN
28	15-Jan	SCC2	ABERCORN	1-1	Ramsay	Smith,A	Fairey	Kennedy	Hyde	Ross	Wilkie	GRAHAM	FLEMING	Simpson	Logan
29	22-Jan	SCC2	Peebles Rovers	3-0	Ramsay	Smith,A	Fairey	Kennedy	Smith	Ross	Wilkie	GRAHAM	Fleming	Simpson	LOGAN
30	29-Jan	SL2	AYR PARKHOUSE	1-0	Ramsay	Smith,A	Fairey	Kennedy	Smith	Ross	WILKIE	Graham	Fleming	Simpson	Logan
31	05-Feb	SCC3	Berwick Rangers	4-1	Ramsay	Smith,A	Fairey	Kennedy	Smith	ROSS	Wilkie	GRAHAM	Fleming	Simpson	LOGAN
32	12-Feb	SCC3	ALBION ROVERS	4-0	Veitch	Smith,A	Fairey	Kennedy	Smith	Ross	Wilkie	Graham	FLEMING 3	Simpson	LOGAN
33	19-Feb	SL2	Dumbarton	0-1	Veitch	Smith,A	Fairey	Kennedy	Smith	Ross	Wilkie	Graham	Fleming	Simpson	Logan
34	05-Mar	PC1	Dunfermline Athletic	2-1	Stanners	Smith,A	Fairey	Kennedy	Smith	Ross	Wilkie	Graham	Fleming	Simpson	Logan
35	19-Mar	SCC5	Arthurlie	1-2	Veitch	Smith,A	Fairey	Kennedy	Smith	Ross	Wilkie	Graham	Fleming	SIMPSON	Logan
36	26-Mar	PC2	Lochgelly United	2-2	Veitch	Smith,A	Fairey	Kennedy	Smith	Ross	Wilkie	Graham	Fleming	Simpson	Logan
37	02-Apr	SL2	RAITH ROVERS	2-1	Logan	Dewar	Fairey	Hyde	Smith	Ross	Wilkie	GRAHAM	FLEMING	Hyde	Logan,D
38	04-Apr	ESSs	Hibernian	0-0	Logan,A	Smith,A	Fairey	Hyde	Smith	Ross	Wilkie	Graham	Fleming	Allan	Logan,W
39	09-Apr	PC2	LOCHGELLY Utd	2-0	Logan,A	Smith,A	Fairey	Hyde	Smith	Ross	Wilkie	Graham	Fleming	Allan	Logan,W
40	16-Apr	SL2	Leith	2-1	Logan,A	Kennedy	Fairey	Hyde	Smith	Ross	Wilkie	GRAHAM	Fleming	White	Logan,W
41	19-Apr		Penicuik Juniors		from Logan, A Smith and Kennedy, Hyde, W Smith and Ross, Wilkie, Graham, Fleming, Allan and Logan.										
42	23-Apr	CCs	Leith	1-2	Logan	Ramsay	Smith,A	Kennedy	Smith	Ross	Wilkie	Allan	Fleming	White	White
43	25-Apr		Midlothian League	5-2	Ramsay	Smith,A	Kennedy	Hyde	Smith	Ross	Wilkie	Ferguson	Fleming	White	Wilson'
44	29-Apr	ESSf	Hearts (2-11c)	1-1	Ramsay	Smith,A	Fairey	Kennedy	Smith	Ross	Wilkie	Ferguson	Thomson	White	Logan
45	04-May	RCC	Leith (n)	1-2	Ramsay	Fleming	Fairey	Kennedy	McNab	Ross	Wilkie	Ferguson	Forrest	Morton	Logan

1917
Charlie Thomson

1882
Jamie Ross

1900
Baines' Cigarette Card

1924
Dr Archie Young

1930
Mascot at Tynecastle
Scottish Cup Tie

1938
Scottish Cup Semi-Final at Tynecastle

1902
Bill Morrison

Goalmouth Incident at the Gymnasium

Half Time attention for Leonard Small

The Grandstand at the Gymnasium being dismantled in 1948 before being moved to Old Meadowbank

1910/11

#	Date	Comp	Opponent	Score												
1	16-Aug	DC	Hibernian	0-1	Ramsay	Philip	Fairley	Kennedy	Smith	Ross	Wilkie	Ferguson	Morton	Fleming	McLennan
2	20-Aug	SL2	EAST STIRLING	5-1	Ramsay	Philip	Fairley	Kennedy	Smith	Ross	Wilkie	FERGUSON 2	MORTON 3	Fleming	Logan
3	27-Aug	SL2	Vale of Leven	2-1	Ramsay	Philip	McLennan	Kennedy	Smith	Ross	Wilkie	Ferguson	Morton	Fleming	LOGAN
4	03-Sep	SQC1	BROXBURN ATH	4-0	Ramsay	Philip	Fairley	Kennedy	SMITH	Ross	Wilkie	FERGUSON 2	MORTON 3	Fleming	Logan
5	10-Sep	SL2	DUNDEE HIBS	4-3	Ramsay	Philip	Fairley	Ross	McLENNAN	McLENNAN	WILKIE	FERGUSON 2	MORTON	Fleming	Logan
6	17-Sep	SL2	DUMBARTON	2-1	Ramsay	Philip	Fairley	Kennedy	Smith	Ross	Wilkie	Ferguson	Morton	McLennan	Logan
7	24-Sep	SL2	Port Glasgow Athletic	0-0	Ramsay	Philip	Fairley	Kennedy	Smith	Ross	Wilkie	Ferguson	Morton	Fleming	Logan
8	01-Oct	SQC3	COLDSTREAM	3-2	Ramsay	Philip	Fairley	Kennedy	Smith	Ross	WILKIE	Ferguson	MORTON	FLEMING	Logan
9	08-Oct	SQC4	ABERCORN	3-2	Ramsay	Scott	Philip	KENNEDY	Smith	McLennan	Wilkie	Ferguson	MORTON 2	Fleming	Logan
10	15-Oct	SQC4	Forfar Athletic	0-0	Ramsay	Scott	Fairley	Kennedy	Smith	Ross	Wilkie	Ferguson	Morton	Fleming	Logan
11	22-Oct	SQC4	FORFAR ATHLETIC	0-0	Ramsay	Philip	Fairley	Kennedy	Smith	McLennan	Fleming	Ferguson	Morton	Ferguson	Logan
12	29-Oct	SQC4	FORFAR ATHLETIC	3-0	Ramsay	Philip	Fairley	Kennedy	Smith	Ross	Fleming	Ferguson	MORTON 3	Ferguson	Logan
13	05-Nov	SQC5	East Stirling	0-2	Ramsay	Philip	Fairley	Kennedy	Smith	Ross	Fleming	Ferguson	Morton	Ferguson	Logan
14	12-Nov	SL2	ALBION ROVERS	0-3	Ramsay	Philip	Fairley	McLennan	Kennedy	Ross	Wilkie	Ferguson	Fleming	Morton	Logan,J
15	19-Nov	SL2	PORT GLASGOW Ath	0-1	Grant	Scott	Fairley	Kennedy	Smith	Ross	Wilkie	Ferguson	Morton	Fleming	McLennan
16	26-Nov	SL2	Arthurlie	0-1	Grant	Scott	Fairley	Kennedy	Smith	Ross	Wilkie	Ferguson	Rodgers	Fleming	Morton
17	03-Dec	SL2	LEITH	1-3	Grant	Scott	Fairley	Kennedy	Smith	Ross	Wilkie	Ferguson	MORTON	Fleming	Logan
18	10-Dec	SL2	Ayr	1-5	Grant	Wilson	Fairley	Kennedy	Smith	Ross	Morton	Wilkie	RODGERS	Fleming	Logan
19	17-Dec	SL2	Cowdenbeath	1-3	Grant	Philip	Fairley	McLennan	Smith	Ross	Morton	Wilkie	FLEMING	Ferguson	Cairns
20	24-Dec	SL2	Dundee Hibs	2-1	Ramsay	Scott	Kennedy	McLennan	Smith	Ross	Morton	WILKIE	FLEMING	Ferguson	Cairns
21	31-Dec	SL2	VALE OF LEVEN	2-0	Ramsay	Kennedy	Fairley	McLennan	Smith	Ross	MORTON	WILKIE	FLEMING	FERGUSON	CAIRNS
22	07-Jan	SL2	AYR	4-1	Ramsay	Kennedy	Fairley	Philip	Smith	ROSS	MORTON	WILKIE	FLEMING	Ferguson	Cairns
23	21-Jan	SL2	Leith	3-2	Ramsay	Kennedy	Fairley	McLennan	Smith	Ross	MORTON	Wilkie	FLEMING	Ferguson	Cairns
24	28-Jan	SC1	Partick Thistle	2-7	Ramsay	Scott	Kennedy	Philip	Smith	Ross	Ferguson	Morton	Fleming	Gibb	Cairns
25	04-Feb	ESSs	Hibernian	0-1	Grant	Scott	Philip	Jack	Smith	Gibb	Wilkie	Fleming	MORTON 2	Ferguson	Cairns
26	11-Feb	SL2	Dumbarton	2-8	Grant	Scott	Philip	Jack	Smith	Ross	MORTON	Fleming	Fleming	GIBB	Cairns
27	18-Feb	SL2	ARTHURLIE	3-0	Grant	Wilson	Philip	Jack	Smith	Ross	Kennedy	FERGUSON	Morton	GIBB	Cairns
28	25-Feb	SL2	Albion Rovers	1-2	Grant	Wilson	Bell	Jack	Smith	Ross	Morton	Ferguson	Rodgers	GIBB	Wilson
29	11-Mar	SL2	COWDENBEATH	0-0	Grant	Philip	Philip	Bell	Smith	Ross	Morton	Ferguson	Fleming	Gibb	Gibb
30	01-Apr	SL2	Abercorn	0-1	Grant	Philip	Bell	Kennedy	Smith	Ross	Morton	Smith	Fleming	Ferguson	Wilson
31	08-Apr		Hearts	1-3	Grant	Scott	Philip	Kennedy	Jack	Gibb	Morton	Rodgers	Fleming	Ferguson	Gibb
32	15-Apr	CC	Hearts	0-7	Grant	Philip	Bell	Kennedy	Smith	Gibb	Wilson	Morton	Rodgers	Ferguson	Cairns
33	22-Apr	SL2	East Stirling	0-2	Grant	Philip	Kennedy	Wilson	Smith, Rodgers, Smith, Morton, Gibb and Wilson		Johnston	Ferguson	Morton	Ferguson	Gibb
34	29-Apr		Midlothian Jnr Lge	2-1	Grant	from Grant, Philip, Bell, Kennedy, Smith, Ross, Rodgers, Smith, Morton, Gibb and Wilson									
35	29-Apr		Bonnyrigg Rose Ath (n)	1-1	Grant	Henderson	Kennedy	Winning	Anderson	Ross	Ferguson	Smith,W	Smith,R	Gibb	Cameron
36	03-May	RCCs	Leith	2-1	Grant	Henderson	Wilson	Kennedy	Corstorphine	Ross	Ferguson	Smith,W	Fleming	Smith,R	Johnston
37	10-May	RCCr	LEITH	0-5	Grant	Henderson	Wilson	Kennedy	Corstorphine	Ross	Ferguson	Gibb	Fleming	Gibb	Dougan
38	13-May	RCCf	Hibernian											Morton	Smith,H	Dougan

1911/12

#	Date	Comp	Opponent	Score											
1	08-Aug		PENICUIK JUNIORS	?-?											
2	15-Aug	DC	HEARTS	1-5	Grant	Penman	Kennedy	Henderson	Corstorphine	Ross	Ferguson	Smith	Lawson	Morton	Dougan
3	19-Aug	SL2	Dumbarton	0-3	Grant	Penman	Philip	Kennedy	Smith	Ross	Ferguson	Smith	Lawson	Morton	Dougan
4	26-Aug	SL2	EAST STIRLING	1-3	Grant	Penman	Philip	Henderson	Smith	Ross	Wilson	FERGUSON	LAWSON	MORTON	DOUGAN
5	02-Sep	SQC1	BROXBURN SHAMROCK	4-0	Grant	Penman	Philip	Henderson	Smith	Ross	Morton	Ferguson	Lawson	FRENCH	DOUGAN
6	09-Sep	SL2	St Johnstone	0-0	Grant	Penman	Muir	Henderson	Smith	Ross	Lawson	Ferguson	Morton	French	Dougan
7	16-Sep	SQC2	Bathgate	1-1	Grant	Penman	Muir	Henderson	Smith	Ross	Lawson	Ferguson	MORTON	French	Dougan
8	18-Sep	ESSs	Hearts	1-0	Grant	Penman	Muir	Henderson	Smith	Ross	Lawson	Ferguson	Morton	FRENCH	Dougan
9	23-Sep	SQC2	BATHGATE	1-3	Grant	Penman	Muir	Henderson	Smith	Ross	Lawson	Ferguson	Morton	French	Dougan
10	30-Sep	SL2	Leith	0-2	Grant	Penman	Muir	Henderson	Corstorphine	Kennedy	Lamb	Ferguson	Morton	Morton	Lawson
11	07-Oct	SL2	VALE OF LEVEN	5-0	Grant	Penman	Philip	Henderson	Corstorphine	Smith	Lamb	FEGUSON 2	MORTON 2	FRENCH	Currie
12	14-Oct	SL2	Dundee Hibs	2-2	Grant	Penman	Muir	Henderson	Corstorphine	Ross	Lamb	FEGUSON 2	Morton	FRENCH	Currie
13	21-Oct	SL2	COWDENBEATH	0-1	Grant	Penman	Muir	Smith	Henderson	Ross	Lamb	Ferguson	Morton	French	Currie
14	28-Oct	SL2	Arthurlie	2-2	Grant	Penman	Muir	Henderson	Corstorphine	Ross	Lamb	Smith	French	Ferguson	CURRIE 2
15	04-Nov	SL2	DUNDEE HIBS	7-1	Grant	Penman	Muir	HENDERSON	Corstorphine	Ross	LAMB	SMITH 3	French	FERGUSON	CURRIE 2
16	11-Nov	SL2	Cowdenbeath	0-5	Grant	Penman	Muir	Henderson	Corstorphine	Ross	Henderson,J	Smith	xxxxxxx	Ferguson	Philip
17	18-Nov	SL2	LEITH	2-1	Grant	Penman	Muir	Henderson	CORSTORPHINE	Ross	Henderson,J	Smith	LAWSON	Ferguson	CURRIE
18	25-Nov	SL2	ST JOHNSTONE	2-1	Grant	Penman	Muir	Henderson	Corstorphine	Ross	Henderson,J	SMITH	LAWSON	Ferguson	Currie
19	02-Dec	SL2	Vale of Leven	2-0	Grant	Penman	Muir	Henderson	Corstorphine	Ross	Henderson,J	Smith	LAWSON	Ferguson	Currie
20	09-Dec	SL2	Albion Rovers	3-2	Grant	Penman	Muir	Henderson	Corstorphine	Ross	HENDERSON,J 2	Smith	LAWSON	Ferguson	Currie
21	16-Dec	SL2	ALBION ROVERS	1-0	Grant	Penman	Muir	Henderson	Corstorphine	Ross	Henderson,J	Smith	LAWSON	FERGUSON	Currie
22	23-Dec	SL2	DUMBARTON	2-1	Grant	Penman	Muir	Henderson	Corstorphine	Ross	Henderson,J	Smith	FRENCH	French	Currie
23	30-Dec	SL2	East Stirling	4-2	Grant	Penman	Muir	Ferguson,John	CORSTORPHINE	Ross	Henderson,J	FERGUSON	LAWSON 2	FERGUSON	Currie
24	01-Jan	SL2	Ayr United	2-3	Grant	Penman	Muir	Smith	Corstorphine	Ross	Henderson	SMITH	LAWSON	French	Currie
25	06-Jan	SL2	ABERCORN	0-1	Grant	Penman	Muir	Henderson	Corstorphine	Ross	Henderson,Jas	Ferguson	Lawson	French	Currie
26	13-Jan	SCC1	WEST LOTHIAN ALBION	5-0	Grant	Penman	Muir	HENDERSON,J	Corstorphine	French	Henderson	SMITH	LAWSON 2	FERGUSON	Currie
27	27-Jan	SL2	ARTHURLIE	1-1	Grant	Penman	Muir	French	Corstorphine	Ross	Morton	Smith	Albert	FERGUSON	Currie
28	10-Feb	SCC2	BROXBURN	2-1	Grant	Penman	Muir	Henderson	Corstorphine	Ross	MORTON	SMITH	Lawson	Ferguson	Currie
29	17-Feb	SCC3	BROXBURN SHAMROCK	8-0	Grant	Penman	Muir	Henderson	Corstorphine	ROSS	Morton	SMITH	ALBERT 4	FEGUSON	CURRIE
30	24-Feb	SCC4	DUNDEE HIBS	1-0	Grant	Penman	Muir	Henderson	Corstorphine	Ross	MORTON	French	Albert	Ferguson	Currie
31	02-Mar	SCC5	Cowdenbeath	1-1	Grant	Penman	Muir	Henderson	Corstorphine	Ross	MORTON	Smith	French	Ferguson	Currie
32	09-Mar	SCC5	COWDENBEATH (n)	0-0	Grant	Philip	Muir	Henderson	Corstorphine	Ross	Morton	Smith	French	Pattison	Currie
33	16-Mar	SL2	Abercorn	0-3	Grant	Corstorphine	Muir	French	Smith	Ross	Lawson	Ferguson	Albert	Pattison	Currie
34	23-Mar	SL2	AYR UNITED	2-2	Grant	Penman	Muir	Henderson	CORSTORPHINE	Ross	Frail	Morton	ALBERT	Pattison	Currie
35	30-Mar	SL2	Leith	2-2	Grant	Penman	Muir	Henderson	Corstorphine	Ross	Frail	Ferguson	Albert	Albert	Currie
36	06-Apr	ESSf	Dunfermline Athletic (n)	0-2	Grant	Penman	Muir	Henderson	Corstorphine	Ross	Frail	Smith	Albert	Ferguson	Currie
37	13-Apr		Hibernian (n)	1-1											
38	20-Apr		THIRD LANARK	1-1	Grant	Penman	Muir	Henderson	Corstorphine	Ross	Morton	Ferguson,J	Albert	Ross,A	Currie
39	24-Apr	CCs	BROXBURN ATHLETIC	4-1	Grant	Penman	Muir	Henderson	French	Ross	Frail	Ferguson,J	Albert	Morton	Currie
40	27-Apr	CCf	Peebles Rovers (n)	0-0	Grant	Penman	Muir	Henderson	Corstorphine	Ross	Henderson,J	Henderson,J	Albert	Morton	Currie
41	29-Apr	CCf	Peebles Rovers 7-3c (n)	1-1	Grant	Penman	Muir	Henderson	Corstorphine	Ross	Frail	Ferguson,J	Albert	Ferguson,D	Currie
42	30-Apr		Midlothian Junior League	1-2											
43	08-May	RCCs	Hibernian	0-2	Grant	Penman	Philip	French	Smith	Ross	Frail	Ferguson,J	Albert	Morton	Currie

1912/13

#	Date	Comp	Opponent	Score											
1	10-Aug	DC	LEITH AMATEURS	?-?											
2	15-Aug	DC	HEARTS	1-1	Grant	Penman	Muir	Henderson	Corstorphine	Ross	Frail	Albert	Morton	McGregor	Currie
3	17-Aug	SL2	LEITH	1-2	Grant	Penman	Muir	Henderson	Corstorphine	Ross	Frail	Albert	MORTON	McGregor	Currie
4	20-Aug	DC	Hearts	0-5	Grant	Penman	Usher	Henderson	Henderson	Ross	Frail	'Black'	Morton	'White'	Thomson
5	24-Aug	SL2	Dunfermline Athletic	2-1	Grant	Penman	Muir	Henderson	Corstorphine	Ross	FRAIL	McGregor	Morton	Thomson,W	Thomson,H
6	31-Aug	SQC1	EAST STIRLING	1-0	Grant	Penman	Muir	Henderson	Corstorphine	Ross	Frail	McGregor	Gilmour	Thomson	Currie
7	07-Sep	SL2	Leith Amateurs	0-3	Grant	Penman	Muir	Henderson	Corstorphine	Ross	Frail	McGregor	Usher	THOMSON	Currie
8	14-Sep	SL2	Leith	2-0	Grant	Penman	Muir	Henderson	Corstorphine	Gilmour	Morton	McGregor	Albert	Thomson	Currie
9	16-Sep	ESSs	Bathgate	2-1	Grant	Penman	Muir	Davie	Henderson	Ross	Morton	McGregor	ALBERT 2	Faulds	McGregor
10	21-Sep	SQC2	DUMBARTON	1-3	Grant	Penman	Muir	Davie	Henderson	Ross	Faulds	FAULDS	ALBERT 2	McGregor	Currie
11	28-Sep	SOC3	Selkirk	3-1	Grant	Penman	Muir	Henderson	Corstorphine	Ross	Gilmour	Faulds	Albert	Thomson	McGregor
12	05-Oct	SOC3	Johnstone	2-1	Grant	Stewart	Muir	Henderson	Corstorphine	Ross	Morton	Faulds	Albert	Thomson	Currie
13	12-Oct	SL2	Dunfermline Athletic	0-0	Grant	Stewart	Muir	Henderson	Corstorphine	Ross	Morton	Faulds	Albert	Thomson	Currie
14	19-Oct	SQC4	Dunfermline Athletic	1-1	Grant	Stewart	Muir	Henderson	Corstorphine	Ross	Morton	Gilmour	ALBERT	Thomson	Currie
15	26-Oct	SQC4	Dunfermline Athletic (n)	0-1	Grant	Stewart	Muir	Henderson	Corstorphine	Gilmour	Morton	McGregor	FERGUSON	THOMSON	Gilmour
16	02-Nov	SQC4	VALE OF LEVEN	0-2	Grant	Penman	Stewart	Henderson	Corstorphine	Gilmour	Morton	Faulds	Albert	Thomson	Gilmour
17	09-Nov	SL2	East Stirling	3-2	Grant	Penman	Stewart	Henderson	Corstorphine	Gilmour	Morton	Faulds	FERGUSON 3	Thomson	Gilmour
18	16-Nov	SL2	ALBION ROVERS	4-0	Grant	Stewart	Muir	Henderson	Corstorphine	Davie	Morton	Ferguson	Albert	Thomson	Currie
19	23-Nov	CCs	WEST CALDER SWIFTS	1-2	Grant	Stewart	Muir	Davie	Henderson	Ross	Faulds	Ferguson	ALBERT	Thomson	Gilmour
20	30-Nov	CCs	Arthurlie	3-0	Grant	Stewart	Muir	Henderson	Corstorphine	Ross	Gilmour	FERGUSON	Albert	Thomson	Currie
21	07-Dec	SL2	DUNDEE HIBS	0-0	Grant	Stewart	Muir	Henderson	Corstorphine	Ross	Morton	Ferguson	Albert	Thomson	Currie
22	14-Dec	SL2	ARTHURLIE	2-1	Grant	Stewart	MUIR	Henderson	Corstorphine	Ross	Morton	DAVIE	FERGUSON	Ferguson	Gilmour
23	21-Dec	SL2	COWDENBEATH	0-3	Grant	Stewart	Muir	Henderson	Corstorphine	Ross	Faulds	Albert	Albert	Ferguson	Gilmour
24	28-Dec	SL2	Ayr United	1-1	Grant	Stewart	Muir	Henderson	Corstorphine	Ross	Davie	ALBERT	ALBERT	Ferguson	Gilmour
25	01-Jan	SL2	Dundee Hibs	0-2	Grant	Stewart	Muir	Henderson	Corstorphine	Ross	Davie	Ferguson	Albert	Thomson	Currie
26	02-Jan	SL2	Cowdenbeath	1-0	Grant	Stewart	Muir	Henderson	Corstorphine	Ross	Davie	MORTON	MORTON	Ferguson	Currie
27	11-Jan	SL2	Hamilton Accies	0-2	Grant	Stewart	Muir	Henderson	Corstorphine	Ross	Gilmour	Thomson	Morton	Ferguson	Currie
28	18-Jan	SL2	ST JOHNSTONE	1-0	Grant	Stewart	Muir	Henderson	Corstorphine	Ross	Thomson	Morton	Morton	Ferguson	Currie
29	25-Jan	SC1	HAMILTON ACCIES	0-0	Grant	Brown	Muir	Henderson	Corstorphine	ROSS	Gilmour	Thomson	Morton	Ferguson	Currie
30	01-Feb	SC1	Albion Rovers	0-3	Grant	Brown	Muir	Henderson	Corstorphine	Ross	Gilmour	Davie	Morton	Ferguson	Currie
31	08-Feb	SL2	JOHNSTONE	2-3	Grant	Brown	Muir	Henderson	Corstorphine	Ross	Gilmour	Ferguson	Morton	Thomson	Currie
32	15-Feb	SL2	DUNFERMLINE ATHLETIC	1-1	Grant	Brown	Muir	Henderson	Corstorphine	Ross	Gilmour	Thomson	MURRAY	Ferguson	Currie
33	22-Feb	SL2	St Johnstone	4-1	Grant	Brown	Muir	Davie	Corstorphine	Ross	Gilmour	Davie	MURRAY 3	Thomson	CURRIE
34	01-Mar	SL2	Vale of Leven	0-1	Grant	Brown	Muir	Henderson	Corstorphine	Morton	Neal	Ferguson	Murray	Thomson	Currie
35	08-Mar	SL2	AYR UNITED	2-0	Grant	Stewart	Muir	Henderson	Corstorphine	McAllister	Ferguson	Ferguson	MURRAY 2	Thomson	Currie
36	15-Mar	SL2	ABERCORN	2-0	Grant	Stewart	Muir	Henderson	Corstorphine	McAllister	Ferguson	FERGUSON 2	MURRAY	Thomson	Currie
37	22-Mar	SL2	AYR UNITED	3-0	Grant	Stewart	Muir	Henderson	Corstorphine	McAllister	FERGUSON 2	FERGUSON	MURRAY	THOMSON 2	Currie
38	05-Apr	SL2	ABERCORN	0-0	Grant	Stewart	Muir	Henderson	Corstorphine	McAllister	Ferguson	Ferguson	Murray	Thomson	Currie
39	12-Apr	CCf	Leith *	3-0	Grant	Stewart	Muir	Henderson	Corstorphine	McAllister	Ferguson	Ferguson	Murray	Thomson	Currie
40	21-Apr	ESSf	Hibernian	2-3	Grant	Stewart	Muir	Henderson	Chambers	Wemyss	Speedie,J	Speedie,J	MURRAY	Black	Currie
41	23-Apr		Broxburn United	2-2	Grant	'Armstrong'	Brown	Gilmour	Corstorphine	Ross	McAllister	Ferguson	Murray	Thomson	Currie
42	26-Apr	SL2	Abercorn	0-3	Grant	Brown	Stewart	Henderson	Corstorphine	Ross	Robertson	Mercer	Murray	Black	Cobban
43	28-Apr		Midlothian Juniors	2-4	Lochhead	Johnstone	Yorston	Williamson	Gilmour	Wemyss	McAllister	Ferguson	Ferguson	Thomson	Currie
44	03-May	RCCs	Hearts	2-3	Grant	Brown	Stewart	Henderson	Corstorphine	Ross	McAllister	Davie	Murray	Thomson	Currie

* cup withheld

1913/14

#	Date	Comp	Opponent	Score											
1	09-Aug	SL2	CIVIL SERVICE	3-0	Grant	Wilson	Stewart,W	Henderson	Corstorphine	Ross	Fairley	Ferguson	Stewart	Wemyss	Black
2	14-Aug	DCs	LEITH AMATEURS	4-0	Lochhead	Wilson	Malcolm	Henderson	Fairley	Davie	Cooper	Ferguson	Adams	Wemyss	Cousins
3	16-Aug	SL2	Leith	1-1	Grant	Wilson	Stewart	Henderson	Corstorphine	Ross	McAllister	Ferguson	DAVIE	Fairley	Cousins,D
4	20-Aug	SL2	HIBERNIAN	0-4	Grant	Wilson	Malcolm	Henderson	Corstorphine	Ross	Wemyss	Ferguson	Stewart	Thomson	Fairley
5	23-Aug	SL2	ABERCORN	1-2	Grant	Wilson	Stewart	Henderson	Corstorphine	Wemyss	Cousins,J	Ferguson	Adams	Malcolm	Fairley
6	30-Aug	SL2	Albion Rovers	0-1	Grant	Wilson	Stewart	Henderson	Corstorphine	Ross	Wemyss	Ferguson	REID	REID	THOMSON
7	06-Sep	SQC1	Armadale	1-1	Grant	Wilson	Stewart	Henderson	Corstorphine	Ross,T	McAllister	Hosie	Reid	Hosie	THOMSON
8	13-Sep	SQC1	ARMADALE	1-0	Grant	Wilson	Stewart	Henderson	Corstorphine	Ross,G	McAllister	Ross,G	Ferguson	Thomson	Goldie
9	20-Sep	SL2	COWDENBEATH	1-2	Grant	Wilson	Stewart	Henderson	CORSTORPHINE	Ross,T	McAllister	Hosie	Ferguson	Thomson	Goldie
10	27-Sep	SL2	St Johnstone	3-1	Grant	Wilson	Stewart	Henderson	Corstorphine	Ross,T	Ross,G	FERGUSON 2	Hosie	HOSIE	Goldie
11	04-Oct	SQC3	Leith	0-1	Grant	Wilson	Cox	Henderson	Corstorphine	Davie	Ross,G	Reid	Reid	Hosie	Goldie
12	11-Oct	SQC3	Abercorn	3-3	Grant	Wilson	Cox	Henderson	Corstorphine	Ross,T	Ross,G	FERGUSON 3	Reid	Hosie	Goldie
13	18-Oct	SL2	JOHNSTONE	3-0	Grant	Prior	Cox	Henderson	Corstorphine	Wemyss	ROSS,G	Thomson	REID	Hosie	GOLDIE
14	25-Oct	SL2	Cowdenbeath	0-3	Grant	Cox	Wilson	Henderson	Corstorphine	Ross,T	McAllister	Ross,G	Reid	Hosie	Goldie
15	01-Nov	SL2	ST JOHNSTONE	1-1	Grant	Cox	Wilson	Henderson	Corstorphine	Ross,T	Ross,G	Greig	Wemyss	Hosie	GOLDIE
16	08-Nov	SL2	DUNFERMLINE ATH	1-0	Grant	Cox	Wilson	Henderson	Corstorphine	Ross,T	GREIG	McAllister	Fairley	Hosie	Goldie
17	15-Nov	SL2	East Stirling	1-1	Grant	Cox	Wilson	Henderson	Corstorphine	Ross,T	GREIG	McAllister	Ross,G	Hosie	GOLDIE
18	22-Nov	SL2	LEITH	4-0	Grant	Cox	Wilson	Henderson	CORSTORPHINE	Ross,T	GREIG	McALLISTER	Ross,G	HOSIE	Goldie
19	29-Nov	CCs	PEEBLES ROVERS	1-0	Grant	Cox	Wilson	Henderson	Corstorphine	Ross,T	GREIG	McAllister	Ross,G	HOSIE	Goldie
20	06-Dec	SL2	Arthurlie	3-3	Grant	Cox	Wilson	Henderson	Corstorphine	Ross,T	Greig	McAllister	Ross,G	HOSIE 2	Goldie
21	13-Dec	SL2	Dunfermline Athletic	1-2	Grant	Cox	Wilson	Henderson	Corstorphine	Ross,T	McAllister	ROSS,G	Greig	Hosie	Goldie
22	20-Dec	SL2	Vale of Leven	1-2	Grant	Cox	Wilson	Henderson	Corstorphine	Ross,T	McAllister	ROSS,G	ROSS,G	Hosie	Goldie
23	27-Dec	SL2	Dundee Hibs	4-2	Grant	Wilson	Cox	Henderson	CORSTORPHINE	Ross,T	McALLISTER	Greig	FAIRLEY	HOSIE	GOLDIE
24	03-Jan	SL2	VALE OF LEVEN	3-1	Grant	Wilson	Cox	Henderson	Corstorphine	Ross,T	McAllister	Greig	Fairley	Hosie	GOLDIE
25	10-Jan	SCC1	BONESS	2-0	Grant	Wilson	Amos	Henderson	Corstorphine	Ross,T	McAllister	FERGUSON 2	Greig	Hosie	Goldie
26	17-Jan	SCC2	BATHGATE	1-1	Grant	Wilson	Amos	Henderson	Corstorphine	Ross,T	McAllister	FERGUSON	GREIG	Hosie	Goldie
27	24-Jan	SL2	Johnstone	1-1	Grant	Wilson	Amos	Henderson	Corstorphine	Ross,T	Cowe	Fairley	GREIG	Hosie	Goldie
28	31-Jan	SCC3	Gala Fairydean	1-3*	Grant	Wilson	Amos	Henderson	Corstorphine	Ross,T	Cowe	Ferguson	Greig	Hosie	GOLDIE
29	07-Feb	SCC3	Gala Fairydean	3-1	Grant	Wilson	Amos	HENDERSON	Corstorphine	Ross,T	COWE	Ferguson	GREIG	Hosie	Goldie
30	14-Feb	SCC4	EAST FIFE	1-0	Grant	Wilson	Amos	Henderson	Corstorphine	Ross,T	Cowe	Ferguson	Greig	Fairley	GOLDIE
31	21-Feb		Ayr United	1-4	Grant	Wilson	Amos	Henderson	Corstorphine	Ross,T	McAllister	Greig	Murray	Hosie	Goldie
32	28-Feb	SCC5	MONTROSE	6-0	Grant	Wilson	Amos	HENDERSON	Corstorphine	Ross,T	Cowe	FERGUSON 3	MURRAY	HOSIE	Goldie
33	07-Mar	CCf	Leith (n)	1-2	Grant	Wilson	Amos	Henderson	Corstorphine	Ross,T	Cowe	Ferguson	Murray	Hosie	Goldie
34	14-Mar	ESSs	Hearts	0-2	Grant	Wilson	Amos	Henderson	Corstorphine	Ross,T	Ross,G	Greig	Cox	Hosie	Goldie
35	21-Mar	SCCs	Vale of Leven	2-0	Grant	Hodge	Amos	Henderson	Corstorphine	Ross,T	COWE	FERGUSON	Cox	Fairley	Hosie
36	28-Mar	SL2	ALBION ROVERS	0-1	Grant	Hodge	Amos	Henderson	Corstorphine	Ross,T	Cowe	Greig	Cox	HOSIE	Goldie
37	04-Apr	SL2	ARTHURLIE	1-0	Grant	Hodge	Amos	Henderson	Wilson	Cox	Cox	Ferguson	Murray	Hosie	Goldie
38	11-Apr	SL2	DUNDEE HIBS	1-2	Grant	Wilson	Amos	Henderson	Corstorphine	Ross,T	Ross,G	Ferguson	Hosie,T	Fairley	Goldie
39	18-Apr	SCCf	St Johnstone (n)	0-0	Grant	Hodge	Amos	Henderson	Corstorphine	Ross,T	McLaughlan	Ferguson	Cox	Hosie,R	Hosie,R
40	20-Apr	BC1L	LEITH	2-0	Grant	Wilson	Amos	Henderson	Corstorphine	Ross,T	Ross,G	Greig	Buchan,CL	Greig	Goldie
41	25-Apr	SCCf	St Johnstone (n)	1-2	Grant	Wilson	Amos	Henderson	CORSTORPHINE	Ross,T	McLaughlan	Ferguson	Cox	Hosie,R	Hosie,R
42	28-Apr	SL2	EAST STIRLING	5-2	Grant	Wilson	Amos	Henderson	Corstorphine	Ross,T	ROSS,G 2	Greig	COX	Fairley	'COWE' 2
43	02-May	RCCs	HEARTS	0-2	Grant	Wilson	Amos	Hosie	Corstorphine	Davie	'Smith'	Greig	Cox	'Forrest'	Goldie

1914/15

#	Date	Comp	Opponent	Score											
1	08-Aug	SL2	LEITH AMATEURS	4-1											
2	15-Aug	SL2	Abercorn	3-1	Grant	Stewart	Amos	Bennett	McGarrity	Ross	COX	Greig	BUCHAN	AIRD	Weir
3	18-Aug	BC	Leith	0-2	Grant	Stewart	Amos	Bennett	Corstorphine	Ross	Cox	Greig	Buchan,CL	Aird	Weir
4	22-Aug	SL2	LEITH	2-0	Grant	Stewart	Amos	Bennett	Corstorphine	Ross	Cox	GREIG	Coupar	TAYLOR	Weir
5	29-Aug	SL2	Lochgelly United	3-1	Grant	Stewart	Amos	Bennett	McGarrity	Ross	Cox	AIRD 2	Coupar	Taylor	Weir
6	05-Sep	SL2	Cowdenbeath	0-2	Grant	Stewart	Amos	Bennett	McGarrity	Ross	Rogers	Aird	Coupar	Taylor	Weir
7	12-Sep	SL2	East Stirling	0-3	Grant	Stewart	Amos	Bennett	McGarrity	Ross	Rogers	Greig	Coupar	Taylor	Weir
8	19-Sep	SQC2	DUNS	WO											
9	19-Sep	SL2	VALE OF LEVEN	2-1	Grant	Stewart	Amos	Corstorphine	McGARRITY	Ross	Rogers	Greig	Taylor	TAYLOR	Weir
10	26-Sep	SL2	Dunfermline Ath	1-2	Grant	Hastie	Amos	Bennett	Corstorphine	Ross	Rogers	McGarrity	COUPAR	TAYLOR	Weir
11	03-Oct	SQC3	Peebles Rovers	3-1	Grant	Stewart	Amos	BENNETT	Corstorphine	Ross	Rogers	AIRD	COUPAR	Taylor	Weir
12	10-Oct	SL2	Dundee Hibs	0-1	Grant	Stewart	Amos	Bennett	McGarrity	Ross	Rogers	Cox	Coupar	Taylor	Weir
13	17-Oct	SL2	CLYDEBANK	2-1	Grant	Hay	Stewart	Bennett	McGarrity	Ross	Coupar	Greig	COX 2	Taylor	Weir
14	24-Oct	SL2	Arthurlie	2-1	Grant	Hay	Stewart	Bennett	McGarrity	Ross	Coupar	Greig	COX	TAYLOR	Weir
15	31-Oct	SQC5	Broxburn United	0-0	Grant	Hay	Stewart	Bennett	McGarrity	Ross	Coupar	McDougall	Cox	Taylor	WEIR
16	07-Nov	SQC5	BROXBURN Utd	4-0	Grant	Hay	Stewart	Bennett	McGarrity	Ross	Cox	McDOUGALL	COUPAR 3	Taylor	Weir
17	14-Nov	SL2	St Johnstone	1-3	Grant	Hay	Stewart	Bennett	McGarrity	Ross	Cox	McDOUGALL	Coupar	Taylor	Weir
18	21-Nov	SL2	ALBION ROVERS	3-1	Grant	Hay	Stewart	Bennett	McGarrity	Ross	COX	McDOUGALL	Coupar	Taylor	WEIR
19	28-Nov	SL2	Leith	0-5	Grant	Hay	Stewart	Bennett	McGarrity	Ross	Flucker	McDougall	Coupar	Taylor	Weir
20	05-Dec	SQC6	EAST STIRLING	2-1	Grant	Hay	Stewart	Bennett	McGarrity	Ross	McDougall	COX	Coupar	Taylor	WEIR
21	12-Dec	SQCs	St Johnstone	4-1	Grant	Hay	Penman	Bennett	McGarrity	Ross	COX	McDougall	COUPAR 2	Taylor	Weir
22	19-Dec	SL2	DUNFERMLINE Ath	2-1	Grant	Hay	Penman	Bennett	McGarrity	Ross	COX	McDougall	Coupar	Taylor	WEIR
23	26-Dec	SL2	Albion Rovers	1-1	Grant	Hay	Penman	Bennett	McGarrity	Ross	Gray	McDougall	Coupar	TAYLOR	Weir
24	02-Jan	SQCf	Dykehead (n)	2-2	Grant	Hay	Penman	Bennett	McGarrity	Ross	Cox	McDOUGALL	COUPAR	Taylor	Weir
25	09-Jan	SQCf	Dykehead (n)	1-1	Grant	Hay	Penman	Bennett	McGarrity	Ross,T	Cox	Ross,A	COUPAR 2	Taylor	Weir
26	18-Jan	SQCf	Dykehead (n)	3-0	Grant	Hay	Penman	Bennett	McGarrity	Ross,T	Cox	Ross,A	COUPAR 2	Taylor	Weir
27	23-Jan	SL2	DUNDEE HIBS	5-1	Grant	Hay	Penman	BENNETT	McGarrity	Ross,T	COX 2	Ross,A	McDOUGALL	TAYLOR	WEIR
28	30-Jan	SL2	ARTHURLIE	6-0	Grant	Hay	Penman	Bennett	McGarrity	Ross,T	Cox	Ross,A	COUPAR 4	McDOUGALL	WEIR
29	06-Feb	SL2	Clydebank	4-1	Grant	Hay	Penman	Bennett	McGarrity	Ross,T	Cox	Ross,A	COUPAR 3	McDOUGALL	Weir
30	13-Feb	SL2	EAST STIRLING	3-2	Grant	Hay	Penman	Bennett	McGarrity	Ross,T	Cox	Ross,A	COUPAR	McDOUGALL	Weir
31	20-Feb	SL2	Vale of Leven	7-1	Grant	Hay	Penman	Bennett	McGarrity	ROSS,T	COX 2	Ross,A	COUPAR 2	McDOUGALL 2	Weir
32	27-Feb	SL2	ABERCORN	4-0	Grant	Hay	Penman	Bennett	McGarrity	Ross,T	Cox	Ross,A	COUPAR 2	McDOUGALL	WEIR
33	06-Mar	SL2	JOHNSTONE	4-2	Grant	Hay	Penman	Bennett	McGarrity	Ross,T	Cox	Ross,A	McDougall	McDougall	Weir
34	13-Mar	SL2	COWDENBEATH	1-0	Grant	Hay	Penman	Bennett	McGarrity	Ross,T	Cox	Ross,A	COUPAR	McDougall	Weir
35	20-Mar	SL2	Johnstone	1-2	Grant	Hay	Penman	Bennett	McGarrity	Ross,T	Cox	Ross,A	COUPAR	McDougall	Weir
36	27-Mar	SL2	ST JOHNSTONE	3-1	Grant	Hay	Penman	BENNETT	McGARRITY	Ross,T	Cox	Ross,A	COUPAR	McDOUGALL	Weir
37	10-Apr	SL2	LOCHGELLY UTD	6-0	Grant	Hay	Penman	Bennett	McGARRITY	Ross,T	Cox	Ross,A 2	COUPAR	McDOUGALL	WEIR
38	17-Apr	SL2po	Leith (n)	1-2	Grant	Hay	Morrison	Bennett	McGarrity	Ross,T	Cox	Ross,A	Coupar	McDougall	WEIR
39	21-Apr	ESSs	HIBERNIAN	0-2	Grant	Hay	Morrison	Bennett	McGarrity	Ross,T	Cox	McDougall	Coupar	Ross,A	Weir
40	24-Apr	SL2po	Cowdenbeath (n)	1-3	Grant	Hay	Morrison	Bennett	McGarrity	Ross,T	Cox	ROSS,A	Coupar	Early	Weir
41	01-May	RCCs	Hearts	3-2	Grant	Amos	Hay	Bennett	Morrison	Ross,T	Cox	Ross,A	Coupar	McDougall	Weir
42	08-May	RCCf	Hibernian (n)	4-3	Grant	Amos	Hay	Bennett	Morrison	Ross,T	Cox	McDougall	Coupar	Ross,A	Weir

1915/16

#	Date	Comp	Opponent	Score												
1	21-Aug	EL	COWDENBEATH	1-0	Grant	Hay	Kennedy	Bennett	McGarity	Ross, T	Messer	Ross, A	COUPAR	Elmore	McDougall
2	28-Aug	EL	Leith	4-1	from Grant, Hay, Kennedy, Bennett, McGARRITY 2, Ross, G, Ross,A, Elmore, COUPAR 2, McDougall and AN Other.
3	04-Sep	EL	ARMADALE	1-3	Grant	Hay	Thomson	Bennett	McGARRITY	Ross, T	Messer	Ross, A	COUPAR	McDougall and AN Other.	Speirs
4	11-Sep	EL	Broxburn United	2-0	Grant	Hay	McGarity	Bennett	Thomson	Ross, T	Messer	Ross, A	COUPAR	McDougall	ELMORE
5	18-Sep	EL	BATHGATE	1-1	Grant	Hay	Kennedy	Bennett	McGarity	Ross, T	Messer	ROSS,A	Coupar	McDougall	Elmore
6	20-Sep	BC	LEITH	2-1	Grant	Hay	Kennedy	Bennett	McGarity	Ross, T	Messer	Ross,A	Coupar	McDougall	Elmore
7	25-Sep	EL	Dunfermline Athletic	4-5	Grant	Hay	Kennedy	Bennett	McGarity	Ross, T	MESSER	ELMORE	COUPAR	McDougall	MCDONALD
8	02-Oct	EL	EAST STIRLING	3-0	Grant	Hay	Penman	'Newman'	Bennett	Ross, T	Messer	Ross,A	COUPAR 2	McDougall	McDonald
9	09-Oct	EL	Lochgelly United	2-1	Grant	Hay	Penman	Bennett	MCGARRITY	Ross, T	Messer	Ross, A	Coupar	McDougall	TAYLOR
10	16-Oct	EL	DUNFERMLINE Ath	5-1	Grant	Hay	Penman	Bennett	Thomson	Ross, T	Cox	Ross, A	COUPAR 4	TAYLOR	Dickson
11	23-Oct	EL	Armadale	0-2	Grant	Hay	Penman	Bennett	Thomson	Ross, T	Messer	Ross, A	Coupar	Taylor	Dickson
12	30-Oct	EL	BROXBURN Utd	2-1	Grant	Hay	Penman	Bennett	Thomson	Ross, T	Messer	Ross, A	COUPAR	McDOUGALL	Weir
13	06-Nov	EL	DUNDEE HIBS	5-0	Grant	Hay	Penman	McGarrity	Thomson	Ross, T	Messer	Ross, A	COUPAR 3	McDougall	WEIR
14	13-Nov	EL	Cowdenbeath	1-2	Grant	Hay	Penman	Bennett	Thomson	Ross, T	Messer	Ross, A	COUPAR	McDougall	Weir
15	20-Nov	BC	LEITH	0-1	from Grant, Hay, Penman, Bennett, Thomson, Ross T, Ross A, Maclean, Coupar, McDougall and Weir.
16	27-Nov	EL	East Stirling	2-1	Grant	Hay	Penman	Bennett	Thomson	Ross, T	Messer	Ross,A	COUPAR	McDOUGALL	Weir
17	04-Dec	EL	Dundee Hibs	1-5	Messer	Hay	Penman	BENNETT	Thomson	Ross, T	Ross,A	Maclean	Coupar	McDOUGALL	Weir
18	11-Dec	EL	LEITH	3-0	Grant	Hay	Penman	Kennedy	Thomson	Ross,A	Ross,A	Maclean	COUPAR	McDougall	Weir
19	18-Dec	GC	Broxburn United	4-2	Grant	Kennedy	Penman	Bennett	Thomson	Ross, T	Ross,A	Maclean	Coupar	McDougall	Weir
20	25-Dec	EL	KIRKCALDY Utd	5-0	Grant	Hay	Penman	Kennedy	Thomson	Ross, T	Ross,A	MACLEAN	COUPAR 4	McDougall	Weir
21	01-Jan	EL	East Fife	2-0	Grant	Hay	Penman	Ross	Thomson	Kennedy	MESSER	Maclean	Coupar	McDOUGALL	Murray
22	08-Jan		CLYDEBANK	1-0	Grant	Hay	Penman	Ross,A	Thomson	Ross, T	Messer	Maclean	Coupar	McDougall	Weir
23	15-Jan	GC	Bathgate	1-2	Grant	Hay	Penman	Ross,A	Thomson	Ross, T	Messer	Maclean	Coupar	McDougall	Weir
24	22-Jan	ELC1	EAST FIFE	3-3	Grant	Hay	Penman	Bennett	Thomson	Ross, T	Messer	Maclean	Coupar	McDougall	Weir
25	29-Jan	EL	Bathgate	2-1	Grant	Hay	Penman	Bennett	Thomson	Ross,A	MACLEAN	COUPAR	McDougall		Murray
26	05-Feb	EL	LOCHGELLY Utd	7-0	Grant	Hay	Penman	Bennett	Thomson	ROSS, A	MESSER	MACLEAN 3	COUPAR	Ross, T	MCDOUGALL
27	19-Feb	ELC1	EAST FIFE	2-1	Grant	Kennedy	Penman	Ross, A	Bennett	Murray	Messer	MACLEAN	Coupar	McDougall	Weir
28	26-Feb	EL	East Fife	5-1	Grant	Hay	Penman	Bennett	Thomson	Ross, T	Ross,A	Maclean	Coupar	McDougall	Weir
29	11-Mar	BC	LEITH	3-0	from Grant, Scott, Penman, Kennedy, Thomson, Ross,T, Ross,A, Maclean, Coupar, McDougall and Weir.
30	18-Mar		Clydebank	?-?	from Grant, Scott, Hay or Penman, Kennedy, Thomson , Ross, Messer, Maclean, Coupar, McDougall and Weir.
31	01-Apr	ELC2	DUNFERMLINE Ath	3-0	Grant	Scott	Penman	Bennett	Thomson	Ross	Messer	Maclean	Coupar	McDougall	Weir
32	08-Apr	GC	BROXBURN Utd	2-0	Grant	Scott	Penman	Bennett	Thomson	Ross	Messer	Maclean	COUPAR 2	McDOUGALL	Weir
33	15-Apr	EL	Kirkcaldy United	3-1	Grant	Kennedy	Penman	Scott	Thomson	Ross	Messer	Maclean	Coupar	McDougall	Weir
34	17-Apr	GC	LEITH	2-2	Grant	Scott	Kennedy	Murray	Thomson	Ross	Messer	Maclean	COUPAR 2	McDOUGALL	Weir
35	22-Apr	ELCs	Leith	2-0	from Grant, Scott, Penman, AN Other, Bennett, Thomson, Ross, Messer, Maclean, Coupar, McDougall and Weir.
36	22-Apr	ELCf	Armadale (n)	1-2	Grant	Scott	McGarrity	Bennett	Penman	Ross,T	Messer	Maclean	McDougall	Ross,A	Weir
37	06-May	RCC	Hibernian	1-6	Grant	Scott	Penman	Kennedy	Drummond	Thomson	Ross	Messer	Maclean	Coupar	McDougall

1916/17

#	Date		Opponent	Score										
1	19-Aug	EL	EAST STIRLING	5-1	Kerr	Hyde	Kennedy	Pearson	McGarrity	McBeth	Morton	MACLEAN	Coupar	ALLAN	McDOUGALL 3
2	26-Aug	EL	Broxburn United	0-1	Kerr	Hickie	Kennedy	Pearson	Gourlay	McBeth	Morton	Allan	Coupar	Maclean	McDougall
3	02-Sep	EL	LOCHGELLY UTD	6-2	?	Hyde	Kennedy	Young	McGarrity	McBeth	MORTON	MACLEAN	COUPAR 2	BLACKHALL	MCDOUGALL
4	09-Sep	EL	Dunfermline Ath	1-1	Kerr	Scott	Kennedy	Hyde	McGarrity	McBeth	Morton	Blackhall	Allan	Maclean	McDougall ?
5	16-Sep	EL	BATHGATE	3-2	Kerr	Scott	Amos	Pearson	McGarrity	McBeth	Cartmell	MACLEAN	COUPAR	Allan	HYDE
6	23-Sep	EL	East Stirling	1-2	Kerr	Scott	Amos	Hyde	'Thomson'	McBeth	Coupar	Maclean	Morton	McDOUGALL	Meagher
7	30-Sep	EL	EAST FIFE	1-0	Kerr	Scott	Amos	Bennett	Smith	McBeth	Cartmell	MACLEAN	Meagher	McDougall	Cartmell
8	07-Oct	EL	Lochgelly United	3-0	Kerr	Cresswell	Amos	Stratford	McGarrity	McBeth	Bennett	Maclean	Hyde	MCDOUGALL 2	Cartmell
9	14-Oct	EL	COWDENBEATH	1-2	Kerr	Scott	Amos	Stratford	McGarrity	McBeth	Sinclair	Maclean	Coupar	Hyde	MCDOUGALL
10	21-Oct	EL	East Fife	0-1	Kerr	Hyde	Amos	Smith	McGarrity	McBeth	Sinclair	Allan	McDougall	Mitchell	Cartmell
11	28-Oct	EL	BROXBURN UTD	1-0	Bruce	Hyde	Amos	Reed	Smith	McBeth	Cartmell	Ritchie	COUPAR	McDougall	Lambert
12	04-Nov	EL	Bathgate	5-0	Kerr	Cresswell	Amos	Smith'	Reed	McBeth	CARTMELL	MACLEAN	HYDE 2	McDOUGALL	Lambert
13	11-Nov	ELC1	Bathgate	2-1	Kerr	Cresswell	Amos	AN Other	Seed	McBeth	COUPAR	MACLEAN	Hyde	McDougall	Lindley
14	18-Nov	EL	Dunfermline Ath	2-1	Kerr	Cresswell	Amos	Reed	Seed	McBeth	Hyde	Maclean	Coupar	McDougall	Lindley
15	25-Nov	EL	Dundee Hibs	1-1	Kerr	Smith	Amos	McDougall	Seed	McBeth	Dunn	Smith	Petrie	McDougall	Lindley
16	02-Dec	EL	DUNDEE HIBS	2-1	Kerr	Cresswell	Amos	Reed	Seed	McBeth	Dunn	MACLEAN	Coupar	McDougall	Lindley
17	09-Dec	EL	ARMADALE	3-0	Kerr	Cresswell	Amos	Lamb	Reed	McBeth	Herbste	MACLEAN 2	Coupar	McDougall	HYDE
18	16-Dec	LC	Dunfermline Ath	0-2	Kerr	Cresswell	Amos	Lamb	Reed	Golding	Herbste	Maclean	Coupar	McDougall	Hyde
19	06-Jan	LC	DUNFERMLINE Ath	4-2	Kerr	Cresswell	Hyde	Seed	McBeth	Herbste	Maclean	Coupar	McDougall	Grant
20	20-Jan	ELC2	BROXBURN UTD	3-0	Kerr	Amos	Cresswell	Seed	Reed	McBeth	Herbste	MACLEAN	COUPAR	McDougall	Hyde
21	27-Jan		ROYAL FUSILIERS	3-1	from Kerr, Cresswell, Amos, Lamb, Scott, McBeth, Herbste, Maclean, Couper, McDougall and Hyde.										
22	03-Feb	GC1	BATHGATE	1-1	Kerr	Cresswell	Amos	Oddy	McLeod	Hyde	Saunders	Coupar	McDougall	Firth
23	10-Feb	EL	Cowdenbeath	0-2	Kerr	Cresswell	Amos	Oddy	McLeod	Thomson	Maclean	Coupar	McDougall	McBeth
24	17-Feb	PC2	Armadale	1-1	Bruce	McLeod	Amos	Hyde	Thomson	McBeth	Herbste	Maclean	Coupar	Saunders	McDougall
25	03-Mar	PC2	ARMADALE	1-1	Kerr	McLeod	Amos	Hyde	Thomson	McBeth	Firth	Maclean	Coupar	McDougall	Ross
26	24-Mar		ROYAL FUSILIERS	4-1	from Kerr, McLeod, Amos, Gordon, Gilhooley, McBeth, Newman, Maclean, Cresswell, Coupar, Maclean and McLeod										
27	31-Mar	GC1	Bathgate	0-1	Kerr	Cresswell	Oddy	Hyde	Gilhooley	McBeth	Herbste	McDougall	Morgan	Coupar
28	07-Apr	ELCs	DUNFERMLINE Ath	2-1	Kerr	Cresswell	Amos	Reed	Gilhooley	McBeth	Herbste	Maclean	McLeod	McDougall	Hyde
29	16-Apr		ARMY XI	2-1											
30	28-Apr		Hibs	0-2	from Kerr, Cresswell, Amos, Reed, Gilhooley, McBeth, Hyde, Herbste, McLeod, McDougall, Maclean, Coupar and Newman.										
31	05-May	RCC	Armadale (n)	2-2*	Slavin	Cresswell	Amos	Reed	Gilhooley	McBeth	Hyde	Maclean	McLeod	McDougall	McGeachin

1919/20

#	Date	Comp	Opponent	Score												
1	01-Jul	Trial	TRIAL	?-?												
2	12-Jul	Trial	TRIAL	?-?												
3	09-Aug	Trial	CIVIL SERVICE		from McNaughton, Dickson, McLeod, Amos, McLean,R, Seed, Dawson, Cox, Ross,G, Coupar, Taylor and Welsh.											
4	16-Aug	CL	ARMADALE	4-1	McNaughton	McLeod	Amos	McLean,R	SEED	Dawson	ROSS,G	MACLEAN,T 2	Coupar	'Watson'	Welsh
5	23-Aug	CL	EAST FIFE	4-2	from McNaughton, McLeod, Amos, McLean,R, Seed, Dawson, Cox, Maclean,T, COUPAR 2, ROSS and Welsh.											
6	30-Aug	CL	Bathgate	1-1	McNaughton	McLeod	Amos	McLean,R	Seed	Dawson	Cox	Maclean,T	Coupar	Ross	Welsh
7	06-Sep	SQC1	Bathgate	0-1	McNaughton	McLeod	Amos	McLean,R	Seed	Cox	Maclean,T	Coupar	Dawson	Welsh
8	13-Sep	CL	East Fife	1-1	McNaughton	McLeod	Amos	McLean,R	Seed	Wilson,J	Cox	Maclean,T	Henderson	Dawson	Welsh
9	20-Sep	CL	BATHGATE	1-0	McNaughton	McLeod	Amos	McLean,R	Seed	Wilson,J	Ross	Maclean,T	HENDERSON	Dawson	Welsh
10	27-Sep	CL	Broxburn United	2-2	McNaughton	McLeod	Amos	McLean,R	Seed	Wilson,J	Cox	Maclean,T	HENDERSON	DAWSON	Welsh
11	11-Oct	CL	Kings Park	3-0	McNaughton	Cox	Amos	Seed	Clow	Wilson	McLean,R	Maclean,T	HENDERSON	Lawson	Welsh
12	18-Oct	CL	BONESS	0-0	McNaughton	Cox	Amos	Seed	McLeod	Wilson	McLean,R	Maclean,T	Henderson	Lawson	Welsh
13	25-Oct	CL	Armadale	0-2	McNaughton	Cox	Amos	Seed	McLeod	Wilson	COX	Maclean,T	Henderson	Dawson	Welsh
14	01-Nov	CL	DUNFERMLINE ATH	3-1	McNaughton	Watson	Amos	Seed	McLeod	Wilson	COX	Maclean,R	HENDERSON 2	Maclean,T	Welsh
15	08-Nov	CL	Clackmannan	5-2	McNaughton	Cox	Amos	Seed	McLeod	Wilson	Thomson	McLean,R	Henderson	MACLEAN,T 3	WELSH 2
16	29-Nov	CL	ALLOA ATHLETIC	3-4	McNaughton	Cox	Amos	Seed	McLeod	Dawson	Ross,G	McLean,R	Henderson	MACLEAN,T 2	Welsh
17	06-Dec	CL	Stenhousemuir	1-1	McNaughton	'Cowan'	Amos	Wilson	McLeod	Dawson	Ross,G	McLean,R	Henderson	Maclean,T	WELSH
18	13-Dec	CL	FALKIRK 'A'	2-1	McNaughton	Anderson	Amos	Wilson	McLeod	Murray	Ross,G	McLEAN,R	HENDERSON	Maclean,T	Welsh
19	20-Dec	CL	Alloa Athletic	1-3	McNaughton	Miller	Amos	McLean,R	McLeod	Murray	Cox	Ross	Henderson	MACLEAN,T	Welsh
20	27-Dec	CL	EAST STIRLING	4-0	McNaughton	Miller	Amos	McLean,R	McLeod	Wilson	Cox	Maclean,T	HENDERSON 3	TAYLOR	Welsh
21	01-Jan	CL	Dunfermline Athletic	1-4	McNaughton	Miller	Amos	McLean,R	McLeod	Wilson	Cox	Maclean,T	Henderson	Taylor	Welsh
22	10-Jan	CLC	Bathgate	3-5	McNaughton	Anderson	Amos	McLean,R	McLeod	Newman, Manson, Ross, Maclean,T, Henderson, Taylor and Welsh.						
23	10-Jan		Hearts 'A'	0-3	from McNaughton, Gilbert, McLeod, McLean,R, Amos, Wilson, Cox, Maclean,T, Henderson, Taylor and Welsh.											
24	24-Jan	SC2	BATHGATE	2-0	McNaughton	Campbell	Amos	McLean,R	McLeod	Wilson	Ross	Maclean,T	HENDERSON	Taylor	WELSH
25	31-Jan	SC2	BROXBURN Utd	2-1	McNaughton	Campbell	Amos	McLean,R	McLEOD	Wilson	Ross	Maclean,T	HENDERSON	Taylor	Welsh
26	07-Feb	CL	Dunfermline Ath	0-4	McNaughton	Campbell	Amos	McLean,R	McLeod	Wilson	Ross	Maclean,T	Henderson	Taylor	Welsh
27	14-Feb		Vale of Leithen	0-5	McNaughton	Campbell	Amos	McLean,R	McLeod	Dawson	Ross	Maclean,T	Henderson	Taylor	Welsh
28	21-Feb	SC3	ALBION ROVERS	1-1	McNaughton	Campbell	Amos	McLean,R	McLeod	Wilson	ROSS	Maclean,T	HENDERSON	Taylor	Welsh
29	25-Feb	SC3	Albion Rovers	1-4	McNaughton	Campbell	Amos	McLean,R	McLeod	Ross,T	Ross,G	Maclean,T	Henderson	Duncan	Welsh
30	28-Feb	CL	KINGS PARK	3-0	from McNaughton, Campbell, Amos, McLean,R, McLEOD, Wilson, Ross, Maclean,T, HENDERSON, Dawson and WELSH.											
31	06-Mar	CL	CLACKMANNAN	0-0	from McNaughton, Campbell, Amos, McLean,R, McLeod, Wilson, Ross,G, Maclean,T, Henderson, Dawson and Welsh											
32	13-Mar		Hearts 'A'	1-1	from McNaughton, Campbell, Amos, McLean,R, McLeod, Wilson, Ross, Maclean,T, Henderson, Dawson, Welsh, Cox, Taylor and Other,AN											
33	20-Mar	CCs	GALA FAIRYDEAN	7-0	McNaughton	Campbell	McLeod	DAWSON 2	Wilson	Cox	Maclean,T	HENDERSON	Henderson	Lawson	Welsh
34	27-Mar	CCf	STENHOUSEMUIR	4-0	McNaughton	Cox	McLeod	DAWSON 2	'Smith'	Ross	Maclean,T	HENDERSON	Henderson	Lawson	WELSH
35	03-Apr	CL	BROXBURN Utd	4-0	McNaughton	Cox	Amos	McLean,R	McLeod	Wilson	Ross	Maclean,T	Henderson	Lawson	Welsh
36	10-Apr		Newcastle United	0-5	McNaughton	McLeod	Amos	Dawson	Wilson	Cox	Lawson	Maclean,T	Henderson	Maclean,T	
37	12-Apr	ESSs	Hibernian	0-1	McNaughton	McLeod	Cox	Dawson	Wilson	Cox	Lawson	Maclean,T	Henderson	Lawson	Welsh
38	15-Apr	CL	Falkirk 'A'	0-0	McNaughton	McQuade	McLeod	Dawson	Wilson	Cox	Ross	Lawson	Inglis	Maclean,T	Lawson
39	17-Apr		Airdrie	1-3											
40	24-Apr	CL	Boness	0-2	McNaughton	McLeod	Amos	McLean,R	Dawson	Wilson	Murray	Williams	Cox	Maclean,T	Welsh
41	28-Apr		Mburgh Bruntonians	1-1											
42	01-May	CL	Edinburgh Emmet	3-0	McNaughton	Cox	McLeod	McLean,R	Dawson	Wilson	Murray	Maclean,T	Henderson	Lawson and Welsh.	
43	03-May	CL	East Stirling	2-2	McNaughton	Cox	McLeod	McLean,R	Dawson	Wilson	Lawson	Maclean,T	Henderson	Maclean,T	Welsh
44	12-May	RCCs	Hearts	0-5	McNaughton	Cox	McLeod	McLean,R	Dawson	Weightman	Murray	Maclean,T	Henderson	Cook	Welsh

1920/21

#	Date	Trial	BLUES	v HOOPS											
1	07-Aug		BLUES	v HOOPS		Stevenson	Henry	Frame	Lawrie	Wilson	Dawson	Weightman	McCulloch	McLean,T	Henderson	Cairns	Imrie
2	16-Aug	CL	BATHGATE		1-3	Lochhead	Cox	Frame		McLean,R	Summers	McLeod	Fisher	Miller	Clark	Black	Welsh
3	21-Aug	CL	ALLOA ATHLETIC		0-0	Stevenson	Henry	Frame		Summers	Dawson	Weightman	Fisher	Stage	Clark	Miller	Welsh
4	24-Aug	CL	Hearts 'A'		3-0	Stevenson	Henry	Frame		McLean,R	Summers	Dawson	Fisher	STAGE	CLARK	MILLER	Welsh
5	28-Aug	CL	East Fife		0-2	Stevenson	Henry	Frame		McLean,R	Summers	Weightman	FISHER	Stage	Clark	MILLER	Welsh
6	04-Sep	SQC1	Armadale		1-1	Stevenson	Henry	McLeod		Miller	Summers	Miller	Fisher	Stage	Clark	McLean,R	Welsh
7	06-Sep		Lochgelly United		0-3	Stevenson	Waterston	McLeod		McLean,R	Summers	Cairns	Fisher	Stage	Clark	McLean,T	Welsh
8	11-Sep	CL	Armadale		1-2	Stevenson	Henry	McLeod		McLEAN,R	Summers	Weightman	Fisher	Moore	Whyte	Wilkinson	Wilson
9	18-Sep	CL	HEARTS 'A'		2-3	Stevenson	Henry	McLeod		McLean,R	Summers	Taylor	Fisher	Miller	Clark	'Logan'	Welsh
10	25-Sep	CL	East Stirling		1-1	Stevenson	Henry	'Penman'		McLean,R	Summers	McLeod	Fisher	Stage	Cairns	CLARK	Welsh
11	02-Oct	CL	Dunfermline Ath		0-4	Stevenson	Henry	McLeod		Summers	Dawson	Cairns	Fisher	Stage	Clark	Wilson	WELSH
12	09-Oct	CL	Dundee Hibs		2-1	Stevenson	Watson	Frame		Cairns	Summers	Miller	Fisher	Wilson	Weightman	Wilson	Welsh
13	16-Oct	CL	COWDENBEATH		4-3	Stevenson	Cairns	McLeod		Miller	Summers	Clark	Fisher	Clark	TURNER 2	Clark	Tennent
14	23-Oct	CL	KINGS PARK		2-0	Stevenson	Watson	Dawson		Miller	Summers	Clark	Fisher	Clark	TURNER 2	WILSON	Welsh
15	30-Oct	CL	Falkirk 'A'		1-0	Stevenson	Watson	McLeod		Miller	Summers	Dawson	Fisher	Clark	TURNER	Wilson	Welsh
16	06-Nov	CL	BONESS		1-1	Stevenson	McLeod	Scott		Dawson	Summers	Dawson	Fisher	Clark	Clark	WILSON	Dawson
17	13-Nov	CL	CLACKMANNAN		2-0	Stevenson	McLeod	McLeod		Miller	Summers	Clark	Fisher	Brogan	WILSON,G	Wilson,A	Welsh
18	20-Nov	CL	ST JOHNSTONE		4-1	Stevenson	McLeod	Gay		Miller	Summers	Clark	FISHER	Brogan	DAWSON	Wilson	Welsh
19	27-Nov	CL	Bathgate		0-0	Stevenson	McLeod	Gay		Miller	Summers	Clark	Fisher	BROGAN	REID	WILSON 2	Welsh
20	04-Dec	CL	STENHOUSEMUIR		1-1	Stevenson	Scott	McLeod		Dawson	Summers	Dawson	Fisher	BROGAN	Reid	WILSON	Dawson
21	11-Dec	CL	BROXBURN Utd		4-0	Stevenson	McLeod	Gay		Miller	Cairns	Clark	Fisher	Brogan	Reid	WILSON	Welsh
22	18-Dec	CL	Clackmannan		1-1	Stevenson	McLeod	Gay		Miller	Summers	Clark	FISHER	BROGAN 2	'NEWMAN'	Wilson	WELSH
23	25-Dec	CL	LOCHGELLY Utd		6-0	Stevenson	McLeod	Gay		Miller	SUMMERS	Clark	Fisher	BROGAN	Cairns	Wilson	Welsh
24	01-Jan	CL	St Johnstone		2-3	Stevenson	McLeod	Gay		Miller	Summers	Clark	FISHER	BROGAN	CAIRNS 2	WILSON	WELSH
25	03-Jan	CL	Cowdenbeath		1-2	Stevenson	McLeod	Gay		Miller	Summers	Clark	Fisher	BROGAN	Nicol	Turner	Welsh
26	08-Jan	CL	Boness		1-2	Stevenson	McLeod	Gay		Miller	Summers	Clark	Fisher	Brogan	Nicol	Wilson	Welsh
27	15-Jan	CL	ARMADALE		1-1	Stevenson	McLEOD	Gay		Miller	Summers	Clark	Fisher	Brogan	Simpson	Wilson	CAIRNS
28	22-Jan	CL	DUNDEE HIBS		1-1	Stevenson	McLeod	Gay		Miller	Summers	Cairns	Nicol	Brogan	'Newman'	Wilson	Cairns
29	29-Jan	CL	Broxburn United		0-2	Stevenson	McLeod	Gay		Miller	Summers	Clark	Fisher	Brogan	'NEWMAN'	Wilson	Nelson
30	05-Feb	CL	FALKIRK 'A'		3-1	Stevenson	McLEOD	Gay		Miller	Summers	Simpson	Fisher	Brogan	Sutherland	Wilson	'Nelson'
31	12-Feb	CL	Lochgelly United		0-0	Stevenson	Wilson	Gay		Miller	Summers	Clark	Fisher	Brogan	Sutherland	Wilson,A	WELSH
32	19-Feb	CL	DUNFERMLINE Ath		0-2	Stevenson	Wilson,J	Gay		Miller	Summers	Clark	Fisher	Brogan	Sutherland	Wilson,A	Welsh
33	26-Feb	CL	Kings Park		1-0	Stevenson	Wilson,J	Gay		Miller	Summers	Clark	Fisher	Brogan	Sutherland	Wilson	Welsh
34	05-Mar	CL	EAST FIFE		0-1	Savage	McLeod	McIlwraith		Miller	Summers	Clark	Fisher	Wilson	Sutherland	Black	Welsh
35	12-Mar	CCs	BERWICK Rangers		6-2	Stevenson	McLeod	McIlwraith		Miller	Summers	Clark	Fisher	Brogan	Sutherland	Wilson	WELSH
36	19-Mar	CL	Stenhousemuir		0-1	Savage	McLeod	McIlwraith		Miller	'Watson'	Clark	Fisher	Wilson	Sutherland	Black	Welsh
37	26-Mar	CLC1	BATHGATE		1-1	Stevenson	McLeod	Gay		Miller	Summers	Clark	Fisher	Brogan	Sutherland	Wilson	WELSH
38	08-Apr	CLC1	Bathgate		0-4	Savage	McLeod	Gay		Miller	Saunders	Black	Fisher	Wilson	Wilson	Black	Welsh
39	09-Apr	CL	EAST STIRLING		2-2	Savage	'Thomson'	Smith		Thomson	Anderson	'Gorman'	Christie	HENDERSON 2	Sutherland	Sutherland	Clark
40	14-Apr	CL	Broxburn United		1-1	Stevenson	McLeod	Gay		Miller	Summers	Watson	Fisher	Brogan	Sutherland	Black	Welsh
41	16-Apr	CCf	Leith Athletic		1-0	from Savage, McLeod, Gay, Miller, Summers, Clark, Fisher, Brogan, Sutherland, Wilson and Welsh.										
42	23-Apr	BC1	LEITH ATHLETIC		1-0	from Stevenson, McLeod, Gay, Miller, Summers, Clark, Fisher, Brogan, Sutherland, Nicol, Wilson and Welsh.										
43	30-Apr	ESSs	Hibernian		2-4	from Savage, Gay, McLeod, Miller, Summers, Clark, Fisher, Brogan, 'Other,AN, Wilson and Welsh.										
44	02-May	CL	Alloa Athletic		1-1	Savage	McLeod	Gay		Miller	Gorman	Campbell	Fisher	Brogan	Black	CLARK	Welsh
45	04-May	BC2	Leith Athletic		2-3	Savage	Miller	Gay		Clark	McNally	Campbell	Nicol	Black	Wilson	Newman
46	07-May	RCCs	Hibernian		3-1	'Williamson'	McLeod	Gay		McLean	Campbell	Rusk	Fisher	Brogan	Henderson	Wilson	McKay
47	14-May	RCCf	Hearts		0-1	Archibald	'Thomson'	Gay		McLean	Campbell	Rusk	Fisher	Brogan	Henderson	Wilson	McKay

1921/22

#	Date	Opponent	Lg	Score											
1	13-Aug	TRIAL													
2	15-Aug	Bathgate		2-0	Archibald	McLean	Campbell	?-?	Black	Henderson	White,C	Cox	Stewart	White,J	Wilson	Robertson
3	20-Aug	Armadale		0-3	Archibald	McLean	Campbell	Law	Henderson	Rusk	Cox	Brogan	Rintoul	Robertson	Wilson
4	27-Aug	ARBROATH	SL2	0-0	Archibald	McLean	Campbell	Law	Henderson	Rusk	Cox	Brogan	Wilson	'Thomson'	Other,AN
5	03-Sep	Vale of Leven	SL2	1-2	Archibald	McLean	Law	Campbell	Henderson	Robertson	Cox	Brogan	RINTOUL	Wilson	Mackay
6	10-Sep	COWDENBEATH	SL2	0-2	Archibald	McLean	Law	Gordon	Henderson	Campbell	Cox	Mackay	Rintoul	Wilson	Smith
7	17-Sep	Broxburn United	SL2	2-1	Archibald	McLean	Law	Gordon	Henderson	Campbell	Cox	Mackay	RINTOUL	Wilson	WIMSETT
8	24-Sep	FORFAR ATHLETIC	SL2	1-5	Archibald	McLean	Law	'Fowler'	Henderson	Campbell	Cox	MACKAY	Rintoul	Wilson	Wimsett
9	01-Oct	St Johnstone	SL2	3-1	Archibald	Law	Campbell,A	Brown	McLean	Campbell,J	COX	Brogan	Donnachie	ROBERTSON	RINTOUL
10	08-Oct	ALLOA ATHLETIC	SL2	2-0	Archibald	McLean	Law	Brown	Gordon	Campbell	Cox	BROGAN	DONNACHIE	Robertson	Rintoul
11	15-Oct	East Fife	SL2	2-4	Archibald	McLean	Law	Brown	Gordon	Campbell	Cox	BROGAN	DONNACHIE	Robertson	Rintoul
12	22-Oct	STENHOUSEMUIR	SL2	3-1	Archibald	McLean	Law	Brown	Henderson	Campbell,J	Cox	Brogan	DONNACHIE	ROBERTSON	Rintoul
13	29-Oct	Bathgate	SL2	2-2	Archibald	McLean	Law	Brown	Henderson	Campbell	COX	Brogan	DONNACHIE	Robertson	Rintoul
14	05-Nov	EAST STIRLING	SL2	0-1	Archibald	McLean	Law	Brown	Henderson	Campbell	Cox	Brogan	Donnachie	Watson	Rintoul
15	12-Nov	Lochgelly United	SL2	0-0	Archibald	McLean	Law	Brown	Henderson	Campbell	Cox	Brogan	DONNACHIE 2	Wilson	Rintoul
16	19-Nov	DUNDEE HIBS	SL2	1-0	Archibald	McLean	Law	Brown	McAvoy	Campbell	Cox	Brogan	Donnachie	Robertson	Rintoul
17	26-Nov	CLACKMANNAN	SL2	1-0	Archibald	McLean	Law	Brown	McAvoy	Campbell	Cox	Logan	DONNACHIE 2	Robertson	Rintoul
18	03-Dec	Johnstone	SL2	0-1	Archibald	McLean	Law	from Archibald, McLean, Law, Brown, McAvoy, Campbell, Cox, Robertson, Donnachie, Wilson and Rintoul.							
19	07-Dec	Hearts		1-2	Archibald	McLean	Law	Brown	McAvoy	Campbell	Cox	Logan	Donnachie	Robertson	Rintoul
20	10-Dec	ST JOHNSTONE	SL2	1-0	Archibald	McLean	Law	Brown	Henderson	McAvoy	Cox	'Smith'	DONNACHIE	Robertson	Newman
21	17-Dec	Boness	SL2	1-0	Archibald	McLean	Law	Brown	Henderson	Turnbull	Cox	Robertson	DONNACHIE	Wilson	'Smith'
22	24-Dec	KINGS PARK	SL2	0-0	Archibald	McLean	Law	Brown	Henderson	Campbell	Scott	Brown	Donnachie	Wilson	Dailley
23	31-Dec	DUNFERMLINE ATH	SL2	1-0	Archibald	McLean	Law	McAvoy	Henderson	Campbell	Rintoul	Brogan	Donnachie	Robertson	Rintoul
24	02-Jan	Forfar Athletic	SL2	3-2	Archibald	McLean	Law	Brown	Campbell,G	Campbell,J	Cox	SMITH	Donnachie	ROBERTSON	Rintoul
25	03-Jan	Cowdenbeath	SL2	0-3	Archibald	McLean	Law	Robertson	Campbell	McAvoy	Cox	Brogan	Donnachie	Wilson	Rintoul
26	07-Jan	JOHNSTONE	SL2	6-0	Archibald	McLean	Law	McAvoy	Campbell,J	BROWN	COX	ROBERTSON	DONNACHIE 2	WILSON	Rintoul
27	14-Jan	Kings Park	SL2	0-0	Archibald	McLean	Law	Campbell	Fairley	Cox	Brogan	Rintoul,D	Wilson	Robertson,G
28	21-Jan	EAST FIFE	SL2	2-1	Archibald	McLean	Law	Brown	Henderson	Campbell	Cox	Brogan	DONNACHIE 2	Wilson	Black
29	28-Jan	Alloa Athletic	SC1	1-3	Savage	Campbell,G	Law	Campbell	Henderson	Campbell,J	Cox	Brogan	DONNACHIE	Wilson	Rintoul
30	04-Feb	LOCHGELLY UTD	SL2	1-1	Savage	Law	Campbell	Brown	Henderson	Fairley	Cox	Robertson	DONNACHIE	Wilson	RINTOUL
31	11-Feb	ARMADALE	SL2	4-0	Archibald	Law	Campbell,J	Brown	Henderson	Fairley	Cox	Robertson	DONNACHIE	Wilson	'Hall'
32	18-Feb	BROXBURN UTD	SL2	1-1	Archibald	McLean	Law	Campbell	Henderson	Fairley	COX	Robertson	DONNACHIE 2	Wilson	'HALL'
33	22-Feb	Dunfermline Athletic	SL2	1-1	Archibald	McLean	Law	Campbell	Henderson	Fairley	Cox	Robertson	Donnachie	Wilson	Newman
34	25-Feb	BONESS	SL2	1-2	Archibald	McLean	Law	Campbell	Henderson	Fairley	Cox	Robertson	Donnachie	Geddes	Rintoul
35	04-Mar	Dundee Hibs	SL2	0-2	Archibald	McLean	Law	Brown	Henderson	Fairley	Cox	Wilson	Donnachie	Geddes	Geddes
36	11-Mar	East Stirling	SL2	0-1	Archibald	McLean	Law	Campbell	Henderson	Fairley	Cox	Brogan	Donnachie	Wilson	Rintoul
37	18-Mar	LEITH ATHLETIC	CC	0-1	Archibald	McLean	Law	Campbell	Henderson	Fairley	Cox	Robertson	Donnachie	Wilson	Rintoul
38	25-Mar	Clackmanan	SL2	3-2	Savage	McLean	Law	Campbell	Henderson	Gilhooley	COX 2	Wilson	DONNACHIE	Logan	Tennant
39	01-Apr	Stenhousemuir	SL2	1-4	Archibald	McLean	Law	Campbell	Henderson	Fairley	COX	ROBERTSON	Donnachie	Millar,AB	Millar,B
40	08-Apr	Arbroath	SL2	2-2	Godfrey	McLean	Law	Campbell	Henderson	Fairley	Cox	WILSON	Grant	Millar,AB	Millar,AB
41	15-Apr	BATHGATE	SL2	1-2	Godfrey	McLean	Law	'Jones'	Henderson	Campbell	Cox	Wilson	DONNACHIE	Fairley	Millar,AB
42	18-Apr	Leith Athletic	ESSs	0-0*	Godfrey	McLean	Law	Brown	Henderson	Fairley	Cox	Wilson	Donnachie	Sinclair,JW	Millar,AB
43	22-Apr	VALE OF LEVEN	SL2	2-1	Godfrey	McLean	Law	Campbell	Henderson	Fairley	Cox	DONNACHIE	SMITH	Wilson	Millar,AB
44	24-Apr	Hibernian	ESSf	2-3	Godfrey	McLean	Law	Brown	Henderson	Fairley	Cox	Donnachie	Wilson	Robertson	Millar,AB
45	29-Apr	Alloa Athletic	SL2	1-2	Godfrey	McLean	Law	Campbell	Henderson	Fairley	Cox	Wilson,A	Donnachie	Wilson,B	FINNERTY
46	03-May	LEITH ATHLETIC	RCCs	2-3	Godfrey	McLean	Law	Campbell	Henderson	Fairley	Cox	Ramsay	Donnachie	Wilson	Blair,J

1922/23

#	Date	Comp	Opponent			Score												
1	12-Aug	Trial	TRIAL			?-?												
2	15-Aug	ESSs	Hearts			0-3	Mason	Law	Hay	Campbell	Henderson		Speirs	Fairley	Campbell	Malcolm	Donnachie	Gordon	Docherty
3	19-Aug	SL2	CLYDEBANK			1-2	Mason	Hay	Law	Campbell	Henderson		Speirs	Fairley	Campbell	Malcolm	DONNACHIE	Gordon	Docherty
4	26-Aug	SL2	East Fife			0-0	Mason	Law	Hay	Campbell	Henderson		Speirs	Fairley	Campbell	McLean	Donnachie	Newman	Docherty
5	29-Aug	BC	LEITH ATHLETIC			2-1	Mason	McLean	Hay	'Park'	Campbell		McKenzie	Fairley	'Park'	'Allan'	Donnachie	Ritchie	Lawrence
6	02-Sep	SL2	VALE OF LEVEN			3-1	Mason	Law	Hay	Campbell	HENDERSON		Speirs	Fairley	Campbell	McRitchie	DONNACHIE	GORDON	Lawrence
7	09-Sep	SL2	Broxtum United			0-1	Mason	Law	Hay	Campbell	Henderson		Speirs	Fairley	Campbell	Stirling	DONNACHIE	Anderson	Lawrence
8	16-Sep	SL2	JOHNSTONE			1-0	Mason	Law	Hay	Campbell	Henderson		Speirs	Fairley	Campbell	Stirling	DONNACHIE	Anderson	Lawrence
9	23-Sep	SL2	Kings Park			0-1	Mason	Law	Hay	Campbell	Henderson		Speirs	Fairley	Campbell	Stirling	Donnachie	Anderson	Lawrence
10	30-Sep	SL2	ARMADALE			0-0	Mason	Law	Hay	Campbell	Henderson		Speirs	Fairley	Campbell	Anderson	Gordon	Malcolm	Lawrence
11	07-Oct	SL2	St Johnstone			1-1	Mason	Law	Hay	Campbell	Henderson		SPEIRS	Fairley	Campbell	Anderson	GORDON	Malcolm	Lawrence
12	14-Oct	SL2	DUNFERMLINE ATH			2-1	Mason	Law	Hay	Campbell	Henderson		SPEIRS 2	Fairley	Campbell	ANDERSON	Gordon	Malcolm	Lawrence
13	21-Oct	SL2	FORFAR ATHLETIC			2-1	Mason	Law	Hay	Campbell	Henderson		Gordon	Fairley	Walker	Anderson	Speirs	Malcolm	Lawrence
14	28-Oct	SL2	Dumbarton			1-0	Mason	Law	Hay	Walker	Henderson		SPEIRS	Campbell	Walker	ANDERSON	Donnachie	Malcolm	Lawrence
15	04-Nov	SL2	LOCHGELLY UTD			1-1	Mason	Law	Hay	Walker	Henderson		Donnachie	Campbell	Walker	ANDERSON	Donnachie	Malcolm	Lawrence
16	11-Nov	SL2	BATHGATE			2-3	Mason	Law	Hay	Stirling	Campbell		SPEIRS	Fairley	Campbell	Stirling	Donnachie	ANDERSON	Malcolm
17	18-Nov	SL2	Arbroath			1-0	Mason	Law	Hay	Campbell	Henderson		Speirs	Fairley	Campbell	Stirling	DOCHERTY	ANDERSON	Lawrence
18	25-Nov	SL2	STENHOUSEMUIR			0-2	Mason	Law	Hay	Campbell	Walker		Speirs	Fairley	McLean	ANDERSON	Speirs	Anderson	Lawrence
19	02-Dec	SL2	East Stirling			1-1	Mason	Law	Hay	Stirling	Campbell		Speirs	Fairley	Stirling	Newman	ANDERSON	Wilson	Lawrence
20	09-Dec	SL2	BONESS			1-1	Mason	Law	Hay	Campbell	Henderson		Speirs	Fairley	Campbell	ANDERSON	Newman	Wilson	Lawrence
21	16-Dec	SL2	Clydebank			1-1	Mason	Law	Hay	Campbell	Henderson		Speirs	Fairley	Campbell	Anderson	PETTIGREW	Wilson	Lawrence
22	23-Dec	SL2	COWDENBEATH			0-0	Mason	Law	Hay	Campbell	Henderson		Speirs	Fairley	Campbell	Anderson	Pettigrew	Wilson	LAWRENCE
23	30-Dec	SL2	Stenhousemuir			1-2	Mason	Law	Hay	Campbell	Henderson		Speirs	Fairley	Campbell	Anderson	Pettigrew	WILSON	Lawrence
24	01-Jan	SL2	Forfar Athletic			2-2	Mason	Law	Hay	Campbell	Henderson		Speirs	Fairley	Campbell	Wilson	Pettigrew	Anderson	LAWRENCE
25	02-Jan	SL2	ARBROATH			2-2	Mason	McLean	Hay	Campbell	Henderson		Speirs	Fairley	Campbell	Stirling	PETTIGREW 2	Wilson	Lawrence
26	06-Jan	SL2	Queens Park			1-1	Mason	Law	Hay	Campbell	Henderson		SPEIRS	Fairley	Campbell	Wilson	Pettigrew	ANDERSON	LAWRENCE
27	13-Jan	SC1	DALBEATTIE STAR			8-1	Mason	Law	Hay	Campbell	Henderson		Speirs	Fairley	Campbell	ANDERSON	PETTIGREW 3	Wilson	Lawrence
28	20-Jan	SL2	EAST STIRLING			0-1	Mason	McLean	Hay	Campbell	Henderson		Speirs	Fairley	Campbell	Anderson	Pettigrew	Wilson	McGibbon
29	27-Jan	SL2	Dundee			0-0	Mason	Law	Hay	Campbell	Henderson		Speirs	Fairley	Campbell	Anderson	Pettigrew	Wilson	McGibbon
30	31-Jan	SC2	DUNDEE			2-3	Mason	Law	Hay	Campbell	Henderson		FAIRLEY	Fairley	Campbell	Anderson	PETTIGREW	WILSON	'Junior'
31	03-Feb	SL2	EAST FIFE			2-2	Mason	Law	Hay	Campbell	Henderson		SPEIRS	Fairley	Campbell	Anderson	Pettigrew	WILSON	Smith
32	14-Feb	SL2	Dunfermline Athletic			1-4	Mason	Law	Hay	Campbell	Henderson		Speirs	Fairley	Campbell	Anderson	PETTIGREW	Wilson	Brown
33	17-Feb	SL2	QUEENS PARK			1-0	Mason	Law	Hay	Campbell	Henderson		SPEIRS	Fairley	Campbell	Anderson	Pettigrew	WILSON	NEWMAN 2
34	24-Feb	SL2	Lochgelly United			0-1	Mason	Law	Hay	Campbell	'Newman'		Speirs	Fairley	Campbell	Wilson	Pettigrew	'Robinson'	McGibbon
35	03-Mar	SL2	ST JOHNSTONE			4-4	Mason	McLean	Henderson	Hay	Campbell		Speirs	Fairley	Campbell	Anderson	PETTIGREW	McGibbon	McGibbon
36	10-Mar	SL2	Armadale			0-3	Mason	Law	Hay	Law	McLean		Speirs	Fairley	Campbell	Anderson	Pettigrew	Dobbie	McGibbon
37	17-Mar	SL2	DUMBARTON			0-1	Steel	Law	Hay	Campbell	Henderson		Speirs	Fairley	Campbell	Anderson	Pettigrew	Dobbie	McGibbon
38	24-Mar	SL2	Cowdenbeath			1-2	Mason	Law	Hay	Campbell	Henderson		Speirs	Fairley	Campbell	Anderson	PETTIGREW	Dobbie	McGibbon
39	31-Mar	SL2	Vale of Leven			0-2	Mason	Law	Hay	Campbell	Henderson		Speirs	Fairley	Pettigrew	Pettigrew	'Junior'	Dobbie	'Newman'
40	07-Apr	SL2	BROXBURN UNITED			0-0	Mason	Law	Hay	Campbell	Henderson		Junior	Fairley	Pettigrew	Anderson,S	Anderson,D	McGibbon	Dobbie
41	09-Apr	SL2	Boness			2-2	Mason	Law	Hay	Campbell	Henderson		Speirs	Fairley	Campbell	Speirs	Anderson,D	ANDERSON,S	Dobbie
42	14-Apr	SL2	KINGS PARK			3-0	Mason	Law	Hay	Campbell	Henderson		Pettigrew	FAIRLEY	Campbell	Pettigrew	Anderson,D	ANDERSON,S 2	Dobbie
43	21-Apr	SL2	Johnstone			1-1	Mason	Law	Hay	Campbell	Henderson		Speirs	Fairley	Campbell	Wilson	PETTIGREW	Anderson	Dobbie
44	28-Apr	SL2	Bathgate			0-2	Mason	Law	Hay	Campbell	Henderson		Pettigrew	Fairley	Campbell	Wilson	Speirs	Anderson,S	Dobbie
45	30-Apr		LOTHIAN AMAT LGE			0-5													
46	05-May	RCCs	Hearts			1-2	Mason	Law	Hay	McNab	Henderson		'Black'	Fairley	Pettigrew	Anderson,D	Anderson,S	Anderson,D	'Brown'

1923/24

#	Date	Opponent	Comp	Score											
1	04-Aug	Trial		?-?											
2	11-Aug	Lothian Amateur Lge		?-?											
3	15-Aug	HIBERNIAN	ESSs	2-2	McAlpine	Law		Hay	Pettigrew	Henderson	Fairley	Murray	McAlister	Don	Jamieson	Williams
4	18-Aug	FORFAR ATH	SL2	2-2	McAlpine	Law		Hay	Pettigrew	Henderson	Fairley	Murray	McALLISTER	Don	Jamieson	WILLIAMS
5	22-Aug	Dunfermline Athletic	SL2	1-1	McAlpine	Law		Hay	Pettigrew	Henderson	Fairley	Murray	McAlister	Don	Dobbie	Williams
6	25-Aug	Cowdenbeath	SL2	1-1	McAlpine	Law		Hay	Pettigrew	Ford	Fairley	Murray	McAlister	Don	Dobbie	WILLIAMS
7	30-Aug	Hibernian	ESSs	1-5	McAlpine	Law		Hay	Pettigrew	Ford	Fairley	Murray	McAlister	Don	Dobbie	Dobbie
8	01-Sep	ARBROATH	SL2	2-0	McAlpine	Law		Hay	Caldwell	Henderson	Fairley	Murray	McAlister	DON 2	McAlister	Dobbie
9	08-Sep	East Fife	SL2	0-2	McAlpine	Law		Hay	Pettigrew	Ford	Fairley	Murray	McAlister	Don	Dobbie	BLACK
10	15-Sep	KINGS PARK	SL2	1-1	McAlpine	Law		Hay	Pettigrew	Henderson	Fairley	Murray	McAlister	Don	Dobbie	Black
11	22-Sep	Albion Rovers	SL2	1-2	McAlpine	Law		Hay	Pettigrew	Henderson	Fairley	Murray	McALLISTER	Don	Dobbie	Black
12	29-Sep	BATHGATE	SL2	0-2	McAlpine	Law		Hay	Newman	Henderson	Fairley	Murray	McAlister	McAlister	Jamieson	Black
13	06-Oct	LOCHGELLY UTD	SL2	1-0	McAlpine	Law		Hay	Newman	Henderson	Fairley	Don	JAMIESON	Don	Dobbie	Dunn
14	13-Oct	BONESS	SL2	2-3	McAlpine	Law		Sloan	Don	Henderson	Fairley	McAlister	JAMIESON	McAlister	DOBBIE	Dunn
15	20-Oct	St Johnstone	SL2	1-4	McAlpine	Law		Sloan	Don	Henderson	Fairley	Pettigrew	Jamieson	YOUNG	Lauder	Dunn
16	27-Oct	VALE OF LEVEN	SL2	3-1	McAlpine	Law		Sloan	Marshall	Paterson	Marshall	Newman	JAMIESON 2	YOUNG	Lauder	Dobbie
17	03-Nov	Dundee United	SL2	2-3	McAlpine	Law		Sloan	Marshall	Henderson	Fairley	Pettigrew	JAMIESON	YOUNG	Lauder	Penman
18	10-Nov	ARMADALE	SL2	0-0	McAlpine	Law		Sloan	Marshall	Paterson	Fairley	Pettigrew	Jamieson	Young	Lauder	Dobbie
19	17-Nov	Alloa Athletic	SL2	1-0*	McAlpine	Law		Sloan	Marshall	Paterson	Fairley	Leitch	Jamieson	Young	Lauder	Penman
20	24-Nov	STENHOUSEMUIR	SL2	1-1	McAlpine	Law		Sloan	Marshall	Paterson	Fairley	Leitch	Jamieson	Young	Lauder	PENMAN
21	01-Dec	DUNFERMLINE ATH	SL2	2-2	McAlpine	Law		Sloan	Newman	Paterson	Fairley	Leitch	Lauder	YOUNG 2	LAUDER	Penman
22	04-Nov	Alloa Athletic	SL2	2-4	McAlpine	Law		Sloan	Newman	Paterson	Fairley	Leitch	Lauder	Young	Dobbie	Penman
23	08-Dec	COWDENBEATH	SL2	0-1	McAlpine	Law		Sloan	Kane	Paterson	Fairley	LEITCH	Jamieson	Young	Dobbie	Penman
24	15-Dec	Broxburn United	SL2	1-3	McAlpine	Law		Sloan	Marshall	Paterson	McLeod	Leitch	Lauder	YOUNG 3	Dobbie	Penman
25	22-Dec	DUMBARTON	SL2	3-0	McAlpine	Law		Sloan	Kane	Paterson	McLeod	Leitch	Newman	Young	Lauder	Penman
26	29-Dec	Stenhousemuir	SL2	0-3	McAlpine	Law		Sloan	Kane	Paterson	McLeod	Leitch	Dunsmuir	Young	Lauder	Penman
27	01-Jan	Forfar Athletic	SL2	0-1	McAlpine	Law		Dunsmuir	Young	Paterson	McLeod	Sloan	'Newman'	Pettigrew	Lauder	Kane
28	02-Jan	Arbroath	SL2	3-0	McAlpine	Law		Dunsmuir	Paterson	Henderson	McLeod	Leitch	Lauder	YOUNG 2	Lauder	KANE 3
29	05-Jan	JOHNSTONE	SL2	2-1	McAlpine	Law		Dunsmuir	Paterson	Henderson	McLeod	Leitch	Newman	Young	Lauder	Kane
30	12-Jan	Boness	SL2	0-2	McAlpine	Law		Dunsmuir	Paterson	Henderson	McLeod	Leitch	Ross	Young	Lauder	Kane
31	19-Jan	ALLOA ATHLETIC	SL2	2-1	McAlpine	Law		Dunsmuir	Paterson	Henderson	McLeod	Leitch	Ross	YOUNG 2	Lauder	Kane
32	26-Jan	FRASERBURGH	SC1	3-0	McAlpine	Law		Dunsmuir	Paterson	Henderson	McLeod	PETTIGREW	Ross	Young	KANE	PENMAN
33	02-Feb	Bathgate	SL2	1-0	McAlpine	Law		Dunsmuir	Paterson	Henderson	McLeod	Leitch	Ross	Young	Kane	PENMAN
34	09-Feb	STENHOUSEMUIR	SC2	0-0	McAlpine	Law		Dunsmuir	Paterson	Henderson	McLeod	Henderson,JA	Henderson,JA	Young	Newman	Penman
35	13-Feb	Stenhousemuir	SC2	0-0	McAlpine	Law		Dunsmuir	Paterson	Henderson,G	McLeod	Leitch	Ross	YOUNG 3	Ross	Penman
36	16-Feb	Vale of Leven	SL2	4-0	McAlpine	Law		Dunsmuir	Paterson	Henderson,G	McLeod	Leitch	Ross	YOUNG 2	Henderson,JA	Penman
37	20-Feb	Stenhousemuir (n)	SC2	2-0	McAlpine	Law		Dunsmuir	Paterson	Henderson,G	McLeod	Leitch	Henderson,JA	YOUNG	Ross	Penman
38	23-Feb	Raith Rovers	SC3	1-0	McAlpine	Law		Dunsmuir	Paterson	Henderson,G	McLeod	Leitch	Ross	Wilson	Lauder	Penman
39	27-Feb	Kings Park	SL2	0-1	McAlpine	Law		Dunsmuir	Paterson	Henderson,G	McLeod	Leitch	Henderson,JA	Newman	Lauder	Penman
40	01-Mar	ST JOHNSTONE	SL2	0-1	McAlpine	Law		Dunsmuir	Paterson	Henderson,G	McLeod	Leitch	Ross	Merrie	Lauder	Penman
41	05-Mar	DUNDEE UNITED	SL2	0-0	McAlpine	Law	Newman	Dunsmuir	Paterson	Henderson,G	McLeod	Leitch	Henderson,JA	Merrie	Lauder	Penman
42	08-Mar	Aberdeen	SC4	0-3	McAlpine	Law		Dunsmuir	Paterson	Henderson,G	McLeod	Penman	Ross	Merrie	Lauder	Kane
43	12-Mar	Dumbarton	SL2	0-1	McAlpine	Law		Dunsmuir	Paterson	Henderson,G	McLeod	LEITCH	KANE	KANE	LAUDER	PENMAN
44	15-Mar	EAST FIFE	SL2	4-3	McAlpine	Law		Dunsmuir	Paterson	Henderson,G	McLeod	Leitch	Henderson,JA	KANE	LAUDER	Penman
45	22-Mar	Armadale	SL2	2-3	McAlpine	Law		Dunsmuir	Paterson	Henderson,G	McLeod	'Junior'	Ross	KANE	Henderson,JA	Lauder
46	29-Mar	ALBION ROVERS	SL2	1-1	McAlpine	Law		Dunsmuir	Paterson	Henderson,G	McLeod	Merrie	Henderson,JA	KANE	Lauder	Penman
47	05-Apr	Lochgelly United	SL2	1-1	McAlpine	Law		Dunsmuir	Paterson	Henderson,G	McLeod	Merrie	HENDERSON,JA	KANE	Lauder	Penman
48	12-Apr	BROXBURN UNITED	SL2	1-2	McAlpine	Law		Dunsmuir	Paterson	Henderson,G	McLeod	Merrie	Kane	Kane	Lauder	Kane
49	19-Apr	LEITH ATHLETIC	BC	1-0	McAlpine	Law		Dunsmuir	Paterson	Henderson,G	McLeod	Merrie	Ross	YOUNG	LAUDER	'Newman'
50	26-Apr	Johnstone	SL2	2-0	McAlpine	Law		Dunsmuir	Henderson,JA	Henderson,G	McLeod	Leitch	Kane	Young	Lauder	
51	30-Apr	WARRENDER AMS		1-0												
52	03-May	Hibernian (n)	RCCs	1-2	McAlpine	Reid		Dunsmuir	Henderson,JA	Henderson,G	McLeod	Leitch	Ross	Young	Lauder	Kane

1922

Law, Hay, Henderson, Speirs, Pettigrew, Lawrence
Mason, Campbell, Fairlie, Anderson, Wilson

1924

Standing: Jimmy Sorbie (Trainer), G Henderson, Paterson, Law, McAlpine, Dunsmuir, McLeod and George Lamont (Chairman).
Seated: Harry Stewart (Director), Leitch, Ross, Young, JA Henderson, Penman and Robert Penman (Director).

1924

Back Row: Directors J Taylor, Robert Penman and Robert Murray.
Standing: Jimmy Sorbie (Trainer), Henderson, Law, McAlpine, Dunsmuir, McLeod and Lauder.
Seated: Leitch, Ross, Paterson, 'Wilson', and Penman.

1924

Standing: Kane, Boyd, Bruce, Gay, Beattie and McInally.
Seated: Duncan, Henderson, Muir, Graham and Peters.

1927

Standing: Jimmy Sorbie (Trainer), Muir, Raeburn, Ramage, Robertson, Simpson and David S Gordon (Manager).
Seated: Burgoyne, W Brown, Duke, J Brown, Mitchell and Gilmour.

1924/25

#	Date	Trial	STRIPES BLUES			McAlpine	Newman	Dunsmuir	Pollock	Ramage	Fordyce	Walker	Johnston	Collins	Brown	Laing
1	09-Aug					McAlpine	Bree	Donaldson	Drummond	Campbell	Johnston	Reid	Kane	Young	Alston	Duncan
2	16-Aug	SL2	ARMADALE	2-3	Douglas	McAlpine	Donaldson	Dunsmuir	McBeath	Ramage	Fordyce	Reid	Kane	Young	Alston	Duncan
3	23-Aug	SL2	Albion Rovers	1-2	McAlpine	Donaldson	Dunsmuir	McBeath	Ramage	Fordyce	Reid	Kane	YOUNG 2	ALSTON	Duncan
4	30-Aug	SL2	EAST STIRLING	3-4	McAlpine	Donaldson	Dunsmuir	McBeath	McInally	Fordyce	Reid	KANE	YOUNG 2	Alston	Duncan
5	03-Sep	ESSs	LEITH ATHLETIC	0-1	McAlpine	Whitehead	Dunsmuir	Ramage	McBeath	Fordyce	Reid	Alston	Collins	Fordyce	Duncan
6	06-Sep	SL2	Broxburn United	1-3	McAlpine	Whitehead	Dunsmuir	McBeath	McInally	Fordyce	Reid	Newman	COLLINS	Alston	Duncan
7	13-Sep	SL2	ALLOA ATHLETIC	1-0	McAlpine	Muir	Donaldson	Kane	McInally	McLeod	Duncan	Kane	YOUNG	Alston	Newman
8	20-Sep	SL2	Stenhousemuir	1-1	McAlpine	Muir	Donaldson	Kane	McInally	McLeod	Duncan	Reid	YOUNG	Alston	Dunsmuir
9	22-Sep	SL2	Arthurlie	2-5	McAlpine	Muir	Donaldson	Smith	Newman	Fordyce	Duncan	Reid	YOUNG 2	Collins	Dunsmuir
10	27-Sep	SL2	DUNFERMLINE ATH	3-0	McAlpine	Muir	Dunsmuir	Newman	McInally	McLeod	Kane	Reid	YOUNG	ALSTON 2	Dunsmuir
11	04-Oct	SL2	Dundee United	0-3	McAlpine	Muir	Dunsmuir	Kane	McInally	McLeod	Kane	Reid	Young	Alston	Duncan
12	06-Oct	SL2	Dunfermline Athletic	2-1	McAlpine	Muir	Dunsmuir	Kane	Campbell	McLeod	Newman	Reid	YOUNG	ALSTON	Duncan
13	11-Oct	SL2	DUMBARTON	2-1	McAlpine	Muir	Dunsmuir	Campbell	McInally	McLeod	Junior	Kane	YOUNG 2	Alston	Duncan
14	18-Oct	SL2	Boness	0-6	McAlpine	Muir	Dunsmuir	Campbell	McInally	McLeod	Boyd	Reid	Young	Alston	Peter
15	25-Oct	SL2	CLYDEBANK	1-2	McAlpine	Muir	Dunsmuir	Campbell	McInally	McLeod	Boyd	Reid	YOUNG	Kane	Peter
16	01-Nov	SL2	FORFAR ATHLETIC	2-1	Bruce	MUIR	Dunsmuir	Allan	McInally	Beattie	Boyd	KANE	Young	Alston	Peter
17	08-Nov	SL2	Kings Park	0-2	Bruce	Muir	Dunsmuir	Allan	McInally	Beattie	Boyd	Ramage	Young	Kane	Duncan
18	15-Nov	SL2	ARTHURLIE	0-1	Bruce	Muir	Gay	Allan	McInally	Beattie	Boyd	Kane	Young	Graham	Duncan
19	22-Nov	SL2	Bathgate	2-5	Bruce	Muir	Gay	Campbell	McInally	Beattie	KANE	Graham	Young	ALSTON	Peter
20	29-Nov	SL2	CLYDE	2-2	Bruce	Muir	Gay	Allan	Campbell	Beattie	Boyd	Graham	KANE	ALSTON	Peter
21	06-Dec	SL2	EAST FIFE	1-2	Bruce	Muir	Gay	Allan	Campbell	Beattie	Boyd	Graham	Kane	ALSTON	Peter
22	13-Dec	SL2	Arbroath	0-2	Bruce	Muir	Gay	Kane	McInally	Beattie	Boyd	Ramsay	Young	Alston	Peter
23	20-Dec	SL2	Johnstone	1-1	Bruce	Junior	Gay	Kane	McInally	Beattie	Duncan	Henderson	MUIR	Graham	Peter
24	27-Dec	SL2	ALBION ROVERS	2-0	Newman	Junior	Gay	Kane	McInally	Beattie	BOYD	Henderson	Muir	Graham	PETER
25	03-Jan	SL2	BROXBURN UNITED	3-2	Newman	Bernard	Gay	Campbell	McInally	Beattie	BOYD	HENDERSON	Muir	GRAHAM	Peter
26	07-Jan	SL2	Clyde	0-1	Weir	Bernard	Gay	Kane	Campbell	Beattie	Boyd	Henderson	Muir	Graham	Peter
27	10-Jan	SL2	Alloa Athletic	0-2	Weir	Bernard	Gay	Kane	KANE	Beattie	Boyd	Henderson	Muir	Graham	Peter
28	17-Jan	SL2	KINGS PARK	1-0	Weir	Bernard	Gay	Kane	McInally	Beattie	Boyd	MUIR	Young	Henderson	Newman
29	24-Jan	SC1	Hamilton Accies	2-5	Weir	Bernard	Gay	Kane	McInally	Beattie	Boyd	Henderson	Muir	ALSTON 2	Peter
30	31-Jan	SL2	Armadale	1-5	Weir	Bernard	Gay	Kane	McInally	Paterson	Boyd	Henderson	Muir	ALSTON	Duncan
31	11-Feb	SL2	Dumbarton	2-0	Weir	Muir	Gay	Kane	Campbell	Paterson	Boyd	GRAHAM	Young	ALSTON	Thomson
33	18-Feb	SL2	STENHOUSEMUIR	1-2	Weir	Muir	Gay	Kane	Campbell	Paterson	Boyd	GRAHAM	Shirlaw	ALSTON	Peter
34	21-Feb	SL2	DUNDEE UNITED	1-2	Weir	Muir	Gay	McInally	Campbell	Paterson	Boyd	Graham	Henderson	ALSTON	Shirlaw
35	28-Feb	SL2	Forfar Athletic	5-1	Weir	Muir	Gay	KANE	McInally	Paterson	Boyd	Graham	Young	ALSTON	Duncan
36	07-Mar	SL2	JOHNSTONE	0-3	Weir	Muir	Gay	Kane	McInally	Paterson	Boyd	GRAHAM 2	Henderson	ALSTON 2	Duncan
37	14-Mar	SL2	East Fife	1-2	Weir	Muir	Gay	Henderson	McInally	Paterson	Boyd	Graham	Henderson	Alston	Duncan
38	21-Mar	SL2	BONESS	2-3	Weir	Muir	Gay	Bernard	McInally	Paterson	Boyd	Duke	YOUNG	Graham	Duncan
39	28-Mar	SL2	Clydebank	2-1	Weir	Muir	Gay	Kane	Campbell	Paterson	Boyd	DUKE 2	Campbell	Alston	Duncan
40	08-Apr	CCs	LEITH ATHLETIC	2-2	Weir	Muir	Gay	Kane	Campbell	Paterson	Shirlaw	Graham	Henderson	Graham	Duncan
41	11-Apr	SL2	BATHGATE	0-2	Weir	Muir	Gay	Kane	Campbell	Paterson	Boyd	DUKE 2	Henderson	Graham	Duncan
42	18-Apr	SL2	East Stirling	2-0	Weir	Muir	Bernard	Henderson	Campbell	Paterson	Boyd	Duke	Other,AN	Kane	Duncan
43	25-Apr	SL2	ARBROATH	1-6	Weir	Muir	Bernard	Kane	Campbell	Paterson	Boyd	DUKE	JUNIOR	Graham	Duncan
44	09-May	RCCs	Hearts		Weir	Muir	Gay	Henderson	McInally	Paterson	Boyd	Duke	Other,AN	Newman	Duncan

1925/26

#	Date	Comp	Opponent	Score	1	2	3	4	5	6	7	8	9	10	11
1	01-Aug	Trial	BLUES v HOOPS	2-0	Weir	Muir	Mitchell	Cumming	Johnstone	Harvey	Paterson	Main	Duke	Simpson	McCulloch	Gilmour
					Anderson	Darling	Campbell	Birrell	Paterson	Edgar	Swanson	Duncan	Fisher	'Smith'	Baker	Hannah
2	08-Aug	Trial	BLUES v HOOPS	2-2	Paul	Campbell	Douglas	Welsh	Cumming	Cumming	Paterson	Crighton	Desson	Fisher	Purves	Duncan
					Weir	Muir	Mitchell	Birrell	Birrell	Birrell	Paterson	Main	Duke	Simpson	McCulloch	Gilmour
3	15-Aug	SL2	Stenhousemuir	1-2	Weir	Muir	Mitchell	Birrell	Harvey	Harvey	Paterson	Main	Duke	SIMPSON	McCulloch	Gilmour
4	18-Aug	CCf	CLERWOOD AMS	8-0	Weir	Birrell	Campbell	Cumming	McCulloch	Cumming	Lumsden	Fisher	Duke	Simpson	Gilmour	Duncan
5	22-Aug	SL2	BROXBURN UNITED	11-1	Weir	Muir	Mitchell	Birrell	Harvey	Harvey	Paterson	Main	DUKE 2	SIMPSON 4	McCULLOCH	GILMOUR
6	26-Aug	ESSs	Hibernian	0-9	Weir	Muir	Mitchell	Birrell	McCulloch	Harvey	McCulloch	Main	Duke	Simpson	Gilmour	Duncan
7	29-Aug	SL2	Dunfermline Athletic	0-3	Weir	Muir	Mitchell	Birrell	Harvey	Harvey	Paterson	Main	Duke	Simpson	McCulloch	Fisher
8	01-Sep	BC1L	LEITH ATHLETIC	2-3	Weir	MUIR	Mitchell	Campbell	Cumming	Cumming	Paterson	Main	Duke	Simpson	McCulloch	Duncan
9	05-Sep	BC2L	EAST STIRLING	6-1	Weir	Muir	Mitchell	Birrell	CUMMING	CUMMING	Paterson	MAIN	DUKE	SIMPSON 2	Gilmour	Duncan
10	08-Sep	SL2	Leith Athletic	2-3	Weir	Muir	Mitchell	Birrell	Cumming	McCulloch	McCulloch	Main	Duke	Simpson	Gilmour	Duncan
11	12-Sep	SL2	Third Lanark	2-4	Weir	MUIR	Mitchell	Birrell	McCulloch	McCulloch	Paterson	Main	Duke	SIMPSON 2	McCulloch	GILMOUR
12	19-Sep	SL2	ARMADALE	6-2	Weir	Muir	Mitchell	Birrell	Harvey	Harvey	Paterson	MAIN	Duke	SIMPSON 2	McCulloch	GILMOUR
13	26-Sep	SL2	Albion Rovers	4-2	Weir	Muir	Mitchell	Birrell	Campbell	Campbell	Paterson	MAIN	Duke	SIMPSON 2	McCulloch	Gilmour
14	03-Oct	SL2	DUMBARTON	3-2	Weir	Muir	Mitchell	Birrell	Harvey	Harvey	Lumsden	MAIN	Duke	SIMPSON 2	McCulloch	Gilmour
15	10-Oct	SL2	Queen of the South	0-2	Weir	Muir	Mitchell	Birrell	Harvey	Harvey	Lumsden	Main	Duke	SIMPSON	McCulloch	Fisher
16	17-Oct	SL2	BONESS	1-1	Weir	Muir	Mitchell	Birrell	Harvey	Harvey	Lumsden	Main	Duke	SIMPSON	Fisher	Duncan
17	24-Oct	SL2	Clyde	2-4	Weir	Muir	Mitchell	Birrell	Harvey	Harvey	Paterson	Main	Duke	Simpson	McCULLOCH	GILMOUR
18	31-Oct	SL2	BATHGATE	4-0	Weir	Campbell	Mitchell	Birrell	Campbell	Harvey	Cumming	Main	FISHER	SIMPSON	McCULLOCH	GILMOUR
19	07-Nov	SL2	Arthurlie	3-2	Weir	Muir	Mitchell	Birrell	Harvey	Harvey	Cumming	Main	DUKE	SIMPSON	McCulloch	Gilmour
20	14-Nov	SL2	Arbroath	1-4	Weir	Muir	Mitchell	Birrell	Harvey	Harvey	Cumming	Main	Duke	SIMPSON	McCulloch	Gilmour
21	21-Nov	SL2	East Fife	0-4	Weir	Muir	Mitchell	Birrell	Harvey	Harvey	Paterson	Main	Duke	Fisher	McCulloch	Gilmour
22	28-Nov	SL2	ALLOA ATHLETIC	2-1	Weir	Campbell	Mitchell	Birrell	Common	Common	Paterson	MAIN	Duke	Fisher	Johnstone	Gilmour
23	05-Dec	SL2	Nithsdale Wanderers	1-2	Weir	Campbell	Mitchell	Birrell	Common	Common	Paterson	Main	DUKE	Muir	JOHNSTONE	Gilmour
24	12-Dec	SL2	Kings Park	0-2	Weir	Muir	Mitchell	Birrell	Harvey	Harvey	Paterson	Fisher	Duke	Simpson	Johnstone	Gilmour
25	26-Dec	SL2	Boness	3-6	Weir	Campbell	Mitchell	Birrell	Duke	BIRRELL	Junior	MUIR 2	Johnstone	Simpson	Johnstone	Gilmour
26	01-Jan	SL2	CLYDE	1-2	Weir	Campbell	Mitchell	Birrell	Harvey	Cumming	Johnstone	MUIR 2	Duke	Simpson	McCulloch	Gilmour
27	02-Jan	SL2	Broxburn United	7-4	Weir	Campbell	Mitchell	Birrell	Harvey	Birrell	Johnstone	Muir	Duke	SIMPSON 4	RAMAGE	GILMOUR
28	04-Jan	SL2	ALBION ROVERS	3-1	Weir	Campbell	Mitchell	Birrell	Harvey	Cumming	Johnstone	MUIR 2	Duke	SIMPSON	Ramage	Gilmour
29	09-Jan	SL2	Armadale	1-5	Weir	MUIR	Mitchell	Birrell	Harvey	Birrell	Paterson	Muir	Duke	SIMPSON	Gilmour	Paterson
30	13-Jan	SL2	AYR UNITED	1-2	Weir	Birrell	Mitchell	Birrell	Harvey	Cumming	Johnstone	Main	Duke	SIMPSON	Ramage	Gilmour
31	16-Jan	SL2	ARTHURLIE	5-3	Weir	Campbell	Mitchell	Birrell	Harvey	Birrell	Paterson	Main	Duke	SIMPSON 2	McCulloch	JOHNSTONE 4
32	23-Jan	SC1	Aberdeen	1-8	Weir	Muir	Mitchell	HARVEY	Harvey	Birrell	Corrigan	Main	Duke	Simpson	Cumming	Johnstone
33	30-Jan	SL2	Ayr United	0-2	Weir	Muir	Mitchell	Mitchell	Johnstone	Birrell	Corrigan	Fisher	Muir	Simpson	Cumming	Johnstone
34	06-Feb	SL2	DUNFERMLINE ATH	1-4	Weir	Muir	Mitchell	Mitchell	Harvey	Campbell	Corrigan	Main	DUKE	Simpson	Henderson	Junior
35	13-Feb	SL2	ARBROATH	0-0	Weir	Muir	Mitchell	Mitchell	Harvey	Birrell	Corrigan	Fisher	Duke	Simpson	Henderson	Junior
36	20-Feb	SL2	QUEEN OF SOUTH	4-1	Weir	Muir	Mitchell	Mitchell	Henderson	CORRIGAN	CORRIGAN	JUNIOR	Duke	SIMPSON	JOHNSTONE	GILMOUR
37	27-Feb	SL2	THIRD LANARK	3-2	Weir	MUIR	MITCHELL	Mitchell	Henderson	Birrell	Johnstone	Burgoyne	DUKE 2	Simpson	Corrigan	Gilmour
38	06-Mar	SL2	Bathgate	3-1	Weir	Muir	Mitchell	Mitchell	Henderson	Birrell	JUNIOR	Burgoyne	DUKE	SIMPSON	Corrigan	Gilmour
39	13-Mar	SL2	KINGS PARK	4-0	Weir	Muir	Mitchell	Mitchell	Henderson	Birrell	Johnstone	BURGOYNE	DUKE	SIMPSON 2	Ramage	Gilmour
40	20-Mar	SL2	Dumbarton	0-1	Weir	Muir	Mitchell	Mitchell	Henderson	Junior	Corrigan	Burgoyne	Duke	SIMPSON	Desson	Paterson
41	27-Mar	SL2	NITHSDALE WANDS	1-1	Weir	Muir	Mitchell	Mitchell	Henderson	Birrell	Johnstone	Gilmour	Duke	SIMPSON	Corrigan	JOHNSTONE 4
42	03-Apr	SL2	STENHOUSEMUIR	0-2	Weir	Campbell	Mitchell	Mitchell	Corrigan	Cumming	Johnstone	Main	Duke	Simpson	Desson	Johnstone
43	10-Apr	SL2	Alloa Athletic	3-3	Newman	Campbell	Mitchell	Mitchell	Harvey	Corrigan	Johnstone	Fisher	Duke	Simpson	DESSON	GILMOUR
44	17-Apr	SL2	EAST FIFE	2-2	Newman	Muir	Mitchell	Mitchell	Henderson	Junior	Corrigan	Young	Duke	SIMPSON	Desson	Gilmour
45	24-Apr	SL2	East Stirling	0-2	Newman	Campbell	Mitchell	Allison	Other,AN	Junior	Corrigan	Muir	Duke	Simpson	Dawson	Gilmour
46	08-May	RCCf	Hearts	2-6	Ramage	Campbell	Mitchell	Allison	Graham	Henderson,A	Dalgleish	Henderson,J	Duke	Simpson	Dawson	Dalziel

1927

Standing: Dickson, McKnight, Boyne, Raeburn, Swanson and Jimmy Sorbie (Trainer).
Seated: Brown, Mitchell, Duke, Drummond, Walker and McCaig.

Standing: Duke, Dickson, McKnight, Raeburn, Boyne, Drummond, Corrigan and Swanson.
Seated: Scott, McCaig, Mitchell, Brown, Walker and Boyle.

Standing: Moffat, Barton, Forrest, RL Small, Gilchrist and Brown.
Seated: Robertson, Eadie, Drummond, Meagher and Walker.

ST. BERNARD'S F.C., 1929-1930

Standing: Gilchrist, Brown, Drummond, R Forrest and MacFarlane.
Seated: Henderson, Moffat, Barton, Crawford, Eadie and Elliot.

1926/27

#	Date	Trial	BLUES v HOOPS	Score	Meiklejohn	Gilmour	Allison	Johnstone	Delauney	Smith	Burgoyne	Duke	Thomson	Robertson	Dobson
1	07-Aug			0-3	Ramage	Muir	Mitchell	Raeburn	Brown,J	Brown,W	Burgoyne	Duke	Eddie	Robertson	Dobson
2	14-Aug	SL2	STENHOUSEMUIR	3-3	Ramage	Muir	Mitchell	Raeburn	Brown,J	Brown,W	Simpson	Walker	EDDIE	Kyle	Taylor
3	18-Aug	ESSs	Hearts	2-3	Ramage	Muir	Mitchell	Raeburn	Brown,J	Brown,W	Eddie	DUKE	Simpson	ROBERTSON	Gilmour
4	21-Aug	SL2	Alloa Athletic	3-2	Ramage	Muir	Mitchell	Raeburn	Brown,J	BURGOYNE	Walker	DUKE	SIMPSON	Robertson	Gilmour
5	24-Aug	CCs	COLDSTREAM	4-0	Ramage	Muir	Allison	Raeburn	Brown	Johnstone	Burgoyne	Duke	Simpson	Robertson	Gilmour
6	28-Aug	SL2	THIRD LANARK	2-0	Ramage	Muir	Mitchell	Raeburn	Brown,J	Brown,W	Burgoyne	Duke	SIMPSON 2	Robertson	Gilmour
7	04-Sep	SL2	Raith Rovers	1-5	Ramage	Muir	Mitchell	Raeburn	Brown,J	Brown,W	Burgoyne	DUKE	Simpson	Robertson	Gilmour
8	07-Sep	CCf	LEITH ATHLETIC	3-2	Ramage	Muir	Mitchell	Raeburn	Brown,J	Brown,W	Eddie	Robertson	Simpson	Duke	Gilmour
9	11-Sep	SL2	QUEEN OF SOUTH	4-1	Ramage	Muir	Johnstone	Mitchell	Raeburn	Brown,W	Burgoyne	WALKER	SIMPSON	DUKE	GILMOUR
10	18-Sep	SL2	East Stirling	2-5	Ramage	Muir	Allison	Mitchell	Raeburn	Brown,W	RUTHERFORD	Walker	Simpson	Duke	Gilmour
11	20-Sep	BC1L	LEITH ATHLETIC	1-1	Ramage	Muir	Allison	Mitchell	Raeburn	Johnstone	Rutherford	Duke	Simpson	Johnstone	Gilmour
12	25-Sep	SL2	ARMADALE	1-2	Ramage	Muir	Mitchell	Allison	Raeburn	Johnstone	Rutherford	Simpson	EDDIE	Duke	Gilmour
13	30-Sep	SL2	Dumbarton	0-3	Ramage	Muir	Mitchell	Raeburn	Brown,J	Brown,W	Rutherford	Duke	Simpson	Gilmour	Sanderson
14	09-Oct	SL2	FORFAR ATHLETIC	3-0	Ramage	Muir	Allison	Raeburn	Brown,J	Brown,W	Rutherford	Robertson	DUKE 2	GILMOUR	Sanderson
15	16-Oct	SL2	Ayr United	1-1	Ramage	Muir	Mitchell	Raeburn	Brown,J	Brown,W	Rutherford	Robertson	DUKE	Gilmour	Sanderson
16	23-Oct	SL2	NITHSDALE WANDS	1-0	Ramage	Muir	Mitchell	Raeburn	Brown,J	Brown,W	Rutherford	ROBERTSON	Duke	Gilmour	Sanderson
17	30-Oct	SL2	Bathgate	1-4	Ramage	Muir	Mitchell	Raeburn	Brown,J	Brown,W	Rutherford	DUKE	Simpson	Gilmour	Sanderson
18	06-Nov	SL2	Clydebank	3-2	Ramage	Muir	Mitchell	Raeburn	Brown,J	Brown,W	Rutherford	DUKE	Simpson	Gilmour	Sanderson
19	13-Nov	SL2	BONESS	2-5	Ramage	Muir	Mitchell	Raeburn	Brown,J	Brown,W	Rutherford	Duke	SIMPSON	Gilmour	SANDERSON
20	20-Nov	SL2	Kings Park	0-5	Ramage	Muir	Mitchell	Raeburn	Junior	Brown	Burgoyne	Robertson	Simpson	Gilmour	Sanderson
21	27-Nov	SL2	ARBROATH	1-2	Ramage	Allison	Mitchell	Raeburn	McKnight	Brown	Burgoyne	Simpson	Muir	GILMOUR	Sanderson
22	04-Dec	SL2	ALBION ROVERS	4-1	Ramage	Allison	Mitchell	Raeburn	McKnight	Brown,W	SIMPSON 3	Duke	Cowan	GILMOUR	Sanderson
23	11-Dec	SL2	Arthurlie	2-3	Ramage	Allison	Mitchell	Raeburn	McKnight	Brown,W	Junior	Duke	SIMPSON	GILMOUR	Sanderson
24	18-Dec	SL2	East Fife	2-3	Ramage	Allison	Mitchell	RAEBURN	McKnight	Brown,W	Walker	Duke	Simpson	GILMOUR	Sanderson
25	25-Dec	SL2	Stenhousemuir	0-0	Boyd	Allison	Mitchell	Raeburn	McKnight	Muir	Muir	Johnstone	Duke	Gilmour	Sanderson
26	01-Jan	SL2	ALLOA ATHLETIC	3-3	Boyd	Allison	Mitchell	Raeburn	McKnight	GILMOUR	MARSHALL	Duke	MUIR	Johnstone	Sanderson
27	03-Jan	SL2	Third Lanark	0-2	Boyd	ALLISON	Mitchell	Raeburn	McKnight	Brown	Marshall	Duke	Muir	Gilmour	Sanderson
28	08-Jan	SL2	RAITH ROVERS	1-2	Boyne	ALLISON	Mitchell	Raeburn	McKnight	Brown	Marshall	Duke	Muir	Gilmour	Sanderson
29	15-Jan	SL2	Queen of the South	0-1	Boyne	Allison	Mitchell	Raeburn	McKnight	Brown	Marshall	Duke	Muir	GILMOUR	Sanderson
30	22-Jan	SC1	VALE OF ATHOLL	3-1	Boyne	Allison	Mitchell	Raeburn	McKnight	Brown	MARSHALL	Duke	MUIR	GILMOUR	Sanderson
31	29-Jan	SL2	EAST STIRLING	2-0	Boyne	Allison	Mitchell	Raeburn	McKnight	Brown	Marshall	Duke	McGrath	Gilmour	Sanderson
32	05-Feb	SC2	ARTHURLIE	0-3	Boyne	Allison	Mitchell	Raeburn	McKnight	Brown	Marshall	Duke	McGrath	Gilmour	Sanderson
33	09-Feb	SL2	ARMADALE	2-2	Boyne	Allison	Mitchell	Raeburn	McKnight	Brown	Muir	DUKE	GILMOUR	Robertson	Johnstone
34	12-Feb	SL2	DUMBARTON	1-1	Boyne	Allison	Mitchell	Raeburn	McKnight	Robertson	Muir	Duke	McGrath	Gilmour	Johnstone
35	19-Feb	SL2	Forfar Athletic	0-1	Boyne	Allison	Mitchell	Raeburn	McKnight	Junior	Newman	Duke	Laidlaw	Robertson	Gilmour
36	26-Feb	SL2	AYR UNITED	2-4	Boyne	Allison	Mitchell	Raeburn	McKnight	Junior	Newman	DUKE	McGrath	GILMOUR	McNeill
37	05-Mar	SL2	Nithsdale Wanderers	3-2	Boyne	Allison	Mitchell	Raeburn	McKnight	Brown	LAIDLAW 2	Duke	Other,AN	ROBERTSON 4	McNeill
38	12-Mar	SL2	BATHGATE	6-3	Boyne	Allison	Mitchell	Raeburn	McKnight	Brown	GILMOUR	DUKE	Laidlaw	Robertson	McNeill
39	19-Mar	SL2	CLYDEBANK	4-1	Boyne	Allison	Mitchell	Raeburn	McKnight	Brown	LAIDLAW 2	DUKE	JUNIOR	Robertson	Gilmour
40	26-Mar	SL2	Boness	1-2	Boyne	Allison	Mitchell	Raeburn	McKnight	Brown	Laidlaw	Duke	Junior	ROBERTSON	GILMOUR
41	02-Apr	CCs	KINGS PARK	3-0	Boyne	Allison	Mitchell	Raeburn	McKnight	Brown	LAIDLAW	Duke	Junior	ROBERTSON	Johnstone
42	06-Apr	SL2	CORSTORPHINE AMS	0-0	Boyne	Allison	Glimour	Raeburn	McKnight	Brown	McNeill	Duke	Henderson	Robertson	Johnstone
43	09-Apr	CCs	Arbroath	2-1	Boyne	Allison	Mitchell	Raeburn	McKnight	Brown	McNeill	Duke	NEWMAN 2	Robertson	Gilmour
44	16-Apr	SL2	Albion Rovers	1-2	Boyne	Allison	Mitchell	Raeburn	McKnight	Brown	Laidlaw	Duke	DRUMMOND	Robertson	McNeill
45	20-Apr	BC2L	Leith Athletic	1-1	Boyne	Allison	Mitchell	Raeburn	McKnight	Brown	McNeill	Robertson	Drummond	GILMOUR	Gilmour
46	23-Apr	SL2	ARTHURLIE	3-2	Boyne	Allison	Mitchell	Raeburn	McKnight	Brown	LAIDLAW 2	Duke	Drummond	ROBERTSON	'Thomson'
47	28-Apr	BCpo	LEITH ATHLETIC	1-2	Boyne	Mitchell,A	Mitchell,S	Raeburn	'Steel'	Brown	McNeill	DUKE 2	'Jackson'	Gilmour	'Thomson'
48	30-Apr	SL2	EAST FIFE	2-1	Boyne	Mitchell	Allison	Raeburn	McKnight	Brown	Laidlaw	DUKE 2	Drummond	Robertson	Junior
49	09-May	RCCs	Hibernian	1-5	Boyne	Allison	Mitchell,A	Cameron	McKnight	Mitchell,S	Mitchell,S	Duke	Drummond	Robertson	Walker

1927/28

#	Date	Comp	Opponent	Score												
1	13-Aug	SL2	Ayr United	4-4	Boyne	Swanson	Mitchell	Raeburn	McKnight	Brown	DICKSON	DUKE 2	Drummond	McCAIG	Walker
2	16-Aug	CCs	CORSTORPHINE	0-2	Boyne	Swanson	Mitchell	Raeburn	Boyle	Brown	Dickson	Duke	Drummond	McCaig	Walker
3	20-Aug	SL2	ARBROATH	1-2	Boyne	Swanson	Mitchell	Raeburn	McKnight	BROWN	Dickson	Duke	Drummond	McCaig	Walker
4	24-Aug	ESSs	Hibernian	1-7	Boyne	Drummond	Mitchell	Duke	McKnight	Brown	Dickson	McCaig	Boyle	Duke	'Thomson'
5	27-Aug	SL2	Dumbarton	3-3	Boyne	Drummond	Mitchell	Raeburn	McKnight	Brown	DICKSON 2	McCAIG	Boyle	Duke	Walker
6	03-Sep	SL2	THIRD LANARK	0-1	Boyne	Drummond	Mitchell	Raeburn	McKnight	Brown	BOYLE	McCaig	Swanson	Duke	Walker
7	10-Sep	SL2	Armadale	1-2	Boyne	Drummond	Mitchell	Raeburn	McKnight	Brown	BOYLE 3	McCaig	Dickson	Newman	Walker
8	17-Sep	SL2	STENHOUSEMUIR	3-1	Boyne	Swanson	Drummond	Raeburn	McKnight	Brown	Boyle	Duke	Newman	Corrigan	Walker
9	19-Sep	BC1L	LEITH ATHLETIC	2-3	Boyne	Drummond	Mitchell	Raeburn	McKnight	Brown	Boyle	DUKE 2	Newman	Corrigan	Walker
10	24-Sep	SL2	East Stirling	2-1	Boyne	Drummond	Mitchell	Raeburn	McKnight	Brown	Boyle	Duke	Scott	Corrigan	WALKER
11	01-Oct	SL2	EAST FIFE	3-5	Boyne	Drummond	Mitchell	Raeburn	McKNIGHT	Brown	Boyle	Duke	SCOTT	McCAIG 2	Walker
12	08-Oct	SL2	Dundee United	1-2	Boyne	Drummond	Mitchell	Raeburn	McKnight	Brown	BOYLE	Duke	Scott	McCaig	Walker
13	15-Oct	SL2	Leith Athletic	0-3	Boyne	Drummond	Mitchell	Raeburn	McKnight	Brown	Boyle	Duke	Scott	Corrigan	Walker
14	22-Oct	SL2	Alloa Athletic	3-2	Boyne	Drummond	Swanson	RAEBURN	McKnight	Brown	BOYLE	DUKE	Junior	SCOTT	Walker
15	29-Oct	SL2	ARTHURLIE	2-5	Boyne	Drummond	Mitchell	RAEBURN	McKnight	Brown	Boyle	McCaig	SCOTT	Corrigan	WALKER
16	05-Nov	SL2	MORTON	2-9	Boyne	Swanson	Mitchell	Raeburn	McKnight	Brown	BOLE	Scott	Drummond	McCaig	Walker
17	12-Nov	SL2	Forfar Athletic	3-6	Boyne	Boyle	Drummond	Mitchell	McKnight	Brown	Dickson	SWANSON	MITCHELL	MOFFAT 2	WALKER
18	19-Nov	SL2	Queen of the South	3-1	Boyne	Drummond	Mitchell	Newman	McKnight	Brown	MITCHELL	Swanson	Junior	Moffat	Walker
19	26-Nov	SL2	ALBION ROVERS	1-1	Boyne	Boyle	Mitchell	Raeburn	McKnight	Brown	Mitchell	Swanson	Junior	McCaig	Walker
20	03-Dec	SL2	Bathgate	2-1	Boyne	Boyle	Mitchell	Raeburn	McKnight	Brown	Mitchell	McCaig	Moffat	McCAIG	WALKER
21	10-Dec	SL2	KINGS PARK	1-7	Boyne	Boyle	Mitchell	Brown	McKnight	Fleming	Dickson	McCaig	MOFFAT	Junior	Walker
22	17-Dec	SL2	Clydebank	0-4	Boyne	Junior	Mitchell	Raeburn	McKnight	Brown	Boyle	Moffat	Moffat	Junior	Walker
23	24-Dec	SL2	AYR UNITED	1-0	Junior	Drummond	Mitchell	Moffat	McKnight	Brown	Boyle	Swanson	Moffat	Fleming	WALKER
24	31-Dec	SL2	Third Lanark	2-1	Boyne	Drummond	Mitchell	Moffat	McKnight	Brown	Boyle	Swanson	Junior	McCAIG	Walker
25	02-Jan	SL2	LEITH ARMADALE	2-1	Boyne	Drummond	Mitchell	Moffat	McKNIGHT	Brown	Boyle	SWANSON 2	Junior	McCaig	Walker
26	03-Jan	SL2	ARMADALE	2-0	Boyne	Drummond	Mitchell	Moffat	McKnight	Brown	Dickson	SWANSON	PATRICK	McCaig	Walker
27	07-Jan	SL2	DUMBARTON	0-2	Boyne	Drummond	Mitchell	Moffat	McKnight	Brown	Boyle	Swanson	Patrick	McCaig	Walker
28	14-Jan	SL2	Stenhousemuir	1-3	Boyne	Drummond	Mitchell	Moffat	McKnight	Brown	BOYLE	Swanson	McCaig	Patrick	Walker
29	21-Jan	SC1	Falkirk	3-2	Boyne	Drummond	Mitchell	Moffat	McKnight	Brown	Boyle	McCaig	EADIE 2	PATRICK	WALKER
30	28-Jan	SL2	DUNDEE UNITED	2-2	Boyne	Drummond	Mitchell	Moffat	McKnight	Brown	Boyle	McCaig	EADIE	Patrick	Walker
31	04-Feb	SL2	East Fife	1-2	Boyne	Other.AN	Mitchell	MOFFAT	McKnight	Brown	Boyle	McCaig	Eadie	Patrick	Walker
32	11-Feb	SL2	EAST STIRLING	4-3	Junior	Drummond	Mitchell	Moffat	McKNIGHT	Brown	Boyle	Swanson	EADIE 3	McCAIG	McCaig
33	18-Feb	SL2	Arthurlie	2-2	Boyne	Drummond	Mitchell	Moffat	McKnight	Brown	Boyle	Swanson	EADIE	Patrick	Other.AN
34	25-Feb	SL2	ALLOA ATHLETIC	2-3	Boyne	Drummond	Mitchell	Moffat	McKnight	Brown	Dickson	McCaig	EADIE 2	McCaig	Newman
35	03-Mar	SL2	Arbroath	1-3	Boyne	Drummond	Mitchell	Moffat	McKnight	Brown	Boyle	Swanson	Eadie	McCaig	OTHER.AN 2
36	10-Mar	SL2	Morton	3-0	Hilligan	Drummond	Mitchell	Moffat	McKNIGHT	Brown	BOYLE	SWANSON	Eadie	McCaig	Scott
37	17-Mar	SL2	FORFAR ATHLETIC	8-2	Hilligan	Drummond	Mitchell	Moffat	McKnight	Brown	Boyle	SWANSON	EADIE 4	McCAIG 2	Scott
38	24-Mar	SL2	QUEEN OF SOUTH	2-6	Hilligan	Drummond	Mitchell	Moffat	McKnight	Brown	Boyle	Swanson	EADIE	McCaig	Scott
39	31-Mar	SL2	Albion Rovers	2-0	Hilligan	Drummond	Mitchell	Raeburn	McKnight	Brown	BOYLE	DUKE	EADIE	McCaig	Scott
40	07-Apr	SL2	BATHGATE	1-8	Hilligan	Drummond	Mitchell	Raeburn	McKnight	Moffat	Moffat	Duke	EADIE	Patrick	Moffat
41	14-Apr	SL2	Kings Park	1-0	Hilligan	Drummond	Mitchell	Raeburn	Junior	Brown	Moffat	Duke	EADIE	McCaig	Scott
42	21-Apr	SL2	CLYDEBANK	1-0	Hilligan	Drummond	Mitchell	Swanson	McKnight	Brown	Moffat	Duke	Eadie	McCaig	Scott
43	24-Apr	CCs	BERWICK Rangers	2-2	Welsh	Drummond	Mitchell	Moffat	McKnight	Brown	Boyle	Swanson	Eadie	McCaig	Moffat
44	30-Apr	CCf	LEITH ATHLETIC	1-0											
45	05-May	RCCs	Hearts	1-2	Hilligan	Drummond	Mitchell	Moffat	McKnight	Brown	Boyle	Swanson	Eadie	Duke	Walker

1928/29

#	Date	Trial	HOOPS v BLUES	Score											
1	06-Aug	Trial	HOOPS v BLUES	4-0	Small,RL	Gilchrist	Drummond	Moffat	Barton	Forrest	Robertson	Watson	Eadie	Ramage	Walker
2	11-Aug	SL2	QUEEN of the SOUTH	1-1	Watt	Letham	McLaren	Peters	Brown	Gibb	Graham	Boyd'	Duff	Richmond	Noble
3	15-Aug	ESSs	Hearts	2-4	Small,RL	Gilchrist	Drummond	Brown	Barton	Forrest	Duke	Thomson	Eadie	Ramage	WALKER
4	18-Aug	SL2	Albion Rovers	2-3	Small,RL	Gilchrist	Drummond	Brown	Barton	Forrest	Duke	Thomson	EADIE 2	Robertson	Moffat
5	25-Aug	SL2	STENHOUSEMUIR	2-2	Small,RL	Gilchrist	Drummond	Brown	Barton	Forrest	Duke	Thomson	EADIE 2	Robertson	Moffat
6	28-Aug		Berwick Rangers	3-2	Small,RL	Barton	Drummond	Robertson	Barton	Forrest	'Brady'	Duke	Ramage	Moffat	Walker
7	01-Sep	SL2	East Fife	1-2	Small,RL	Gilchrist	Drummond	Moffat	Brown	Forrest	Duke	Thomson	EADIE	Moffat	Walker
8	08-Sep	SL2	DUNDEE UNITED	2-2	Small,RL	Drummond	Gilchrist	Brown	Barton	Forrest	Duke	Thomson	EADIE 2	Robertson	Walker
9	15-Sep	SL2	East Stirling	2-2	Small,RL	Gilchrist	Brown	Moffat	Barton	Forrest	Ramage	THOMSON	Eadie	Robertson	Walker
10	17-Sep	CCf	Leith Athletic	4-0	Small,RL	Gilchrist	Brown	Moffat	Barton	Forrest	Duke	Thomson	Eadie	Robertson	Walker
11	22-Sep	SL2	FORFAR ATHLETIC	2-1	Small,RL	Gilchrist	Drummond	Moffat	Barton	Forrest	Ramage	Thomson	EADIE 2	Ramage	WALKER
12	29-Sep	SL2	CLYDEBANK	1-2	Small,RL	Gilchrist	Drummond	Moffat	Barton	Forrest	Robertson	Thomson	Eadie	Ramage	Walker
13	01-Oct	SL2	Dundee United	1-3	Small,RL	Gilchrist	Drummond	Moffat	Barton	Forrest	Robertson	JUNIOR	Eadie	Ramage	Walker
14	06-Oct	SL2	Arbroath	1-0	Drummond	Gilchrist	Brown	Moffat	Barton	Forrest	Duke	Eadie	RAMAGE	Robertson	WALKER
15	13-Oct	SL2	Alloa Athletic	3-0	Drummond	Gilchrist	Drummond	Moffat	Barton	Forrest	DUKE	Thomson	Eadie	ROBERTSON	WALKER
16	20-Oct	SL2	Leith Athletic	0-0	Drummond	Gilchrist	Brown	Moffat	Barton	Forrest	Duke	Thomson	EADIE 2	Robertson	Walker
17	27-Oct	SL2	ARMADALE	5-1	Drummond	Gilchrist	Brown	Moffat	Barton	Forrest	DUKE	Thomson	RAMAGE 2	ROBERTSON 2	Walker
18	03-Nov	SL2	KINGS PARK	4-1	Small,RL	Gilchrist	Brown	Robertson	Barton	Forrest	Duke	DRUMMOND	MOFFAT	MEAGHER	Walker
19	10-Nov	SL2	Bathgate	0-0	Small,RL	Gilchrist	Brown	Robertson	Barton	Forrest	Drummond	Drummond	Moffat	Meagher	Walker
20	17-Nov	SL2	DUNFERMLINE ATH	3-0	Small,RL	Gilchrist	Brown	Moffat	Barton	Forrest	Robertson	Drummond	EADIE 2	MEAGHER	Walker
21	24-Nov	SL2	ARTHURLIE	5-1	Small,RL	Gilchrist	Brown	Moffat	Barton	Forrest	ROBERTSON	DRUMMOND	EADIE 3	Meagher	Walker
22	01-Dec	SL2	MORTON	7-3	Small,RL	Gilchrist	Brown	Moffat	Barton	Forrest	ROBERTSON 2	DRUMMOND	EADIE 3	MEAGHER 2	Walker
23	08-Dec	SL2	Dumbarton	1-2	Small,RL	Gilchrist	Brown	Moffat	Barton	Forrest	Robertson	Drummond	EADIE	Meagher	Walker
24	15-Dec	SL2	BONESS	2-2	Drummond	Gilchrist	Brown	Robertson	Barton	Forrest	DUKE	DRUMMOND	Eadie	Ramage	Walker
25	22-Dec	SL2	ALBION ROVERS	1-1	Small,RL	Gilchrist	Brown	Moffat	Barton	Forrest	Thomson	Thomson	EADIE	Meagher	Walker
26	29-Dec	SL2	Queen of the South	1-3	Small,RL	Gilchrist	Brown	Moffat	Barton	Forrest	Junior	Thomson	EADIE	Meagher	Walker
27	01-Jan	SL2	LEITH ATHLETIC	1-1	Small,RL	Gilchrist	Brown	Moffat	Barton	Forrest	ROBERTSON	JUNIOR	EADIE 2	Meagher	Walker
28	05-Jan	SL2	Stenhousemuir	4-3	Small,RL	Gilchrist	Brown	Moffat	Barton	Forrest	ROBERTSON	Drummond	Eadie	Meagher	Walker
29	12-Jan	SL2	EAST FIFE	2-1	Small,RL	Gilchrist	Brown	Moffat	Barton	Forrest	ROBERTSON 2	Drummond	Eadie	Meagher	Walker
30	19-Jan	SC1	FALKIRK	1-2	Small,RL	Gilchrist	Brown	Moffat	Barton	Forrest	ROBERTSON	Thomson	Eadie	Meagher	Walker
31	26-Jan	CCs	Murrayfield Amateurs	2-2	Drummond	Gilchrist	Brown	Moffat	BARTON	Forrest	Duke	Drummond	Eadie	Meagher	Walker
32	06-Feb	SL2	EAST STIRLING	2-0	Junior	Gilchrist	Brown	Moffat	Barton	Forrest	Junior	Drummond	EADIE	Meagher	Thomson
33	09-Feb		Forfar Athletic	1-3	Small,RL	Gilchrist	Brown	Moffat	Barton	Forrest	ROBERTSON	Drummond	EADIE	Meagher	Junior
34	16-Feb	SL2	Clydebank	3-1	Small,RL	Gilchrist	Brown	Moffat	Barton	Forrest	Thomson	Eadie	DRUMMOND	MEAGHER	Walker
35	23-Feb	SL2	ARBROATH	3-2	Small,RL	Gilchrist	Brown	Moffat	Barton	Forrest	Eadie	Eadie	DRUMMOND 2	MEAGHER	Walker
36	02-Mar	SL2	ALLOA ATHLETIC	2-0	Small,RL	Gilchrist	Brown	Moffat	Barton	Forrest	Eadie	ROBERTSON 2	Drummond	Meagher	Walker
37	09-Mar	SL2	Kings Park	4-2	Small,RL	Gilchrist	Brown	Moffat	Barton	Forrest	Eadie	Eadie	DRUMMOND 2	MEAGHER	Walker
38	23-Mar	SL2	Dunfermline Athletic	1-3	Small,RL	Gilchrist	Brown	Moffat	Barton	Newman	Dippie	Dippie	DRUMMOND	Meagher	Walker
39	30-Mar	SL2	Arthurlie	1-1	Small,RL	Gilchrist	Brown	Moffat	Barton	Newman	Dippie	Dippie	EADIE	Meagher	Walker
40	06-Apr	SL2	Morton	1-4	Small,RL	Gilchrist	Brown	Moffat	Barton	Drummond	Duke	Dippie	EADIE	Meagher	Walker
41	12-Apr	SL2	Armadale	3-0	Small,RL	Gilchrist	Drummond	Brown	Barton	Drummond	Thomson	Dippie	EADIE 2	Meagher	WALKER
42	15-Apr		Mid/E Lothian Select	1-0	Small,RL	Drummond	Brown	Moffat	Barton	Miller	Dippie	Dippie	Eadie	Walker	Forrest
43	20-Apr	SL2	DUMBARTON	3-0	Small,RL	Gilchrist	Drummond	Moffat	Barton	Drummond	Newman	Thomson	EADIE 2	Meagher	WALKER
44	23-Apr	ESCs	Murrayfield Amateurs	0-4	Small,RL	Moffat	Brown	Duke	Barton	Drummond	Dippie	Thomson	Eadie	Meagher	Walker
45	27-Apr	SL2	Boness	0-1	Drummond	Gilchrist	Brown	Duke	Barton	Newman	Junior	Junior	Eadie	Meagher	Walker
46	04-May	RCCs	Hibernian	1-2	Small,RL	Gilchrist	Brown	Moffat	Barton	'Newman'	Duke	Henderson	Eadie	Meagher	Walker

1929/30

#	Date	Comp		Score	Opponent										
1	05-Aug	Trial	PROBABLES v SCRAP	7-1	Newbigging Watt	Macfarlane Hall	Brown Roxburgh	Moffat 'Scott'	Barton 'Murray'	Reid 'Telfer'	Drummond 'Brown'	Henderson 'White'	Eadie 'Harrower'	Watson 'Birrell'	Forrest 'Penman'
2	10-Aug	SL2	DUNFERMLINE ATH	1-0	Small,RL	Macfarlane	Brown	Moffat	Barton	McCaig	Drummond	Henderson	EADIE	Watson	Forrest
3	17-Aug	SL2	Boness	0-1	Small,RL	Macfarlane	Brown	Moffat	Gilchrist	Reid	Drummond	Henderson	Eadie	Watson	Forrest
4	21-Aug		Newtongrange Star	4-0	Drummond	Macfarlane	Gilchrist	Moffat	Duke	Brown	Reid	Henderson	McCaig	McCaig	Forrest
5	24-Aug	SL2	MONTROSE	0-1	Small,RL	Macfarlane	Gilchrist	Moffat	Barton	Drummond	Reid	Henderson	Eadie	McCaig	Forrest
6	27-Aug	ESSs	HIBERNIAN	3-4	Small,RL	Macfarlane	Brown	Moffat	Drummond	Brown	Forrest,G	Henderson	McCaig	Reid	Forrest,R
7	31-Aug	SL2	Stenhousemuir	2-4	Small,RL	Macfarlane	Brown	Moffat	DRUMMOND	McCaig	Forrest,G	Henderson	EADIE	Watson	Forrest,R
8	07-Sep	SL2	FORFAR ATHLETIC	1-2	Small,RL	Macfarlane	Gilchrist	Moffat	Drummond	Brown	FORREST,G	Henderson	McCaig	Duke	Forrest,R
9	14-Sep	SL2	Clydebank	1-1	Small,RL	Gilchrist	Macfarlane	Moffat	Barton	Brown	Eadie	Forrest,G	ELLIOTT	McCaig	Forrest,R
10	21-Sep	SL2	EAST FIFE	1-2	Small,RL	Gilchrist	Macfarlane	Moffat	Barton	Brown	Drummond	Eadie	ELLIOTT	Crawford	Forrest,R
11	28-Sep	SL2	Alloa Athletic	1-0	Drummond	Gilchrist	Macfarlane	Moffat	Barton	Brown	Henderson	Watson	Eadie	Elliott	Forrest,R
12	05-Oct	SL2	Kings Park	2-3	Drummond	Gilchrist	Macfarlane	Moffat	Barton	Brown	Henderson	McCaig	EADIE 2	Elliott	Forrest,R
13	12-Oct	SL2	RAITH ROVERS	2-2	Drummond	Gilchrist	Macfarlane	McCaig	Barton	BROWN	Henderson	Watson	EADIE	Elliott	Forrest,R
14	19-Oct		Armadale	0-1	Drummond	Gilchrist	Macfarlane	Moffat	Barton	Brown	Henderson	Elliott	Eadie	Crawford	Forrest,R
15	26-Oct	SL2	LEITH ATHLETIC	0-1	Drummond	Gilchrist	Macfarlane	Moffat	Barton	Brown	Henderson	Elliott	Eadie	Crawford	Forrest,R
16	02-Nov	SL2	East Stirling	0-4	Drummond	Gilchrist	Macfarlane	Moffat	Crawford	Brown	Henderson	Elliott	Watt	Watson	Forrest,R
17	09-Nov	SL2	QUEEN of the SOUTH	1-2	Drummond	Gilchrist	Macfarlane	Moffat	Barton	Brown	Henderson	Elliott	NEWMAN	Crawford	Forrest,R
18	16-Nov		Arbroath	0-1	Drummond	Gilchrist	Macfarlane	Moffat	Barton	Brown	Henderson	Elliott	Sweeney	Junior	Forrest,R
19	23-Nov	SL2	THIRD LANARK	3-2	Drummond	Gilchrist	Macfarlane	Moffat	Barton	McCaig	Eadie	Henderson	SWEENEY 2	MORRISON	IMRIE
20	30-Nov	SL2	BRECHIN CITY	3-1	Drummond	Gilchrist	Macfarlane	McCaig	Barton	Brown	EADIE	Moffat	Sweeney	FORREST,R	IMRIE
21	07-Dec	SL2	Albion Rovers	1-2	Drummond	Gilchrist	Macfarlane	Henderson	Sweeney	Brown	EADIE	Crawford	Forrest	Morrison	IMRIE
22	14-Dec	SL2	DUMBARTON	5-0	Drummond	Gilchrist	Macfarlane	Moffat	Sweeney	Brown	EADIE 2	Crawford	FORREST	MORRISON	IMRIE
23	21-Dec	SL2	Dunfermline Athletic	2-1	Drummond	Gilchrist	Macfarlane	Moffat	Sweeney	Brown	FORREST	Crawford	EADIE	Morrison	IMRIE
24	28-Dec	SL2	BONESS	4-2	Drummond	Gilchrist	Macfarlane	Moffat	Barton	Brown	FORREST	Crawford	EADIE 2	Morrison	Imrie
25	01-Jan	SL2	Leith Athletic	0-0	Drummond	Gilchrist	Macfarlane	Moffat	Barton	Brown	Forrest	Crawford	Eadie	Morrison	Imrie
26	02-Jan	SL2	ARMADALE	5-1	Drummond	Macfarlane	Brown	Moffat	Barton	McCaig	Eadie	Crawford	NEWMAN 5	Morrison	Imrie
27	04-Jan	SL2	Montrose	3-5	Drummond	Macfarlane	Brown	Sweeney	Barton	McCaig	Forrest	CRAWFORD	Newman	Morrison	Imrie
28	11-Jan	SL2	STENHOUSEMUIR	3-3	Drummond	Macfarlane	Brown	Moffat	Barton	Brown	Eadie	Crawford	DUFF 2	Morrison	IMRIE 2
29	18-Jan	SC1	THIRD LANARK	5-3	Drummond	Gilchrist	Macfarlane	Moffat	Barton	Brown	EADIE	Crawford	DUFF 3	Morrison	Imrie
30	25-Jan	SL2	Forfar Athletic	2-3	Drummond	Sweeney	Macfarlane	Moffat	Barton	Brown	EADIE	CRAWFORD	DUFF 3	Morrison	IMRIE
31	01-Feb	SC2	Hearts	0-0	Drummond	Gilchrist	Macfarlane	Moffat	Barton	Brown	Eadie	Crawford	Duff	Morrison	Imrie
32	05-Feb	SC2	Hearts	1-5	Drummond	Sweeney	Macfarlane	Moffat	Barton	Brown	EADIE	Henderson	DUFF	Morrison	Imrie
33	08-Feb	SL2	East Fife	1-3	Drummond	Gilchrist	Macfarlane	Moffat	Barton	Brown	Forrest	Henderson	Duff	Crawford	Imrie
34	15-Feb	SL2	ALLOA ATHLETIC	1-2	Drummond	Gilchrist	Macfarlane	Moffat	Barton	Brown	HENDERSON	Watson	Duff	Morrison	IMRIE 2
35	22-Feb	SL2	KINGS PARK	0-0	Newman	Gilchrist	Macfarlane	Drummond	Sweeney	Brown	Eadie	Crawford	DUFF 2	Morrison	Imrie
36	01-Mar	SL2	Raith Rovers	1-2	Newman	Gilchrist	Macfarlane	Drummond	Sweeney	Brown	Forrest	Duff	DUFF	Watson	Junior
37	08-Mar	SL2	EAST STIRLING	4-2	Junior	Drummond	Macfarlane	Barton	Sweeney	Brown	Eadie	Moffat	EADIE 3	McCaig	IMRIE
38	15-Mar	SL2	Queen of the South	1-2	Junior	Drummond	Macfarlane	Barton	Sweeney	Brown	Eadie	Moffat	DUFF	Forrest	Imrie
39	22-Mar	SL2	ARBROATH	5-2	McLean	Drummond	MACFARLANE 2	Barton	Sweeney	Brown	EADIE	Henderson	DUFF	Forrest	IMRIE
40	29-Mar	SL2	Third Lanark	4-1	Drummond	Gilchrist	Macfarlane	Barton	Sweeney	Brown	EADIE	Henderson	Duff	Forrest	IMRIE 2
41	05-Apr	SL2	Brechin City	1-0	Drummond	Gilchrist	Macfarlane	McCaig	Sweeney	Brown	EADIE	Henderson	Duff	Forrest	Imrie
42	12-Apr	SL2	ALBION ROVERS	1-1	McLean	Gilchrist	Macfarlane	Moffat	Barton	Drummond	Eadie	HENDERSON	Duff	Newman	IMRIE 2
43	14-Apr	SL2	CLYDEBANK	3-2	McLean	Drummond	Macfarlane	Sweeney	Barton	Brown	Eadie	HENDERSON	Duff	Forrest	Imrie
44	19-Apr	SL2	Dumbarton	0-3	McLean	Gilchrist	Macfarlane	McCaig	Sweeney	Drummond	Eadie	Crawford	Duff	Forrest	Imrie
45	22-Apr	SL2	CLERWOOD AMS	3-3	McLean	Drummond	Macfarlane	Barton	Sweeney	Brown	Eadie	Henderson	Duff	Morrison	Imrie
46	06-May	RCCs	Hearts	0-1	Smith	Drummond	Macfarlane	McCaig	Barton	Forrest	Eadie	Henderson	Duff	Morrison	Imrie

1933

Standing: Robert Tait (Director), Fitzsimmons, King, Keenan, Murray, T Robertson, Drummond.
Seated: Davidson, Brown, Marley, Marshall and Weir.

1931 — THE GYMNASIUM SAINTS

Standing: Marley, King, Keenan, Robertson and Dunn.
Seated: Brown, Walls, Davidson, Drummond, Duff and Eadie

1932

Standing: King, Marley, Weir, Keenan, Fitzsimmons and Brown.
Seated: ?, T Robertson, Murray, Davidson and Eadie.

1932

Standing: Marley, King, Keenan, Weir, Drummond and Fitzsimmons.
Seated: McCallum, Davidson, Murray, A Robertson and Eadie.

1930/31

#	Date	Trial	Hoops v Blues / Probables v Possibles	Score	Lg	Opponent							Clark		Brown,W Green	Pryce Eadie	Brown,J Henderson	Johnston Duff		Robertson Forrest	Newlands Imrie
1	26-Jul	Trial	Hoops v Blues	2-2			Loudon	Robb	Drummond	Macfarlane	Walls	Ross	Clark	Mitchell						Robertson	Newlands
2	02-Aug	Trial	Probables v Possibles	4-1			'Fraser' Robb	Richardson Robertson	Drummond Duff,J	Sweeney Macfarlane	Ross Mitchell	Walls Clark	Sweeney		'Ross' Green	Eadie McAtee	'Brown,J' Grant	Duff,I Pryde		Forrest Robertson	Imrie Newlands
3	09-Aug		Third Lanark	0-2	SL2		Robb	Drummond	Macfarlane	Newman			Sweeney		Walls	Eadie	Nicol	Duff		Forrest	Imrie
4	12-Aug		Hearts	2-3	ESS		Robb	Drummond	Macfarlane	Marshalsey			Sweeney		Walls	Eadie	Nicol	Duff		FORREST	Imrie
5	16-Aug		CLYDEBANK	6-1	SL2		Robb	Drummond	Macfarlane	Marshalsey			Sweeney		WALLS 2	Henderson	NICOL 2	DUFF		FORREST	Imrie
6	23-Aug		Alloa Athletic	0-2	SL2		Robb	Drummond	Macfarlane	Marshalsey			Sweeney		Walls	Henderson	Nicol	DUFF		Forrest	Imrie
7	30-Aug		FORFAR ATHLETIC	0-2	SL2		Robb	Drummond	Macfarlane	Marshalsey			Barton		Walls	Junior	Nicol	Sweeney		Forrest	IMRIE
8	06-Sep		St Johnstone	1-5	SL2		Robb	Drummond	Macfarlane	Walls			Barton		Brown	Eadie	Marshalsey	DUFF		Forrest	Imrie
9	13-Sep		STENHOUSEMUIR	2-2	SL2		Robb	Drummond	Macfarlane	MARSHALSAY			Barton		Brown	Forrest	Walls	DUFF		Newman	IMRIE
10	20-Sep		Raith Rovers	2-4	SL2		Robb	Drummond	Macfarlane	Marshalsey			Sweeney		Brown	Forrest	Walls	DUFF		Newman	Imrie
11	27-Sep		ARMADALE	3-1	SL2		Newman	Macfarlane	Brown	Marshalsey			Sweeney		Drummond	DUFF	Walls	EADIE 2		AN Other	Imrie
12	04-Oct		Montrose	3-1	SL2		Newman	Macfarlane	Brown	Marshalsey			Sweeney		Drummond	Duff	Walls	EADIE 3		Cannon	Imrie
13	11-Oct		EAST STIRLING	1-1	SL2		Newman	Macfarlane	Brown	Marshalsey			Sweeney		Drummond	Duff	Walls	EADIE		Cannon	Imrie
14	18-Oct		ALBION ROVERS	2-4	SL2		Newman	Macfarlane	Brown	Marshalsey			Sweeney		Drummond	Duff	WALLS	EADIE		Cannon	Imrie
15	25-Oct		Kings Park	1-3	SL2		Newman	Macfarlane	Brown	WALLS			Sweeney		Cannon	Newman	Henderson	Eadie		Cannon	Imrie
16	01-Nov		Boness	1-0	SL2		Newman	Macfarlane	Brown	Walls			Marshalsey		Cannon	Junior	AN Other	Eadie		Drummond	IMRIE
17	08-Nov		BRECHIN CITY	2-3	SL2		Keenan	Drummond	Macfarlane	Brown			Drummond		Cannon	Clark	Newman	EADIE		Walls	Imrie
18	15-Nov		Dundee United	3-5	SL2		Keenan	Drummond	Macfarlane	Brown			MARSHALSAY		Cannon	Clark	Forrest	DUFF		CANNON	Imrie
19	22-Nov		QUEEN OF SOUTH	1-2	SL2		Keenan	Drummond	Macfarlane	Brown			Sweeney		Brown	Clark	Forrest	Eadie		CANNON	Imrie
20	29-Nov		Dunfermline Ath	2-1	SL2		Keenan	Drummond	Macfarlane	Brown			Sweeney		Brown	Walls	Robertson	Eadie		Forrest	IMRIE 2
21	06-Dec		DUMBARTON	2-2	SL2		Keenan	Drummond	Macfarlane	Brown			SWEENEY		Brown	Walls	Robertson	EADIE		Forrest	Imrie
22	13-Dec		Arbroath	4-4	SL2		Keenan	Drummond	Macfarlane	Walls			Sweeney		Brown	WALLS	ROBERTSON	EADIE 2		Forrest	Imrie
23	20-Dec		THIRD LANARK	0-1	SL2		Keenan	Drummond	Macfarlane	Brown			Marshalsey		Cannon	Walls	Robertson	EADIE		Forrest	Imrie
24	27-Dec		Clydebank	1-2	SL2		Keenan	Drummond	Macfarlane	Walls			Sweeney		Brown	Walls	Robertson	EADIE		Duff	FORREST
25	01-Jan		RAITH ROVERS	1-1	SL2		Keenan	Drummond	Macfarlane	Newman			Sweeney		Cannon	Eadie	ROBERTSON	Duff		Cannon	Forrest
26	03-Jan		ALLOA ATHLETIC	5-0	SL2		Keenan	Drummond	Macfarlane	Newman			Sweeney		BROWN 2	WALLS 2	Robertson	Eadie		Cannon	Forrest
27	05-Jan		Armadale	1-2	SL2		Keenan	Drummond	Macfarlane	Newman			Sweeney		Brown	Eadie	Newman	Duff		Walls	Forrest
28	10-Jan		Forfar Athletic	0-1	SL2		Keenan	Drummond	Brown				Sweeney		Cannon	Junior	Newman	Duff		Cannon	Imrie
29	17-Jan		STRANRAER	6-2	SL2		Keenan	Drummond	Macfarlane	Dunn			Marley		BROWN 2	WALLS	Robertson	EADIE 3		Cannon	Imrie
30	24-Jan		ST JOHNSTONE	1-1	SC1		Keenan	Drummond	Brown	Dunn			Newman		Weir	WALLS	Robertson	EADIE		Cannon	Imrie
31	04-Feb		Kings Park	3-0	SL2		Sweeney	Drummond	Brown	DUNN 2			Marley		Weir	WALLS 2	Robertson	EADIE		Cannon	Newman
32	07-Feb		Hearts	0-3	SC2		Keenan	Drummond	Brown	Dunn			Marley		Weir	WALLS	Johnston	EADIE		Watts	Smith
33	11-Feb		KINGS PARK	1-0	SC2		Keenan	Drummond	Brown	King			Marley		Weir	WALLS	Robertson	DUFF		Cannon	Forrest
34	14-Feb		Cowdenbeath	0-3	SC3		Keenan	Drummond	Brown	Dunn			Marley		Weir	Eadie	Robertson	Duff		Cannon	Walls
35	21-Feb		Albion Rovers	4-4	SL2		Keenan	Drummond	Brown	Dunn			Marley		Weir	WALLS 4	Robertson	Duff		ROBERTSON	Imrie
36	25-Feb		MONTROSE	7-2	SL2		Keenan	Drummond	Brown	Dunn			Marley		Weir	WALLS 3	CANNON	DUFF 2		Robertson	Imrie
37	28-Feb		KINGS PARK	3-0	SL2		Keenan	Drummond	Brown	Dunn			Marley		Weir	WALLS 2	Cannon	Duff		Robertson	Newman
38	07-Mar		BONESS	2-2	SL2		Keenan	Drummond	Brown	Dunn			Marley		Weir	WALLS 2	Cannon	DUFF 2		ROBERTSON	Imrie
39	18-Mar		Brechin City	4-1	SL2		Keenan	Drummond	Brown	King			Marley		Weir	WALLS	Cannon	DUFF		Robertson	Eadie
40	21-Mar		DUNDEE UNITED	2-1	SL2		Keenan	Drummond	Brown	King			Marley		Weir	WALLS	Cannon	DUFF 2		Robertson	Eadie
41	28-Mar		East Stirling	1-0	SL2		Keenan	Drummond	Brown	King			Marley		Weir	WALLS	Cannon	Duff		Robertson	Eadie
42	04-Apr		Queen of South	4-0	SL2		Keenan	Drummond	Brown	Dunn			Marley		WEIR	WALLS	King	Duff		CANNON	EADIE
43	11-Apr		DUNFERMLINE ATH	2-2	SL2		Keenan	Drummond	Brown	Dunn			Marley		King	WALLS 2	Robertson	Duff		Weir	EADIE
44	15-Apr		Stenhousemuir	0-1	SL2		Keenan	Drummond	Brown	King			Marley		Weir	WALLS	King	King		ROBERTSON	Eadie
45	18-Apr		Dumbarton	3-0	SL2		Keenan	Drummond	Brown	Dunn			Marley		Weir	WALLS 2	King	MACFARLANE 2		ROBERTSON 3	EADIE 2
46	25-Apr		ARBROATH	8-0	SL2		Keenan	Drummond	Brown	Dunn			Marley		Weir	WALLS	King	Duff		Robertson	Eadie
47	06-May	RCC	Hibernian	3-2			Keenan	Drummond	Brown	Dunn			Marley		Weir	Walls	King	Duff		Robertson	Eadie
48	09-May	RCC	Hearts	2-1			Keenan	Drummond	Brown	Dunn			Marley		Weir	Walls	King	Duff		Robertson	Eadie

1931/32

#	Date	BLUES v HOOPS	Comp	Score	'White'	'Black' / 'Johnson'	'Bennett'	'Reid'	'Morrison'	'Grey'	'Crooks'		'Menzies'	'McKay'	
1	01-Aug	BLUES v HOOPS	Trial	0-4											
2	08-Aug	Dumbarton	SL2	1-1	Keenan	Drummond	Brown	King	Marley	Dunn	Walls	Davidson	Duff	Robertson	Eadie	Imrie
3	11-Aug	HIBERNIAN	ESSs	3-0	Keenan	Drummond	Brown	King	Marley	Dunn	Walls	DAVIDSON	Duff	Robertson	Eadie
4	15-Aug	BRECHIN CITY	SL2	5-1	Keenan	Drummond	Brown	King	Marley	DUNN	WALLS	DAVIDSON 2	Duff	Robertson	EADIE
5	18-Aug	Alloa Athletic	SL2	3-1	Keenan	Drummond	Brown	King	Marley	Dunn	Walls	DAVIDSON 2	Duff	Robertson	Eadie
6	22-Aug	Albion Rovers	SL2	1-2	Keenan	Drummond	Hume	King	MARLEY	Brown	Walls	DAVIDSON	Duff	Robertson	Eadie
7	26-Aug	FORFAR ATHLETIC	SL2	1-2	Keenan	Drummond	Hume	Dunn	Marley	Brown	Walls	King	Eadie	Davidson	IMRIE 2
8	29-Aug	EAST FIFE	SL2	4-2	Keenan	Hume	Brown	King	Marley	Dunn	WALLS	DAVIDSON 2	EADIE	Robertson	KING,A
9	05-Sep	Hibernian	SL2	3-1	Keenan	Drummond	Brown	King	Marley	Dunn	EADIE	DAVIDSON	Walls	Robertson	KING,A
10	12-Sep	ARBROATH	SL2	1-5	Keenan	Drummond	Brown	King	Marley	Dunn	Walls	Davidson	Eadie	Robertson	King,A
11	15-Sep	Hearts	ESSf	2-2	Keenan	Drummond	Brown	King	Marley	Dunn	WALLS	Davidson	Walls	Cannon	CANNON
12	19-Sep	Kings Park	SL2	1-3	Keenan	Drummond	Brown	King	Marley	Dunn	Walls	Davidson	Eadie	Cannon	King,A
13	26-Sep	BONESS	SL2	1-1	Keenan	Drummond	Brown	Dunn	Marley	Cannon	Walls	Davidson	Scoular	MURRAY	EADIE
14	03-Oct	Dunfermline Athletic	SL2	1-0	Keenan	Drummond	Brown	King	Marley	Dunn	Walls	Davidson	Scoular	Robertson	EADIE
15	10-Oct	QUEEN of the SOUTH	SL2	3-4	Keenan	Hume	Brown	King	Marley	Dunn	SCOULAR	DAVIDSON	MURRAY	ROBERTSON	Eadie
16	17-Oct	Raith Rovers	SL2	4-2	Newman	Drummond	Brown	King	Marley	Dunn	Scoular	DAVIDSON 2	Murray	Robertson	Newman
17	24-Oct	EDINBURGH CITY	SL2	2-1	Keenan	Hume	Brown	King	Marley	Dunn	Walls	Davidson	MURRAY	Robertson	Eadie
18	31-Oct	Montrose	SL2	1-3	Keenan	Drummond	Brown	King	Marley	Dunn	Scoular	Davidson	Murray	Robertson	MacLachlan,AS
19	07-Nov	ST JOHNSTONE	SL2	1-3	Keenan	Drummond	Brown	King	Marley	DUNN	Walls	Davidson	Murray	Robertson	MacLachlan,AS
20	14-Nov	Stenhousemuir	SL2	0-4	Keenan	Hume	Brown	King	Marley	Dunn	Walls	Davidson	Murray	Scoular	MacLachlan,AS
21	21-Nov	EAST STIRLING	SL2	3-4	Keenan	Hume	Brown	Drummond	Marley	Dunn	Walls	King	Scoular	Dunn	Eadie
22	28-Nov	Armadale	SL2	0-2	Johnstone,JR	Hume	Brown	King	Marley	Brown	Walls	Davidson	MURRAY 3	Dunn	EADIE
23	05-Dec	ALLOA ATHLETIC	SL2	3-0	Johnstone,JR	Drummond	Drummond	King	Marley	Dunn	Walls	DAVIDSON 2	Murray	Cannon	EADIE 3
24	12-Dec	Forfar Athletic	SL2	3-5	Keenan	Drummond	Brown	Robertson	MARLEY	Dunn	Eadie	Davidson	MURRAY	Dunn	MacLachlan,AS
25	19-Dec	DUMBARTON	SL2	0-0	Keenan	Drummond	Hume	King	Marley	Brown	WALLS	Davidson	Murray	Cannon	Eadie
26	26-Dec	Brechin City	SL2	2-0	Keenan	Drummond	Brown	King	Marley	Dunn	Walls	Davidson	Murray	MURRAY	EADIE
27	01-Jan	HIBERNIAN	SL2	1-0	Keenan	Drummond	Hume	King	Marley	Dunn	Scoular	Davidson	Murray	Meagher	Eadie
28	02-Jan	Arbroath	SL2	0-3	Keenan	Drummond	Hume	King	Marley	Dunn	WALLS	Cannon	MURRAY 2	Meagher	Eadie
29	09-Jan	ALBION ROVERS	SL2	3-2	Keenan	Drummond	Hume	King	Marley	Dunn	Scoular	Davidson	MURRAY 2	Meagher	EADIE
30	16-Jan	BEITH	SC1	4-3	Keenan	Drummond	Hume	King	Marley	Dunn	Scoular	Davidson	MURRAY 3	Robertson	EADIE 2
31	23-Jan	East Fife	SL2	2-0	Keenan	Drummond	Hume	King	Marley	Dunn	WALLS	Robertson	MURRAY 2	Meagher	EADIE
32	30-Jan	Edinburgh City	SC2	3-2	Keenan	Drummond	Hume	King	Marley	Dunn	Scoular	Davidson	MURRAY	ROBERTSON	EADIE
33	06-Feb	Boness	SL2	2-1	Keenan	Drummond	Hume	King	Marley	Dunn	Scoular	DAVIDSON	MURRAY	Robertson	Eadie
34	13-Feb	Clyde	SC3	0-2	Keenan	Drummond	Hume	King	Marley	Dunn	Davidson	Robertson	Murray	Meagher	Eadie
35	20-Feb	Queen of the South	SL2	2-2	Keenan	Drummond	Brown	Walls	MARLEY	Dunn	Walls	DAVIDSON	MURRAY 2	Meagher	Scoular
36	27-Feb	RAITH ROVERS	SL2	2-0	Keenan	Drummond	Brown	Robertson	Marley	Robertson	WALLS	Davidson	MURRAY	Meagher	EADIE 2
37	05-Mar	Edinburgh City	SL2	6-1	Keenan	DRUMMOND	Brown	King	Marley	Robertson	King	DAVIDSON 2	Murray	Meagher	Eadie
38	12-Mar	MONTROSE	SL2	1-2	Keenan	Drummond	Brown	King	Marley	Dunn	Scoular	Davidson	MURRAY 2	Murray	Eadie
39	19-Mar	St Johnstone	SL2	2-0	Keenan	Drummond	Brown	King	Marley	Dunn	Walls	Davidson	Murray	Murray	Eadie
40	26-Mar	STENHOUSEMUIR	SL2	3-1	Keenan	Drummond	Brown	King	Marley	Dunn	Scoular	Davidson	Murray	ROBERTSON	EADIE 2
41	02-Apr	East Stirling	SL2	1-5	Keenan	Drummond	Brown	King	Marley	Dunn	Scoular	DAVIDSON	MURRAY	Newman	EADIE
42	09-Apr	ARMADALE	SL2	3-1	Keenan	Drummond	Brown	King	Marley	Robertson	Scoular	Davidson	MURRAY 2	Murray	Eadie
43	16-Apr	KINGS PARK	SL2	4-0	Keenan	Drummond	Brown	King	Marley	Dunn	Walls	Davidson	MURRAY 2	WALLS	EADIE
44	19-Apr	LEITH ATHLETIC	CC1	1-1	Keenan	Drummond	Brown	King	Marley	Dunn	Walls	Davidson	Murray	Robertson	Eadie
45	23-Apr	DUNFERMLINE ATH	SL2	4-0	Keenan	Drummond	Brown	Wallis	Marley	Dunn	Scoular	Davidson	MURRAY 2	Robertson	EADIE 2
46	27-Apr	Peebles Rovers		1-3	Eadie	Eadie	Peterkin	Wallis	Hume	Lindsay	Murray,R	Meagher	Murray,D	Cannon	Eadie
47	28-Apr	LEITH ATHLETIC	CC1	4-1	Keenan	Drummond	Hume	King	Marley	Dunn	Walls	Davidson	Scoular	Reid	Scoular
48	30-Apr	HIBERNAN	CCs	3-0	Keenan	Drummond	Brown	King	Marley	Dunn	Walls	Davidson	Scoular	Robertson	Eadie
49	04-May	Hearts	RCCs	1-4	Keenan	Drummond	Brown	King	Marley	Dunn	Walls	Davidson	Scoular	Robertson	Eadie

1932/33

#	Date	Trial	BLUES v HOOPS	Score		Newman	Smith	Brown	Dunn	Devine	Stevenson	Eadie	Davidson	Paterson	Robertson	McCallum
1	06-Aug	Trial	BLUES v HOOPS			Newman	Smith	Brown	Dunn	Devine	Stevenson	Eadie	Davidson	Paterson	Robertson	McCallum
2	13-Aug	SL2	ALBION ROVERS	2-2		Keenan	Drummond	Fitzsimmons	King	Marley	Weir	Johnstone	Black	Simpson	Brown	Haldane
3	16-Aug	ESSs	HEARTS	4-1		Keenan	Drummond	Fitzsimmons	King	Marley	Weir	McCallum	Davidson	MURRAY 2	ROBERTSON	EADIE
4	20-Aug	SL2	East Fife	0-2		Keenan	Drummond	Fitzsimmons	King	Marley	Brown	McCallum	Davidson	Murray	Robertson	Eadie
5	23-Aug	SL2	QUEEN of the SOUTH	2-2		Keenan	Fitzsimmons	Brown	King	Marley	Weir	Knox,HA	Davidson	Murray	Robertson	Eadie
6	27-Aug	SL2	KINGS PARK	1-0		Keenan	Fitzsimmons	Brown	Dunn	Drummond	Weir	Newman	DAVIDSON	Murray	ROBERTSON	Eadie
7	03-Sep	SL2	Boness $	6-3		Keenan	Fitzsimmons	Brown	Marshalsey	Marshalsey	Weir	McCALLUM	Davidson	MURRAY 3	Robertson	EADIE 2
8	07-Sep	CCf	PENICUIK ATHLETIC	1-1		Keenan	Fitzsimmons	Brown	Marshalsey	Marley	Weir	McCallum	Davidson	Murray	Robertson	Eadie
9	10-Sep	SL2	EDINBURGH CITY	8-1		Keenan	Fitzsimmons	Brown	Marshalsey	Marley	Weir	Knox	Robertson	MURRAY 2	DAVIDSON 3	EADIE 3
10	14-Sep	SL2	Raith Rovers	2-4		Keenan	Drummond	Brown	Marshalsey	Marley	Weir	Drummond	Robertson	MURRAY 2	Davidson	EADIE
11	17-Sep	SL2	Arbroath	2-1		Keenan	Drummond	Fitzsimmons	King	Marley	Weir	Knox	Robertson	Murray	Davidson	McGlynn
12	19-Sep	CCf	PENICUIK ATHLETIC	6-0		Keenan	Drummond	Brown	King	Marley	Weir	Knox	Robertson	Murray	Davidson	Eadie
13	24-Sep	SL2	LEITH ATHLETIC	0-1		Keenan	Fitzsimmons	Brown	King	Marley	Weir	Eadie	Robertson	Murray	Davidson	McGlynn
14	01-Oct	SL2	Dundee United	0-1		Keenan	Fitzsimmons	Brown	Dunn	Marley	Weir	Eadie	King	MURRAY	DAVIDSON	McGlynn
15	08-Oct	SL2	DUNFERMLINE ATH	2-0		Keenan	Fitzsimmons	Brown	Dunn	Marley	Weir	Eadie	King	MURRAY	Drummond	McGlynn
16	15-Oct	SL2	Brechin City	1-3		Keenan	Fitzsimmons	Brown	King	Marshalsey	Weir	Eadie	Robertson	Murray	Drummond	McGlynn
17	22-Oct	SL2	Stenhousemuir	0-1		Keenan	Fitzsimmons	Brown	King	Marley	Weir	Eadie	Robertson	MURRAY 2	Robertson,T	EADIE
18	29-Oct	SL2	DUMBARTON	4-0		Keenan	Fitzsimmons	Brown	King	Marley	Weir	DRUMMOND	Robertson,A	Murray	Robertson,T	Eadie
19	05-Nov	SL2	Queen of the South	2-2		Keenan	Fitzsimmons	Brown	King	Marley	Weir	Marshall	ROBERTSON,A 2	MURRAY	Robertson,T	Eadie
20	12-Nov	SL2	RAITH ROVERS	3-2		Keenan	Fitzsimmons	Brown	King	Marley	Weir	Davidson	Robertson,A	Murray	Robertson,T	Eadie
21	19-Nov	SL2	HIBERNIAN	0-1		Keenan	Fitzsimmons	Brown	King	Marley	Weir	NEWMAN	Robertson,A	Murray	Robertson,T	Eadie
22	26-Nov	SL2	Montrose	1-1		Keenan	Fitzsimmons	Brown	King	Marley	Marshalsey	O'Brien	Robertson,T	Other,AN	Davidson	Eadie
23	03-Dec	SL2	FORFAR ATHLETIC	0-1		Keenan	Fitzsimmons	Brown	King	Marley	Weir	O'Brien	DAVIDSON	MURRAY	Robertson,T	Eadie
24	17-Dec	SL2	ALLOA ATHLETIC	2-2		Keenan	Fitzsimmons	Brown	King	Marley	Weir	O'BRIEN	Davidson	EADIE 3	Robertson,T	Murray
25	24-Dec	SL2	Albion Rovers	1-3		Keenan	Drummond	Brown	King	Marley	Weir	O'Brien	Davidson	EADIE 3	Robertson,T	MURRAY
26	26-Dec	SL2	Edinburgh City	8-2		Keenan	Fitzsimmons	Brown	King	MARLEY	WEIR	Murray	ROBERTSON,A	DAVIDSON 2	Robertson,T	Eadie
27	31-Dec	SL2	EAST FIFE	3-1		Keenan	Fitzsimmons	Brown	King	Marley	Weir	O'Brien	ROBERTSON,A	MURRAY	Robertson,T	Eadie
28	03-Jan	SL2	ARBROATH	0-0		Keenan	Fitzsimmons	Brown	King	Marley	Weir	O'Brien	Davidson	Murray	Murray	Marshall
29	07-Jan	SL2	Kings Park	4-2		Keenan	Fitzsimmons	Brown	KING	Marley	Weir	O'Brien	DAVIDSON	MURRAY	Robertson,T	Eadie
30	14-Jan	ESC1	BERWICK RANGERS	5-1		Keenan	Fitzsimmons	Brown	King	Marley	Weir	Drummond	Davidson	Murray	Robertson,T	EADIE
31	21-Jan	SC1	PARTICK THISTLE	2-2		Keenan	Fitzsimmons	Brown	King	Marley	Weir	DRUMMOND	Davidson	MURRAY	Robertson,T	Eadie
32	25-Jan	SC1	Partick Thistle	0-3		Keenan	Fitzsimmons	Brown	King	Marley	Weir	Drummond	Davidson	Murray	Robertson,T	Eadie
33	28-Jan	SL2	Leith Athletic	1-1		Keenan	Fitzsimmons	Brown	King	Marley	Weir	O'Brien	DAVIDSON	MURRAY 2	Robertson,T	Eadie
34	11-Feb	SL2	DUNDEE UNITED	3-2		Keenan	Fitzsimmons	Brown	King	Marley	Weir	O'Brien	Davidson	Murray	ROBERTSON,T	Eadie
35	18-Feb	CCs	LEITH ATHLETIC	3-1		Keenan	Fitzsimmons	Brown	King	Marley	Weir	O'Brien	Robertson,T	MURRAY 4	Davidson	Eadie
36	25-Feb	SL2	BRECHIN CITY	8-0		Keenan	Fitzsimmons	Brown	King	MARLEY	Weir	O'Brien	Robertson,T	MURRAY 2	DAVIDSON 2	Newman
37	11-Mar	SL2	STENHOUSEMUIR	3-2		Keenan	Fitzsimmons	Brown	King	Marley	Weir	O'Brien	Robertson,A	Murray	DAVIDSON	Newman
38	18-Mar	SL2	Dumbarton	0-6		Keenan	Fitzsimmons	Brown	King	Marley	Weir	O'Brien	Robertson,A	Murray	Marshall	Eadie
39	25-Mar	SL2	Hibernian	1-4		Keenan	Fitzsimmons	Brown	King	Marley	Weir	Murray	Tait	Murray	Robertson,T	EADIE
40	08-Apr	SL2	MONTROSE	1-3		Keenan	Brown	Fitzsimmons	Dunn	Marley	Weir	O'Brien	King	Dobbie	King	Eadie
41	15-Apr	SL2	Forfar Athletic	0-4		Keenan	Drummond	Fitzsimmons	Dunn	Marley	Weir	Murray	King	Murray	Robertson,T	McDonald,JH
42	22-Apr	SL2	Dunfermline Athletic	0-4		Keenan	Drummond	Fitzsimmons	Dunn	Marley	Weir	O'Brien	Robertson,T	Paterson	'Brown'	MURRAY
43	29-Apr	SL2	Alloa Athletic	1-2		Keenan	Drummond	Fitzsimmons	King	Newman	Weir	Eadie	Robertson,T	Fleming	Murray	Eadie
44	10-May	RCCs	Hearts	0-4		Keenan	Drummond	Fitzsimmons	Weir	Marley	'Sutherland'	Riddle	Marshalsey			

1933/34

#	Date	Trial	BLUES v HOOPS	Score	Cassidy	Wilson	Ford	McLeod	Ramage	Naughty	Forbes	Rankine	Murray	Bow	Brown
1	07-Aug	Trial	BLUES v HOOPS			Marshalsey	Allen	King	Marley	Weir	Duncan	Paxton	Murray	Bow	McKane
2	12-Aug	SL2	Kings Park	2-3	Keenan	Drummond	Fitzsimmons	King	Marley	Weir	FORBES	Wilson	Oliver	Tullis	BROWN,A
3	16-Aug	ESSs	HEARTS	2-3	Keenan	Fitzsimmons	Brown,W	Drummond	Marley	Weir	Forbes	King	Murray	Bow	Brown,A
4	19-Aug	SL2	BRECHIN CITY	2-1	Keenan	Fitzsimmons	Brown,W	King	Marley	Weir	Forbes	Stevenson	Murray	Bow	Brown,A
5	26-Aug	SL2	Leith Athletic	1-4	'Lawrence'	Fitzsimmons	Brown,W	Drummond	Marley	Weir	Forbes	King	MURRAY	BOW 2	Brown,A
6	02-Sep	SL2	ARBROATH	1-0	Keenan	Fitzsimmons	Brown,W	King	Marley	Weir	Forbes	Tait	MUIR	Bow	Bow
7	05-Sep	CCf	MURRAYFIELD AMS	3-0	Keenan	Fitzsimmons	Brown,W	King	Marley	Weir	FORBES 2	'Sinclair'	Murray	Brown,A	Brown,A
8	09-Sep	SL2	Edinburgh City	5-0	Keenan	Fitzsimmons	Drummond	Newman	Marley	Weir	Forbes	King	MURRAY 2	BOW	Brown,A
9	16-Sep	SL2	DUNDEE UNITED	3-0	Keenan	Fitzsimmons	Brown,W	Newman	Marley	Weir	Forbes	Wilson	MURRAY 3	Bow	Brown,A
10	23-Sep	SL2	Albion Rovers	1-1	Keenan	Fitzsimmons	Brown,W	King	Marley	Weir	Forbes	Wilson	Murray	Bow	Brown,A
11	30-Sep	SL2	RAITH ROVERS	0-1	Keenan	Fitzsimmons	Brown,W	King	Marley	Weir	Forbes	Wilson	Murray	Bow	Brown,A
12	07-Oct	SL2	Dunfermline Athletic	1-4	Keenan	Fitzsimmons	Brown,W	Drummond	Marley	Weir	Forbes	Bow	Murray	Bow	Campbell
13	14-Oct	SL2	MORTON	10-1	Keenan	Fitzsimmons	Brown,W	Drummond	Marley	Weir	FORBES	King	MURRAY 3	BROWN,A 5	CAMPBELL
14	21-Oct	SL2	KINGS PARK	2-0	Loudon	Fitzsimmons	Brown,W	King	Marley	Weir	FORBES	Bow	MURRAY	BROWN,A	Campbell
15	28-Oct	SL2	Forfar Athletic	1-2	Loudon	Fitzsimmons	Brown,W	Drummond	Marley	Weir	Forbes	Bow	Murray	BROWN,A	Campbell
16	04-Nov	SL2	ALLOA ATHLETIC	5-1	Loudon	Fitzsimmons	Brown,W	King	Marley	WEIR	FORBES 2	Bow	MURRAY 2	Brown,A	Campbell
17	11-Nov	SL2	East Stirling	0-2	Loudon	Fitzsimmons	Brown,W	Newman	Marley	Weir	Wilson	King	Murray	Bow	CAMPBELL
18	18-Nov	SL2	EAST FIFE	2-2	Loudon	Fitzsimmons	Brown,W	Newman	Marley	WEIR	DRUMMOND	Bow	Murray	Brown,A	Campbell
19	25-Nov	SL2	Stenhousemuir	0-3	Loudon	Fitzsimmons	Brown,W	Bell	Marley	Weir	Forbes	Drummond	Murray	Brown,A	Campbell
20	02-Dec	SL2	LEITH ATHLETIC	0-1	Loudon	Fitzsimmons	Brown,W	Bell	Marley	Weir	Forbes	Wilson	King	Bow	Brown,A
21	09-Dec	SL2	Brechin City	1-2	Loudon	Fitzsimmons	Drummond	Brown,W	Marley	Brown,W	FORBES	Newman	Campbell	MURRAY	CAMPBELL 2
22	16-Dec	SL2	DUNFERMLINE ATH	4-1	Loudon	Fitzsimmons	Brown,W	Drummond	Marley	Weir	FORBES	King	NEWMAN	Murray	Campbell
23	23-Dec	SL2	ALBION ROVERS	2-0	Loudon	Fitzsimmons	Brown,W	Drummond	Marley	Weir	Forbes	King	MURRAY	Russell	Campbell
24	30-Dec	SL2	Raith Rovers	1-3	Keenan	Fitzsimmons	Brown,W	Bell	Marley	Weir	Forbes	BOW	Murray	Russell	Campbell
25	01-Jan	SL2	EDINBURGH CITY	5-0	Keenan	King	Brown,W	Bell	Marley	Weir	FORBES	King	MURRAY 3	Russell	CAMPBELL
26	06-Jan	SL2	Dundee United	1-4	Keenan	Fitzsimmons	Brown,W	Drummond	Marley	Weir	Forbes	King	Murray	Russell	Campbell
27	13-Jan	SL2	EAST STIRLING	1-1	Loudon	Fitzsimmons	Brown,W	Newman	Marley	Weir	Forbes	Russell	BOW	BOW	Campbell
28	20-Jan	SC1	WICK ACADEMY	3-0	Loudon	Fitzsimmons	Brown,W	McGirr	Marley	Weir	Forbes	Russell	MURRAY 2	BOW	Campbell
29	27-Jan	SC2	Alloa Athletic	3-1	Loudon	Fitzsimmons	Brown,W	King	Marley	Weir	Forbes	McGirr	MURRAY 3	RUSSELL	Campbell
30	03-Feb	SC2	Cowdenbeath	1-2	Loudon	Fitzsimmons	Brown,W	Drummond	Marley	WEIR	Bell	McGirr	MURRAY	Russell	CAMPBELL
31	10-Feb	SL2	Morton	2-2	Loudon	Fitzsimmons	Brown,W	McGirr	Marley	Weir	Forbes	Wilson	Murray	Russell	Campbell
32	17-Feb	BC1L	LEITH ATHLETIC	1-1	Loudon	Fitzsimmons	Brown,W	McGirr	Drummond	Bell	Forbes	Bow	MURRAY	Russell	Campbell
33	24-Feb	SL2	FORFAR ATHLETIC	0-2	Loudon	Fitzsimmons	Brown,W	McGirr	Marley	Weir	Forbes	Newman	Murray	Russell	Campbell
34	03-Mar	SL2	Dumbarton	7-2	Loudon	Fitzsimmons	Drummond	McGirr	Marley	Weir	FORBES 2	NEWMAN	MURRAY 2	RUSSELL 2	Campbell
35	10-Mar	SL2	DUMBARTON	2-4	Loudon	Fitzsimmons	Newman	Drummond	Marley	Weir	Forbes	McGirr	Murray	Russell	CAMPBELL
36	17-Mar	SL2	Montrose	2-0	Loudon	Fitzsimmons	Brown,W	Bell	Marley	Russell	Forbes	McGirr	MURRAY	Bow	CAMPBELL
37	24-Mar	SL2	MONTROSE	7-2	Loudon	Fitzsimmons	Brown,W	McGirr	Marley	Russell	Forbes	Wilson	Murray	BOW	Eadie
38	31-Mar	CC1	MOSSEND SWIFTS	3-1	Loudon	Fitzsimmons	Brown,W	Drummond	Marley	Russell	Forbes	Newman	Eadie	Bow	EADIE
39	07-Apr	SL2	STENHOUSEMUIR	2-3	Loudon	Fitzsimmons	Brown,W	Bell	Marley	Weir	EADIE 2	Newman	MURRAY	Murray	Campbell
40	14-Apr	SL2	East Fife	2-5	Loudon	Fitzsimmons	Drummond	Russell	Marley	Russell	MURRAY 2	Forbes	Eadie	Bow	Campbell
41	21-Apr	SL2	Arbroath	2-4	Loudon	Drummond	Brown,W	Bell	Marley	Weir	Forbes	Russell	Eadie	Bow	Murray
42	28-Apr	BC2L	Leith Athletic	2-4	Loudon	Fitzsimmons	Brown,W	Drummond	Marley	Weir	EADIE	'Newman'	Eadie	Murray	Campbell
43	02-May	RCCq	Hibernian	0-1	Loudon	Fitzsimmons	Brown,W	Drummond	Marley	Weir	Forbes	Russell	Murray	Russell	Eadie

1934

THE ST BERNARDS' PLAYERS

Standing: Weir, Russell, Loudon, Murray, Noble, Fitzsimmons and Keenan.
Seated: Brown, Eadie, Marley, Igoe and Hay.

1935

Standing: Fitzsimmons, Allan, Cunningham, Igoe, Marley and Weir.
Seated: Laidlaw, Russell, Eadie, Noble and Hay.

1935

Back Row: ?, Weir, ? and Fitzsimmons.
Standing: Willie Brown (Trainer), M Langton, ?, Symons, ?, Murray, ?, L Langton, Cunningham, ?,?, Allan and Bob Innes (Manager).
Seated: Brooks. ?. Russell. Marlev. Noble. ? and Hav.   (Pre-Season Trial)

1935

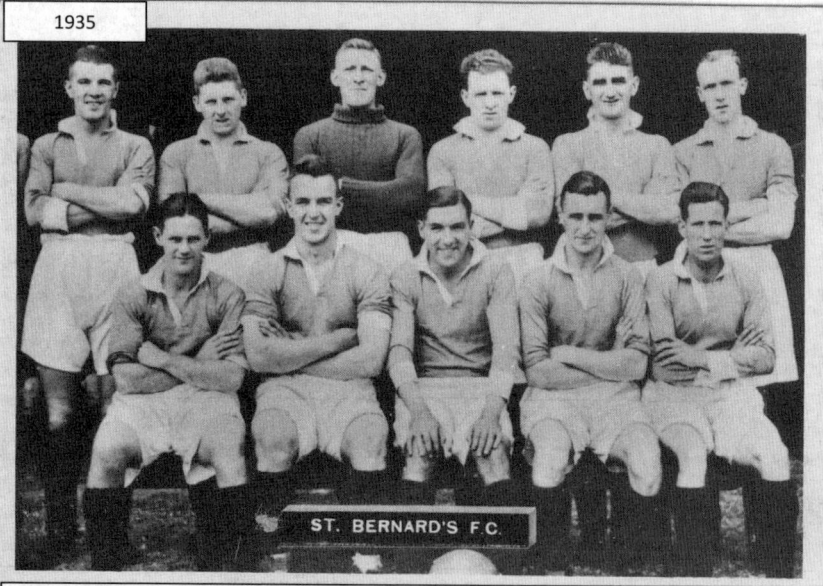

Standing: Fitzsimmons, Allan, Cunningham, Langton, Marley and Weir.
Seated: Brooks, Russell, Murray, Noble and Hay.

1934/35

#	Date	Trial 'A' v 'B'		Opponent	Score		Loudon	Fitzsimmons	Brown	Johnson	Marley	'Wood' Drummond	England	McIvor	Eadie	Laidlaw	Houston
1	04-Aug					1-2	Loudon	Fitzsimmons	Brown	Penman	Tait	Drummond	Forbes	Igoe	Murray	Noble	Pryde
2	11-Aug	SL2	LEITH ATHLETIC			0-1	Keenan	King	Russell	Russell	Marley	Weir	Forbes	Laidlaw	Murray	Noble	Hay
3	18-Aug	SL2	Arbroath			5-2	Loudon	Fitzsimmons	Brown	Russell	Marley	Weir	Eadie	Igoe	MURRAY 3	NOBLE	HAY
4	25-Aug	SL2	STENHOUSEMUIR			4-1	Loudon	Fitzsimmons	Brown	Russell	Marley	Weir	EADIE 2	Igoe	MURRAY 2	Noble	Hay
5	29-Aug	ESSs	Hearts			1-5	Loudon	Fitzsimmons	Brown	Russell	Marley	Weir	Eadie	Igoe	Murray	Noble	Hay
6	01-Sep	SL2	Cowdenbeath			10-1	Loudon	Fitzsimmons	Brown	Russell	Marley	WEIR	Eadie	LAIDLAW	MURRAY 4	Noble	HAY 3
7	08-Sep	SL2	BRECHIN CITY			5-1	Loudon	Fitzsimmons	Brown	Russell	Marley	Weir	Eadie	LAIDLAW	MURRAY 4	Noble	Hay
8	15-Sep	SL2	East Fife			1-1	Loudon	Fitzsimmons	Brown	Russell	Marley	Weir	FORBES	Laidlaw	Murray	Noble	Hay
9	17-Sep	BC1L	LEITH ATHLETIC			7-1	Loudon	Fitzsimmons	Brown	Igoe	Marley	Weir	Forbes	Laidlaw	Eadie	Noble	Hay
10	22-Sep	SL2	DUNDEE UNITED			1-0	Keenan	Fitzsimmons	Russell	Igoe	Marley	Weir	Forbes	Laidlaw	EADIE	Noble	Hay
11	29-Sep	SL2	East Stirling			0-0	Loudon	Fitzsimmons	Brown	Igoe	Russell	Weir	Forbes	Laidlaw	Eadie	Noble	Hay
12	06-Oct	SL2	EDINBURGH CITY			6-2	Loudon	Fitzsimmons	Brown	Igoe	Marley	Weir	Pryde	Laidlaw	EADIE 4	Noble	HAY 2
13	13-Oct	SL2	Morton			4-3	Loudon	Fitzsimmons	Brown	Russell	Marley	WEIR	Eadie	Igoe	MURRAY 3	Noble	Hay
14	20-Oct	SL2	Kings Park			2-4	Loudon	Newman	Fitzsimmons	Russell	Marley	Weir	Eadie	Igoe	MURRAY	NOBLE	Hay
15	27-Oct	SL2	MONTROSE			1-1	Loudon	Fitzsimmons	Allan	Igoe	RUSSELL	Weir	Pryde	Laidlaw	Murray	Noble	Hay
16	03-Nov	SL2	Alloa Athletic			1-2	Loudon	Fitzsimmons	Allan	Russell	Marley	Weir	EADIE	Laidlaw	Murray	Noble	Hay
17	10-Nov	SL2	RAITH ROVERS			6-2	Loudon	Fitzsimmons	Allan	Russell	Marley	Weir	EADIE 2	MURRAY	MURRAY	NOBLE 2	Hay
18	17-Nov	SL2	FORFAR ATHLETIC			0-0	Loudon	Fitzsimmons	Allan	Russell	Marley	Weir	Eadie	Igoe	Murray	Noble	Hay
19	24-Nov	SL2	EAST FIFE			6-1	Loudon	Fitzsimmons	Allan	Igoe	Marley	Weir	EADIE 3	RUSSELL	MURRAY	Noble	HAY
20	01-Dec	SL2	Third Lanark			1-2	Loudon	Fitzsimmons	Allan	Igoe	Russell	Weir	Forbes	Laidlaw	MURRAY	Noble	Hay
21	08-Dec	SL2	DUMBARTON			5-0	Loudon	Fitzsimmons	Allan	Laidlaw	Igoe	Weir	Eadie	RUSSELL 4	MURRAY	Noble	Hay
22	15-Dec	SL2	Dumbarton			4-1	Loudon	Fitzsimmons	Allan	Laidlaw	Igoe	Weir	Eadie	Russell	MURRAY 4	Gordon	Hay
23	22-Dec	SL2	Leith Athletic			1-2	Loudon	Fitzsimmons	Allan	Igoe	Marley	Weir	EADIE 2	Russell	Murray	Noble	Hay
24	25-Dec	SL2	Edinburgh City			6-2	Junior	Fitzsimmons	Allan	Igoe	Igoe	WEIR	EADIE 2	RUSSELL 2	MURRAY	Noble	Hay
25	29-Dec	SL2	KINGS PARK			4-1	Loudon	Fitzsimmons	Allan	Igoe	Marley	Weir	Forbes	RUSSELL 2	MURRAY	Noble	EADIE
26	05-Jan	SL2	Montrose			4-0	Loudon	Fitzsimmons	Allan	Igoe	Marley	Weir	EADIE	Russell	MURRAY 2	Laidlaw	HAY
27	12-Jan	SL2	ALLOA ATHLETIC			2-1	Loudon	Fitzsimmons	Allan	Igoe	Marley	Weir	EADIE	Russell	Murray	Noble	HAY
28	19-Jan	SL2	Stenhousemuir			2-1	Loudon	Fitzsimmons	Allan	Igoe	Marley	Weir	Eadie	Russell	Murray	Noble	Hay
29	26-Jan	SC1	AIRDRIE			1-3	Newman	Fitzsimmons	Allan	Igoe	Marley	Weir	EADIE	Russell	MURRAY	Noble	HAY 2
30	02-Feb	SL2	COWDENBEATH			2-0	Newman	Fitzsimmons	Allan	Newman	Marley	Weir	Other,AN	RUSSELL	MURRAY 2	NOBLE	Hay
31	16-Feb	SL2	Dundee United			3-3	Cunningham	Fitzsimmons	Allan	Davidson	Marley	Weir	Forbes	Russell	Murray	Noble	Hay
32	23-Feb	CCs	VALE OF LEITHEN			1-0	Cunningham	Fitzsimmons	Allan	Davidson	Marley	Weir	Eadie	Russell	Murray	Noble	Hay
33	02-Mar	SL2	MORTON			0-1	Cunningham	Fitzsimmons	Allan	Laidlaw	Marley	Weir	Eadie	RUSSELL 2	Murray	Noble	HAY 2
34	09-Mar	SL2	THIRD LANARK			3-2	Cunningham	Fitzsimmons	Allan	Igoe	Marley	Weir	Laidlaw	Russell	Murray	Noble	Hay
35	16-Mar	SL2	Forfar Athletic			4-4	Cunningham	Fitzsimmons	Allan	Russell	Marley	Weir	Eadie	Newman	EADIE 2	Noble	HAY 2
36	23-Mar	SL2	ARBROATH			0-0	Cunningham	Fitzsimmons	Allan	Davidson	Marley	Weir	Eadie	Russell	Murray	Noble	Hay
37	30-Mar	SL2	Raith Rovers			0-3	Newman	Fitzsimmons	Allan	Igoe	MARLEY	Weir	Forbes	Russell	Murray	Noble	Hay
38	13-Apr	SL2	EAST STIRLING			7-0	Cunningham	Brown	Allan	Igoe	Marley	Weir	Davidson	RUSSELL 2	MURRAY 2	NOBLE	Hay
39	20-Apr	SL2	Brechin City			3-2	Cunningham	Brown	Allan	Igoe	Marley	Weir	Davidson	RUSSELL	MURRAY	NOBLE	HAY
40	23-Apr	SL2	Vale of Leithen			2-2	Cunningham	Dickson	Allan	Nicolson	McDonald	Laidlaw	Davidson	Russell	Murray	Noble	Eadie
41	27-Apr	BC2L	LEITH ATHLETIC			2-2	Cunningham	Brown	Allan	Igoe	Marley	Weir	Davidson	Russell	Murray	Noble	Hay
42	01-May	RCC1	Hamilton Accies			2-7	Cunningham	Fitzsimmons	Allan	Laidlaw	Marley	Weir	Pryde	Russell	Murray	Noble	Hay

1935/36

#	Date	Div	HOOPS v BLUES	Score	Cunningham	Fitzsimmons	Allan			Marley	Weir	Sinclair	Davidson	Mitchell	Ferguson	Noble
1	03-Aug	Trial	HOOPS v BLUES	0-1	Symons	Clark	Mills	'Tait'	Langton	McPherson	Davis	Brooks	Russell	Murray	Noble	Hay
2	10-Aug	SL2	Dundee United	2-2	Cunningham	Fitzsimmons	Allan	Langton	Marley	Marley	Weir	Brooks	RUSSELL	Murray	Noble	Hay
3	14-Aug	CCf	LEITH ATHLETIC	3-0	Cunningham	Fitzsimmons	Allan	Langton	Marley	Marley	Weir	Brooks	Russell	MURRAY	Noble	Hay
4	17-Aug	SL2	EAST STIRLING	4-0	Cunningham	Fitzsimmons	Allan	Langton	Marley	Marley	Weir	Brooks	RUSSELL 2	MURRAY	NOBLE	Hay
5	21-Aug	ESSs	HIBERNIAN	1-1	Cunningham	Fitzsimmons	Allan	Langton	Marley	Marley	Weir	Brooks	Russell	Murray	Noble	Hay
6	24-Aug	SL2	Montrose	3-1	Cunningham	Fitzsimmons	Allan	Langton	Marley	Marley	Weir	BROOKS	RUSSELL	Murray	Noble	HAY
7	27-Aug		Duns	1-4	Cunningham	Nicholson	Allan	Newman	Marley	Marley	Newman	Davidson	Newman	Mitchell	Murray	Hay
8	31-Aug	SL2	EAST FIFE	2-2	Cunningham	Fitzsimmons	Allan	Langton	Marley	Marley	Weir	Brooks	Russell	MITCHELL 2	NOBLE	Hay
9	04-Sep	ESSs	Hibernian	0-0	Cunningham	Fitzsimmons	Allan	Langton	Marley	Marley	Weir	Brooks	Russell	Mitchell	Noble	Murray
10	07-Sep	SL2	Stenhousemuir	6-3	Cunningham	Fitzsimmons	Allan	Langton	Marley	Marley	Weir	BROOKS 4	Russell	MURRAY	NOBLE	Hay
11	14-Sep	SL2	COWDENBEATH	2-3	Cunningham	Fitzsimmons	Allan	Langton	Marley	Marley	Weir	Brooks	Russell	Murray	NOBLE	Hay
12	21-Sep	SL2	Leith Athletic	6-2	Cunningham	Fitzsimmons	Allan	Langton	Davidson	Marley	Langton	BROOKS 2	RUSSELL 2	Mitchell	NOBLE 2	Hay
13	28-Sep	SL2	FORFAR ATHLETIC	3-0	Cunningham	Fitzsimmons	Allan	Davidson	Davidson	Marley	Weir	Brooks	RUSSELL 2	Mitchell	NOBLE	HAY
14	05-Oct	SL2	Edinburgh City	6-1	Cunningham	Fitzsimmons	Allan	Langton	Langton	Marley	Weir	Brooks	RUSSELL 2	MURRAY	NOBLE	HAY 2
15	12-Oct	SL2	MORTON	3-2	Cunningham	Fitzsimmons	Allan	Langton	Langton	MARLEY	Weir	Brooks	Russell	Murray	Noble	HAY
16	19-Oct	SL2	STENHOUSEMUIR	1-2	Cunningham	Fitzsimmons	Allan	Langton	Langton	MARLEY	Weir	Brooks	Russell	Murray	Noble	Hay
17	26-Oct	SL2	Brechin City	8-2	Cunningham	Fitzsimmons	Allan	Langton	Langton	Marley	Weir	Brooks	RUSSELL 2	MITCHELL 3	NOBLE 2	HAY
18	02-Nov	SL2	Alloa Athletic	3-4	Cunningham	Fitzsimmons	Langton	Davidson	Langton	Marley	Weir	Brooks	RUSSELL	Mitchell	NOBLE 2	HAY
19	09-Nov	SL2	RAITH ROVERS	6-2	Cunningham	Fitzsimmons	Allan	Langton	Langton	Marley	Weir	Brooks	RUSSELL	Mitchell	Noble	HAY
20	16-Nov	SL2	Forfar Athletic	2-3	Cunningham	Fitzsimmons	Allan	Langton	Langton	Marley	Weir	Brooks	Russell	MURRAY 3	NOBLE	HAY
21	23-Nov	SL2	FALKIRK	2-3	Cunningham	Fitzsimmons	Allan	Langton	Russell	Marley	Weir	Brooks	RUSSELL	Mitchell	NOBLE	HAY 2
22	30-Nov	SL2	ALLOA ATHLETIC	1-2	Cunningham	Langton	Allan	JUNIOR 2	JUNIOR 2	Marley	Weir	Brooks	Davidson	NEWMAN	Noble	HAY
23	07-Dec	SL2	St Mirren	2-4	Cunningham	Fitzsimmons	Allan	RUSSELL	RUSSELL	Marley	Weir	Brooks	Noble	NEWMAN	NOBLE	Murray
24	14-Dec	SL2	East Stirling	2-1	Cunningham	Langton	Fitzsimmons	Langton	Langton	Marley	Weir	Brooks	Junior	NEWMAN	Russell	HAY
25	21-Dec	SL2	MONTROSE	2-5	Cunningham	Fitzsimmons	Allan	Langton	Langton	Marley	Weir	Brooks	JUNIOR	Russell	Noble	Hay
26	28-Dec	SL2	East Fife	2-0	Cunningham	Fitzsimmons	Allan	Langton	Langton	Marley	Weir	BROOKS	Murray	MURRAY 2	NOBLE	Hay
27	01-Jan	SL2	EDINBURGH CITY	5-3	Cunningham	Fitzsimmons	Allan	Langton	Langton	Marley	Weir	BROOKS 2	Russell	MURRAY 2	NOBLE	HAY
28	04-Jan	SL2	KINGS PARK	3-1	Cunningham	Fitzsimmons	Allan	Langton	Langton	Marley	Weir	Brooks	NELSON	PATERSON	NOBLE	HAY
29	11-Jan	SL2	DUNDEE UNITED	4-3	Cunningham	Fitzsimmons	Allan	Langton	Newman	Marley	Weir	Brooks	Nelson	MURRAY 2	NOBLE	HAY
30	18-Jan	SL2	Cowdenbeath	5-0	Newman	Fitzsimmons	Allan	Langton	Russell	Marley	WEIR	Brooks	Nelson	MURRAY 3	NOBLE 2	HAY 2
31	01-Feb	SC1	Ross County	0-3	Newman	Fitzsimmons	Allan	Langton	Langton	Marley	Weir	Brooks	Nelson	Murray	NOBLE	HAY
33	08-Feb	SC2	Motherwell	2-3	Cunningham	Fitzsimmons	Allan	Langton	Langton	Marley	Weir	Nelson	Russell	Murray	NOBLE	Hay
33	15-Feb	SL2	BRECHIN CITY	4-5	Cunningham	Fitzsimmons	Allan	Langton	Langton	Marley	Weir	Brooks	Russell	Murray	Noble	Brooks
34	22-Feb	CC1	LEITH ATHLETIC	1-7	Newman	Fitzsimmons	Allan	Langton	Langton	Marley	Weir	Nelson	NELSON	PATERSON	Noble	Hay
35	29-Feb	SL2	Falkirk	5-2	Cunningham	Fitzsimmons	Allan	Langton	Langton	Marley	Weir	Brooks	Nelson	NELSON 2	NOBLE 2	HAY
36	07-Mar	SL2	Raith Rovers	7-0	Cunningham	Fitzsimmons	Allan	Langton	Newman	Marley	Weir	BROOKS	RUSSELL	NELSON 2	NOBLE 2	HAY 2
37	14-Mar	SL2	LEITH ATHLETIC	4-2	Newman	Fitzsimmons	Allan	Langton	Russell	Marley	Weir	Brooks	Nelson	MURRAY	NOBLE	HAY
38	21-Mar	SL2	DUMBARTON	2-0	Cunningham	Fitzsimmons	Allan	Langton	Langton	Marley	Weir	Brooks	Russell	NELSON	NOBLE	Hay
39	28-Mar	SL2	Kings Park	2-6	Cunningham	Fitzsimmons	Allan	Langton	Langton	Marley	Weir	Brooks	Nelson	McPHERSON	NOBLE 2	HAY 2
40	04-Apr	SL2	ST MIRREN	3-3	Cunningham	Marley	Allan	Marley	Nelson	McPherson	Davidson	Murray	Hogg	Brooks	Noble	Hay
41	11-Apr	SL2	Morton	0-2	Cunningham	Fitzsimmons	Allan	Langton	Langton	Marley	Weir	Brooks	Nelson	McPherson	Russell	Hay
42	18-Apr		Coldstream	3-2	Cunningham	Fitzsimmons	Allan	Langton	Langton	Marley	Weir	Davidson	Nelson	McPherson	Brooks	Hay
43	20-Apr	BC1L	LEITH ATHLETIC	2-2	Cunningham	Fitzsimmons	Allan	Langton	Langton	Marley	Weir	Brooks	Nelson	McPherson	Noble	Hay
44	25-Apr	SL2	Dumbarton	3-2	Cunningham	Fitzsimmons	Allan	Langton	Langton	Marley	Davidson	Brooks	Nelson	McPherson	Russell	Hay
45	27-Apr	ESSs	Hibernian	2-2	Cunningham	Fitzsimmons	Allan	Langton	Langton	Marley	Weir	Brooks	Nelson	McPherson	Brooks	Hay
46	30-Apr	ESSf	Hearts	3-2	Cunningham	Fitzsimmons	Allan	Langton	Langton	Marley	Weir	Brooks	Nelson	McPherson	Noble	Hay
47	06-May	RCCs	Hibernian	0-2	Cunningham	Riddle	Allan	Langton	Langton	Shepherd	Weir	Brooks	Nelson	McPherson	Noble	Hay
48	15-May	RCCf	Hearts	3-2	Cunningham	Fitzsimmons	Allan	Langton	Nelson	McPherson	Weir	Brooks	Nelson	Paterson,L	Noble	Hay

1936/37

#	Date	Comp	Opponent	Score												
1	01-Aug	Trial	HOOPS v BLUES	5-0	Cunningham	Fitzsimmons	Allan	Langton		Strathie	Weir	Brooks	Johnston	Flucker	Noble	Hay
2	08-Aug	Trial	MONTROSE	7-1	Keenan	Fitzsimmons	Allan	Philp	LANGTON	McPherson	Mills	Paterson,L	Russell	McGregor	Hogg	Scott
3	11-Aug		Gala Fairydean	5-1	Cunningham	Fitzsimmons	Allan	Langton	Strathie	Smith,TG	Weir	BROOKS 2	Johnston	FLUCKER 2	NOBLE 2	Hay
4	15-Aug	SL2	East Fife	1-6	Smith,TG	Rogers	Paterson,H	Philp	Smith,TG	Strathie	Russell	Paterson,L	Hogg	McPherson	Noble	Hay
5	22-Aug	SL2	STENHOUSEMUIR	3-2	Cunningham	Fitzsimmons	Allan	Langton	Smith,TG	Strathie	Weir	Brooks	Johnston	FLUCKER 3	Noble	Brooks
6	26-Aug	ESSf	Hearts	1-3	Smith,TG	Fitzsimmons	Allan	Philp	Smith,TG	Strathie	Weir	Paterson,L	Russell	Flucker	Noble	Hay
7	29-Aug	SL2	Cowdenbeath	0-2	Smith,TG	Fitzsimmons	Allan	Philp	Smith,TG	Strathie	Weir	Brooks	Johnston	Flucker	Noble	Paterson,L
8	01-Sep	ESSs	HIBERNIAN	0-1	Smith,TG	Fitzsimmons	Allan	Philp	Langton	Strathie	Weir	Brooks	Russell	Flucker	Noble	Hay
9	05-Sep	SL2	EDINBURGH CITY	4-1	Smith,TG	Fitzsimmons	Allan	Philp	Smith,TG	Strathie	Weir	Paterson,L	RUSSELL	FLUCKER 3	Johnston	JOHNSTON
10	12-Sep	SL2	Forfar Athletic	8-1	Smith,TG	Fitzsimmons	Allan	Philp	Smith,TG	Strathie	Weir	BROOKS 2	Russell	FLUCKER 3	NOBLE 2	Johnston
11	19-Sep	SL2	LEITH ATHLETIC	2-0	Smith,TG	Fitzsimmons	Allan	Philp	Smith,TG	Strathie	Weir	BROOKS	Russell	FLUCKER	Noble	JOHNSTON
12	26-Sep	SL2	East Stirling	1-1	Smith,TG	Langton	Allan	Philp	Smith,TG	Strathie	Weir	McPherson	Johnston	Flucker	Russell	Hay
13	03-Oct	SL2	DUNDEE UNITED	3-0	Smith,TG	Fitzsimmons	Allan	Philp	Smith,TG	STRATHIE	Weir	Newman	Johnston	FLUCKER	Russell	HAY
14	10-Oct	SL2	Alloa Athletic	0-0	Smith,TG	Fitzsimmons	Allan	Philp	Smith,TG	Strathie	Weir	Flucker	Johnston	Paterson,L	Russell	Hay
15	17-Oct	SL2	MORTON	2-1	Smith,TG	Fitzsimmons	Allan	Philp	Smith,TG	Strathie	Weir	Paterson,L	Johnston	FLUCKER 2	Russell	Hay
16	24-Oct	SL2	Kings Park	2-3	Smith,TG	Fitzsimmons	Allan	Philp	Smith,TG	Strathie	Weir	Paterson,L	JOHNSTON 2	Flucker	Russell	Hay
17	31-Oct	SL2	RAITH ROVERS	3-0	Smith,TG	Rogers	Fitzsimmons	Philp	Smith,TG	Strathie	Weir	GRANT 2	Johnston	Flucker	Russell	PINKERTON
18	07-Nov	SL2	Brechin City	1-1	Smith,TG	Fitzsimmons	Allan	Philp	Smith,TG	Strathie	Weir	GRANT	Johnston	Flucker	Russell	Pinkerton
19	14-Nov	SL2	Dumbarton	4-1	Smith,TG	Fitzsimmons	Allan	Philp	Smith,TG	Strathie	Weir	GRANT	Johnston	FLUCKER 2	Newman	Pinkerton
20	21-Nov	SL2	BRECHIN CITY	6-0	Smith,TG	Fitzsimmons	Allan	Philp	Smith,TG	Strathie	Weir	GRANT 2	Johnston	HOGG	NEWMAN	Pinkerton
21	28-Nov	SL2	AYR UNITED	2-5	Smith,TG	Fitzsimmons	Allan	Philp	Smith,TG	Strathie	Weir	GRANT	JOHNSTON	Flucker	HOGG	Pinkerton
22	12-Dec	SL2	KINGS PARK	6-1	Smith,TG	Fitzsimmons	Allan	PHILP	Smith,TG	Strathie	Weir	GRANT	Johnston	FLUCKER 3	Russell	PINKERTON
23	19-Dec	SL2	Montrose	3-1	Smith,TG	Fitzsimmons	Allan	Philp	Smith,TG	Strathie	Weir	GRANT	Johnston	Flucker	RUSSELL 2	Pinkerton
24	26-Dec	SL2	DUMBARTON	4-0	Smith,TG	Fitzsimmons	Allan	Philp	Smith,TG	Strathie	Weir	GRANT 2	Johnston	Flucker	HOGG 2	Pinkerton
25	01-Jan	SL2	Edinburgh City	3-0	Smith,TG	Fitzsimmons	Allan	Philp	Smith,TG	STRATHIE	Weir	Grant	JOHNSTON	ROGERS	Russell	Pinkerton
26	02-Jan	SL2	FORFAR ATHLETIC	3-1	Smith,TG	Fitzsimmons	Allan	Langton	Smith,TG	STRATHIE	Weir	GRANT	JOHNSTON	Flucker	Newman	Pinkerton
27	09-Jan	SL2	Stenhousemuir	1-2	Smith,TG	Fitzsimmons	Allan	Philp	Smith,TG	Strathie	Weir	Grant	Johnston	ROGERS	Dawson	Pinkerton
28	16-Jan	SL2	COWDENBEATH	2-2	Smith,TG	Fitzsimmons	Allan	Philp	Smith,TG	Strathie	Weir	Grant	Langton	McPherson	Dawson	JOHNSTON
29	23-Jan	SL2	Leith Athletic	4-2	Smith,TG	Fitzsimmons	Allan	Philp	Smith,TG	STRATHIE	Weir	GRANT 2	Johnston	Flucker	Hogg	HAY
30	30-Jan	SC1	Hearts	1-3	Smith,TG	Fitzsimmons	Allan	Philp	Smith,TG	Strathie	Weir	Grant	Johnston	Flucker	Russell	Hay
31	06-Feb	SL2	EAST STIRLING	4-3	Smith,TG	Fitzsimmons	Allan	Philp	Smith,TG	STRATHIE 2	Weir	Grant	Johnston	FLUCKER 2	Dawson	Hay
32	13-Feb	SL2	Ayr United	2-5	Smith,TG	Fitzsimmons	Allan	Philp	Smith,TG	STRATHIE 2	Weir	GRANT	Johnston	FLUCKER	DAWSON	Hay
33	20-Feb	SL2	Raith Rovers	1-0	Smith,TG	Strathie	Fitzsimmons	Philp	McPherson	Strathie	Langton	Grant	Johnston	Flucker	Dawson	Hay
34	06-Mar	SL2	EAST FIFE	3-0	Smith,TG	Fitzsimmons	Allan	Philp	Smith,TG	STRATHIE	Weir	GRANT	Johnston	Flucker	Dawson	PINKERTON
35	20-Mar	SL2	AIRDRIE	6-1	Smith,TG	Fitzsimmons	Allan	PHILP	Smith,TG	Strathie	Weir	Grant	JOHNSTON	Flucker	DAWSON	Pinkerton
36	27-Mar	SL2	ALLOA ATHLETIC	3-0	Cunningham	Fitzsimmons	Allan	Philp	Smith,TG	STRATHIE 2	Weir	Grant	JOHNSTON	Flucker	Dawson	Pinkerton
37	10-Apr	SL2	Dundee United	3-0	Smith,TG	Fitzsimmons	Allan	Philp	Smith,TG	Strathie	Weir	GRANT 3	Johnston	Flucker	Dawson	Pinkerton
38	14-Apr	SL2	Morton	1-4	Smith,TG	Fitzsimmons	Allan	Philp	Smith,TG	Strathie	Weir	Grant	JOHNSTON	Flucker	Dawson	Pinkerton
39	23-Apr	SL2	Airdrie	2-4	Smith,TG	Rogers	Allan	Philp	Smith,TG	STRATHIE	Weir	Grant	McPHERSON	Flucker	Dawson	Pinkerton
40	29-Apr	SL2	Berwick Rangers	6-1	Smith,TG	Strathie	Allan	Philp	Johnston	McPherson	Johnston	Flucker	Scobie	Russell	Hogg	Pinkerton
41	01-May	RCCs	Hearts	2-6	Smith,TG	Newman	Allan	Philp	Smith,TG	Strathie	Weir	Grant	Johnston	Flucker	Dawson	Pinkerton

1937/38

#	Date	Trial	BLUES v HOOPS	Score	Keenan	Anderson	Kerr	Wood	Chilcott	Russell	Dee	Fairley	Hoy	Baker	Flynn
1	07-Aug	Trial	BLUES v HOOPS	3-3	Smith,TG	Allan	Mills	Philp	McPherson	Aird	Grant	Johnston	Flucker	Dawson	Pinkerton
2	14-Aug	SL2	Dundee United	7-1	Smith,TG	Allan	Mills	Philp	McPherson	Weir	GRANT 2	JOHNSTON 2	FLUCKER 2	DAWSON	Pinkerton
3	17-Aug		Vale of Leithen	1-2	Smith,TG	Allan	Mills	McPherson	Ormiston	Flucker	Sayers	Baker	Hoy	Scobie	Flynn
4	21-Aug	SL2	COWDENBEATH	3-2	Smith,TG	Allan	Kerr	Philp	McPherson	Weir	Grant	Johnston	FLUCKER 3	Dawson	Pinkerton
5	25-Aug		Duns	2-3											
6	28-Aug	SL2	Leith Athletic	1-1	Smith,TG	Allan	Kerr	Philp	Christie	Weir	Grant	Johnston	Flucker	Dawson	Pinkerton
7	31-Aug	CCs	Edinburgh City	6-1	Smith,TG	Allan	Kerr	Philp	Christie	Weir	Grant	Johnston	Flucker	Dawson	Pinkerton
8	04-Sep	SL2	FORFAR ATHLETIC	0-1	Smith,TG	Allan	Kerr	Philp	Christie	Weir	Grant	Johnston	Flucker	Dawson	Pinkerton
9	11-Sep	SL2	Stenhousemuir	1-2	Smith,TG	Allan	Kerr	Aird	Philp	WEIR	Grant	JOHNSTON	FLUCKER	DAWSON	PINKERTON
10	18-Sep	SL2	EAST FIFE	3-1	Smith,TG	Allan	Kerr	Philp	Aird	Weir	Grant	Russell	Flucker	Russell	Pinkerton
11	22-Sep	ESSs	Hearts	1-5	Smith,TG	Allan	Kerr	Philp	Aird	Weir	Grant	JOHNSTON	FLUCKER	JOHNSTON	Pinkerton
12	25-Sep	SL2	East Stirling	1-1	Smith,TG	Allan	Kerr	Philp	Aird	Weir	Russell	Russell	Flucker	KEMP	PINKERTON
13	02-Oct	SL2	AIRDRIE	3-2	Smith,TG	Allan	Kerr	Philp	Aird	Weir	Grant	Johnston	FLUCKER	DAWSON	PINKERTON
14	09-Oct	SL2	Brechin City	3-2	Smith,TG	Allan	Kerr	Mills	Philp	McPherson	GRANT	Johnston	FLUCKER	Dawson	PINKERTON
15	11-Oct		Selkirk	2-0	Libberton	Allan	Mills	Philp	Aird	WEIR	Sayers	Thompson	Grant	Plant	Pinkerton
16	16-Oct	SL2	DUNDEE UNITED	3-0	Smith,TG	Allan	Kerr	Philp	Aird	Weir	Grant	Johnston	FLUCKER	Dawson	Pinkerton
17	23-Oct	SL2	Albion Rovers	0-5	Smith,TG	Allan	Kerr	Philp	Aird	Weir	Grant	Johnston	Flucker	Dawson	Pinkerton
18	30-Oct	SL2	ALLOA ATHLETIC	6-1	Smith,TG	Allan	Kerr	Philp	Aird	Weir	JOHNSTON 2	Newman	GRANT 3	DAWSON	Pinkerton
19	06-Nov	SL2	LEITH ATHLETIC	1-0	Smith,TG	Allan	Kerr	Philp	Aird	Weir	Flucker	Johnston	Flucker	Dawson	Sayers
20	13-Nov	SL2	Dunfermline Athletic	1-2	Smith,TG	Allan	Kerr	Philp	Aird	Weir	Flucker	Johnston	GRANT	Russell	FLUCKER
21	20-Nov	SL2	Raith Rovers	2-4	Smith,TG	Allan	Kerr	Philp	Aird	Weir	Sayers	Johnston	GRANT	Russell	Johnston
22	27-Nov	SL2	DUMBARTON	1-0	Smith,TG	Allan	KERR	PHILP	Aird	Weir	Flucker	Dawson	Grant	KEMP	Flucker
23	04-Dec	SL2	Edinburgh City	4-0	Smith,TG	Allan	Kerr	Philp	Russell	Weir	Grant	JOHNSTON	Dawson	Kemp	Kemp
24	18-Dec	SL2	MONTROSE **	1-1	Smith,TG	Allan	Kerr	Philp	Russell	Weir	Sayers	Johnston	GRANT	Dawson	KEMP
25	25-Dec	SL2	Alloa Athletic	1-0	Smith,TG	Allan	Kerr	Philp	Russell	Weir	Sayers	Johnston	Grant	Dawson	Kemp
26	01-Jan	SL2	STENHOUSEMUIR	4-2	Smith,TG	Allan	Kerr	Philp	Aird	Weir	GRANT 2	JOHNSTON 2	Flucker	Dawson	Kemp
27	03-Jan	SL2	EDINBURGH CITY	4-0	Smith,TG	Allan	Kerr	Philp	Aird	Weir	GRANT 2	Aird	Flucker	JOHNSTON	Kemp
28	08-Jan	SL2	Airdrie	0-3	Smith,TG	Allan	Kerr	Philp	Aird	Weir	Grant	Johnston	Flucker	Dawson	Kemp
29	15-Jan	SL2	EAST FIFE	3-3	Smith,TG	Allan	Kerr	Philp	Aird	Aird	Grant	Johnston	PINKERTON	DAWSON 2	Kemp
30	22-Jan	SC1	VALE OF LEITHEN	1-0	Smith,TG	Allan	Kerr	Philp	Aird	Aird	FLUCKER	Pinkerton	Pinkerton	DAWSON	KEMP
31	29-Jan	SL2	ALBION ROVERS	1-1	Smith,TG	Allan	Kerr	Philp	Aird	Aird	Grant	Johnston	Newman	Dawson	Kemp
32	05-Feb	SL2	EAST STIRLING	3-0	Smith,TG	Allan	Kerr	Philp	Aird	Aird	FLUCKER	Johnston	GRANT 2	Dawson	KEMP
33	12-Feb	SC2	KINGS PARK	1-1	Smith,TG	Dick	Kerr	Aird	Philp	Kemp	GRANT 3	Johnston	Grant	Dawson	Kemp
34	16-Feb	SC2	KINGS PARK	4-3	Smith,TG	Millar	Kerr	Aird	Aird	Kemp	Grant	Johnston	FLUCKER	Dawson	KEMP
35	19-Feb	SL2	Kings Park	1-0	Smith,TG	Millar	Kerr	Aird	Aird	Kemp	FLUCKER	Johnston	Grant	Dawson	Kemp
36	26-Feb	SL2	RAITH ROVERS	0-3	Smith,TG	Allan	Kerr	Aird	Dick	Aird	Grant	Johnston	GRANT	Dawson	Dawson
37	05-Mar	SL2	MONTROSE	2-1	Smith,TG	Allan	KERR	Kerr	Aird	Kemp	Grant	Johnston	Grant	Dawson	Pinkerton
38	12-Mar	SL2	Cowdenbeath	2-2	Smith,TG	Allan	Kerr	Kerr	Dick	Kemp	FLUCKER 2	Johnston	FLUCKER 2	Dawson	Pinkerton
39	19-Mar	SC4	MOTHERWELL	3-1	Smith,TG	Allan	Kerr	Kerr	Aird	Kemp	GRANT	Johnston	Grant	Dawson	PINKERTON
40	26-Mar	SL2	Dumbarton	2-1	Smith,TG	Allan	Kerr	Kerr	Aird	Kemp	Sayers	Johnston	FLUCKER	Dawson	Pinkerton
41	02-Apr	SL2	East Fife	1-1	Smith,TG	Allan	Kerr	Kerr	Aird	Kemp	Grant	JOHNSTON	Flucker	Dawson	Pinkerton
42	06-Apr	SCs	East Fife	1-1	Smith,TG	Allan	Kerr	Aird	Aird	Kemp	KERR	Grant	PINKERTON	Thomson	Flynn
43	09-Apr	SCs	BRECHIN CITY	2-1	Smith,TG	Dick	Millar	Dick	Aird	Kemp	Grant	Johnston	Flucker	Dawson	Pinkerton
44	13-Apr	SCs	East Fife	1-2	Smith,TG	Allan	KERR	Kerr	Aird	Kemp	GRANT	Johnston	FLUCKER	Dawson	Pinkerton
45	16-Apr	SL2	Forfar Athletic	2-1	Smith,TG	Allan	Kerr	Kerr	Dick	Aird	GRANT	Johnston	Newman	Dawson	KEMP
46	20-Apr	SL2	DUNFERMLINE ATH	4-0	Smith,TG	Allan	Kerr	Kerr	Aird	Johnston	FLUCKER	JUNIOR 2	BROWN	Dawson	Kemp
47	23-Apr	SL2	Montrose	2-1	Smith,TG	Allan	Kerr	Kerr	Aird	Johnston	GRANT	GRANT	Millar	Dawson	Kemp
48	25-Apr	CCf	LEITH ATHLETIC	0-1	Smith,TG	Allan	Kerr	Kerr	Aird	Johnston	Flucker	Grant	Newman	Dawson	Kemp
49	30-Apr	SCs	KINGS PARK	3-4	Smith,TG	Allan	Millar	Aird	Aird	Clark	FLUCKER	GRANT 2	Other,AN	Walls	Kemp
50	07-May	RCCs	Hibernian	1-0	Smith,TG	Allan	Kerr	Aird	Aird	Russell	Brooks	Johnston,T	Newman	Dawson	Kemp
51	14-May	RCCf	Leith Athletic	4-0	Smith,TG	Allan	Kerr	Aird	Aird	Russell	Brooks	Johnston,T	Flucker	Dawson	Kemp

1936 — THE ST BERNARDS TEAM

Standing: Russell, Philp, Fitzsimmons, Cunningham, Rogers and Strathie.
Seated: L Paterson, Flucker, Weir, Noble and Brooks.

1937 — THE ST BERNARD'S TEAM

Standing: Allan, Kerr, TG Smith, Philp, McPherson and Weir.
Seated: Grant, Johnston, Flucker, Dawson and Pinkerton.

1939

THE GYMNASIUM COMBINE

Standing: Dick, Philp, McKay, Flucker, Aird and Gilchrist.
Seated: S Johnston, J Johnston, Walker, Dawson and Kemp.

1938

EDINBURGH SAINTS' BID FOR PROMOTION

Standing: Allan, Kerr, TG Smith, Philp, Russell, Aird and Robert Tait (Director).
Seated: Flucker, Johnston, 'Newman', Dawson and Kemp.

1938/39

#	Date	Trial	HOOPS v BLUES	Score												
1	06-Aug	Trial		3-4	Smith,TG	Libberton	Allan	Kerr	Aird	Russell	Johnston,J	Clark	Baker	Brown	Dawson	Sutherland
2	13-Aug	SL2	Leith Athletic	2-1	Smith,TG	Libberton	Ross	Millar	Philp	Flucker	Spence	Morton	Johnston,T	Dunsire	Whyte	Kemp
3	16-Aug	PC1	Leith Athletic	2-2	Smith,TG	Libberton	Allan	Millar	Aird	RUSSELL	Johnston,J	Flucker	JOHNSTON,T	Dunsire	Dawson	Kemp
4	20-Aug	SL2	Forfar Athletic	2-2	Smith,TG	Libberton	Allan	Kerr	Aird	Russell	Johnston,J	Dunsire	Flucker	Newman	Dawson	Kemp
5	24-Aug		Penicuik Athletic	1-1		Libberton	Allan	Kerr	Philp	Russell	Johnston,J	Newman	Johnston,T	DUNSIRE	Dawson	KEMP
6	27-Aug	SL2	BRECHIN CITY	7-1		Libberton	Allan	Kerr	Aird	Russell	Aird	NEWMAN	Johnston,J	Rutherford	Newman	Dunsire
7	30-Aug	ESSs	Hibernian	0-2		Libberton	Allan	Kerr	Philp	Russell	Johnston,J	Dunsire	Johnston,T	BROOKS 4	WHYTE	KEMP
8	03-Sep	SL2	East Stirling	2-5		Libberton	Allan	Kerr	Philp	Russell	Johnston,J	Flucker	Johnston,T	BROOKS 2	Dawson	Kemp
9	10-Sep	SL2	STENHOUSEMUIR	1-0		Libberton	Allan	Kerr	Johnston,J	Russell	Millar	Johnston,S	Johnston,T	Dunsire	Dawson	KEMP
10	17-Sep	SL2	Morton	2-2		Libberton	Allan	Kerr	Johnston,J	Russell	Millar	Johnston,S	JOHNSTON,T	DUNSIRE	Brooks	Kemp
11	24-Sep	SL2	DUNFERMLINE ATH	3-1		Libberton	Allan	Kerr	Aird	Russell	Kemp	Johnston,S	Johnston,T	DUNSIRE	BROOKS	KEMP
12	01-Oct	SL2	Edinburgh City	4-0		Libberton	Allan	Kerr	Aird	Russell	KEMP	Johnston,S	Johnston,T	DUNSIRE 2	MILLAR	Kemp
13	08-Oct	SL2	DUNDEE UNITED	5-3		Libberton	Allan	Kerr	Aird	Russell	Johnston,J	JOHNSTON,S	BROOKS 2	Dunsire	Millar	Flucker
14	15-Oct	SL2	Montrose	2-2		Libberton	Allan	Kerr	Aird	Russell	Kemp	Johnston,S	DAWSON 3	Dunsire	Brooks	Kemp
15	22-Oct	SL2	Brechin City	1-4		Libberton	Allan	Kerr	Aird	Russell	Johnston,J	JOHNSTON,S	Johnston,J	Dunsire	Whyte	Kemp
16	29-Oct	SL2	MORTON	5-0		Libberton	Allan	Kerr	Aird	Russell	Kemp	JOHNSTON,S	Johnston,J	Dunsire	Johnston,J	BROOKS 2
17	05-Nov	SL2	COWDENBEATH	1-2		Libberton	Allan	Kerr	Aird	Russell	Kemp	JOHNSTON,S	Dawson	Brooks	Johnston,J	Brooks
18	12-Nov	SL2	Dundee United	2-5		Libberton	Allan	Kerr	AIRD	Russell	Millar	Dawson	Dawson	Brooks	DUNSIRE	Kemp
19	19-Nov	SL2	KINGS PARK	5-4		Libberton	Allan	Kerr	Philp	Russell	JOHNSTON,J	JOHNSTON,S	Dawson	FLUCKER 2	DUNSIRE	BROOKS
20	26-Nov	SL2	DUMBARTON	2-4		Libberton	Allan	Kerr	Philp	Russell	Johnston,J	JOHNSTON,J	Dawson	Flucker	DUNSIRE	Brooks
21	03-Dec	SL2	Dundee	0-3		Shepherd,KC	Millar	Kerr	Philp	Russell	Kemp	Johnston,S	Dawson	Dunsire	Johnston,J	Brooks
22	10-Dec	SL2	EAST FIFE	0-1		Shepherd,KC	Millar	Kerr	Philp	Russell	Kemp	Johnston,S	Dawson	Dunsire	Johnston,J	DUNSIRE
23	17-Dec	SL2	Airdrie	3-4		Shepherd,KC	Allan	Millar	Philp	Russell	Kemp	BROOKS	Johnston,S	Johnston,S	DAWSON	Dunsire
24	24-Dec	SL2	Alloa Athletic	1-6		Libberton	Allan	Millar	Philp	Russell	Kemp	Brooks	Johnston,J	TAMS,W	Dawson	KEMP
25	31-Dec	SL2	EAST STIRLING	3-2		Shepherd,KC	Millar	Kerr	Philp	Russell	Aird	Brooks	Johnston,J	TAMS,W 2	Dawson	Kemp
26	02-Jan	SL2	Stenhousemuir	2-2		Shepherd,KC	Millar	Kerr	Philp	Flucker	Aird	Johnston,S	Johnston,J	TAMS,W	Dawson	Kemp
27	21-Jan	SC1	Dundee	0-2		Shepherd,KC	Millar	Kerr	Philp	Flucker	Aird	Brooks	Russell	Tams,W	Dawson	Kemp
28	28-Jan	SL2	Dunfermline Ath	2-1		Libberton	Allan	Millar	Philp	Flucker	Aird	Dunsire	JOHNSTON,S	Tams,W	Dawson	JOHNSTON,J
29	11-Feb		MONTROSE	2-1		Libberton	Dick	Millar	Philp	Flucker	AIRD	Dunsire	Dawson	Dunsire	JOHNSTON,J	Kemp
30	18-Feb	SL2	FORFAR ATHLETIC	6-2		Libberton	Dick	Millar	Philp	Flucker	Aird	Brown	Johnston,S	JOHNSTON,J 6	Dawson	Kemp
31	25-Feb	SL2	ALLOA ATHLETIC	0-5		Libberton	Dick	Millar	Philp	Flucker	Aird	Johnston,S	JOHNSTON,S	JOHNSTON,J	Dawson	Kemp
32	04-Mar	SL2	Kings Park	1-1		Libberton	Dick	Millar	Philp	FLUCKER	Kemp	Johnston,S	Russell	Johnston,J	Dawson	Kemp
33	11-Mar	SL2	EDINBURGH CITY	4-3		Newman	Dick	Millar	Kerr	Flucker	Aird	JOHNSTON,S	Junior	JOHNSTON,J 2	Dawson	Dunsire
34	18-Mar	SL2	Cowdenbeath	1-3		Newman	Dick	Millar	Kerr	Flucker	Aird	Brown	OTHER,AN	JOHNSTON,J	Dawson	Kemp
35	25-Mar	SL2	East Fife	4-3		Newman	Millar	Kerr	Philp	Flucker	Aird	JOHNSTON,S	JOHNSTON,S	JOHNSTON,J	DAWSON 2	Kemp
36	01-Apr	SL2	Dumbarton	2-1		McKay	Dick	Kerr	Philp	Russell	Aird	Brooks	Johnston,S	MILLAR	Dawson	KEMP
37	08-Apr	SL2	DUNDEE	1-1		McKay	Dick	Kerr	Philp	Russell	Aird	Brooks	Johnston,S	JOHNSTON,J	Dawson	Kemp
38	15-Apr	SL2	AIRDRIE	0-1		McKay	Dick	Kerr	Philp	Russell	Aird	Johnston,S	Newman	JOHNSTON,J	Dawson	Kemp
39	19-Apr	SL2	Leith Athletic	1-1		McKay	Dick	Kerr	Philp	Russell	Aird	Johnston,S	Newman	Flucker	Johnston,J	Kemp
40	22-Apr	CCf	PEEBLES ROVERS	4-3		Libberton	Dick	Kerr	Philp	Russell	Aird	Johnston,S	Newman	Flucker	Johnston,J	Kemp
41	25-Apr	PC1	LEITH ATHLETIC	3-2		McKay	Dick	Kerr	Philp	Flucker	Aird	Johnston,S	Johnston,S	Johnston,S	Dawson	Kemp
42	29-Apr	PCsf	East Fife	0-1		Shepherd,KC	Dick	Kerr	Philp	Russell	Aird	Brooks	Brooks	Johnston,S	Dawson	Kemp
43	03-May	RCCs	Hearts	2-5		McKay	Dick	Kerr	Philp	Flucker	Aird	Johnston,S	Johnston,S	Brooks	Dawson	Kemp

1939/40

#	Date	Trial	HOOPS BLUES	Score											AN Other
1	05-Aug	Trial	HOOPS BLUES	2-1	McKay	Dick	Newman	Philip	Russell	Aird	Johnston,S	Johnston,J	Walker	Dawson	McKnight
2	12-Aug	SL2	Brechin City	0-0	O'Brien	Russell	Kemp	Gilchrist	Hudson	Martin	Hay	Allan	Curran	Ross	Kemp
3	15-Aug	PC1	LEITH ATHLETIC	2-2	McKay	Dick	Gilchrist	Philip	Flucker	Aird	Johnston,S	Johnston,J	Walker	Dawson	Kemp
4	19-Aug	SL2	FORFAR ATHLETIC	6-2	McKay	Dick	Gilchrist	PHILP	Flucker	Aird	Johnston,S	Johnston,J	WALKER	Dawson	KEMP 2
5	22-Aug	CC1	PENICUIK ATHLETIC	3-3	McKay	Dick	Gilchrist	Philip	Flucker	Russell	JOHNSTON,S 2	JOHNSTON,J	Walker	Dawson	Kemp
6	26-Aug	SL2	East Fife	1-5	McKay	Dick	Gilchrist	Philip	Flucker	Aird	Johnston,S	Johnston,S	Walker	Dawson	Kemp
7	29-Aug	ESSs	HIBERNIAN	0-1	McKay	Dick	Gilchrist	Philip	Flucker	Aird	Walker	Johnston,S	Newman	Dawson	Kemp
8	02-Sep	SL2	QUEENS PARK	0-0	McKay	Dick	Gilchrist	Philip	Flucker	Aird	Johnston,S	Johnston,J	Walker	Dawson	Kemp
9	07-Oct	PC1R	Leith Athletic	1-4	McKay	Newman	Gilchrist	Philip	Flucker	Aird	Johnston,S	Johnston,J	Walker	Linton	Kemp
10	21-Oct	ERL	Cowdenbeath	0-4	Wallace	Flucker	Yorke	Philip	Aird	Johnston,J	Johnston,J	Logie	Hay	Linton	Kemp
11	28-Oct	ERL	STENHOUSEMUIR	6-2	Wallace	Abbie	Yorke	Philip	Flucker	Aird	Johnston,S	LOGIE	HAY 4	Linton	KEMP
12	04-Nov	ERL	Hearts	2-2	Wallace	Abbie	Yorke	Philip	Flucker	Aird	Johnston,J	Logie	HAY 2	Linton	Kemp
13	11-Nov	ERL	EAST FIFE	2-1	Wallace	Abbie	Yorke	Philip	Flucker	Aird	Theurer	Logie	HAY 2	Linton	Kemp
14	18-Nov	ERL	Aberdeen	3-3	Wallace	Abbie	Yorke	PHILP	Flucker	Aird	THEURER	Logie	HAY	Linton	Kemp
15	25-Nov	ERL	ST JOHNSTONE	1-1	Wallace	Abbie	Yorke	Philip	Flucker	Aird	REGAN	Logie	Hay	Linton	Kemp
16	02-Dec	ERL	Alloa Athletic	0-5	Wallace	Abbie	Kemp	Aird	Flucker	Johnston	Regan	Logie	Hay	Linton	Linton
17	09-Dec	ERL	Arbroath	4-0	Wallace	Abbie	Kemp	Philip	Flucker	Aird	Regan	LOGIE	HAY 3	Johnston	Kemp
18	16-Dec	ERL	DUNDEE UNITED	4-2	Wallace	Abbie	Yorke	Philip	Flucker	AIRD	Regan	LOGIE	HAY 2	Linton	Kemp
19	23-Dec	ERL	FALKIRK	1-2	Wallace	Abbie	Yorke	Philip	Flucker	Aird	Regan	Logie	Hay	Johnston,J	Kemp
20	30-Dec	ERL	HIBERNIAN	1-6	Wallace	Yorke	Walker	PHILP	Flucker	Aird	REGAN	Buchan	HAY	Logie	Kemp
21	02-Jan	ERL	Dundee	2-2	Wallace	Abbie	Yorke	Philip	Flucker	Aird	Regan	Logie	Hay	Linton	Kemp
22	13-Jan	ERL	Raith Rovers	0-6	Wallace	Abbie	Yorke	Philip	Flucker	Aird	Flucker	Yorke	Hay	Linton	Kemp
23	03-Feb	ERL	East Fife	1-2	Wallace	Abbie	Yorke	Philip	Johnstone	Aird	Flucker	Abbie	HAY	BUCHAN	Linton
24	17-Feb	ERL	ABERDEEN	3-1	Wallace	Yorke	Walker	Philip	Johnstone	Aird	Flucker	Theurer	HAY	Buchan	Linton
25	24-Feb	WC1	MORTON	1-5	Wallace	Yorke	Walker	PHILP	Johnstone	Aird	Flucker	Abbie	Hay	Buchan	Kemp
26	02-Mar	WC1	Morton	0-5	Wallace	Yorke	Walker	Philip	Johnstone	Walker	Regan	Abbie	Hay	Linton	KEMP
27	09-Mar	ERL	ARBROATH	2-0	Wallace	Abbie	YORKE	Philip	Aird	Walker	Johnston,J	Buchan	Hay	Linton	Kemp
28	16-Mar	ERL	Dundee United	0-1	Wallace	Abbie	Yorke	Philip	Aird	Walker	Theurer	Buchan	Hay	Linton	Kemp
29	23-Mar	ERL	Falkirk	1-8	Wallace	Abbie	Yorke	Russell	Aird	Buchan	JOHNSTON	Johnstone	HAY	Linton	Kemp
30	27-Mar	ERL	Kings Park	1-4	Wallace	Abbie	Yorke	Russell	Russell	Walker	Johnston	Cringan	Hay	Glass	Kemp
31	30-Mar	ERL	KINGS PARK	3-4	Wallace	Abbie	Yorke	Aird	Russell	Walker	Hay	Buchan	HAY	Buchan	Kemp
32	06-Apr	ERL	Stenhousemuir	0-4	Wallace	Abbie	Walker	Cringan	Cringan	Walker	Johnston	Buchan	HAYWOOD	WHITELAW	KEMP
33	10-Apr	ERL	DUNDEE	0-0	Wallace	Abbie	Walker	Buchan	Buchan	Walker	Haywood	Johnston,J	Haywood	Strang	Kemp
34	13-Apr	ERL	HEARTS	0-2	Wallace	Abbie	Walker	Buchan	Buchan	Aird	Haywood	Russell	Adlem	Hay	Kemp
35	15-Apr	ERL	Dunfermline Athletic	1-3	Wallace	Abbie	Walker	Philip	Cringan	Aird	Johnston	Buchan	Adlem	Johnston,J	Kemp
36	20-Apr	ERL	St Johnstone	1-6	Wallace	Abbie	Walker	Philip	Cringan	Aird	Johnston	Buchan	Theurer	Russell	Kemp
37	24-Apr	ERL	RAITH ROVERS	1-0	Wallace	Abbie	Walker	Philip	Cringan	Aird	PRYDE	Buchan	Theurer	STRANG	Kemp
38	27-Apr	ERL	ALLOA ATHLETIC	2-0	Wallace	Abbie	YORKE	Philip	Cringan	Walker	Buchan	Logie	Logie	Gilchrist	Kemp
39	04-May	ERL	DUNFERMLINE ATH	1-3	Wallace	Abbie	Yorke	Gilchrist	Cringan	Walker	Buchan	PRYDE	FITZGERALD	PRYDE	Haywood
40	14-May	RCCs	Hibernian	2-4	Wallace	Abbie	Yorke	Gilchrist	Cringan	Aird	Dougan	Logie	Hay	Fitzgerald	Walker

Rosebery Juniors 1940/41

#	Date	Comp	Opponent	Score										
1	24-Aug	MJL	BATHGATE THISTLE	2-4	Pottie	Cairns	Finlayson	Sands	White	Purves	McIntee	Bannatyne	Hoy	Sim	Gibson
2	31-Aug	MJL	Bonnyrigg Rose Athletic	2-2											
3	07-Sep	MJL	ARMADALE THISTLE	1-1	Walkinshaw	Cairns	Davidson	Sands	White	Purves	Duncan	Bannatyne	Hoy	Robertson	McIntee
4	14-Sep	EJC	Polkemmet Juniors	0-4	Walkinshaw	Davidson	Finlayson	Innes	Cairns	Purves	McIntee	Bannatyne	Hoy	Sim	Robertson
5	21-Sep	EJC	POLKEMMET JUNIORS	2-0	Walkinshaw	Davidson	Finlayson	Sands	White	Sim	Hoy	Henderson	Cairns	Robertson	McIntee
6	28-Sep	MJL	Haddington Athletic	3-4											
7	05-Oct	MJL	MUSSELBURGH ATHLETIC	3-3	Matthews	Davidson	Finlayson	Sands	Cairns	Purves	Smart	Henderson	Hoy	Robertson	Sim
8	12-Oct	SJC2	Bowhill Rovers	4-2											
9	19-Oct	MJL	WINCHBURGH JUNIORS	1-5	Matthews	Davidson	Finlayson	Sands	Cairns	Purves	Bannatyne	Robertson	Herbert	Sim	McIntee
10	26-Oct	StMC	MUSSELBURGH ATHLETIC	3-0											
11	02-Nov	MJL	Armadale Thistle	1-11	Prentice	Davidson	Finlayson	Sands	Cairns	Sim	Hoy	Bannatyne	Morrish	Robertson	McIntee
12	09-Nov	StMC	Musselburgh Athletic	2-2	Matthews	Cairns	Davidson	Hoy	Buchan	McIntee	Walkinshaw	Bannatyne	Morrish	Robertson	Greenhorn
13	16-Nov	SJC3	Armadale Thistle	0-4	Matthews	Davidson	Finlayson	Cairns	Sherlaw	Purves	McIntee	Hoy	Morrish	Sim	Greenhorn
14	30-Nov	MJL	Polkemmet Juniors	1-8											
15	07-Dec	MJL	HADDINGTON ATHLETIC	1-1											
16	14-Dec	StMCs	ARMADALE THISTLE	1-6	Matthews	Cairns	Davidson	Devlin	Buchanan	Purves	Morrish	Robertson	Hoy	Sim	Greenhorn
17	21-Dec	MJL	Winchburgh Juniors	1-4											

1941/42

#	Date	Comp	Opponent	Score														
1	02-Aug	Trial	BLUES v HOOPS	?-?														
2	09-Aug	NEL 1s	Dunfermline Athletic	3-7	Matthews	Hall,GA	McDermott	Veitch,DD	Junior	Harvey	WILKIE,W	LOGIE	WILKIE,J	Dougan	Geetie
3	16-Aug	NEL 1s	DUNDEE UNITED	1-4	Matthews	Hall,GA	Mackie	Harvey	Veitch,DD	Hamilton,W	WILKIE,W	Logie	Wilkie,J	Dougan	Dally,H
4	23-Aug	NEL 1s	Raith Rovers	4-3	Matthews	Hall,GA	Mackie	Brown	Veitch,DD	Hamilton,W	DINGWALL	Logie	WILKIE,J 2	Dougan	WILKIE,W
5	30-Aug	NEL 1s	LEITH ATHLETIC	5-3	Mathieson	Dick	Mackie	Brown	Cringan	Hall,GA	RAMSAY	LOGIE 3	Wilkie,J	HALDANE	Wilkie,W
6	06-Sep	NEL 1s	East Fife	2-4	Matthews	Junior	Mackie	Dingwall	Veitch,DD	Duffy,Jas	Ramsay	Logie	Wilkie,J	Brown	WILKIE,W
7	13-Sep	NEL 1s	Aberdeen	1-7	Matthews	Junior	Mackie	Dingwall	Wood	Hall,GA	WILKIE,J	Logie	Davie	Dougan	Dally,H
8	20-Sep	NEL 1s	RANGERS RESERVES	2-3	Matthews	Hall,GA	Mackie	Dingwall	VEITCH,DD	VEITCH,DD	Wilkie,J	LOGIE	WILKIE,J 3	Newman	VEITCH,DD
9	27-Sep	NEL 1s	DUNFERMLINE ATH	5-3	McKay	Hall,GA	Mackie	Dingwall	Junior	Veitch,DD	Wilkie,W	LOGIE	WILKIE,J	NEWMAN	Veitch,DD
10	04-Oct	NEL 1s	EAST FIFE	1-1	Matthews	Hall,GA	Mackie	Other,AN	Wood	Hamilton,W	WILKIE,W	Logie	Wilkie,J	DOUGAN	JUNIOR
11	11-Oct	NEL 1s	Dundee United	2-2	Matthews	Hall,GA	Newman	Dingwall	Wood	Junior	WILKIE,W	Logie	WILKIE,J	Dougan	Duffy,John
12	18-Oct	NEL 1s	Leith Athletic	3-3	Matthews	Newman	Newman	Dingwall	Wood	Junior	WILKIE,W	Logie	WILKIE,J	DOUGAN	Duffy,John
13	25-Oct	NEL 1s	Rangers Reserves	2-0	Matthews	Newman	Newman	Dingwall	Wood	Dingwall	WILKIE,W	Logie	WILKIE,J	Dougan	Duffy,John
14	01-Nov	NEL 1s	RAITH ROVERS	3-2	Matthews	Newman	Mackie	Veitch,DD	Dingwall	Duffy,Jas	Wilkie,W	LOGIE	WILKIE,J	Dougan	Duffy,John
15	08-Nov	NEL 1s	ABERDEEN	2-6	Matthews	Newman	Mackie	Veitch,DD	Dingwall	Duffy,Jas	Wilkie,W	LOGIE	WILKIE,J	Dougan	Duffy,John
16	15-Nov	NEC	Dundee United	1-7	Matthews	Philp	Mackie	Dingwall	Wood	Duffy,Jas	Wilkie,W	LOGIE	WILKIE,J	Dougan	Newman
17	22-Nov	NEC	EDINBURGH CITY	3-3	Matthews	Veitch,DD	Philp	Dingwall	Wood	Veitch,DD	WILKIE,W 2	Logie	Wilkie,J	Dougan	Duffy,John
18	29-Nov	ESS1	LEITH ATHLETIC	7-1	Matthews	Abbie	Philp	Dingwall	Wood	Duffy,Jas	WILKIE,W 2	Johnston	WILKIE,J	'Junior'	Duffy,John
19	06-Dec	BC1	ABERDEEN	2-4	Matthews	Newman	Mackie	Dingwall	Wood	Veitch,DD	Wilkie,W	Logie	Wilkie,J	Dougan	Newman
20	01-Jan	NEL 2s	Rangers Reserves	3-3	Matthews	Veitch,DD	Duffy,Jas	Dingwall	Wood	Hamilton,W	Wilkie,W	Dougan	Wilkie,J	Sharkey	VEITCH,DD
21	03-Jan	NEL 2s	Leith Athletic	1-5	Matthews	Junior	Other,AN	Dingwall	Wood	Veitch,DD	Wilkie,W	Logie	WILKIE,J	Dougan	Dally,H
22	17-Jan	NEL 2s	East Fife	0-3	Matthews	Harrower	Mackie	Stewart	Duffy	Duffy,John	WILKIE,J 2	Newman	WILKIE,W 2	'Junior'	Smith
23	14-Feb	NEL 2s	RANGERS RESERVES	5-6	Matthews	Harrower	Duffy,Jas	Dingwall	Wood	Hamilton,W	WILKIE	Other,AN	WILKIE,W	Smith	VEITCH,DD 2
24	21-Feb	NEL 2s	Leith Athletic	1-2	Matthews	Harrower	Duffy,Jas	Dingwall	Wood	Junior	WILKIE,J 2	Morgan	Newman	Duffy,Jas	Veitch,DD
25	28-Feb	NEL 2s	East Fife	2-3	Matthews	Junior	Harrower	Stewart	Dingwall	Dingwall	WILKIE	Logie	Falconer	Morgan	Duffy,John
26	14-Mar	NEL 2s	DUNDEE UNITED	1-3	Matthews	Abbie	Harrower	Dingwall	Murphy	Gilbert	WILKIE	Wilkie	Wilkie	Morgan	DUFFY,JOHN
27	21-Mar	NEL 2s	RAITH ROVERS	0-0	Matthews	Abbie	Harrower	Ireland	Murphy	Gilbert	Wilkie	Logie	WILKIE	Morgan	Duffy,John
28	28-Mar	NEL 2s	Dunfermline Athletic	2-2	Matthews	Harrower	Duffy,Jas	Stewart	Murphy	Gilbert	Moonie	Moonie	WILKIE	Moonie	DUFFY,JOHN
29	04-Apr	NEL 2s	Dundee United	0-2	Matthews	Harrower	Duffy,Jas	Newman	Murphy	Gilbert	Moonie	Dingwall	Wilkie	Moonie	WILKIE
30	11-Apr	NEL 2s	DUNFERMLINE ATH	1-2	Matthews	Abbie	Harrower	Newman	McCaig	Junior	Newman	'Smith'	Falconer	Moonie	Other,AN
31	18-Apr	NEL 2s	Raith Rovers	2-5	Matthews	Abbie	Newman	Newman	Murphy	Gilbert	Moonie	Moonie	WILKIE 2	Junior	McDonald
32	20-Apr	ESSs	Hibernian	1-7	Matthews	Harrower	Morgan,A	Wilkie	Murphy	Hadley	'Newman'	Other,AN	Falconer	Morgan,J	Duffy,J
33	25-Apr	NEL 2s	Aberdeen	0-8	Junior	Newman	Harrower	Wilkie	Murphy	McDonald	Morgan	Falconer	WILKIE 2	Gilbert	DUFFY,JOHN
34	16-May	NEL 2s	East Fife	2-3	Matthews	Other,AN	Duffy,Jas	Gillies	Murphy	Gilbert	DOUGAL	Dingwall	Moonie	Junior	

St Bernards 2nd and 3rd XI Results 1879/86

1879/80

Date	Team		Opponent	Score
06-Sep		EDINA 2nd		1-1
04-Oct		RAEBURN		2-1
18-Oct		ROSE		2-8
08-Nov		RANGERS		4-1
15-Nov		ROVERS 2nd		4-1
29-Nov		Caledonian 2nd		5-0
20-Dec		HANOVER 2nd		1-1
07-Feb		CALEDONIAN 2nd		2-1
28-Feb		ROVERS 2nd		1-1
20-Mar		EDINA 2nd		2-0
27-Mar		BUCCLEUCH 2nd		2-1

1880/81

Date	Team		Opponent	Score
?	E 2nd XI C1		Bellevue 2nd	Win
11-Sep		HANOVER 2nd		2-1
02-Oct		WEST CALDER 2nd		4-2
09-Oct		Edina 2nd		4-3
23-Oct	E 2nd XI C2		Rovers 2nd	12-0
11-Dec	E 2nd XI C2		Burntisland Thistle 2nd	3-2
11-Dec St B 3rd XI v		ADVENTURERS		2-1
08-Jan	E 2nd XI C2		Burntisland Thistle 2nd	5-1
15-Jan		West Calder 2nd		1-1
12-Feb	E 2nd XI C3		Hanover 2nd	4-0
19-Feb		HEARTS 2nd		0-4
19-Feb		Rose		3-0
12-Mar	E 2nd XI C4		West Calder 2nd	5-3
19-Mar		North Star		Draw
19-Mar St B 3rd XI v		Leith Baltic		6-1
16-Apr St B 3rd XI v		Midlothian		0-3
23-Apr		ADVENTURERS		4-0
?	E 2nd XI CF		Hibernian 2nd	1-7

1881/82

Date	Team		Opponent	Score
?	E 2nd XI C2		Trafalgar 2nd	6-0
?	E 2nd XI C3		Norton Park 2nd	9-2
17-Sep		Hearts 2nd		0-5
24-Sep		KINLEITH 2nd		8-1
01-Oct		ADDIEWELL 2nd		8-0
29-Oct E 2nd XI C1		Edina 2nd		5-1
12-Nov		Harp		5-0
19-Nov St B 3rd XI v		Selkirk		4-1
10-Dec St B 3rd XI v		Western		2-0
17-Dec		UNIVERSITY 2nd		11-0
24-Dec		ST JAMES (Scratch)		7-1
14-Jan	E 2nd XI C3		Hibernian 2nd	1-1
21-Jan		DUMBARTON 2		?
21-Jan St B 3rd XI v		Mayflower		3-2
28-Jan	E 2nd XI C3		HIBERNIAN 2nd	3-1
04-Feb St B 3rd XI v		Albany		5-0
11-Feb St B 3rd XI v		Easter		8-2
18-Feb		NORTON PARK 2nd		14-0
18-Mar		Lennox		2-3
25-Mar St B 3rd XI v		LORNE STAR		11-1
08-Apr	E 2nd XI CF		Hearts 2nd (n)	0-2

1882/83

Date	Team		Opponent	Score
?	E 2nd XI C2		Harp 2nd	WO
02-Sep		Third Lanark 2nd		0-3
02-Sep St B 3rd XI v		EASTER		3-2
23-Sep		ST GEORGE		12-1
07-Oct E 2nd XI C1		East Linton 2nd		8-0
14-Oct		ROSE		5-2
14-Oct St B 3rd XI v		MARMION (Scratch)		9-0
14-Oct St B 3rd XI v		ADVENTURERS 2nd		8-0
21-Oct St B 3rd XI v		Our Boys		2-5
04-Nov St B 3rd XI v		Belltane Birds		0-4
04-Nov		ST BERNARDS 1st		7-3
11-Nov		EDINA 2nd		13-1
18-Nov St B 3rd XI v		Easter		0-6
25-Nov		DUMBARTON 2nd		1-8
02-Dec		Hanover 2nd		4-2
23-Dec		AVONDALE		2-0
30-Dec St B 3rd XI v		Avondale 2nd		1-0
03-Feb E 2nd XI C3		DUNFERMLINE 2nd		14-1
17-Feb		ST JAMES		3-2
24-Feb		AVONDALE		6-2
03-Mar E 2nd XI C4		Hearts 2nd		1-2
10-Mar		EDINA 2nd		3-5
28-Apr		ST MIRREN 2nd		1-5

1883/84

Date	Team		Opponent	Score
01-Sep		THIRD LANARK 2nd		6-2
15-Sep S 2nd XI C?		ROYAL ALBERT 2nd		7-2
22-Sep		LEITH THISTLE		3-1
27-Oct S 2nd XI C?		DUNBLANE 2nd		12-1
03-Nov St B 3rd XI v		HEARTS Valleyfield		0-4
17-Nov S 2nd XI C?		COWLAIRS 2nd		4-1
24-Nov E 2nd XI C?		Selkirk 2nd		9-0
05-Jan E 2nd XI C?		HIBERNIAN 2nd		0-4

1884/85

Date	Team		Opponent	Score
19-Jan		NORTHERN		2-4
16-Feb		DUMBARTON 2nd		2-2
29-Nov		HARP		1-3
13-Dec		ST JAMES		1-3
27-Dec E 2nd XI CSF		HIBERNIAN 2nd		1-5
21-Feb		Glencairn 2nd		1-1

1885/86

Date	Team		Opponent	Score
29-Aug		Third Lanark 2nd		2-2
03-Oct		HIBERNIAN 2nd		1-2
17-Oct E 2nd XI C?		HEARTS 2nd		2-1
07-Nov		HEARTS 2nd		2-1
16-Jan		West Calder 2nd		2-0
06-Feb		Hearts 2nd		0-6
27-Feb		S HIGHLANDERS		10-0
06-Mar E 2nd XI CF		Hibernian 2nd		0-2

St Bernards 2nd XI 1886/87 and 1887/1888

Date	Competition	Opponent	Score	Team
1886/87				
04-Sep		2 Cambuslang	?	from Hutchison, Cuthbertson, McKail, McEwan, Jenkinson, Sutherland, Mackay,R. Bruce, Cannon, Carruthers and Greig.
18-Sep		2 POLTON VALE	?	
25-Sep		DALRY ALBERT	Win	
02-Oct		2 NORTON PARK	0-3	
09-Oct		2 Hearts	?	from Hutchison, Cuthbertson, Fleming, Ritchie, Garlick, Ramage, Kilgour, Pratt, Douglas, Neaves and Carruthers.
23-Oct		2 Adventurers	Win	
30-Oct E 2XI C?		WOODBURN	?	from Hutchison, Cuthbertson, Fleming, McKail, Jenkinson, Ritchie, Wight, Garlick, Bruce, Pratt and McIntosh.
13-Nov		2 Dunfermline	4-1	
20-Nov Cup tie		NORTHERN	?	
11-Dec		2 Falkirk	?	from Hutchison, Cuthbertson, Fleming, Garlick, Jenkinson, Ritchie, Wight, McIntoh, Bruce, Kilgour and Pratt.
18-Dec		2 PARTICK THISTLE	?	from Hutchison, Fleming, Cuthbertson, Ritchie, Jenkinson, Neaves, Wight, Bruce, Garlick, Kilgour and Pratt.
08-Jan		2 Hearts	?	from Hutchison, Fleming, Cuthbertson, Neaves, Garlick, Ritchie, Wight, McIntosh, Bruce, Kilgour and Pratt.
15-Jan		2 Broxburn Shamrock	?	from Hutchison, Fleming, Cuthbertson, Neaves, Garlick, Ritchie, Wight, McIntosh, Bruce, Kilgour and Pratt.
22-Jan E 2XI C?		LORNE STAR	Win	from Hutchison, Fleming, Cuthbertson, ?, ?, ?, Wight, Garlick, Bruce, Kilgour and Pratt. Res McIntosh and Lang.
05-Feb		2 HEARTS	?	
12-Feb		HIBS ATHLETIC	1-3	
19-Feb		Hibs Athletic	3-0	from Miller, Fleming, Cuthbertson, Jenkinson, Ritchie, Garlick, Kilgour, Pratt, Bruce, Wight and McIntosh.
26-Feb		2 Glencairn	Win	from Miller, Fleming, Cuthbertson, Ritchie, O'Donnell, Garlick, Wight, McIntosh, Lee, Kilgour and Pratt
05-Mar E 2XI Cs		2 Hearts	2-6	from Miller, Fleming, Cuthbertson, Ritchie, O'Donnell, Garlick, Wight, McIntosh, Lee,J, Pratt and Kilgour.
19-Mar E 2XI CF		2 CLAREMONT PARK	?	
23-Apr				
1887/88				
20-Aug		Raith Rovers	6-2	from Coltherd, McMurtrie, Fleming, Ritchie, McMillan, Garlick, Lamb, Bruce, Jenkinson, Pratt and Kilgour.
27-Aug		Leith Windsor	8-0	from Baillie, Ross, Fleming, Ritchie, McMurtrie, Garlick, Lamb, Bruce, Arthur, Pratt and Kilgour.
03-Sep		MID LOTHIAN	8-0	from Baillie, Schobread, Fleming, Ritchie, Ritchie, McMillan, Garlick, Lamb, Bruce, Wight, Pratt and Kilgour.
10-Sep		BONNYRIGG ROSE	8-1	from Sutherland, McMurtrie, Fleming, Ritchie, McMillan, Garlick, Bruce, Lamb, Wight, Pratt and Kilgour.
17-Sep		2 Hibernian	3-2	McMurtrie Sutherland Fleming Ritchie McMillan Garlick Lamb Bruce McIntosh Kilgour
24-Sep		LORNE STAR	4-1	McMurtrie, Anderson, Fleming, Ritchie, McMillan, Garlick, Lamb, Bruce, McIntosh, Pratt and Kilgour.
01-Oct S 2XI C		2 BONESS	2-0	McMurtrie Anderson Fleming Ritchie McMillan Sutherland Garlick Bruce McIntosh Pratt Kilgour
08-Oct		2 LEITH ATHLETIC	10-2	
15-Oct		2 MOSSEND SWIFTS	8-0	
22-Oct S 2XI C3		2 HEARTS	1-5	McMurtrie Anderson Fleming Ritchie McMillan Garlick Lamb Bruce McIntosh Pratt Kilgour
29-Oct EC		2 BROXBURN THISTLE	2-2	
05-Nov		Pling		
12-Nov EC		2 Broxburn Thistle	2-1	
19-Nov		ST BERNARD'S 1st XI	0-9	McMurtrie Anderson Fleming Garlick Ritchie Ross Mathieson Lamb Jenkinson Bruce Kilgour
26-Nov		2 Norton Park	5-2	
03-Dec		SCOTIA	3-1	
10-Dec		2 UNIVERSITY	?	
17-Dec		DALRY ALBERT	?	
24-Dec		2 ATHENIANS	10-1	
07-Jan		2 Leith Athletic	4-5	from McEwan, Anderson, Fleming, McMurtrie, Sutherland, AN Other, Ritchie, Bruce, Jenkinson, Pratt and McIntosh.
14-Jan EC SF		2 HEARTS	2-2	McEwan Muir Reid McMurtrie Kennedy Sutherland Lamb Bruce Tevioltdale McIntosh
21-Jan EC SF		2 Hearts	1-4	McEwan Muir Reid McMurtrie Kennedy Sutherland Lamb Tevioddale Bruce McIntosh Garlick
28-Jan		POLTON VALE	0-1	
04-Feb		WOODBURN	0-1	
11-Feb		2 UNIVERSITY	?	
25-Feb		Raith Rovers	4-2	from McEwan, Anderson, Reid, Corson, McMurtrie, Sutherland, Lamb, Teviotdale, Garlick, McNeil and Fleming.
03-Mar		DALRY ALBERT	?	from McEwan, Anderson, Reid, Corson, McMurtrie, Sutherland, Lamb, Baird, Muir, Garlick and McNeill.
10-Mar		2 CLAREMONT PARK	?	
17-Mar		2 Mossend Swifts	1-3	
24-Mar		Linlithgow Atheltic	3-4	
31-Mar		2 HEARTS	0-2	
07-Apr		2 Burntisland Thistle	?	
14-Apr		Bonyrigg Rose	?	
28-Apr		WOODBURN	?	

St Bernards 2nd XI 1888/1889 and 1889/1890

Date		Opponent	Score	Team
25-Aug	1888/89	2 CHAMPFLEURIE	Can	from McEwan, Anderson, Fleming, Sutherland, Rennie, Childe, Lamb, Colthart, Garlick, Lyle and Kilgour.
08-Sep	S 2XI C2	2 HIBERNIAN	6-1	McDiarmid Anderson Muir Lamb,T Colthart Childe Mathieson Arthur
15-Sep		2 LEITH WINDSOR	?	from McEwan, Childe, Sutherland, McKail, McDougall, Garlick, Lamb, Colthard, Cant, Mathieson and Lyall.
22-Sep		2 Renton	1-8	from McEwan, Smith, Graham, Garlick, McKail, McDougall, Lamb, Colthard, Cant, Anderson and Lyle.
29-Sep		WOODBURN	1-12	
06-Oct		Victoria (Haddington)		
13-Oct	E 2XI C	2 LEITH ATHLETIC	2-1	from Jamieson, Anderson, AN Other, Garlick, McKail, Ritchie, McIntosh, Dorkin, Irvine, Cant and Colthart.
20-Oct	S 2XI C3	2 Renton	0-6	from Jamieson, Guild, Anderson, Taylor, Garlick, Fleming, McIntosh, Arthur, Riddle, Lamb and Cant.
27-Oct		PILRIG	?	from Grant, Guild, Gough, Garlick, McKail, Fleming, McIntosh, Lyle, Cant, Lamb and Colthart.
03-Nov	E 2XI C	2 Broxburn	3-2	
10-Nov		ST BERNARDS 1st XI	1-2	
17-Nov		2 Champfleurie	2-5	from Jamieson, Guild, AN Other, McKail, Greenshields, Garlick, Colthart, Cant, Dorkin, Forbes, and Arthur.
24-Nov		2 RENTON	4-2	from Scoales, Anderson, Guild, Ritchie, Greenshields, McKail, Colthart, Cant, Dorkin, Irving and Forbes.
01-Dec		2 ADVENTURERS	0-4	
22-Dec		DUNROBIN	?	
12-Jan		2 MOSSEND SWIFTS	1-0	from Jamieson, Guild, Goodfellow, Ritchie, Tait, Geenshields, Lamb, Baird, Baillie, Cant and Colthart.
19-Jan		2 HEARTS	1-1	from Jamieson, Goodfellow, Guild, Garlick, Ritchie, Greenshields, McIntosh, Colthard, Dorkin, Lamb and Cant.
02-Feb	E 2XI CSF	2 ADVENTURERS	1-0	from Scoales, Goodfellow, Guild, Garlick, Ritchie, McKail, Irving, Lamb, Cant, Colthart and Forbes.
09-Feb		2 Leith Athletic	?	from Jamieson, Denholm, Goodfellow, Fleming, Ritchie, McKail, Taylor, Forbes, Dorkin, Colthart and Irving.
16-Feb		ST BERNARDS 1st XI	2-4	from Jamieson, Denholm, Goodfellow, Fleming, Ritchie, McKail, Garlick, Mathieson, Aitken, Cant and Colthart.
23-Feb		DALRY ALBERT		Scoales Goodfellow Guild McKail Ritchie Fleming Colthart Cant McEwan Forbes Irving
02-Mar		2 CAMBUSLANG	draw	from Jamieson, Goodfellow, Denholm, McKail, Anderson, Ritchie, Cant, Colthart, Garlick, Irving and Mathieson.
09-Mar	E 2XI CF	2 HEARTS	3-2	from Scoales, Guild, Goodfellow, Fleming, Ritchie, McKail, Irving, Forbes, Garlick, Colthart and Cant.
16-Mar		WOODBURN	?	Jamieson Guild Goodfellow Fleming Ritchie McKail Irving Forbes Dorkin Cant Colthart
30-Mar		2 Hearts	0-1	from Jamieson, Guild, Goodfellow, Fleming, Garlick, McKail, Cant, Bayliss, Jenkinson, Colthart and McMurtrie.
31-Aug	1889/90	2 Leith Athletic	1-3	
14-Sep	S 2XI C1	2 Leith Athletic	1-6	from Baillie, Adams, Whitelaw, Walker, Roberts, Fleming, Lamb, Colthart, McMurtrie, Bruce and McIntosh.
21-Sep		Haddington Wanderers	0-1	from Heatherill, Adams, Smith, Walker, McKail, Brown, Porter, Colthart, AN Other, Bruce and McIntosh.
28-Sep		2 NORTON PARK	Win	from Heatherill, Adams, Smith, Walker, Fleming, Brown, Colthart, Porter, Baillie, Mathieson and McIntosh.
05-Oct		Polton Vale	?	
12-Oct	E 2XI C1	2 HIBERNIAN	3-2	from Scoales, Adams, Smith, Walker, Fleming, Brown, Black, Colthart, AN Other, Porter ad McIntosh.
19-Oct		Penicuik Athletic	6-0	from Scoales, Adams, Smith, Walker, McMurtrie, Brown, Porter, Colthart, Robertson, Bishop, and McIntosh.
26-Oct		BAINFIELD	?	from Scoales, Adams, Smith, Brown, McMurtrie, McKail, Porter, Colthart, Miller, Fleming and McIntosh.
02-Nov		2 NORTON PARK	3-2	
09-Nov		2 CLYDE	?	
16-Nov	E 2XI C3	2 MOSSEND SWIFTS	lost	from Scoales, Adams, Smith, Walker, Jacob, Brown, Simpson, Colthart, Forbes, McIntosh and Calder.
23-Nov		2 Leith Athletic	?	from Scoales, Adams, Walker, Jacob, Brown, Porter, Marshall, Angus, Forbes, McIntosh and Colthart.
07-Dec		2 EDINBURGH UNIV	?	from Scoales, Adams, 'Smith', 'Walker', Jacob, Cleuch, Porter, Robertson, Forbes, Bruce and Lowe.
21-Dec		2 Hearts	2-4	from Scoales, Adams, Smith, Brown, Jacob, Stevenson, Porter, Bell, Forbes, Lowe and McIntosh.
01-Jan		2 UDDINGSTON	4-1	Hall Brown Fleming Jacob Forbes Hutton Black Lamb Scoales Porter Lindsay
04-Jan		2 RENTON	?	from Scoales, Adams, Fleming, Brown, Jacob, Walker, Lowe, McIntosh, Forbes, Bell and Fee. Reserves Dudgeon and Porter.
25-Jan		DUNROBIN	?	from Scoales, Adams, Smith, Brown, Hill, Fleming, Porter, Colthart, McMurtrie, McIntosh. Lowe and Robertson.
01-Feb		Muirhouse Rovers	?	
08-Feb		NORTH WESTERN	?	
08-Mar		Queens Park Strollers (n)	?	
29-Mar		2 Leith Athletic	3-2	

St Bernards 2nd XI 1890/1891 and 1891/1892

1890/91

Date	Opponent	Score	Team
23-Aug	NORTH WESTERN	4-3	from Robertson, Scott, McKail, Milne, Moodie, Garlick, Lowe, Scott, Forbes, Baxter and McDonald.
30-Aug	2 Hibernian	3-1	
20-Sep E 2XI C	2 Armadale	?	
27-Sep	2 HEARTS	?	
17-Jan	CAROLINE	?	from Cantley, McLean, AN Other, Dunlop, Moodie, Davis, Taylor, Archibald, J Scott, Allan and Martin.
14-Feb	Muirhouse Rovers	2-6	

1891/92

Date	Opponent	Score	Team
15-Aug	BAINFIELD	2-3	Noble McLean,J Lawrie Smeaton
22-Aug	Lochgelly United	Win	
29-Aug	NORTH WESTERN	?	from McQueen, Mair, McLean, Lawrie, Dick, McFarlane, Smeaton, Baird, Purvis, Dobie and Shand.
05-Sep	4th VBRS	?	
12-Sep S 2XI C1	2 Leith Athletic	3-3	McQueen Mure Robertson Edgar Baird Lawrie Hogg Dobie Baxter Shand McDonald
26-Sep S 2XI C1	2 LEITH ATHLETIC	3-5	McQueen Robertson Reid Lawrie Baird Edgar Hogg Dobie Baxter Shand McDonald
03-Oct	2 HEARTS	1-3	Robertson McLean
10-Oct E 2XI C	2 Adventurers	?	from McQueen, Robertson, McLean, Lawrie, Baird, Edgar, Hogg, Dobie, Bell, Baxter and Shand.
17-Oct	Burntisland Thistle	?	from McQueen, Robertson, McLean, Lawrie, Baird, Edgar, Hogg, Dobie, Baxter, Christie and Shand.
07-Nov	2 University	?	from McQueen, Robertson, McLean, Lawrie, Baird, Edgar, Hogg, Dobie, Reid, Christie and Shand.
14-Nov E 2XI C	2 Bathgate Rovers	5-1	from McQueen, Robertson, McLean, Lawrie, Baird, Edgar, Notman, Dobie, Baxter, Christie and Shand.
21-Nov	WEST CALDER	5-1	
28-Nov E 2XI C	Cowdenbeath	?	from Cantley, Robertson, Hogg, Reid,C, McDonald, Edgar, Reid,J, Taylor, Baxter, Christie and Shand.
12-Dec	Penicuik Athletic	0-1	from McQueen, Robertson, Hogg, Reid,C, McDonald, Edgar, Reid,J, Dobie, Baxter, Taylor and Shand.
19-Dec	2 Leith Athletic	WO	
26-Dec E 2XI CSF	2 Dunfermline Athletic	?	from McQueen, Robertson, Hogg, Reid,C, McDonald, Edgar, Reid,J, Taylor, Baxter, Dobie, Shand, Cantley, McLean, Lumsden.
26-Dec	MILTON HOUSE	3-1	
01-Jan	2 RENTON	Can	
16-Jan	2 LEITH ATHLETIC	3-1	from McQueen, Robertson, Watson, McLean, Lawrie, McDonald, Reid, Taylor, Hogg, Summers, Dobie and Shand.
23-Jan	2 Broxburn	10-1	from McQueen, Robertson, Watson, McLean, Reid, McDonald, Edgar, Taylor, Reid, Hogg, Dobie and Shand.
30-Jan	Dalkeith Thistle	3-0	from McQueen, Robertson, Watson, McLean, Reid, McDonald, Edgar, Taylor, Lawrie, Hogg, Dobie and Shand.
06-Feb	PRIMROSE	?	from Walker, Robertson, McLean, Lawrie, Watson, Reid, Taylor, Hogg, McFarlane, Dobie and Shand.
13-Feb	Polton Vale	2-4	McQueen Robertson McLean Lawrie Turner Edgar Dobie Fairley Young Shand
27-Feb E 2XI CF	2 Hearts	?	from McQueen, Robertson, McLean, Lawrie, Tait, Edgar, Taylor, Reid, Finlay, Dobie and Shand.
02-Apr	Pathhead Utd (Kirk)	0-4	from McQueen, Robertson, McLean, Lawrie, Tait, Edgar, Taylor, Hogg, Finlay, Dobie and Shand.
09-Apr	2 LEITH ATHLETIC	4-2	from McQueen, Robertson,T, Lawrie, Reid,J, Edgar, Taylor, Hogg, Baxter, Dobie and Shand.
23-Apr	VIRGINIANS	?	from McQueen, Robertson, Hogg, Lawrie, Cantley, Edgar, Taylor, Dobie, Baxter, Shand and Lamb.
30-Apr	MUIRHOUSE ROVERS	?	
07-May	2 Hearts	0-2	

St Bernards 2nd XI 1892/1893 and 1893/1894

1892/93

Date	Opponent	Score	Team
06-Aug	Penicuik Athletic	?	from McQueen, Robertson, Kennedy, McDonald, Gray, Ballantine, Shand, Hogg, Baxter, Laverock and Lamb.
20-Aug	Pumpherston	1-5	
27-Aug	Bonnyrigg Rose	?	from Cantley, Malcolm, Williams, Ballantine, McDonald, Baxter, Hogg, Reid, Johnstone, Scott and Alexander
03-Sep	Haddington Wanderers	0-8	from McQueen D, Hogg G, Robertson T, Baxter A, McDonald G, Ballantine J, Brookes G, Reid J, Johnston, McFarlane and Scott T.
10-Sep S 2XI C1	2 Leith Athletic	?	McQueen Hogg Ballantine Cantley Baxter McDonald Robertson Reid Johnston Scott Melville
17-Sep	Peebles	?	
24-Sep	PORTOBELLO	2-0	from McQueen D, Hogg, Robertson W, McKail, McDonald, Govan, Reid, Melville, Johnston, Lawrie J and McLean.
01-Oct	LEITH CELTIC	?	from McQueen, Robertson, Lawrie, Ritchie, McDonald, Walker, Melville, Scott J, Hogg, Robertson and Reid
08-Oct E 2XI C1	2 ADVENTURERS	3-1	from McQueen, Robertson T, Lawrie, McDonald, Reid, Brooke, Melville, Johnston, Scott and Hogg.
15-Oct	Dunfermline Juniors	8-1	from McQueen, Robertson T, Lawrie, McDonald, Purvis, Brooke, Melville, AN Other, Scott and Baxter.
05-Nov	R&R CLARK'S	?	
19-Nov E 2XI C3	2 LEITH ATHLETIC	1-3	McQueen Robertson,W Robertson,T Lawrie Hogg McDonald Brooke Tait Johnston Baxter Landells
03-Dec	MUIRHOUSE ROVERS	3-0	from Cantley, Robertson W, Melrose, Lawrie, McDonald, McGinlay, Brook, Tait, Baxter, Laverock and Landells.
10-Dec	Bonnyrigg Rose	3-1	from McQueen, Robertson W, Robertson T, Lawrie, Baxter, McGinlay, Brook, Hogg, Melville, Melrose and Laverock.
17-Dec	2 LARKHALL	1-2	from McQueen, Robertson W, Robertson T, Lawrie, McDonald, McGinley, Brook, "Hogg", Collins, Landells and Laverock.
24-Dec	West Calder Wanderers	0-3	from McQueen, Robertson W, Robertson T, Robb, Cantley, McDonald, Hogg, Brooke, Thomson, Smith, 'Small' and Landells
31-Dec	Portobello	4-1	from McQueen, Robertson W, Robertson T, Cantley, McDonald, Robb, Hogg, Johnston, 'Small', Smith and Landells
03-Jan		Can	
07-Jan E 2XI C3	2 RENTON	?	
21-Jan	2 LEITH ATHLETIC	2-3	McQueen Robertson,W Robertson,T Lawrie Cantley Hogg Melrose Johnston Collins Laverock Landells
11-Feb	Heriotonians	1-2	from McQueen, Robertson W, Robertson T, Lawrie, McDonald, Robb, Brooke, Gibson, Collins, Tait and Landells.
18-Mar	HERIOTONIANS	1-2	from McQueen, Robertson W, Robertson T, Lawrie, McDonald, McGinley, Brooke, Hogg, Collins, Laverock and Landells.
25-Mar	Bathgate Athletic	0-3	from McQueen, Robertson T, Robb, Cantley, McDonald, Hogg, Brooke, Thomson, Smith, 'Small' and Landells
01-Apr	2 HIBERNIAN	7-0	from McQueen, Robertson W, Robertson T, Cantley, McDonald, Robb, Hogg, Johnston, 'Small', Smith and Smith.
08-Apr	Muirhouse Rovers	3-2	from McQueen, Robertson W, Robertson T, Lawrie, McDonald, Robb, Brooke, Hogg, 'Small', Robertson and Smith.
15-Apr	Arniston Rangers	?	from McQueen, Robertson W, Robertson T, Hogg, Cantley, Robb, Brooke, Robertson A, 'Small', Collins and Landels
22-Apr	HADDINGTON WANDS	6-0	from McQueen, Robertson W, Robertson T, Cantley, Baxter, Robb, Brooke, Robertson A, Collins, AN Other and Landels
29-Apr	Newtongrange Ath		
	Bonnyrigg Rose	3-3	from McQueen, Robertson W, Robertson T, Baxter, Cantley, Robb, Brooke, Robertson A, 'Small', Collins and Landels

1893/94

Date	Opponent	Score	Team
19-Aug	DUNFERMLINE ATH JNRS	6-6	from Fyfe, Robertson, Phillips, Ritchie, Murdoch, Martin, Landells, Steel, Collins, Laverock and Phillips. Res. Foy and Lyon.
26-Aug	Rangers Swifts	2-2	from Fyfe, Phillips, Robertson, Martin, Ritchie, McDonald, Laverock, Dobie, Steel, Landells and Phillips
02-Sep	DUMBARTON RANGERS	5-1	from Fyfe, Phillips, Robertson W, Martin, Ritchie, McDonald, Landells, Laverock, Smeaton, Foy and Phillips.
09-Sep	PORTOBELLO	10-2	from Fyfe, Phillips, Robertson, Martin, McDonald, AN Other, Smeaton, Laverock, Steel, Dobie and Phillips.
23-Sep	Linlithgow Athletic	4-3	
30-Sep S 2XI C2	2 Leith Athletic (n)	4-1	from Fyfe, Phillips, Robertson, Martin, McDonald, Moyes, Landells, Laverock, Johnston, Dobie and Phillips.
14-Oct E 2XI C	2 PENICUIK ATHLETIC	18-0	
21-Oct S 2XI C3	2 East Stirling	3-1	from Fyfe, Phillips, Hogg, Martin, McDonald, Moyes, Phillips, Laverock, Steel, Dobie and Landels.
28-Oct E 2XI C1	2 Bathgate	5-3	from Fyfe, Robertson, AN Other, Martin, McDonald, Moyes, Phillips, Laverock, Steel, Dobie and Landels.
04-Nov	Dumbarton Rangers	?	
11-Nov S 2XI C4	2 ALBION ROVERS	2-1	from Fyfe, Robertson, Cowan, Martin, McDonald, Moyes, Wilson, Laverock, Steel, Dobie and Phillips.
18-Nov	2 LEITH ATHLETIC	3-2	
25-Nov	A&S HIGHLANDERS	6-1	from Fyfe, Robertson, Cowan, Martin, McDonald, Moyes, Landells, Steel, Johnston, Dobie and Phillips.
02-Dec S 2XI C5	2 St Mirren	0-3	from Fyfe, Robertson, Cowan, Martin, McDonald, Moyes, Landells, Steel, Johnston, Laverock and Phillips.
09-Dec E 2XI CSF	2 Edinburgh University	9-1	from Fyfe, Robertson, Cowan, Martin, McDonald, Moyes, Landells, Steel, Johnston, Dobie and Laverock.
16-Dec	HERIOTONIANS	6-0	from Fyfe, Robertson, Cowan, Martin, Johnston, Moyes, Landells, Laverock, Steel, Dobie and Laverock.
30-Dec	Broxburn	2-2	from Rust, Robertson, Cowan, Martin, Johnston, Moyes, Landells, Laverock,Somerville, Dobie and Phillips.
01-Jan	2 Port Glasgow Athletic	6-1	
13-Jan	Penicuik Athletic	5-0	from Weatherhead, Robertson, Cowan, Martin, McDonald, Moyes, Landells, Johnston, Somerville, Laverock and Phillips.
20-Jan	2 Hearts	2-2	from Dobie, Robertson, Cowan, Martin, McDonald, Moyes, Landells, Johnston, Somerville, Laverock and Phillips.

St Bernards 2nd XI 1893/1894 and 1894/1895

	1893/94			
27-Jan		Polton Vale	7-4	from Dobie, Robertson, Cowan, Martin, McDonald, Moyes, Johnston, Steel, Somerville, Laverock and Phillips.
03-Feb		Dykehead	3-3	from Dobie, Robertson, Cowan, Martin, McDonald, Moyes, Johnston, Steel, Somerville, Laverock and Phillips.
10-Feb		RANGERS SWIFTS	3-2	from Reid, Robertson, Cowan, Martin, McDonald, Moyes, Johnston, 'White', Somerville, Laverock and Phillips.
17-Feb		BROXBURN ATHLETIC	?	
24-Feb		Linlithgow Athletic	7-5	from Reid, Robertson, Cowan, Martin, Sibbald, McDonald, Moyes, Johnston, Steel, Johnston, Laverock and Phillips.
03-Mar	E 2XI CF	2 Hearts (n)	3-4	Reid, Robertson, Cowan, Martin, McDonald, Moyes, Johnston, Steel, Somerville, Laverock and Phillips.
10-Mar		2 Edinburgh Univerers	10-3	Gilbert Robertson Cowan Martin McDonald Moyes Johnstone Steel Somerville Laverock Phillips
17-Mar		Armadale Volunteers	0-3	
24-Mar		BROXBURN ATHLETIC	3-1	from Gilbert, Robertson, Martin, Johnston, McDonald, Moyes, Landels, Steel, Somerville, Dobie and Phillips.
31-Mar		Bonnyrigg Rose	1-0	from Gilbert, Robertson, Martin, Johnston, Urquhart, Moyes, Landels, Laverock, Steel, Dobie and Phillips.
07-Apr		DUNFERMLINE JUNIORS	7-1	from Gilbert, Robertson, Martin, Johnston, Urquhart, Moyes, Landels, Dobie, Somerville, Laverock and Phillips.
14-Apr		Kirkcaldy	4-7	from Gilbert, Martin, Robertson, Urquhart, McDonald, Moyes, Landels, Dobie, Somerville, Laverock and Phillips.
21-Apr		2 Leith Athletic	2-9	
28-Apr		Polton Vale	2-1	
	1894/95			
01-Sep	S 2XI C1	BROXBURN ATH	1-3	
08-Sep		2 Mossend Swifts	3-4	
15-Sep		NEWTONGRANGE ATH	3-2	from Ramage, Brown, Robertson, Kirkwood, Reid, Middleton, Flynn, Craigie, McGill, Seaton and Learmonth.
22-Sep		Bonnyrigg Rose	5-6	from Ramage, Brown, Robertson, Martin, Middleton, Flynn, Craigie, Flynn, Reid, Seaton Learmonth. Res Ferguson Adams.
29-Sep		HERIOTONIANS	8-3	from Ramage, Brown, Robertson, Kirkwood, Middleton, Linton, Flynn, Craigie, McGill, Reid and Seaton.
06-Oct		LOCHGELLY UNITED	1-1	from Rutherford, Brown, Robertson, Kirkwood, Middleton, Linton, Reid, Craigie, Flynn, Wilson and Learmonth.
13-Oct		Woodburn	Can	
20-Oct		MUSSELBURGH Windsor	5-2	from Rutherford, Brown, Robertson, Kirkwood, Martin, Middleton, Reid, Craigie, Flynn, Law and Learmonth.
27-Oct		2 Leith Athletic	5-5	from Rutherford, Brown, Robertson, Middleton, Reid, Linton, Inglis, Craigie, Flynn, Seaton and Learmonth.
03-Nov		Newtongrange Athletic	4-1	from AN Other, Brown, Robertson, Middleton, Martin, Linton, Craigie, Inglis, Flynn, Law Learmonth. Res Brown Ferguson.
10-Nov		BONNYRIGG ROSE	1-3	
17-Nov		Trinity	?	
01-Dec		Dunfermline Juniors	0-5	from Ruxton, Mechan, Robertson, Martin, Middleton, Linton, Inglis, Law, Flynn, Hogg Learmonth Ferguson.
15-Dec		2 Leith Athletic	2-3	from Ruxton, Robertson, Linton, Martin, Middleton, Ferguson, Inglis, Law, Flynn, Adams, Hogg and Learmonth.
22-Dec		HERIOTONIANS	4-1	from Hunter, Robertson, Learmonth, Martin, AN Other, Linton, Inglis, Law, Adams, Lafferty and Sharp.
29-Dec		LEITH CELTIC	Can	from Hunter, Mechan, Learmonth, Martin, Urquhart, Middleton, Inglis, Richards, Adams, Law Sharp. Res Ferguson Flynn.
12-Jan		LEITH RANGERS	2-1	from Hunter, Mechan, Linton, Urquhart, Grelicha, Middleton, Flynn, Inglis, Adams, Henderson, Sharp and Ferguson.
19-Jan		EDINBURGH RENTON	Can	
02-Feb		2 LEITH ATHLETIC	Can	from Hunter, Mechan, Robertson, Martin, Middleton, Linton, Urquhart, Ferguson, Adams, Richards, Law, Sharp and Learmonth.
09-Feb		WOODBURN	5-0	from Hunter, Stewart, Robertson, Martin, Urquhart, Middleton, Campbell, Adams, Richards, Law, Sharp, Learmonth and Ferguson.
23-Feb		WOODBURN	5-0	
02-Mar		2 LEITH ATHLETIC	0-3	from Hunter Mechan 'Robertson' Learmonth Stevenson Urquhart Middleton Campbell Adams 'AN Other' Richards Law Ferguson.
23-Mar		Musselburgh Windsor	3-1	from Hunter, Linton, Learmonth, Urquhart, Malcolm, Middleton, Campbell, Ferguson, McNab, Law, Sharp, Richards, Adams.
30-Mar		Penicuik Athletic	3-4	from Hunter, Linton, Learmonth, Urquhart, Malcolm, Duke, Ferguson, Adams, Richards, Law, Craigie, McFarlane.
06-Apr		Polton Vale	5-5	from Hunter, Linton, Learmonth, Urquhart, Malcolm, Middleton, Duke, Campbell, Ferguson, Adams, McFarlane, Law, Craigie.
13-Apr		DUNFERMLINE ATHLETIC	1-2	
27-Apr		2 Leith Athletic	2-4	
11-May				

St Bernards 2nd XI 1895/1896 and 1896/1897

Date	Opponent	Score	Team
			1895/96
24-Aug	DUNFERMLINE	9-1	from Hunter, O'Brien, Dundas, Ward, Middleton, Reid, Law, Muirhead, Lyons, McNamee and Campbell.
31-Aug	2 LEITH ATHLETIC	6-0	from Hunter, Dundas, Hall, Middleton, Wark, Reid, Campbell, Muirhead, Law, Laing and Ferguson.
14-Sep	2 CAMELON (S 2XI C)	3-3	
21-Sep	2 Camelon (n) (S 2XI C)	4-1	
28-Sep	2 Leith Athletic (S 2XI C)	1-3	
05-Oct	PEEBLES	6-1	
12-Oct	BROXBURN	4-2	
26-Oct	2 Leith Athletic	1-9	
16-Nov	BLACK WATCH	1-3	from Hunter, McLean, Kinross, Wilson, McManus, Russell, Campbell, Muirhead, Ferguson, Wark and Richards.
23-Nov	LENZIE	4-0	from Hunter Kinross Welsh Wilson McKinnon Middleton Campbell Brooks Smeaton McLean Muirhead Res Richards Ferguson Hogg
30-Nov	Dunfermline Ath Jnrs	3-2	from Hunter, Kinross, Smeaton, Wilson, McManus, Middleton, Campbell, Otto, McIntosh, Mclean and Wark
07-Dec	HAMILTON ACCIES	1-2	from Hunter 'McGowan' Kinross Backie McManus Middleton McKinnon 'Donnell' Wilkie McLean Wark Smeaton Ferguson Richards
14-Dec	Penicuik	3-3	from Hunter, Smeaton, Middleton, McEwan, McManus, Backie, Kinross, Wilkie, Brown, McLean and Ferguson.
21-Dec	ARNISTON RANGERS	4-3	from Hunter, Kinross, Phillips, Wilson, McEwan, Backie, Wilkie, McQueen', 'Thomson', McLean and Muirhead.
28-Dec	Perthshire	1-3	from Hunter, Hall, Phillips, Middleton, McEwan, Backie, Wilkie, McQueen', 'Thomson', McLean, Ferguson, Richards and Ferguson
01-Jan	Duns	0-4	
11-Jan	Dalkeith Rangers	4-2	from Hunter, Kinross, Phillips, McManus, McEwan, Middleton, Kirkham, Wilkie, McLean and Cunningham.
18-Jan	TRINITY	3-1	Hunter Kinross Pillar McManus Middleton McEwan Wilson Wilkie Brown McLean Cunningham
25-Jan	2 Dundee	2-2	from Hunter, McLean, Pillar, Wilson, McEwan, Middleton, Wilkie, Brown, Cunningham, Phillips and Kirkham.
01-Feb	Arniston Rangers	4-3	from Hunter, McLean, Phillips, Wilson, Middleton, Wilkie, Ferguson, Downie, McManus, Hall, McEwan, Richards and Cunningham.
15-Feb	Dunfermline	2-1	from Hunter, McLean, Phillips, McManus, McEwan, Middleton, Wilson, Wilkie, Brown, Cunningham, Richards and Ferguson.
22-Feb	Kirkcaldy	2-4	from Hunter, McLean, Hall, Russell, McEwan, Middleton, Richards, Wilkie, Brown, Cunningham and Martin.
29-Feb	PENICUIK ATHLETIC	off	
07-Mar	Hamilton Accies	?	from Hunter, McLean, 'Thomson', McEwan, Baird, Middleton, McGraw, Wilkie, Ferguson, Martin, Cunningham, Richards and Seaton.
14-Mar	Armadale	3-1	
28-Mar	Clackmannan	5-1	from Hunter, Hall, Pillar, Russell, McEwan, Robertson, McGraw, Ferguson, Laing, Muirhead and Martin.
04-Apr	BROXBURN SHAMROCK	2-4	
18-Apr	Lenzie	5-0	from Hunter, Hall, Bennett, ?, ?, Robertson, McGraw, Brown, Laing, ?, ?.
25-Apr	Cowdenbeath	1-6	from Hunter, Campbell, 'Moodie', Murdoch, Low, Middleton, McGraw, Law, Brown, Muirhead, Martin and McEwan.
			1896/97
22-Aug	BATHGATE	11-2	from Rutherford, Middleton, Russell, Murdoch, Low, Jack, Scott, Walker, Provan, Peden, Martin, Neilson, Ferguson and McGraw.
29-Aug	Lanark	?	from Rutherford, Middleton, Barton, Murdoch, Low, Scott, Jack, Peden Barbour, Wark, Neilson, Martin, Ferguson and McGraw.
05-Sep	Fair City Athletic	0-0	Rutherford Middleton Murdoch Wark Jack Scott Wilson Peden Laing Barbour McGraw
12-Sep	Cambuslang	4-4	from Rutherford, Middleton, Graham, Murdoch, Jack, Scott, Wilson, Barbour, Provan, Russell, Martin, Lowe and McGraw.
19-Sep	Kilsyth Wanderers	6-3	from Rutherford, Middleton, Kennedy, Christie, Lowe, Scott, Wilson, Peden, Provan, Bell, Barbour, Jack and Laing.
26-Sep	POLTON VALE (ESS 1)	9-0	Rutherford Murdoch Middleton Wark Lowe Scott Wilson Peden Provan Laing Dobie
03-Oct	Kirkcaldy	4-6	
10-Oct	TRINITY (ESS 2)	3-1	from Rutherford, Scott, Kinross or Wark, Lowe, Russell, Wilson, Peden, Jack, Barbour and Dobie. Res. Stewart. Martin.
24-Oct	Adventurers (KC 1)	2-1	
24-Oct	DUNIPACE		
31-Oct	Peebles (ESS 4)	5-1	from Rutherford, Middleton, Russell, Kinross, Lowe, Scott, Murdoch, Wilson, Peden, Jack, Bell, Barbour, McGraw, McEwing Fisher.
07-Nov	PEEBLES (KC 2)	WO	from Rutherford, Pillar, Russell, Mudoch, Lowe, Scott, Wilson, Paton, Barbour, Hutton, Fisher, McGraw and Kinross.
14-Nov	Penicuik Athletic	2-3	from Rutherford, Kinross, Russell, Murdoch, Lowe, Scott, Wilson, Paton, Barbour, Henderson, Neilson, Jack and McGraw.
21-Nov	BROX. Shrock (ESS sf)	5-1	Rutherford 'Alexander' Russell Murdoch Lowe Scott Provan Peden Henderson Neilson Barbour
28-Nov	Dunfermline Athletic	6-2	
05-Dec	Clackmannan (KC3)	2-1	
19-Dec	Mossend Swifts	0-4	from Hunter, Pillar, Kinross, Murdoch, Lowe, Scott, Wilson, Henderson, Robertson, Barbour and Neilson.
26-Dec	Raith Rovers	2-3	from Rutherford, Pillar, Hogg, Kinross, Lowe, Scott, Wilson, Henderson, Robertson, Barbour and Black.

St Bernards 2nd XI 1896/1897 and 1898/1899

Date	Opponent	Score	Team
16-Jan	2 LEITH ATHLETIC	3-2	Buxton Hogg Wood Christie Tumbull Lowe Henderson Wilson Robertson McGraw Barber
06-Feb	2 Leith Athletic	4-3	Hastie Adams Wood Middleton Lowe Murdoch Brady Wilson Neilson McGraw Henderson
20-Feb	ROYAL SCOTS	0-1	Borer Adams Duncan Murdoch Lowe Middleton Wilson Ferguson Colthard 'Newman' Wood
27-Feb	CAMBUSLANG	0-4	Rutherford, Adams, Duncan, Middleton, Murdoch, Lowe, Christie, Wilson, Brady, Colthard, Wilson, Buchanan, Henderson Barbour.
06-Mar	Cowdenbeath (n) (ESSf)	2-2	Rutherford Duncan Kinross Wark Lowe Murdoch Wilson Brady Provan Henderson Neilson
13-Mar	Cowdenbeath (n) (ESSf)	3-2	Rutherford Duncan Kinross Wark Lowe Murdoch Wilson Brady Provan Neilson Henderson
20-Mar	LOCHGELLY Utd (KCsf)	1-0	
27-Mar	Raith Rovers	0-4	from Rutherford, Ross, Duncan, Brodie, Middleton, Murdoch, Wilson, Coltherd, McLeod, Neilson and Henderson.
03-Apr	Polton Vale (n) (KCf)	2-2	Rutherford Duncan Reece Brodie Lowe Murdoch Wilson Brady Neilson McGraw Henderson
17-Apr	2 HEARTS (E 2XI C)	0-3	Rutherford Duncan Kinross Middleton Murdoch Ramsay Wilson Brady 'Steen' McMillan Neilson
14-May	2 HEARTS (E 2XI C)	1-11	

1898/99

Date	Opponent	Score	Team
03-Sep	Dumfries	1-3	
10-Sep	Dunfermline Ath Jnrs	2-1	from Barclay, Kay, Young, Alexander, Williams, Phillips, Edmonds, McKenzie, Newman, Walls and Cameron.
17-Sep	Leven Thistle	6-1	from Barclay, Kay, Wood, Stewart, 'Williams', Phillips, Bell, Edmonds, Cameron, Walls and McDonald.
24-Sep	Selkirk	0-2	Barclay Young Wood Eadie Buchanan Phillips Beveridge Edmonds Bell Cameron Walls
01-Oct	2 Hearts (S 2XI C2)	8-1	Barclay Buchanan Young Eadie Phillips Beveridge Edmonds Bell Cameron Walls McDonald
08-Oct	LENZIE	9-1	from Barclay, Eadie, Young, Buchanan, Phillips, Cairns, Coltharn, Tweedie, Cameron, Walls and Hall. Res. Edwards and McDonald.
15-Oct	ARMADALE	6-2	from Barclay, Young, Newman, Buchanan, Phillips, Cairns, Coltharn, Beveridge, Cameron, Walls and Bell.
22-Oct	Peebles	10-2	from Barclay, Young, Buchan, Eadie, Phillips, Beveridge, Gifford, McDonald, Brown, McKenzie, Walls, Murray, McGraw and Smith.
19-Nov	MOSSEND SWIFTS	15-1	from Barclay, Young, Buchanan, Young, Eadie, Phillips, Beveridge, Cartyle, McDonald, McKenzie, Walls and Smith.
26-Nov	SLAMANNAN	5-0	from Barclay, Young, Buchan, Eadie, Phillips, Beveridge, 'Carlyle', McKenzie, McDonald, Bell and Smith.
03-Dec	GLASGOW UNIV	2-3	from Barclay, Young, Buchan, Eadie, Phillips, Robertson, Bell, Gifford, Davidson, McKenzie, Scott, Smith and McGraw.
17-Dec	Penicuik	3-2	
24-Dec	Musselburgh Fern	5-2	from Barclay, Young, Newman, Carlyle, Phillips, Robertson, Beveridge, Davidson, McKenzie, Walls and Bell.
14-Jan	ADVENTURERS	5-2	from Barclay, Young, Buchan, Johnstone, Phillips, Robertson, Beveridge, Davidson, Houston, McKenzie, Walls, McGraw and Bell.
21-Jan	Dunfermline Juniors	4-2	
28-Jan	West Calder	2-6	from Barclay, Young, Robertson, Gray (ex Hearts), Phillips, Houston, Tarvit, Carmichael, McKenzie, Walls and Beveridge.
25-Feb	2 Hearts (E 2XI C1L)	?	
22-Apr	Vale of Leithen	1-0	
02-May	2 Hearts (E 2XI C2L)	?	
13-May	2 HEARTS		

APPENDIX 3

Prominent Officials

Some prominent officials of St Bernard's Football Club

Name	Secretary	Manager	Trainer	Comments
Anderson, J	1901/02			
Anderson, Robert G	1896/97			also Committee member.
Ashmole, TS	1895/96			prominent football referee at time of appointment.
Baillie, James				Ex player (See St Bernard's Players Section). Director 1909/11. Sculptor.
Banks, John	1899/00			
Brandon, Tommy			1914/22	Ex pedestrian runner. Real name Ross. Lived at the Gymnasium
Brown, Willie			1935/40	Ex player (See St Bernard's Players Section)
Burns, John Archibald				A member of the syndicate. Director 1908/17. Wholesale Stationer.
Carroll, George			1896/03	Moved to Airdrie FC as trainer. From Winchburgh
Clark, David				Director 1912/20. Spirit Merchant - Clark's Bars, Dundas Street and Laurieston Vice President East of Scotland Football Association 1920/21.
Cooper, James				Ground Company Trustee 1924/1943. Financial benefactor to club. Coal Merchant
Creyk, John	1885/86			also Committee member. Match Secretary 1885/88. Founder member
Dalziel, Jock			1920	
Darlington, William				Trustee of the Ground Company 1924/43. House Furnisher.
Dawson, James M		1919/20		Player Manager - ex Liverpool and Hearts. (See St Bernards Players Section)
Dobbie, James			1928/33	
Fleming, John Guthrie				Director 1924/40. Leather Merchant.
Fraser, Thomas	1885/87			President 1890/92. Director 1908/09. President of SAAA 1898/99. Teacher
Gordon, David S	1925/28	1925/28		former Leith Ath, Hull City and Hibs player. Also Manager of Hibs and Hartlepools
Gordon, Louis				Scout for St Bernard's in the minor grades of football in 1920/30s.
Gordon, William				Director 1908/20 and 1938/43. Gas Meter Inspector.
Gray, Thomas James	1902/22			A member of the syndicate. Director 1908/22. President 1911/12. President of the East of Scotland Football Association 1911/13. A founder of the the St Bernard's FC Supporters Club 1924. ' Mr St Bernard's'. Storekeeper.
Greenshields, Timmy L	1878/79			The first Secretary who eventually moved to London.
Guild, George				Also player. Heriot's cricket player. Match Secretary 1888/89. School Teacher.
Gumley, Louis S	1897/98			Lord Provost of Edinburgh in 1935. Knighted 1937. House Agent.
Heatlie, Thomas	1923/24			formerly Secretary of Broxburn United
Hume, George	1890/92			
Innes, Robert	1930/39	1931/39		former senior referee. Currier.
Keenan, James			1933/35	Ex player (See St Bernard's Players Section)
Kemp, Robert	1927/32			Also carried out managerial duties.
Kemp, Walter				A member of the syndicate. Director 1908/24. President 1926/29. Merchant
Kirkwood, James	1928/31			Supporters Club nominee. Also carried out managerial duties.
Lamb, Tom	1889/90			President 1893/94 and 1912. Director 1912/13. Builder. A prominent cyclist who is credited with bringing Walter Arnott to the club.
Lamont, George Rankin				Director 1915/24. Wine Merchant. President of the East of Scotland Football Association 1928/32.
Lapsley, William M				President 1884/88 and 1896/99. Sports Promoter at Powderhall and Gymnasium.
Main, Robert	1917/18			Director 1915/21. Clerk.
Mathieson, John				A member of the syndicate. Director 1908/11. President 1901. Credited with saving the club when the syndicate was formed. Printsellar.
McDonald, Roderick	1896/97			Director 1909/12. Ordinance Surveyor.
McFarlane, John				President of the Scottish Football League 1899/1900
McIntosh, Alexander S	1891/94			Committee member. Match Secretary 1891/94
Mentiplay, James Calder	1914/20			Director 1908/21. Plumber
Moir, CC	1896/97			
Munro, DD	1907/08			Interim Secretary St Bernards Football and Athletic Club Ltd
Paton, Tom	1893/94			Also Match Secretary 1889/90. Employed with a legal firm.
Payne, Richard P	1891/92			former Hibs' official.
Penman, Robert Muir				Director 1924/44. Gentleman
Pringle, George A				A member of the syndicate. Director 1908/1911. Joiner in Leith.
Reid, Jack	1940/46			Also Secretary of St Bernards FC Grand Stand Co Ltd 1926/43. Clerk
Robertson, William T	1881/88			Committee member. Also acted as club treasurer. Tobacconist. Founder member.
Sorbie, Jim			1922/28	Father of 'George McCrae' famous marathon runner.
Stewart, Harry Leith	1923/26			Director 1924. Clerk.
Tait, Robert Donaldson				Director 1924/44. President 1929/38. Leather Merchant.
Tavendale, Archie			1909/15	former Edinburgh Rosebery Juniors trainer. Assistant Trainer at St Bernards
Thomas, C			1903	Ex pedestrian runner. From Lasswade
Wilson, James			1894/96	Became trainer of Rangers FC and Scotland. From Broxburn.
Young, Dr Archie C				Ex player (See St Bernard's Players Section). Supporters Club nominee on the Board in 1930s. Medical practitioner based in the vicinity of the ground.

1928

St Bernards F.C. Directors—Left to right—Front—Messrs M'Laren, Kemp (president), and Kirkwood (secretary). Back—Messrs Sinclair, Murray, Penman, Lamont, and Skerritt.

Mr Tom Gray, secretary of the St Bernards for thirteen years, and at present president of the Second Division of the Scottish League.

Alexander S McIntosh